# The Causes and Consequences of Group Violence

# The Causes and Consequences of Group Violence

## *From Bullies to Terrorists*

Edited by James Hawdon, John Ryan, and Marc Lucht

LEXINGTON BOOKS
Lanham • Boulder • New York • London

Published by Lexington Books
An imprint of The Rowman & Littlefield Publishing Group, Inc.
4501 Forbes Boulevard, Suite 200, Lanham, Maryland 20706
www.rowman.com

16 Carlisle Street, London W1D 3BT, United Kingdom

British Library Cataloguing in Publication Information Available

**Library of Congress Cataloging-in-Publication Data**
The hardback edition of this book has previously been cataloged by the Library of Congress as
follows:

The causes and consequences of group violence : from bullies to terrorists / edited by James Hawdon,
John Ryan, and Marc Lucht.
pages cm
Includes bibliographical references and index.
1. Violence. 2. Small groups—Psychological aspects. 3. Collective behavior. I. Hawdon, James.
HM1116.C38 2014
303.6—dc23
                                    2014020135

ISBN 978-0-7391-8896-5 (cloth : alk. paper)
ISBN 978-1-4985-0043-2 (pbk. : alk. paper)
ISBN 978-0-7391-8897-2 (electronic)

∞ ™ The paper used in this publication meets the minimum requirements of American
National Standard for Information Sciences Permanence of Paper for Printed Library
Materials, ANSI/NISO Z39.48-1992.

Printed in the United States of America

# Contents

Acknowledgments      vii

Introduction: Working Toward Understanding Group Violence      ix
*James Hawdon and John Ryan*

**I: Perpetrators of Group Violence**      **1**

  **1**   On the Forms and Nature of Group Violence      3
      *James Hawdon*

  **2**   Hate Groups: From Offline to Online Social Identifications      21
      *Atte Oksanen, Pekka Räsänen, and James Hawdon*

  **3**   Violence and Street Groups: Gangs, Groups, and Violence      49
      *David Kennedy*

  **4**   Intergroup Contact and Genocide      71
      *Wenona Rymond-Richmond*

  **5**   Group Violence Against the State: The Hindsight Story of the
      Thirty-Year War in Sri Lanka      91
      *Tharindi Udalagama and Premakumara de Silva*

  **6**   (Non)Violence and Conflict: A Theoretical Assessment of Civil
      Resistance and the Syrian Conflict      109
      *Jeanne Chang and Alec Clott*

  **7**   Killing Before an Audience: Terrorism and Group Violence      125
      *Mark Juergensmeyer*

**II: The Victims of Group Violence**      **141**

  **8**   Gender, Weight, and Inequality Associated with School Bullying      143
      *Anthony A. Peguero and Lindsay Kahle*

**9** Victims of Online Hate Groups: American Youth's Exposure to
Online Hate Speech    165
*James Hawdon, Atte Oksanen, and Pekka Räsänen*

**10** Selecting Targets: The Influence of Judgments, Mobility, and
Gender on Intragroup Violence Among Tamil Refugees    183
*Christian Matheis, Virginia Roach, Michelle Sutherland, and
James Hawdon*

**III: Consequences of Group Violence**    **197**

**11** Consequences of Group Violence Involving Youth in Sri Lanka    199
*Siri Hettige*

**12** Gender Dimensions of Group Violence    209
*Donna Pankhurst*

**13** Communities: Examining Psychological, Sociological, and
Cultural Consequences after Mass Violence Tragedies    221
*Pekka Räsänen, Atte Oksanen, and James Hawdon*

**IV: Reflections on Group Violence**    **239**

**14** Group Violence Revisited: Common Themes Across Types of
Group Violence    241
*James Hawdon*

**15** Humanistic Reflections on Understanding Group Violence    255
*Marc Lucht*

Index    267

About the Editors    273

About the Contributors    275

# Acknowledgments

Several people should be thanked for allowing this project to move from idea to finished product. First, we thank the Lacy Foundation for their continued generous support of the Center for Peace Studies and Violence Prevention at Virginia Tech. We also thank Toy, Joe, and Mary Lou Cobbe for their support. They have been champions for the center since its creation, and their continued benevolence allows us to work toward our goals of researching the causes of violence, informing our local community and the world about critical issues of peace and violence, and educating the next generation of peace scholars. The center's work, including this book, is possible because of the generosity of our donors, but we are not only extremely grateful for the financial support we receive, we are very appreciative of the continued moral support and encouragement they provide us.

In addition to our funders, we would like to thank Sue Ott Rowlands. She was dean of the College of Liberal Arts and Human Sciences when the idea for this project was first formed, and her encouragement and support helped shape it. For example, she encouraged us to include young scholars, and that decision turned out to be a very good one. Over the years, Dean Ott Rowlands was a strong supporter of the Center for Peace Studies and Violence Prevention, and we would like to thank her for the long-term support and guidance she provided as well as her valuable contributions to this project. We were sorry to see her leave Virginia Tech to become the provost at Northern Kentucky University.

We also thank Ms. Zineb Boujrada, Ms. Ihssane Guennoun, Ms. Rim Riouch, Mr. Muhammad Berrada, Mr. Hassan Karim Naciry, and Mr. Hamza Alami Hassani, students from the École de Gouvernance et D'Économie de Rabat (EGE-Rabat). Under the direction of their faculty mentor, Dr. Joanna Buisson, the students provided valuable feedback on the student-authored chapters. Dr. Buisson is an assistant professor and research fellow at EGE-Rabat.

We also would like to thank Amy Splitt, office manager and grants coordinator. Amy was extremely helpful at so many junctions of this project. She organized all the travel arrangements for our contributors to make sure scholars from all over the world got to Morocco. She also worked closely with the staff of the Riad Kalaa in Rabat to make sure the event went smoothly. Once we returned from Rabat, Amy's skills as a technical editor were put to use. She provided valuable editorial suggestions, formatted the texts, and checked and corrected citations and references. We are grateful for all of this work and the professionalism she displayed while doing it.

We are very grateful to the staff at the Riad Kalaa for providing a wonderful space to hold our discussions. Their hospitality was greatly appreciated as they consistently went above our expectations. We also thank Lotfi Lamrani, president and exchange director of Friendship Force Club of Azrou, Morocco, for his hospitality and friendship. We also thank our colleagues at Virginia Tech for creating a wonderful working environment. Finally, we extend our love and gratitude to our families for always being there for guidance, encouragement, support, and insight. Thank you.

# Introduction

*Working Toward Understanding Group Violence*

## James Hawdon and John Ryan

Early in 2013, the Center for Peace Studies and Violence Prevention at Virginia Tech (CPSVP) invited some of the world's leading scholars to write articles that presented their research and theorizing on violence that is perpetrated by or that target groups. Such violence ranges from hate crimes committed by one or two individuals to riots, revolutions, and terroristic acts committed by well-organized groups. We therefore invited leading scholars in areas as varied as bullying to terrorism. These scholars each produced chapters for this volume; however, instead of doing these in isolation, this group of scholars shared them with each other.

Then, in September of 2013, through the generous support of the Lacy Foundation, the CPSVP brought this select group of scholars to Rabat, Morocco, to discuss the papers. The primary goal of our meeting in Rabat was to produce this interdisciplinary manuscript that would present contemporary research and theory on group violence. At the workshop, the invited scholars presented their work, and the group discussed each paper to identify common themes. Each author then had the opportunity to revise her or his paper based on our discussions. The revised papers, now chapters in this volume, bring to bear perspectives informed both by interdisciplinary and international collaboration. Our vision for this book is that it will become a useful volume that professionals and students access when researching or teaching about violence generally and group violence specifically.

This book is not only about what we currently know, but the authors also explore relatively unknown dimensions of the antecedents, processes, and consequences of various types of group violence. It includes both empirical studies and theoretical discussions. The book covers a wide range of topics related to group violence, from school bullying to school shootings, hate crimes, vigilantism, and terrorism. It also looks at consequences for various groups including women, children, and nation states.

In organizing this book, we had three primary goals. First, we wanted to assemble some of the world's leading experts on group violence to give them an opportunity to not only reflect on what they know about violence as individual scholars, but to also generate an intellectual synergy that would provide cutting-edge insights into the causes and consequences of violence. The scholars who contributed to this volume formed a cross-national team that provided perspectives from multiple disciplines, from the developed and developing worlds, from men and women, from qualitative and quantitative perspectives, and from experienced scholars and emerging scholars.

Second, we wanted to fill a gap in the existing literature. There are numerous books available on specific forms of violence, and several books focused on collective violence exist. While each of these volumes has merit, most were published some time ago and none offer what we propose. First, these works are on collective, not group, violence. As described above, group violence is broader than what is typically covered in works on collective violence because it includes violence *committed by collectives or groups* as well as violence *committed against groups*. Thus, in addition to topics typically covered by works on collective violence such as riots, revolutions, terrorism, and gangs, we also include topics such as hate groups and hate crimes. Second, while we focus on *the causes of group violence*, we also consider the *consequences of group violence* by including chapters on the consequences of group violence for youth, for women, and for communities.

Finally, we wanted to stimulate additional analyses that can contribute to our understanding of violence. Indeed, we believe this volume is an important contribution to the study of one of the most pressing issues of our time. The World Health Organization estimates that nearly 1.4 million people lose their lives each year to violence. Despite thousands of volumes devoted to it, we still lack sufficient understanding to effectively curb or prevent it. While we do not claim that this book provides such understanding, we are confident that it significantly contributes to that collective understanding. We hope this book stimulates others to likewise press the boundaries of our knowledge so we may better resolve the core issues that lead to violence and respond to it in ways that heal rather than divide.

## ORGANIZATION OF THE BOOK

The book is divided into four parts. The first part focuses on the perpetrators of group violence and analyzes the situations in which various groups enact violence. The first chapter offers a working definition of group violence. In this chapter, James Hawdon defines group violence and contrasts it with other types of violence. The chapter provides a concise review of extant scientific research that summarizes the fundamental causes and conditioning factors for several types of group violence. Taking an interdisciplinary perspective, Hawdon reviews studies on group bullying, vigilantism, hate crimes, gangs, revolutions, and terrorism. He includes research that focuses on micro, meso, and macro-level processes. He then discusses similarities in the reported causes of these forms of violence. Finally, specific topics for future research and the barriers we confront in conducting this research are identified.

Chapter 2 examines offline and online hate groups that target groups of people based on characteristics such as their ethnicity, religion, or sexual orientation. The chapter contributes a new perspective on online hate groups and their formation. Concentrating on YouTube school-shooting fans that glamorize mass murders, Oksanen, Räsänen, and Hawdon demonstrate the highly structured, yet fluid, networks of hate groups.

Chapter 3, by David Kennedy, is dedicated to urban street gangs. Kennedy documents that a very small group of offenders, often referred to as "gangs," are the primarily drivers of serious urban violence in the United States. These groups are found almost entirely in historically damaged and troubled minority communities, where relationships with legal authorities, especially the police, are always troubled and can be toxic. After reviewing what is known about gangs, their structure, and their members, Kennedy describes a proven approach for addressing that violence and core related issues. The chapter emphasizes a deep underlying truth: that the three parties most involved in the violence problem—neighborhoods, the street groups, and law enforcement—share important common ground. Realizing this leads to new framing of the problem and how to address it.

In chapter 4, Wenona Rymond-Richmond offers a chapter focusing on an extreme form of intergroup violence: genocide. Specifically, she documents the causes and consequences of the Darfur genocide. In particular, the author examines, 1) what, if any, effect close physical proximity of victim (black Africans) and perpetrator (Arabs) had on total victimization rates including sexual victimization; and 2) the dynamics of racial protection and racial targeting. Rymond-Richmond finds that in Darfur, victimization, including sexual victimization and torture, was heightened when the victims and perpetrators lived in close physical proximity.

Tharindi Udalagama and Premakumara de Silva offer a novel insight to the decades-long Sri Lankan civil war in chapter 5. The authors analyze the violent war waged against the state by the Liberation Tamils of Tamil Eelam (LTTE) as a classic case study in "separatism"; however, unlike most scholars of the Sri Lankan conflict, they analyze the combatants as political groups rather than ethnic groups. While ethnic tensions were the root cause of the conflict, the authors document how it expanded to political aspirations and separatist ideals based on the premise that one nation-state should represent one ethnicity.

Chapter 6 is the first chapter primarily authored by students. Here Jeanne Chang and Alec Clott use Ackerman and Rodal's argument concerning the specific criteria necessary for nonviolent civil resistance to be successful and Chenoweth and Stephen's six mechanisms of leverage as defining characteristics of nonviolent movements to analyze the extent to which these factors are applicable and identifiable in the context of the current Syrian Civil War. They apply these mechanisms to offer a better understanding of why violence has come to characterize the conflict.

The part's final chapter focuses on a fundamental cause of terrorism in today's world. Interviews with activists involved in recent terrorist acts show that there were similarities in their thinking. Unlike earlier periods of terrorism in the twentieth century when the activists were inspired by secular ideologies such as nationalism, socialism, and anarchism, the recent activists are in some way religious. But what does religion have to do with it? Mark Juergensmeyer argues "nothing," and "everything." "Nothing," because their struggles are over political and social issues, not conflicts over belief. And yet "everything," since religious histories, ideas, and organization are part of the identities, ideologies, and leadership of the groups. Juergensmeyer contends that to understand the religious roots of terrorism, one has to appreciate the logic of cosmic war.

Part II provides a consideration of the victims of group violence. Chapter 8 is an empirical analysis of how physical characteristics such as height and weight factor into target selection for bullies. Although research has established how these characteristics are constructed as a "suitable target" for bullying in the United States, little is known about how the intersection of gender, height, and weight contributes to the bullying victimization. Anthony Peguero and Lindsay Kahle use the Health Behavior in School-Aged Children (HBSC) data to investigate how gender, height, and weight contribute to being a "suitable target" for bullying victimization.

In chapter 9, Hawdon, Oksanen, and Räsänen report the results of newly collected data on online hate group victimization. While there has been a documented growth of hate material online, few have tracked if this material is actually seen or heard. Using a nationally representative sample of American youth and young adults, the authors investigate the extent to which they have been exposed to online hate speech. They then empirically demonstrate how lifestyle exposure theory helps predict exposure to online hate. They demonstrate how lifestyle variables mediate the relationship between demographic characteristics and exposure to online hate material, thereby verifying that lifestyle exposure theory applies to the online world as well as it does the offline.

Chapter 10 is a theoretical discussion of target selection. Various individual and environmental elements influence the way members of groups select targets of violence. Using Sri Lanka as a case study, the authors consider three distinct groups: Tamils living in internal refugee camps, Tamil refugees living in London, and the leaders and members of the Liberation Tamils of Tamil Eelam (LTTE). By considering how structural factors such as social mobility influence epistemic evaluations of group identity, the authors demonstrate the complexity of circumstances that contribute to intragroup violence and the selection of victims.

Chapter 11 is the first in part III, which deals with the consequences of group violence. Siri Hettige explores the rise of distinct identity groups among post-independence Sri Lankan youth. Specifically, he considers the consequences of the civil war within several sub-themes: state-society relations, the erosion of liberal democracy, insecurity and vulnerability of youth, migration of youth, identity segregation and marginalization, and the future prospects of youth. Hettige concludes that while some of the war's consequences directly influence youth, other consequences relate to the wider social and political context of the country. Specifically, the weakening of the liberal democratic tradition, which bears on governance, development, and reconciliation. He recognizes that there are clear signs of new group conflicts developing in the country, and that these conflicts will likely draw on marginalized youth from diverse groups, thereby affecting their well-being and future prospects.

In chapter 12, Donna Pankhurst argues that the self-evident fact that group violence is most often committed by young men against other men is not often brought into analyses of the causes and consequences of such violence. She argues that using the lens of gender allows us to move beyond a binary understanding of male versus female behavior, and this understanding provokes questions concerning why some men actively choose to participate in violence while others choose to resist it. Pankhurst then explores the highly gendered and varied impacts of group violence.

Chapter 13 addresses the consequences of group violence for communities. Here, Räsänen and Oksanen discuss some recent mass tragedies such as school shootings and terrorist attacks in the United States, Europe, and Asia. The authors identify key psychological, sociological, and cultural consequences that such group-targeted violence generates in communities. While focusing on small communities, they argue that these consequences of violence also apply to larger communities and online communities. Noting that both the size and type of community influence the consequences of group violence, they argue that communities with lower levels of community solidarity are less affected by violence than communities with more solidarity. Simultaneously, however, physical proximity among community members does not necessarily play a crucial role in determining the consequences of group-targeted violence.

The book's final part consists of reflections on the previous materials. In chapter 14, Hawdon identifies common themes that emerge through the chapters of the book. He notes similarities in both the causes of violence as well as the selection of victims. Specifically, it appears that group violence commonly occurs when state power is ineffective. In addition, issues of group formation, identification, and loyalty assume critically important positions when trying to understand the causes of group violence. Similarly, issues of status make group violence particularly intractable. With respect to target selection, the defining of suitable targets appears to be a group-level process. Even in situations where individuals attack other individuals, the definition of who "should be" attacked is linked to processes of group formation and boundary maintenance.

In the final chapter, Marc Lucht, a philosopher, considers the work presented here from a humanistic perspective. All of the previous chapters adopt a social science approach. Lucht reflects on how the humanities can extend or broaden the social scientific understanding of group violence. He argues that while understanding the motivations and purposes of those who perpetrate group violence is important, this understanding does not, nor need not, ground the "toleration of the intolerable." Instead, Lucht argues that recalling our common humanity can allow us to avoid simple demonization and instead find better ways of responding to violence effectively and humanely.

Taken together, the chapters in this volume offer a transdisciplinary, international perspective on group violence. It offers a breadth of scholarship that is atypical as it brings together an array of scholars from several social scientific disciplines and from several countries. We believe the scope of scholarship increases the theoretical and empirical importance of our work.

*I*

# Perpetrators of Group Violence

*Chapter One*

# On the Forms and Nature of Group Violence

## James Hawdon

Violence takes on many forms. Some of it is overt, some covert. Some is clearly visible while other forms are far less so. We know it when we see it, and certainly know it when we feel it. While much of it remains out of sight, it nevertheless seems to be everywhere. Despite considerable scholarly work on the topic, scholars have struggled with definitions of and classification schemes for violence. There are numerous definitions of violence and a considerable variety of ways its types can be classified. There are also countless efforts devoted to understanding its causes and consequences. Our efforts are more in line with the efforts to understand it than they are to define or classify it; however, while we do not wish to be bogged down in conceptual debates, we nevertheless need to operationalize our terms so we can meaningfully participate in the scholarly discussion of violence, its causes, and its consequences. This chapter offers a definition of violence and proposes a theoretical approach to understanding its causes.

## ON VIOLENCE

There are a number of definitions of violence (see, for example, Galtung 1969; Weiner, Zahn, and Sagi 1990; Iadicola and Shupe 2003; Thorton, Voigt, and Harper 2013). A healthy debate has ensued over these definitions as scholars try to define an element of social life that seems ubiquitous. The problem—as with all definitions—is a matter of balance. We wish to include what we know to be violence while not including too much; yet, we wish to exclude that which is clearly not what we mean by violence without becoming so restrictive that we exclude all but the most obvious cases of violence.

For example, Galtung's (1969) classic definition of violence is, in my opinion, too broad. He states,

> Violence is here defined as the cause of the difference between the potential
> and the actual, between what could have been and what is. Violence is that
> which increases the distance between the potential and the actual, and that
> which impedes the decrease of this distance. (Galtung 1969, 168)

While ambitious and the original source for the fundamental distinction between "direct violence" and "structural violence," it seems to include, at least
potentially, any and all acts of power. To me, this makes violence too broad
and undermines our ability to explain its causes and consequences (for a
similar argument, see Tilly 2003 or Martin, McCarthy, and McPhail 2009).

Other definitions of violence are similarly problematic from the perspective of using them in the scientific pursuit of understanding the phenomenon.
For example, Iadicola and Shupe (2003, 23) state that, "violence is any action
or structural arrangement that results in physical or nonphysical harm to one
or more persons." This definition not only includes actions committed by
individuals or groups of individuals, it also includes the institutional and
structural arrangements of society that result in harm to people. The problem
with this and similar definitions is revealed if we consider the classifications
of violence these definitions imply.

Just as there are numerous definitions of violence, there are also several
classifications schemes for the types of violence. Indeed, violence can be
classified across several dimensions. One common scheme that is compatible
with a typical definition similar to Iadicola and Shupe's definition makes
distinctions between interpersonal, institutional, and structural violence.
Interpersonal violence are violent acts occurring between and among individuals, such as fights, corporal punishment, aggravated assault, rape, robbery,
and homicide. This is the type of violence most people envision when they
speak of violence. Institutional violence is violent acts that originate within
the patterns of interactions and social relationships within the basic social
institutions. Institutional violence includes actions that are often commonly
accepted as legitimate forms of interaction within an institutional setting such
as spanking a child or hazing a fraternity brother or military recruit. It can
also include actions such as religious-based terrorism or the violation of the
human rights of workers by their employing corporation. Any act of violence
that is committed in the routine enactment of institutional roles can be considered institutional violence. Finally, structural violence is violence that is
embedded in the established patterns of social organization that aim to pre-
serve the status quo (Iadicole and Shupe 2003). Most, if not all, acts of
structural violence are considered by many to be fundamental and essential
parts of society. They are seen as indispensable for social and individual

survival. They are, as Iadicole and Shupe (2003) say, "violence of the status quo." Acts of structural violence often reinforce and legitimate patterns of social inequality, and they often deny the civil, criminal, or human rights of individuals or groups (Thorton et al. 2013). Examples of structural violence include the policies that give rise to or fail to diminish homelessness and poverty in affluent nations such as the United Sates, laws that limit citizenship and voting rights, and the systematic violation of the human rights of migrant workers (see, Walsh, Thorton, and Voigt 2010).

While this classification system is widely acknowledged and undoubtedly useful, there are potential issues that make it difficult to know exactly the proper classification of some acts of violence. As numerous scholars have noted, the categories are not mutually exclusive. For example, if fraternity members haze their pledges by beating them severely with paddles, is this not both interpersonal and institutional violence? While some consider marital rape an act of institutional violence (e.g., Easteal and McOrmond-Plummer 2006), it is clearly interpersonal violence. Similarly, most acts of structural violence require someone acting in an institutional role to behave in a manner that perpetuates the violence. For example, a police officer must racially profile and arrest someone and a judge must willfully follow harsh sentencing guidelines to create and perpetuate the structural violence of the mass incarceration of disenfranchised groups. The concepts of institutional and structural violence tend to reify institutions. Institutions and structures do not act (or fail to act), people do. The educational institution does not track students, real teachers and real administrators make real decisions about which students are placed in which classes. In this sense, then, all acts of violence are interpersonal: someone behaves in a manner that hurts someone or some group of people.

The lack of mutual exclusion among the categories of interpersonal, institutional, and structural violence make it difficult not only to classify acts of violence, it clouds the potential casual factors and consequences of the various forms of violence. Poverty, homelessness, human rights violations, and other forms of structural violence, while important, are not, in my opinion, violence, even if they are rooted in the system and legitimated by the hegemonic ideology. These factors are potential "precipitating factors" of violence, but to call them violence conflates cause and effect. They are conditions that may result in harm, but they do so indirectly. Political decisions regarding the distribution of food that result in the purposeful starvation of a group are undoubtedly malicious, harmful acts; however, they are fundamentally and consequentially different than violence, per se. To call these structural conditions violence is equivalent to calling the underbrush of an uncut forest "fire." While the underbrush of an uncut forest provides fuel for and indeed may even be a precipitating cause of the fire, it is underbrush, not fire.

Instead of conflating distal causes of the phenomenon in question with the phenomenon itself, I prefer definitions that focus solely on the use of physical force (e.g., Weiner et al. 1990; Black 2012). Thus, I define violence as the use of physical force against people, including threats and attempts. It is, according to this definition, the application of physical power. It leaves out of consideration the use of economic or ideological power. While the use of these forms of power can obviously lead to harm, they are not acts of violence under this definition. What causes one to use ideological or economic power and not physical power seems to be fundamentally different factors. In fact, it is likely that violence occurs in the absence of effective ideological or economic power. One benefit of this definition is it directly links us to the study of a fundamental element of social life: power. As such, this definition links the study of violence to the study of other social acts of power, including, for example, the circulation of economic capital or the rhetorical manipulation of public opinion (see Hawdon 2001). While I am not hypothesizing that physical force necessarily follows the social laws of economic or ideological power, these are potential hypotheses to be explored that may prove fruitful. Thus, in this chapter, I adopt Black's relatively simple definition of violence as the use of physical force.

Recognizing that violence is the act of using physical force has an additional benefit. It leads logically to a classification scheme, and accurate classification is fundamental to a scientific understanding of a given phenomenon. The application of physical force requires an actor and a target. Thus, a typology of violence can be derived by cross-classifying who commits the violence and who those committing the act of violence target. For this typology to be useful in determining the distinctions among types of violence and the primary factors that lead to each type of violence, it must accurately reflect the forms of violence in categories that are distinct and mutually exclusive. I believe the following typology achieves this goal.

## A TYPOLOGY OF VIOLENCE

Violence is committed either by an individual or a group of individuals. Similarly, violence targets either an individual or a group. These forms of violence are clearly different, and they are likely to have different causes and consequences. Realizing this and cross-classifying these types of violence, we arrive at the following typology presented in table 1.1.

This cross-classification results in four types of violence: individual perpetrator–individual target; individual perpetrator–group target; group perpetrator–individual target; and group perpetrator–group target. Typical street crimes such as murders and robberies are examples of individual perpetrator–individual target acts of violence. Similarly, most cases of domestic vio-

|        |            | Perpetrator | |
|--------|------------|-------------|---|
|        |            | Individual | Group |
| Victim | Individual | Street Crime / Domestic Violence | Lynching / Vigilantism / Capital Punishment |
|        | Group      | Rampage Killings | Feud / Gangs / Genocide / Terrorism / Warfare |

**Table 1.1. A Typology of Violence.**

lence or marital rape would be examples of individual perpetrator–individual target violence. Many rampage killings are examples of individual perpetrator–group target acts of violence: such vicious acts as those committed by Anders Breivik, who murdered seventy-seven attending a political rally in Utøya, Norway; or James Holmes, who killed twelve and injured seventy others in a Colorado movie theater. Group perpetrator–individual target violence includes acts of lynching and vigilantism. For example, lynchings are typically group-based and commonly follow an accusation against (typically) a lower-status individual (see Senechal de la Roche 2001). Finally, gang violence, terrorism, and warfare are examples of group perpetrated–group targeted violence.

There appear to be benefits of focusing on the actors involved in violence. First, and most obviously, it avoids reification of institutions and structures. As argued earlier, individuals and individuals acting in groups commit violent acts, not institutions. This truism is explicitly recognized in the proposed typology, and researchers using it will avoid making reifying statements such as "capitalism is a violent system." People interacting in a capitalist system routinely commit acts of violence; however, the system of capitalism organizes behaviors and patterns interactions, it does not behave or interact. Similarly, individuals committing violence while performing some institutional role, such as a soldier or police officer, are doing so as a member of a group. Individual soldiers do not wage war; groups of soldiers do.

Second, the categories are based on easily observable and empirically verifiable behaviors, at least in most cases. While there are some acts of murder, for example, that involve multiple murderers and these may not be easy to detect or verify, these cases are rare. Most homicides involve one perpetrator and one victim. Similarly, in terms of victims, some acts are meant to harm more than one person but do not. Several attempts at rampage killings, for example, resulted in no deaths or injuries. For example, in 2009, a nine-year-old student at Kanebogen Elementary School in Harstad, Norway, fired a shotgun into a crowded schoolyard. No one was hurt, but the youth's intention was to inflict harm on multiple people (the *Independent*, 10 September, 2013). The actor's or actors' intentions in some such cases may be difficult to discern; however, once again, these cases are likely very rare.

While perpetrators do not always succeed in harming more than one person, it is usually obvious if they intended to do so. It therefore seems useful to focus on the involved actors because in most cases the distinction between individual and group is easy to determine and empirically verifiable.

There appear to be other benefits to this typology as well. First, as Martin, McCarthy, and McPhail (2009) argue, most scholars do not distinguish between the various targets of violence. Often, for example, researchers treat violence targeting people and violence targeting property as the same phenomenon. However, conflating targets is problematic because it fails to recognize the diverse causal mechanisms involved in various forms of violence. For example, Walker, Martin, and McCarthy (2008) found that the tactical choices made by social movement actors—including the use of violence—varied considerably depending on the protest's target. Similarly, the interactions that lead to violence targeting persons are quite different from those that lead to attacks on property (Martin et al. 2009). Thus, the typology disentangles the targets of violence, which may lead to theories that are better specified.

In addition, the benefits of focusing on the actors committing the act of violence also seem clear. There is a clear difference between acts of violence perpetrated by an individual and those perpetrated by groups. Several researchers make the distinction between individual violence and "collective violence." For Tilly (2003, 3), collective violence "involves at least two perpetrators of damage" and results "in part from coordination among persons who perform the damaging acts." Unlike acts of violence committed by individuals, acts of collective violence require coordination, and coordination amplifies power. Thus, as a general rule, groups can cause far more damage than individuals can.

If this typology is indeed scientifically useful, we should see considerable similarity in the underlying causal processes leading to the specific types of violence within any given cell, but we should see considerable variation between the types of violence across the different cells. That is, if the typology is useful, similar processes should lead to street crime and domestic violence, but these are likely to be different than the processes that lead to genocide or political assassinations. In addition, we should see more similarities in the precipitating factors within a column than we do between columns. Thus, the processes that lead to vigilantism should be more similar to those that lead to terrorism than they are to those that lead to war. These are empirical questions, of course, and detailing the underlying causes of the wide variety of violence covered by the typology is undoubtedly an arduous task. The rest of this chapter and book is devoted to beginning that task by discussing group violence, and this chapter specifically focuses on only one type of group violence defined in table 1.1: *violence with a group perpetrator*.

## TOWARD AN UNDERSTANDING OF GROUP VIOLENCE

Group violence is violence that is committed by or targets a group. It ranges from rampage killings committed by one or two individuals to riots, revolutions, and terroristic acts committed by well organized groups. Similar to what is often called "collective violence," group violence is, in one sense, broader than collective violence. It not only includes acts of violence *committed by groups*, it also includes acts of *violence that target groups*. Thus, in addition to acts of collective violence such as riots, revolutions, terrorism, and gangs, group violence also includes acts such as hate crimes and the activities of hate groups.

I will now begin identifying the "social geometry" of several types of group violence (see Black 1995). That is, I will try to identify the factors that predict types of group violence based on how these aspects of social life vary with other dimensions of social life such as vertical distance or inequality, relational distance, cultural distance, and radial distance (see Black 1976). I will specifically focus on the relationship between the perpetrators and targets of violence. Is group violence more likely to occur among equals or between those socially unequal? Is it likely to occur when social relations are fluid or more immobile? Are intimates more or less likely to commit group violence against each other? These are the types of relational variables that comprise the social geometry of life, and I seek to identify those that comprise the social geometry of group violence. There is already considerable work in the social geometry of group violence. What follows is an attempt to add to this research.

## ON COLLECTIVE VIOLENCE

First, we can identify what leads violence to move from acts between individuals to acts between collectives. That is, what leads to collective violence? Senechal de la Roche (1996, 106), argues that, "collective violence varies directly with relational distance." That is, collective violence tends to be more likely and more severe when the parties involved are strangers rather than intimates. Similarly, collective violence is more likely to occur when the perpetrators and target or targets are culturally distant, unequal, and functionally independent. Thus, lynchings and other types of vigilantism, terrorism, and riots are more likely to occur when those involved are socially and relationally distant. Moreover, these events also tend to be more violent when they are between socially and relationally distant actors (Campbell 2013; Senechal de la Roche 1996; Senechal de la Roche 1997; Senechal de la Roche 2001; Black 2004a; Black 2012).

In addition, "the collectivization of violence is a direct function of strong partisanship" (Senechal de la Roche 2001, 129). That is, violence becomes collective when one of the parties involved can attract allies, and third-party support occurs when the third party is socially close to one belligerent and socially distant from the other. In addition, it is more likely to occur when the third parties have solidary among themselves, and solidarity is directly related to intimacy, cultural homogeneity, and interdependence (Senechal de la Roche 2001, 129). Situations where a group is highly solidified can be particularly dangerous to non-members. Indeed, violence tends to be extremely severe when relatively isolated, homogeneous groups encounter "outsiders" (see Black 2012).

While collective violence generally occurs among relationally distant actors with allies, we can further specify the social fields of violence by considering specific types of group violence. For example, the distribution of partisanship is related to the type of collective violence. While wars and feuds typically have bilateral distribution of partisanship where both sides have allies, lynching typically occurs when there is a combination of strong partisanship toward the perpetrators (or their advocates) and weak partisanship toward the target of the violence (Senechal de la Roche 2001). Let us now consider specific forms of group violence.

## Violence with a Group Perpetrator

As noted above, violence committed by or targeting a collective is group violence. Violence with a group as perpetrator can target individuals, other groups, or the state. What are the social fields of this type of violence? Is there variation across the types that can help us understand why they occur? We will consider the cases of vigilantism, gangs and feuds, and terrorism.

### *Vigilantism*

Vigilantism is a form of collective violence in which an informal group punishes an individual for some perceived wrong. It typically occurs in situations of strong partisanship where the perpetrators are solidified while the victim is solitary. Since strong partisanship is more likely to occur when the alleged offender is socially distant and inferior to the alleged victim, vigilantism often targets "outsiders." For example, among the Munda and Oraon of eastern India, theft or attempted theft could result in an outsider being lynched; however, those from the village would not be lynched for an economic crime (Saran 1974). Similarly, in the American south and west, violence between transients was *often* treated with indifference, but if a transient killed a member of the community, vigilante justice typically resulted (Brundage 1993; Pfeifer 2004; Senechal de la Roche 2001). The lack of allies can also explain the frequent lynching of witches throughout history and across numerous cultures since "witches typically have no supporters" (Sene-chal de la Roche 2001, 135; also see Heald 1986a).

Vigilantism targets those without strong allies, and, because high status attracts allies, vigilantes often attack those of lower social standing. For example, in the American Midwest and West during the mid-nineteenth century, the landed lynched the landless accused of crimes, and wealthy cattle operators used lynch mobs to intimidate lower-class ranchers and farmers (Pfeifer 2004). As Pfeifer (2004, 26) notes about lynching in southern Iowa, "victims of mob murder tended to be individuals on the margins of the rural economy, and their low status may have accentuated the repercussions for their alleged actions." Similarly, in a number of east African societies, reputed thieves or witches are often legitimate targets for vigilantism, and, among the Gisu of Uganda, allegations of witchcraft and theft are leveled against "the unfortunate or impoverished who lack sufficient resources to maintain themselves independently" (Heald 1986a, 75). While accusations of being a thief are primarily aimed at young men and accusations of being a witch target the old, Gisu men become vulnerable to such accusations if they fail to gain or maintain sufficient resources to establish their positions as adult men (Heald 1986a).

Moreover, vigilantism is often used to exert social control. Specifically, vigilantism can be used to maintain an existing hierarchy, especially when established groups feel threatened by changing social values or the upward mobility of competing sectors of society (Rosenbaum and Sederberg 1974). As Rosenbaum and Sederberg say, it is "conservative violence . . . designed to create, maintain, or recreate an established sociopolitical order." For example, whites used lynching to maintain their superior social position over black laborers in the northern Louisiana parishes in the late nineteenth century and in the West during the first decades of the twentieth century (Pfeifer 2004). Not only did whites use lynching to assert their power over black laborers, these lynch mobs were "backed by a white consensus favoring racial hierarchy and the drastic enforcement of the social control of African Americans" (Pfeifer 2004, 15; also see Rosenbaum and Sederberg 1974). This type of vigilantism is generally a response by those who feel threatened by "social outcasts" or "inferiors." For example, recent vigilantism in South Africa is a result of targeting those perceived to be behind soaring crime rates (Schärf and Nina, 2001). Many lynch mobs in the American South formed after someone of lower status was accused of assaulting or killing someone of high status such as an employer or police officer (see Brundage 1993; Senechal de la Roche 2001). Similarly, vigilante groups in Uganda formed in the 1960s to eradicate "thieves and witches" that threatened the community (Heald 1986b). More recently, ultranationalistic vigilante groups emerged in Turkey after Kurdish nationalists became increasingly visible and Kurdish separatists launched several terrorist attacks (Dönmez 2008).

Vigilantism also occurs in a specific social space that is largely absent of effective state organization. That is, vigilantism emerges in "frontier" conditions ripe with state failure or perceived state failure (Abrahams 1998; Pfeifer 2004). Vigilantism arises in response to the state's incapacity to police and secure citizens' rights. When the system is challenged by movements to alter the status quo, the groups being challenged find governmental efforts to confront the challenge to be insufficient. The state's inability to protect their interests drives them to enact self-help. For example, *sungusungu* groups in Tanzania and Kenya formed to control theft in the absence of state power, and the state even permitted the *sungusungu* groups to codify their own laws and established punishments (see Heald 2006). Similarly, much of the vigilantism in Latin American in the 1960s was due to the absence of effective state structures of protection (Huggins 1991). The recent emergence of "self-defense forces" in numerous Mexican towns and villages are also an apparent response to the lack of effective state control over drug traffickers (Tuckman 2013).

Indeed, vigilantism is not only a response to state failure; it is often a critique of the moral and ethical foundations of the law itself (Buur 2008). For example, vigilantism was rampant in the American West, Midwest, and South through the late nineteenth century as rural working-class supporters of "rough justice" battled middle-class advocates of abstract notions of "due process" (see Pfeifer 2004). Some believe the vigilantism in Mexico is also more than an attempt to protect communities from violent drug cartels. Some governmental officials believe these groups are the beginnings of an anti-government guerrilla force (see Tuckman 2013).

Thus, vigilantism is a form of self-help used to control groups or protect one's position or belongings. It appears that vigilantism occurs in settings with high levels of inequality and heterogeneity. It typically occurs when a great deal of social distance separates the perpetrators and victim, especially if the victim is a social inferior. Moreover, it occurs in the absence or perceived absence of state power. The combination of these social fields results in a situation of strong partisanship against weak partisanship; yet, it is likely to occur only when those with allies feel the need to "take the law into their own hands." Law, like vigilantism, maintains the status quo as law disproportionately punishes those who are disreputable, marginal, and socially inferior (see Black 1976). Typically the powerful—those with status and allies—use law; but when law fails them or is perceived as ineffective, they resort to more drastic means such as lynching or other forms of vigilantism.

## Gangs

Street gangs are most typical in larger urban areas, but they can also be found in smaller cities, suburbs, and rural areas (Klein and Maxson 2006; FBI

2011). The Eurogang network defines a gang as a durable, street-oriented youth group who organize their identity around involvement in illegal activity (see Wood and Alleyne 2010). According to the FBI (2011, 9), there are over 33,000 gangs in the United States, and gangs are responsible for an average of 48 percent of violent crime in most jurisdictions and up to 90 percent in areas where gangs are especially active. Or, as David Kennedy notes in his chapter of this volume, groups collectively representing under 0.5 percent of the city population will be connected with at least half of all homicides in the city.

Contrary to popular conceptions, gangs are typically small (consisting of fewer than fifty members and often as few as ten), non-hierarchal, and largely disorganized. While some may claim allegiance to larger, national groups, in reality they have few if any connections (Sullivan 2005). There tends to be little cohesion, and individual members drift in and out of active membership (Deuchar 2009). Most gangs lack formal leaders, hierarchy, or any meaningful division of labor. Gangs are typically territorial, often limited to a small neighborhood or a single housing project. Gang members join because their family or close friends are members. They are most typically male and from the lower social classes. Being neighborhood-based, gang membership often reflects the ethnic make-up of the neighborhood and are most typically intra-racial (Alleyne and Wood 2010; Hughes and Short 2005). Despite the lack of organization, there is a collective liability in the sense that rival gangs and authorities treat everyone in a geographic area as gang members (Kennedy current volume). There tends to be a strong sense of loyalty among members, and gang members frequently talk about their co-members as "family" (Vigil 2002).

Scholars widely recognize that gangs are adaptations to industrial shifts in the occupational structure and the resulting absence of jobs, failures in the education system, hyper-segregation, outmigration of middle class members, the absence of alternative activities, and the lack of community and informal controls (see Klein and Maxson 2006). In this sense, gangs, like vigilantism, occur in the absence of an effective state. Yet, instead of a means of social control by those in socially superior positions who wish to maintain the status quo, gangs are reactions to oppression, deprivation, and a schism with the society.

Gang violence is generally expressive rather than instrumental (Decker 1996; Papachristos, 2009; Hughes and Short 2005). It typically begins with a symbolic slight, disrespect, challenge, or other "beef" against one or a few members that then spreads to include the entire gang and those allied with it. Gang violence is a form of self-help (see Black 1998) that results from a withdrawal from the dominate society's criminal justice system and the adoption of a street code that requires any violence directed at the group be met with retaliatory violence (see Anderson 1999; Bourgois 2003). Combined, these factors lead addressing grievances through violence instead of legal means. As Kennedy writes in this volume:

> This withdrawal (from the police), coupled with the street code and group dynamics, can produce an escalated cascade of reciprocal violence, in which an initial event—a group member's fellow group member is killed—produces a subsequent killing which is seen by the perpetrating group as justice, by the recipient group as an affront requiring payback, and can grow to involve multiple group members on each side and even groups allied with those groups.

Thus, gang violence typically occurs among equals that are marginalized and isolated from the dominant society. That is, both gangs involved in the violence are disenfranchised. Unlike vigilantism that occurs when one party has strong allies while the other lacks allies, both gangs involved in a dispute have numerous supporters; thus, the gangs tend to have equal partisanship. Gang violence therefore happens among socially distant equals. It is therefore understandable why researchers find that most inter-gang violence results from challenges to one's status (see, for example, Hughes and Short 2005). In a world where the routes to traditional forms of status are largely closed, the honor of one's gang and one's position in it are vehemently protected.

Similar to gang violence, feuds are also group-perpetrated/group-targeted violence. While feuding clans invoke images of pre-modern, rural societies and street gangs conjure visions of modern urban decay, feuding clans and youth gangs "engage in significantly similar forms of violence (Black, 2004a, 163; also see Cooney 1998; Decker and Van Winkle 1996). Although they are not strictly equivalent, there are striking similarities, and feuds and gangs are found in similar social fields.

Feuds are extended and open exchanges of violence, typically involving one assault or murder at a time (Black 2004). They involve clan-like units such as extended families or large homesteads that may include nonfamily members (see Ericksen and Horton 1992; Otterbein and Otterbein 1965; Pospisil 1968). Classic blood feuds occurred everywhere, but they were most common prior to the twentieth century in the Mediterranean region and North America (Erikson and Horton 1992). Like gangs, they occur in areas with limited state controls, and they typically involve groups of equal status. Classic blood feuds literally involve families just as gangs involve members who share familial-like ties. Also like gangs, feuds are often attempts to retain symbolic capital. As Bourdieu (1979) argued, feuds are intimately linked to marriage arrangements between kin groups, especially when arrangements involve intangibles such as chastity and honor. Indeed, cross-cultural research reveals that feuds are most common where there is intense concern over female chastity and the groom contributes limited tangible goods to the marriage transaction (see Ericksen and Horton 1992). Finally, like gangs, feuds most frequently result in violence that targets young males.

## Terrorism

There are, of course, definitional issues with the term "terrorism." Turk (2002; 2004) defines terrorism as the deliberate targeting of randomly selected victims to weaken an opponent's will in a persistent political conflict. Conversely, Black (2004b, 14) defines "pure terrorism" as "unilateral self-help by organized civilians who covertly inflict mass violence on other civilians." Regardless of the definition one adopts, I agree with Turk (2004, 271) when he says that one of the most significant contributions of sociological thinking to our understanding of terrorism "is the realization that it is a social construction." Terrorism, in other words, is in the eye of the beholder, and one group's "terrorism" is another's "liberation struggle." Nevertheless, "terrorism" does differ in many ways from other forms of violence, and, as such, it has a unique social geometry (see Black 2004b for a detailed discussion).

As most scholars recognize, terrorism is an attempt to address some long-standing grievance. Black (2004b, 18–19) states, "terrorists represent an aggrieved collective (such as an ethnicity or religion) and attack civilians associated with another collectivity (such as an ethnicity, religion, or nation-state). As Juergensmeyer argues in this volume, even a "lone wolf" terrorist has "an audience in mind and a larger network of imagined supporters for whom the act is meant to impress." Whether the attacks are politically strategic or, as Juergensmeyer (2003; and this volume) argues, more symbolic of a "grander conquest" or cosmic battle, they are meant to express or symbolize the attackers' position in some conflict.

Terrorism is a form of self-help used when other forms of addressing the grievance are unavailable or believed to be ineffective. Kruger and Maleckova (2003) note, terrorism is a response to feelings of indignity in political contexts.

Like other forms of self-help, terrorism occurs when social distances are large (i.e., high levels of inequality, vertical segmentation, and cultural distance) while physical distance is small (Black 1998). Specifically, terrorism "arises with a high degree of cultural distance, relational distance, inequality and functional independence" (Black, 2004b, 16, 18; Black 2004c; Senechal de la Roche, 1996). Thus, terrorists differ from their targeted victims in culture (language, ethnicity, religion, etc.) and resources (i.e., terrorists tend to be of lower social status, at least with respect to the status structure of the targeted society). Yet, unlike in the past when social distance typically corresponded with physical distance, modern technology has shrunk the physical world and now socially distant groups are able to bridge vast physical distances. Consequently, terrorists are socially distant but physically close, and "terrorism arises only when a grievance has a social geometry distant enough and a physical geometry close enough for mass violence against civilians" (Black, 2004b, 21). This, according to Black (2004b), explains why international terrorism is a relatively recent phenomenon and one whose form has changed radically since the early 1980s (see Juergensmeyer, 2003).

Consequently, in many ways, terrorism resembles vigilantism. They are both forms of self-help. They are both means of "taking the law in one's hands." They both arise when there are high levels of inequality and vast differences in culture separating two groups. In addition, these acts of violence occur when one of the groups feel threatened by the other and when the aggrieved party believes there is no other recourse. As discussed above, vigilantism is used by social superiors against social inferiors when social inferiors threaten social superiors' positions and the state cannot adequately protect their interests. Similarly, terrorism occurs when a social inferior attempts to address a grievance with a social superior. As Smelser and Mitchell (2002) observe, terrorism is most likely to emerge in regions that have a history of Western colonialism and recent postcolonial economic and cultural penetration. In other words, terrorism tends to emerge in regions that are in weak economic, military, and cultural positions relative to their Western targets. It is, as Black (2004b, 19) says, "a form of social control from below."

## CONCLUSION

I hope that the proposed typology focuses scholarly attention on both the perpetrators and the targets of violence. While most scholars do not consider the targets of violence (Martin, McCarthy, and McPhail 2009), the proposed typology explicated does. By doing so, we see there is a fundamental difference between vigilantism and feuds, for example, and that these varying types of group violence have different underlying causes. In addition to introducing a typology that explicitly includes a consideration of the perpetrators and targets of violence, the above discussion also extends a specific strategy for studying and understanding types of violence. Namely, the above discussion is an exercise in "social geometry" that attempts to explain human behavior by referencing its location and direction in social space. Therefore, vigilantism, gang violence, and terrorism are related to the degree of inequality, social distance, cultural distance, intimacy, and so forth between the parties involved in a violent episode.

Of course, there are other ways of explaining or predicting violence; however, I believe the social geometry approach can be extremely fruitful. I believe it can highlight similarities and differences between types of violence. For example, we can see from the above discussion that one major difference in the social fields of vigilantism and terrorism is the *direction of the violence*. Vigilantism is the violent social control of a social inferior while terrorism is the violent social control of a social superior. Another difference is in the level of partisanship. Vigilantism occurs when partisanship is unequal (i.e., the attacker has allies while the attacked has far fewer). Terrorism, however, occurs when partisanship is relatively equal (even if the allies are only imagined as Jergensmeyer argues about "lone wolf" terrorists). With terrorism, the difference in partisanship is not in absolute numbers; instead, the difference between the parties' allies is in relative status. Terrorists have supporters, but they too lack power.

Another example of the possible power of such an approach is comparing "group violence" with "individual violence." As the discussion of vigilantism, gangs and feuds, and terrorism argued, group violence occurs among socially distant actors. Even gang violence and feuds, which typically occurs among equals, often pit culturally distant groups that are largely uninvolved in each other's lives against each other. This is not the case in most cases of individual-perpetrated violence. Most individually committed street crimes, for example, are intraracial and committed by acquaintances, friends, or intimates. For example, acquaintance rape is more common than stranger rape. In fact, in 2010, strangers perpetrated only 39 percent of violent victimizations (Bureau of Justice Statistics 2010). Similarly, domestic violence, which is relatively common, obviously occurs among intimates. Therefore, intimacy appears to be dangerous for individuals; social distance is dangerous for groups.

Although the above discussion only addressed group-perpetrated violence, a similar approach could address group-targeted violence, individual-perpetrated, and individual-targeted violence. I suspect there will be distinct social fields for each of these types of violence. In addition, future research should address the role of the state. While I believe the proposed simple typology can help in our pursuit of explaining violence theoretically, the distinctions may be insufficient. Combining state actors with other groups could potentially be problematic. As Weber notes, the state has a monopoly on the use of lethal violence. Indeed, much of the state's bureaucratic apparatus is dedicated to the efficient use of violence. In addition, the state possesses resources that can be used to enact violence that far outstrips the capabilities of other groups. Although some well-armed rebel groups can match the firepower of the nation-state in which they operate, none can match the violence-making abilities of the most advanced militaries. Similarly, some American gangs can outmatch the police; however, they do not control and operate cruise missiles. Thus, as a perpetrator of violence, the state stands alone. It may be similarly unique when it is the target of violence. Very few targets of violence can appeal to "rules of engagement" like the state can and does. International law recognizes that warfare is a "legitimate" act of violence; however, this mutually agreed upon "sport" must follow pre-established rules for it to be legitimate. It is fine to attack a state, provided you announce it, treat its prisoners "humanly," care for their wounded, and so forth (see, for example, Kalshoven and Zegveld 2011). There is no similar parallel with other forms of group violence. It therefore may be wise to distinguish between "group violence" and "state violence." However, it is possible that the same social geometry applies to both types of collective violence. This empirical question remains unanswered.

While there is work in detailing the geometry of various types of violence, there is no work that I know of that discusses the social geometry of the consequences of violence. Violence has obvious negative effects on individuals, communities, and nations; however, violence can also serve as a source of social change (see Ginsberg 2013) and even social solidarity (see Hawdon, Ryan and Agnich 2010). Future research should investigate if violence that emerges from specific social fields is more likely to result in social fields of change and solidarity. At this point, however, this too remains an unanswered empirical question.

# REFERENCES

Abrahams, R. 1998. *Vigilant Citizens: Vigilantism and the State*. Cambridge: Polity.

Alleyne, E., and J. Wood. 2010. "Gang Involvement: Psychological and Behavioral Characteristics of Gang Members, Peripheral Youth, and non-gang Youth." *Aggressive Behavior* 36: 423–36.

Anderson, E. 1990. *Code of the Street: Decency, Violence, and the Moral Life of the Inner City*. New York: W.W. Norton.

Black, D. 1976. *Behavior of Law*. New York: Academic.

———. 1983. "Crime as Social Control." *American Sociological Review* 48: 34–45.

———. 1998. *The Social Structure of Right and Wrong*. New York: Academic.

———. 1995. "The Epistemology of Pure Sociology." *Law and Social Inquiry* 20: 829–70.

———. 2004a. "Violent Structures." In *Violence: From Theory to Research,* edited by Margaret Zahn, Hennry Brownstein, and Shelly Jackson, 145–58. Newark, NJ: LexisNexis/Anderson.

———. 2004b. "The Geometry of Terrorism." *Sociological Theory* 22: 14–25.

———. 2004c. "Terrorism as Social Control." *Sociology of Crime, Law, and Deviance* 5: 9–18.

———. 2012. *Moral Time*. Oxford: Oxford University Press.

Bourdieu, P. 1979. *Outline of a Theory of Practice*. Cambridge, UK: Cambridge University Press.

Bourgiois, P. 2003. *In Search of Respect: Selling Crack in El Barrio*. New York: Cambridge University Press.

Brundage, W. F. 1993. *Lynching in the New South: Georgia and Virginia, 1880–1930*. Urbana, IL: University of Illinois Press.

Bureau of Justice Statistics. 2010. *National Crime Victimization Survey*. Accessed December 3, 2013, bjs.ojp.usdoj.gov/index.cfm?ty=pbdetail&iid=2224.

Buur, Lars. 2008. "Democracy and its Discontents: Vigilantism, Sovereignty and Human Rights in South Africa." *Review of African Political Economy* 35: 571–84.

Campbell, B. 2013. "Genocide and Social Time." *DILEMAS: Revista de Estudos de Conflito e Controle Social* 6: 465–88.

Cooney, M. 1998. *Warriors and Peacemakers: How Third Parties Shape Violence*. New York: New York University Press.

Decker, S. 1996. "Collective and Normative Features of Gang Violence." *Justice Quarterly* 13: 243–64.

Decker, S. H., and B. Van Winkle. 1996. *Life in the Gang: Family, Friends, and Violence*. Cambridge: Cambridge University Press.

Deuchar, R. 2009. *Gangs, Marginalized Youth and Social Capital*. Stoke-on-Trent, U.K.: Trentham Books.

Dönmez, R. Ö. 2008. "Vigilantism in Turkey: Totalitarian Movements and Uncivil Society in a Post-9/11 Democracy." *Totalitarian Movements and Political Religions* 9: 551–73.

Easteal, P., and L. McOrmond-Plummer 2006. *Real Rape, Real Pain: Help for Women Sexually Assaulted by Male Partners*. Melbourne: Hybrid.

Ericksen, K. P., and H. Horton. 1992. "'Blood Feuds': Cross-Cultural Variations in Kin Group Vengeance." *Cross-Cultural Research* 26: 57–85.

Federal Bureau of Investigation. 2009. *Hate Crime Statistics, 2009*. Washington, DC: U.S. Department of Justice.

———. 2011. *2011 National Gang Threat Assessment: Emerging Trends*. Washington, DC: Federal Bureau of Investigation.

Galtung, J. 1969. "Violence, Peace, and Peace Research." *Journal of Peace Research* 6: 167–91.

Ginsberg, B. 2013. *The Value of Violence*. Amherst, New York: Prometheus.

Hawdon, J. 2001. "The Role of Presidential Rhetoric in the Creation of a Moral Panic: Reagan, Bush, and the War on Drugs." *Deviant Behavior* 22: 419–45.

Hawdon, J., J. Ryan, and L. Agnich. 2010. "Crime as a Source of Solidarity: A Research Note Testing Durkheim's Assertion." *Deviant Behavior* 31: 679–703.

Heald, S. 1986a. "Witches and Thieves: Deviant Motivations in Gisu Society." *Man* 21: 65–78.

———. 1986b. "Mafias in Africa: The Rise of Drinking Companies and Vigilante Groups in Bugisu District, Uganda." *Africa* 56: 446–67.

———. 2006. "State, Law, and Vigilantism in Northern Tanzania." *African Affairs* 105: 265–83.

Huggins, M. 1991. "Introduction: Vigilantism and the State—A look South and North." In *Vigilantism and the State in Modern Latin America: Essays on Extralegal Violence*, edited by Martha Huggins, 1–19. New York: Praeger.

Hughes, L., and J. Short. 2005. "Disputes Involving Youth Street Gang Members: Micro-Social Contexts." *Criminology* 43: 43–75.

Iadicola, P., and A. Shupe. 2003. *Violence, Inequality and Human Freedom*. Lanham: Rowman and Littlefield.

Juergensmeyer, M. 2003. *Terror in the Mind of God: The Global Rise of Religious Violence* Berkeley: University of California Press.

Kalshoven, F., and L. Zegveld. 2011. *Constraints on the Waging of War*. New York: Cambridge University Press.

Klein, M., and C. Maxson. 2006. *Street Gang Patterns and Policies*. Oxford: Oxford University Press.

Krueger, A., and J. Maleckova. 2003. "Education, Poverty and Terrorism: Is There a Causal Connection?" *The Journal of Economic Perspectives* 17: 119–44.

Martin, A., J. McCarthy, and C. McPhail. 2009. "Why Targets Matter: Toward a More Inclusive Model of Collective Violence." *American Sociological Review* 74: 821–41.

Otterbein, K., and C. S. Otterbein. 1965. "An Eye for an Eye, a Tooth for a Tooth: A Cross-Cultural Study of Feuding." *American Anthropologist* 67: 1470–82.

Papachristos, A. V. 2009. "Murder by Structure: Dominance Relations and the Social Structure of Gang Homicide." *American Journal of Sociology* 115: 74–128.

Pfeifer, M. 2004. *Rough Justice: Lynching and American Society 1874–1947*. Champaign, IL: University of Illinois Press.

Pospisil, L. 1968. "Feuds." In *International Encyclopedia of Social Sciences*, edited by D. L. Sills, 389–93, New York: MacMillan.

Rosenbaum, H. J., and P. Sederberg 1974. "Vigilantism: An Analysis of Establishment Violence." *Comparative Politics* 6: 541–70.

Saran, A. B. 1974. *Murder and Suicide among the Munda and the Oraon*. Delhi, India: National Publishing House.

Schärf, W. and D. Nina. 2001. *The Other Law: Non-State Ordering in South Africa*, Cape Town: Juta and Co.

Senechal de la Roche, R. 1990. *The Sociogenesis of a Race Riot: Springfield, Illinois, in 1908*. Urbana, IL: University of Illinois Press.

———. 1996. "Collective Violence as Social Control." *Sociological Forum* 11: 97–128.

———. 1997. "The Sociogenesis of Lynching." In *Under Sentence of Death: Lynching in the South*, edited by W. Fitzhugh Brundage, 48–76. Chapel Hill, NC: University of North Carolina Press.

———. 2001. "Why is Collective Violence Collective?" *Sociological Theory* 19: 126–44.

Smelser, N. J., and F. Mitchell. 2002. *Terrorism: Perspectives from the behavioral and social sciences*. National Academies Press.

Sullivan, M. L. 2005. "Maybe We Shouldn't Study 'Gangs': Does Reification Obscure Youth Violence?" *Journal of Contemporary Criminal Justice* 21: 170–90.

The Independent. 2013. *Nine-Year-Old Fires Shotgun at Norwegian School*. Accessed December 18, 2013, www.independent.co.uk/news/world/europe/nineyearold-fires-shotgun-at-norwegian-school-1675420.html.

Thorton, W., L. Voigt, and D. Wood Harper. 2013. *Leading Question Regarding the Conceptualization and Reality of Violence in Society*. Durham, NC: Carolina Academic Press.

Tilly, C. 2003. *The Politics of Collective Violence*. Cambridge: Cambridge University Press.

Tuckman, J. 2013. "Mexican Vigilantes Take on Drug Cartels and Worry Authorities: Militias Spring up across Mexico to Defend Communities but Authorities Fear 'Rebel Force' and an 'Undeclared Civil War.'" *The Guardian*, October 28, 2013. Accessed December 18, 2013, www.theguardian.com/world/2013/oct/28/mexican-militias-vigilantes-drug-cartels.

Turk, A. T. 2002. *Encyclopedia of Crime and Justice*. New York: Macmillan.

———. 2004. "Sociology of Terrorism." *Annual Review of Sociology* 30: 271–86.

Vigil, J. D. 2002. *A Rainbow of Gangs*. Austin: University of Texas Press.

Walker, E. T., A. W. Martin, and J.D. McCarthy. 2008. "Confronting the State, the Corporation, and the Academy: The Influence of Institutional Targets on Social Movement Repertoires." *American Journal of Sociology* 114: 35–76.

Walsh, P., W. E. Thorton, and L. Voigt. 2010. "Post-Hurricane Katrina and Human Rights Violations in New Orleans, Louisiana." In *Corruption and Human Rights: Interdisciplinary Perspective*, edited by M. Boersma and H. Nelen, 144–48. Cambridge: Intersentia.

Weber, Max. 1918. "Politics as a Vocation." In *From Max Weber: Essays in Sociology*, translated by H. H. Gerth and C. Wright Mills, 77–128. New York: Routledge.

Weiner, N., M. A. Zahn, and R. J. Sagi. 1990. *Violence: Patterns, Causes, and Public Policy*. New York: Harcourt Brace Jovanovich.

Wood, J., and E. Alleyne. 2010. "Street Gang Theory and Research: Where Are We Now and Where Do We Go From Here?" *Aggression and Violent Behavior* 15: 100–11.

*Chapter Two*

# Hate Groups

*From Offline to Online Social Identifications*

Atte Oksanen, Pekka Räsänen, and James Hawdon

Group-perpetrated violence has reached historically dreadful dimensions. Men have slaughtered each other in civil wars and other atrocities for centuries. In addition, especially subordinated social groups and ethnic minorities have been targets of violence. For example, the United States has a violent history involving the persecution of Native Americans, Asian Americans, Hispanic Americans, and African Americans. In Europe, Nazi Germany built one of the most lethal death machines to date targeting ideologically grounded victims including Jewish and Romani populations. More recently in Rwanda in the early 1990s, Hutus killed almost one million Tutsis, whom they called "cockroaches" and blamed them for economic and social problems in public propaganda (Green and Seher 2002; Timmermann 2005).

Even today, Western democracies are not strangers to group-perpetrated violence. Hate targeting specific groups of people is realized in both speech and action. It is grounded on ideology and prejudices that are modified culturally and are enforced in everyday interaction. The basic group distinction made between ingroup (*us*) and outgroup (*them*) may, in specific social conditions, increase prejudices against others, as noted in social psychology (Tajfel, 1970). Hate as a special form of bigotry is known throughout history, but law and other social norms have often regulated its expressions. Legal systems may, however, fail in a "state of exception" (Agamben 2003; Benjamin 1940/1974), which may give rise to new kinds of social evils. The recent Greek economic crisis, for example, gave rise to the Golden Dawn far-right extremist organization, which has fascist and neo-Nazi roots (Xenakis, 2012).

The United States has been a safe haven for organized hate groups such as the Ku Klux Klan, Holocaust Denial, and Christian Identity. With the passage of the first hate crime law in 1980, the United States has seen the rise of hate crime legislation (Gerstenfeld 2013). While these laws seek to control actual violence, the First Amendment of the U.S. Constitution protects the expression of hate in speech and symbols. Partly due to historical reasons, many European societies regulate statements that threaten or degrade a specific group of people (Foxman and Wolf 2013; Waldron 2012).

The rise of far right political populism and associated acts of terror has especially increased public concern over hate speech both offline and online in Europe (see Bartlett, Birdwell, and Littler 2011; Caiani and Parenti, 2013). Although the concept of hate speech is difficult to define, the Council of Europe has tried setting proper guidelines for hate speech, which covers "all forms of expression which spread, incite, promote or justify racial hatred, xenophobia, anti-Semitism, or other forms of hatred based on intolerance, including: intolerance expressed by aggressive nationalism and ethnocentrism, discrimination and hostility against minorities, migrants and people of immigrant origin" (Weber 2009, 3).

Defining hate groups is a sensitive and complex task (Citron and Norton, 2011; Foxman and Wolf 2013; Waldron 2012). Hate groups do not necessarily consider themselves hate groups, (Blazak 2009) and they find ways to justify their arguments. Hate groups consist of different individuals who together disseminate hate speech or hate material. This hate material expresses harmful and threatening statements or defamatory statements targeting individuals or larger human collectives. These groups may themselves act violently or simply concentrate on the dissemination of hate propaganda. The boundary between hate groups and terrorist groups is sometimes vague.

This chapter examines offline and online hate groups targeting specific groups of people based on their ethnicity, religion, sexual orientation, or other characteristics. The chapter aims to contribute a new perspective to the ongoing discussion of online hate groups (Brown 2009; Foxman and Wolf 2013; Gerstenfeld 2013; Hawdon 2012). We start from classic social psychological experiments and theories of intergroup conflicts and continue with examples of both offline and online hate communities. Our main analysis concentrates on the YouTube school-shooting fan community that spreads hateful thoughts and glamorizes mass murders. The YouTube case demonstrates changes in hate group phenomena in contemporary societies.

# SOCIAL PSYCHOLOGY OF INTERGROUP
# CONFLICTS AND VIOLENCE

Group behavior is at the core of social behavior. It is the human tendency to seek social connection (Baumeister and Leary 1995). People are directly influenced by their primary groups, including their families and close friends. They also have much wider group memberships, including social groups (e.g., group memberships based on work, studies, and hobbies). They also belong to broader social categories based on similarities in, for example, gender, ethnicity, religion, and nationality. Stereotypical and prejudicial associations regarding social groups may exist in specific sociocultural environments and affect children and adolescents growing up in those environments (Bodenhausen and Richeson 2010, 349–50). Intergroup conflicts are one consequence of such prejudices.

Group-forming behavior is part of everyday human social interaction. People who have a mutual goal or interest, for example, often form groups. Similarities among people, physical proximity and shared threat may facilitate group formation. Classic social psychological experiments show how easily groups are formed and organized. Muzafer Sherif (1961) and his research group conducted a natural experiment to study intergroup conflict. A homogenous group of eleven to twelve-year-old boys were divided into two groups in summer camp. Both groups formed intragroup hierarchies. They built close connections to the members of their own group and avoided members of the other group. Competition between the groups reinforced the conflict between the groups while increasing intragroup solidarity. Cooperation between the groups gradually lessened the friction between them.

Sherif's natural experiment was followed by studies aimed at establishing minimal conditions in which people distinguish between ingroup and outgroup. Laboratory settings involved participants divided into two groups on an unimportant basis, and they did not interact within their own group or with the other group during the experiment. They were rather simply asked to distribute resources to other participants who were only marked with a number and group name. The results underlined the ingroup favoritism and revealed that even arbitrary group divisions could lead to ingroup favoritism (Tajfel et al. 1971).

The minimal group paradigm was a starting point for the broader social identity theory (SIT) proposed by Henri Tajfel and his colleague John C. Turner (Billig 2002; Turner and Reynolds 2010). SIT proposes that individuals make sense of their social environment by categorizing themselves and others into groups that can be contrasted with others. Social identity theory argues that people establish a positively valued distinctiveness toward their own groups compared to outgroups (Tajfel and Turner 1979). Tajfel (1974) understood social identity as being part of an individual's self-concept that is drawn from the emotional significance he or she attaches to being a member of the group. Hence, social identity is the social self, which may be based on one or several group memberships. Social identity is what allows intergroup behavior to take place (Turner 1982). For example, political identity makes political behavior possible (Simon and Klandermans 2001).

SIT was not a theory of prejudice or bigotry, but rather a theory of positive group identifications, and Tajfel, for example, used it to explain the black power movement and the women's movement (Billig 2002, 179). Tajfel's starting points were, however, grounded on understanding prejudice (Tajfel 1970). He noted how in war members of outgroups are depersonalized—and sometimes dehumanized (Tajfel 1974; 1981). Depersonalization may also occur intragroup, causing a person to self-stereotype (Turner 1985). Such depersonalization (or de-individuation) may be an especially important factor for explaining group-perpetrated violence. Being a member of a group may facilitate violent acts, as a person acts not as an individual, but rather as part of the group. Belonging to a group diffuses the responsibility for the actions, and groups often have a division of labor that separates decision making from carrying out acts (Baumeister 1999, 325–26).

Of course, group action itself can be used for both good and evil. Ingroup favoritism may sometimes be beneficial for individuals and it does not necessarily lead to harmful societal effects. SIT and more recent group theories underline the importance of social and historic conditions. Sherif's (1956) experiments showed that it was possible to manipulate the social conditions that could lead to intergroup conflict by increasing the competition between two groups. Perceived conflict of interest and competition are often grounds for group conflicts. Intergroup conflict may also be rooted in either realistic or imaginary threats from other groups (Brewer 2010, 545). Recent studies demonstrate the complexity of intergroup conflicts arising from ingroup favoritism. Ingroup favoritism and outgroup hostility are not two sides of the same coin but rather independent of each other. Marilynn B. Brewer notes:

> Ingroup love is not a necessary precursor of outgroup hate. However, the very factors that make ingroup attachment and allegiance important to individuals also provide a fertile ground for antagonism and distrust of those outside the ingroup boundaries. The need to justify ingroup values in the form of moral superiority to others, sensitivity to threat, the anticipation of interdependence under conditions of distrust, social comparison processes, and power politics all conspire to connect ingroup identification and loyal to disdain and overt hostility toward outgroups. (1999, 442)

Emotion is an important factor in all group behavior, and recent studies underline the importance of the emotional investments people have (see Billig 2002). First, it is likely that members of the same group are exposed to the same kinds of emotional objects and events. Second, emotions are facilitated by intragroup social interaction. Third, the group's social norms and values influence the emotions that are displayed. Fourth, shared emotions may form the basis of group membership (Manstead 2010, 121). In other words, emotions are socially shared and expressed and they are used to glue the group together. This becomes especially evident in hate groups, which are defined by common enemies, potential threats, and emotional hatred towards others.

As we have seen, in specific social and historic conditions, outgroup members are depersonalized or even dehumanized. In such conditions, ingroup attachment to violent ideologies can facilitate violence. Ever since the horrors of World War II, social scientists have strived to understand how people have, in the worst contextual settings, succumbed to violence (Nurmi and Oksanen 2013). Social psychological evidence points out that, in groups, even otherwise normal individuals can lose their sense of self and commit hateful acts they would not have necessarily done alone. In other words, group membership facilitates evil acts (Baumeister 1999; Zimbardo 2007). However, even in normative group situations, some individuals chose to resist violence (Zimbardo 2007). Furthermore, we have to understand how they become members of such groups in the first place and how group membership radicalizes them further (Haslam and Reicher 2007).

## A BRIEF HISTORY OF HATE GROUPS

Hate groups have a long history in both the United States and Europe, well before our current network and technologically advanced societies. Various organizations, political parties and groups have directly espoused open hatred toward specific groups. The most obvious example of a hate group is the Nazi party (1920–1945), which started as a small political movement after the First World War and later gained power during the politically and economically turbulent Weimar Republic Era. The rise and eventual political dominance of Nazism in Germany is important, because it exemplifies how hate groups use propaganda to disseminate hateful ideology. Nazi ideology was based on sharp binary opposition (*us vs. them*) and an ideology that dehumanized others (Theweleit 2000).

In the United States, the Ku Klux Klan (KKK) exemplifies how hate groups exist when there is something to oppose. If a state is openly racist or bigoted, there is obviously no need for other types of bigoted organizations (Gerstenfeld 2013, 138). The Ku Klux Klan began to flourish in the late 1860s and the early 1870s after the U.S. Civil War ended slavery. Members gradually adopted more serious measures and became a terrorist organization dedicated to white supremacy (Baumeister 1999, 251–54; Gerstenfeld 2013, 139). The original Klan died out by 1872. Gerstenfeld (2013, 140) suspects this was probably because a series of laws that disenfranchised and disempowered blacks rendered the group unnecessary. The clan rose again after 1915, and by 1922 it had 1.5 to 5 million members (Berlet and Lyons 2000, 97). The new Klan did not limit its hate to blacks; instead, the new Klan also opposed Jews, immigrants, Catholics, communists, and anyone who was not considered 100 percent American. The new Klan lost much of its power at the end of 1920s, but revived again in the 1950s after the Supreme Court declared segregated public schools unconstitutional. Today there is no single Klan organization, but rather several smaller organizations. These groups oppose, for example, Jews, nonwhite people, and gays (Gerstenfeld, 2013).

Both the history of KKK and Nazism in Germany exemplify how the rise of hate groups involves both a power struggle and hateful ideologies that are used to attract a wider audience. These groups used successfully the newest available technology: radio and film (Levin 2002). For example, the rise of the KKK during the early 1920s was associated with the successful *The Birth of a Nation* film (1915), the impact of First World War patriotism, and racist theories about the superiority of white people (Gerstenfeld 2013, 140–41). Similarly, in Europe, Nazis were not ideologically distinct from the racist theories of an era. They cleverly used existing prejudices and available technologies, and exploited economic and social crises to help them gain power.

The world around has changed considerably since the Second World War, but the message of hate groups has changed little. Hate groups are really one group trying to take advantage of a social situation by openly stereotyping and depersonalizing another. Many hate groups in the United States and Europe target "nonwhite" people, immigrants, Jews, and recently, Muslims. In addition, there are also nonwhite hate groups, including, for example, Islamist groups such as the Nation of Islam, black separatist groups, and religious groups that target sexual minorities. Notably some religious groups, which themselves often claim to be victims of hate speech, openly target others. The Westboro Baptist Church, for example, has made statements against Jews, blacks, and gays (Gerstenfeld 2013, 133). According to the Southern Poverty Law Center (2013) there are 1,007 hate groups operating in all fifty states of the United States. These include neo-Nazis, Klansmen, white nationalists and racist skinheads, black separatists, and others.

Despite the existence of numerous types of hate groups, there are common features among them. First, they build a strong boundary between in-group and outgroup (*us* vs. *them*), and specific outgroups are targeted with violence. Second, outgroup members are not seen as individuals, but rather become stereotyped members of their group (Gerstenfeld 2013, 101). Third, their viewpoints are based on the moral superiority over others, and they seek to justify criminal acts against their targets. Fourth, these groups are normative and their members identify strongly with their goals. This means that open dialog within the group is not necessarily accepted and the dominant viewpoint is not contested.

The spread of hate material in society is a deceptively slow process. Even the horrors of the Second World War are an example that the consequences of hate often do not have an impact in a day or two, but rather over the course of the years to follow. Abraham H. Foxman and Christopher Wolf (2013, 4) compare it to a virus that may not kill directly but it "normalizes bigotry, diminishes discourse, misleads kids, and blight the lives of its (. . .) targets." Hate speech has broader societal consequences, as Jeremy Waldron points out:

> [R]acist or religious defamation is not just an idea contributed to a debate. In its published, posted, or pasted-up form, hate speech can become a world-defining activity, and those who promulgate it know very well—this is part of their intention—that the visible world they create is a much harder world for the targets of their hatred to live in. (2012, 74)

Waldron (2012, 66) notes that a society that permits hate speech looks very different from a society that does not. We have to ask, do we really want to have a society in which open hatred and death threats are not condemned? Despite the attempts to combat hate groups, many hate groups have existed for a long time, and they have been quite persistent in revitalizing themselves in suitable social and historical contexts. In Europe, for example, recent decades witnessed a re-appearance of far-right political parties whose ideals are not radically different from their fascistic predecessor of the early twentieth century. The Internet and social media may have facilitated the political success of such parties and associated hate groups.

## THE RISE OF ONLINE HATE GROUPS

Hate groups have always been skilled users of mass media and technological innovations. Technological developments during the past thirty years have facilitated their task remarkably. White supremacists in the United States were among the very early users of electronic communication networks. For example, as early as 1983, neo-Nazi publisher George Dietz established the first dial-up bulletin board system (BBS) as a method of online communication (Levin, 2002). The first online hate site appeared soon after the introduction of the World Wide Web. Stormfront.org, thought to be the first hate group with a Web presence, started in 1995. It had over 159,000 members by 2009 (Bowman-Grieve 2009), and it is still one of the most frequently visited hate sites on the Internet (Brown 2009).

The development of the Internet and other communication technologies has in many ways changed the patterns of social interaction in the Western world. People can create and form social relationships online and build their own interest groups and communities. Researchers already talked about online communities in the early period of the Internet (Baym 2000; Haythornth-waite 2007; Rheingold 2000). The Internet had many advantages that were previously unknown: it allowed fast communication and provided user ano-nymity. In other words, prior to the rise of the Internet, recruitment of mem-bers took place in face-to-face-meetings; now, it was possible to recruit people from geographically distant places. During the "Web 1.0 era," web-sites and discussion forums became the main channels to spread hateful ideologies.

With the introduction of Web 2.0, our lives became linked with other people like never before. It is the very nature of social media that it creates a user-generated platform for Internet users. Today most of the content dis-cussed and shared online is not provided by private or public companies, or other third-party players. The most successful companies generate only emp-ty boards for individual users, which are meant to be continually edited, updated and commented on (Tapscott and Williams 2006; Ritzer and Jurgen-son 2010). The leading social networking sites (SNSs) attract millions of users and continue to expand simply by offering a platform where users can discuss, share, and edit material of their own interests.

Online communication is not dependent on physical proximity. It offers increased possibilities to seek company outside your daily circles, and people may develop strong interpersonal ties in Internet communities (Lehdonvirta and Räsänen 2011; Williams et al. 2006). Younger users are especially likely to identify strongly with online communities (Näsi et al. 2011). For young people, participation in online communities is part of their everyday life, and it is no less real than their offline world. In fact, the notion that online reality would be artificial, less factual, and less real is not supported by the literature (Boellstorff 2010; McKenna and Bargh 2000).

Social media has made online hate communication more viral and visible. There is evidence that the Internet promotes the creation of an international extremist community (Burris, Smith, and Strahm 2000). Social media has allowed hate groups to be increasingly visible and successful at reaching and recruiting significant numbers of Internet users. Online hate groups have been gaining popularity since the early 2000s. They actively recruit young people using online technology (Lee and Leets 2002), and the young may be the most vulnerable to their influence. The existence of these groups has become a permanent online phenomenon and they appear to be recruiting members at rapid rates (Chau and Xu 2007). In the United States alone, the number of active hate groups increased by 66 percent between 2000 and 2010, and by 2010 there were over one thousand active hate groups online (Potok 2011). Even one active "lone wolf" can produce an impressive amount of material that is disseminated through different mainstream social networking sites, such as Facebook. As Foxman and Wolf state, the rise of the social media has been the game changer:

A few years back, we might have dismissed the anti-Semitic groups, racist organizations, and other vicious hater on the Internet as outliers . . . not worth taking seriously or responding to. But today we live in the world of Web 2.0, which has transformed the way the Internet is being used. In the interactive community environment of Web 2.0, social networking connects hundreds of millions of people around the globe; it takes just one "friend of a friend" to infect a circle of hundreds or thousands of individuals with weird, hateful lies that may go unchallenged, twisting minds in unpredictable ways. And with the users of Web 2.0 comprised largely of younger people, the impact of the misinformation contained there may persist for generations to come. (2013, 11)

Hate speech and hate material have a broader context as they does not solely concern organized hate groups or highly active individuals publishing hateful and threatening material online. Much of the hate speech or hate material may be disseminated within everyday online settings. Hate speech may sometimes overlap with cyberbullying and online harassment, which by definition involves the threats or other offensive behavior targeted at individuals (see Jones, Mitchell, and Finkelhor, 2013). Hence, we should not only pay attention to the most radical organized hate groups or lone wolves, but also to the ways in which such rhetoric is openly used in social media (see Hawdon 2012; Hawdon et al. forthcoming).

## SIGNIFICANCE OF ANONYMITY IN ONLINE HATE

Anonymity is useful for users who wish to disseminate hateful or politically radical messages because these messages can be disseminated without sharing one's personal information. The level of anonymity on the Web ranges from visual anonymity and pseudonymity to full anonymity. Although some SNSs, such as Facebook, have brought along a new user culture where users are not anonymous, some social media users prefer a higher degree of anonymity. Users may, for example, fake their identities and discerning real identities has become a difficult task. Other media companies such as Google allow a much higher degree of anonymity for their users. YouTube or Flickr provide good examples of such online sites that encourage users to create and maintain pseudonymous profiles (Lange 2007; Thelwal et al. 2012).

The anonymous environment of a SNS makes the viral spread of new ideas possible, including ideas that Western democracies do not normally tolerate. By using information and communication technologies (ICTs), it is possible to bypass the control and censorship of public bodies and state officials. Much of the control of social media is in the hands of active users who report criminal or harassing material to police or other authorities, but not all the material gets suspended, even in the mainstream sites such as YouTube, because uploaded material is increasing rapidly and it is difficult to detect illegal or otherwise deviant material without actively trying to find it.

Now, online hate communities should be understood as any other community, group or subculture within society. While they are potentially transnational and multilingual, they nevertheless have norms and conformist behaviour. Social psychologists have underlined that anonymous behaviour can be highly regulated on the Internet (e.g., Spears et al. 2002). Indeed, it can be argued that anonymity is the most important characteristic that creates strict rules for online discussions. The social identity model of deindividuation effects (SIDE) aims to explain the social effects of anonymity. According to SIDE, anonymity promotes a shift from a personal to a group self (Lea et al. 2001; Postmes et al. 2001). Empirical evidence suggests anonymity in the group enhances conformity to group norms (Postmes and Spears 1998).

SIDE assumes that anonymity intensifies the attraction to the group (Spears et al. 2002). Therefore, the model has important implications for the study of online hate groups. First, subjects are more prone to follow the norms of the group if they desire to be members. This is because anonymity intensifies the attraction to the group (Spears et al. 2002). Previous research on online communities shows that newcomers have to show that they know the common language used in a particular group or community (Cherny 1999; Haythornthwaite 2007). Second, it is important to note that the common language is used if users lack additional knowledge about the other group members since visual cues and other ways to build community are often missing. Hence, common interests and shared goals make it possible for an online hate group to exist.

## SCHOOL SHOOTINGS AND ONLINE GROUPS

School shootings are often dismissed as acts of disturbed young students who act alone or in pairs, like in Columbine. Before the Internet, this certainly was the case, but the developments after Columbine show that these acts should be understood in the broader context of severe targeted violence. Their radicalization has taken place in both on and offline environments (Oksanen et al. 2013). Belonging to radical online social groups has played a role at least in some recent cases, including Montreal (2006), Emsdetten (2006), Jokela (2007), Kauhajoki (2008), and Rio de Janeiro (2011).

The Columbine shooters Eric Harris and Dylan Klebold were the first to use the Internet, and school shooters since then have been active online. The Montreal school shooter, for example, kept an online diary and was active in social media (Cohen-Almagor and Haleva-Amir, 2008; Paton, 2013). The Emsdetten (2006) shooter was active online and posted videos on YouTube (Böckler and Seeger, 2013; Paton, 2013), and the Jokela shooter also had an online identity (Kiilakoski and Oksanen, 2011a). Both Finnish shooters found encouraging communities online, but offline, their fellow students or friends disapproved of their talk about school shootings (Kiilakoski and Oksanen, 2011b; Oksanen et al. 2013).

School shooters have been influenced by terrorist attacks, for example, the Jokela shooter Pekka-Eric Auvinen mentions various white mass killers and serial killers, including Theodore Kaczynski (Unabomber), Timothy McVeigh (Oklahoma City bomber), Eric Robert Rudolf (American anti-abortion and anti-gay terrorist) and Franz Fuchs (Austrian xenophobic terrorist) (Oksanen et al. 2013). School shootings may have influenced some terrorist and rampage shooters, including Anders Behring Breivik who killed sixty-seven children at the island of Utøya in Norway in 2011 (Sandberg et al. forthcoming). Like terrorism, school shooters have espoused their hatred before their violent acts. The Jokela shooter, for example, declared a total war against humanity in his Natural Selector's Manifesto:

> Hate, I'm so full of it and I love it. That is one thing I really love. Some time ago, I used to believe in humanity and I wanted to live a long and happy life . . . but then I woke up. I started to think deeper and realized things. But it was not easy to become existential . . . knowing as much as I know has made me unhappy, frustrated and angry. I just can't be happy in the society or the reality I live. Due to long process of existential thinking, observing the society I live and some other things happened in my life . . . I have come to the point where I feel nothing but hate against humanity and human race.

School shooting fans have been active internationally, especially on YouTube. Böckler and Seeger (2013) studied thirty-one active school shooting fans on YouTube in 2008–2009. Paton (2013) followed eighty-one YouTube users that were active online from 2007 to 2010. She concluded that school shooting fans disappeared after the several shootings that occurred in 2007 and 2008 due to increased social control. Indeed, there are cases in Finland where students have been arrested because of the material they published online (Oksanen et al. forthcoming).

## THIS STUDY

Our explanatory study aims to show how school shooting fans continue to be active online and how they are interconnected. In addition, we examine what kind of material and communication patterns make some profiles more significant than others in the network.

The data were collected from YouTube, from April 15 to June 15, 2012, by following daily sites' content. We looked into YouTube profiles that included positive or sympathizing comments about school shootings or school shooters. For example, comments that were explicitly pro-school shooting or indicated that some school shooters were the user's "hero" were included. Only the profiles that had been active during the previous two years were included in the sample. In other words, these selected users had uploaded material or written comments during the two years prior to data collection (meaning ca. April 2010–June 2012). Since previous school shooters in Jokela, Kauhajoki, and Emsdetten were active on YouTube (Böckler and Seeger 2013; Paton 2013), we collected information included in the shooter profiles. School shooters after Columbine have often mentioned similar objects of fascination, including previous school shootings and lone-wolf terrorism, films and documents, music, videogames, and philosophy (Kiilakoski and Oksanen 2011a). We particularly looked for profile names and pictures, profile texts, videos, and playlists related to a previous school shooting. We also looked for pro-school shooting comments made in school shooting videos.

Our systematic search concentrated on the publicly available material of YouTube. Hence, all the material was uploaded without logging in as a YouTube user. First, we used YouTube and Internet search engines to find the profiles by using key words associated with school shootings. These key words included: a) famous American and European cases, b) dates related to famous school shootings, c) perpetrators by name or nickname (e.g., Eric Harris/REB; Dylan Klebold/VoDKa; Pekka-Eric Auvinen/Sturmgeist89), d) cultural products associated with school shootings including films (e.g., Natural Born Killers), bands (e.g., KMFDM) and first-person shooter videogames (e.g., Battlefield), and e) well-known phrases used by the school shooters (e.g., natural selection). Second, we used the comments and feed sections of the profile pages to find other possible profiles. This snowballing technique proved to be useful, since many school shooting fans commented on each other's pages and videos.

We will first provide descriptive information about the profiles including the information about what school shootings were mentioned and whether other similar acts by lone-wolf terrorists (e.g., Timothy McVeigh, Anders Behring Breivik) were mentioned. Since there are many school shootings, we decided to categorize the incidents into shootings before and after Columbine. Given the frequency with which it is mentioned and its obvious symbolic place in the network's culture, the Columbine school shooting was marked as a separate category. We also coded the data for other radical ideologies (e.g., neo-Nazi ideology) and checked if the profiles were active in January 2007, approximately seven months after the original data collection. After this descriptive analysis, we use social network analysis (SNA) to describe the network as a whole and to identify the network's key actors. We conclude with a thematic analysis of these key actors' profiles.

## IDENTIFYING THE SCHOOL SHOOTING FANS

Contrary to some authors' predictions (Paton 2013), school shooting fan communities were still active on YouTube in 2012. One hundred and thirteen pro-school shooting profiles were identified during the data collection period. Many of the profile names include direct references to school shootings, especially the Columbine shooters. For example DylanVoDKaKlebold666, EricAndDylanRip, and RebHarris2012 refer to the Columbine shooters. Photos of school shooters are used as profile pictures and profile main-page background pictures. The profile main pages also directly indicated that they glorify school shootings and school shooters.

Table 2.1 shows that most of the profiles (89.4 percent, 101 profiles) either mentioned or were completely dedicated to the Columbine shooters. Hence, Columbine has kept its position as the most important school shooting case (see Fast, 2008; Larkin 2009; Muschert and Larkin 2007). In our data, only two pre-Columbine cases were cited. Post-Columbine cases gained more support from the YouTube users (19.5 percent, twenty-two profiles). They included German, Finnish, and U.S. school shootings. In total eight profiles (7.1 percent) mentioned other similar acts such as the 1995 Oklahoma City bombing. Fourteen profiles (12.3 percent) included explicit material related to neo-Nazi ideology, such as swastikas or radical right wing profile names such as 14AryanBrotherhood88.

**Table 2.1.   General information about the data.**

| | |
|---|---|
| Profiles | 113 |
| Months active (Date joined – June 2012) | Range: 0-79<br>Mean: 27 |
| Subscribers | Range: 0–1,477<br>Mean: 46 |
| Average video views | Range: 0–480,073<br>Mean: 22,005 |
| Country (information given in the profile) | US: 51 (45.1%)<br>Europe: 35 (31.0%)<br>Australia: 2 (1.8%)<br>South-America: 1 (0.9%)<br>No information: 24 (21.2%) |
| School shootings, other similar cases and radical ideologies mentioned | Columbine: 101 (89.4%)<br>Pre-Columbine: 2 (1.8%)<br>Post-Columbine: 22 (19.5%)<br>Other similar acts: 8 (7.1%)<br>Neo-Nazi: 14 (12.3%) |

The profiles rarely included information about the owner's gender or age. Although school shooters have been predominately males, their fans include females. However, we must be careful with drawing conclusions about the personal information found on YouTube since such information can easily be falsified. This concerns holds for the country information as well. Although there are tools to locate the IP-addresses, we decided to provide only the information mentioned in the profiles. The profiles were most commonly from the United States. Almost one-third were from Europe, especially from Germany (15.0 percent, seventeen profiles), but also, from the United Kingdom (3.5 percent, four profiles), Finland (3.5 percent, four profiles) and Poland (2.7 percent, three profiles). The languages used included German, Finnish, Polish, and Spanish, although English was the most commonly used language.

Although some profiles were active since 2006 and 2007, on average, profiles were seventeen months old. Overly radical YouTube profiles tend to be shut down because people report them (see also Paton 2013). In fact, such account closures are topics discussed by the fans. For example, NBKNatural-Selection posted a comment to SERVANTOFTHEGODSEAND:

> M WM hoever got your channel down is a piece of shit I wanna fucking kill them. I hate when people don't understand the truth about people like Reb & VoDkA and judge you and shit. We're a family, so we have to stick together . . . LONG LIVE THE REBEL & VODKA FAMILY.

School shooting fans do not have a large following on YouTube. Only seven profiles had more than one hundred subscribers, and on average they have relatively few subscribers (M = 46). The range of video views varied considerably (Rang e = 0–480,073). Many profiles had no uploaded videos and 41 percent of the 113 profiles had no video views. One-fourth of the profiles had over ten thousand video views. Some profiles were able to attract a relatively wide audience of fans. For example, CallyKun had 256,832 video views, including a popular Columbine video. Not all of the videos were necessarily about school shootings. Some of the most popular videos were first-person shooter videogame clips, rock videos, or movie clips. Although the average number of subscribers and video views were rather low, school shooting fans are not a secret society within YouTube. Some of them are active in commenting, especially about school shooting related videos, and they do not hide their controversial views. For them, YouTube is clearly not only a tool to network with other users but also a means to disseminate their ideas.

# NETWORKS OF HATE ON YOUTUBE

YouTube no longer provides the list of "friends" and, even if it did, such lists are misleading, since, for example, a friend of a school shooting fan might not be a school shooting fan. We found that comments sections are particularly useful for identifying links among fans because they include discussions among the users and often contain both positive and negative comments about school shootings. We analyzed the positive school shooting comments made in the comments section of each channel between April 2010 and June 2012. Hence, only positive and active social ties were included, and the network includes only the public communication between the school shooting fan profiles. We were then able to build a directed network based on who commented to whom.

Of the 113 selected profiles, one hundred (88.5 percent) were connected to the same network based on their public comments to each other. In total, there are 360 edges in the network (i.e., 360 connections between one hundred nodes/profiles). A visualization of the graph and the connections between the actors is presented in figure 2.1. The nodes are sized to represent the extent to which each member is active in the network in terms of his or her comments to other network members (out-degree). The figure shows the top ten profiles marked with sphere shapes and darker shades. The top ten profiles are selected on the basis of betweenness centrality, which measures a node's centrality in a network by calculating how many times a node sits on the shortest path linking two other actors (Prell 2012, 104). This measure is commonly used to identify a network's leaders (Freeman 1978/1979).

Table 2.2 reports basic network measures of school shooting fans. On average, each member's profile is commented on by approximately three other members and each member comments on approximately three other network members' pages (in-degree = 3.6, out-degree = 3.6, respectively). The actors are separated by relatively short paths (average path length = 3.27). The network's density is 0.036. Density is the number of edges in a network compared to the maximum number of possible edges in a network of that size. Thus, only 3.6 percent of the possible connections among the YouTube profiles are actually realized.

As can be seen in the figure 2.1, the network is relatively sparse in that there are several members who are connected to only one or two other members. However, we can also see several clusters of highly connected actors. We separated the top ten profiles from the rest of the network to analyze their connections to each other (see figure 2.2 and table 2.2). These ten nodes have twenty-nine edges among them. They are quite connected to each other (in-degree = 2.9; out-degree = 2.9). The network density is high (0.32), meaning that almost one third of the possible connections are actually realized. Maximum path length is six in this directed network; in other

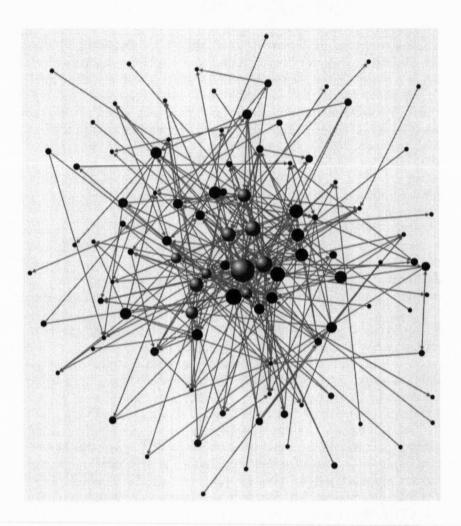

**Figure 2.1.   YouTube School Shooting Fan Network. Top ten nodes are gray spheres. Node sizes are based on the outdegree. Figure created in NodeXL™.**

words, relatively long. Thus, for example, it takes six steps for TheRebvod-ka1999 to get to LynnAnn222. Most of the nodes are still within max three steps from each other. LynnAnn222 who has the highest out-degree (7), is well connected in this network. Only bathtownship and TheRebvodka1999 do not have a direct contact with her.

Table 2.2.   General metrics of the YouTube school shooting fan network.

| Graph Metrics | Whole Network | Top 10 Profiles Only Network |
|---|---|---|
| Nodes (profiles) | 100 | 10 |
| Edges | 360 | 29 |
| In-degree | | |
| – maximum | 18 | 5 |
| – average | 3.60 | 2.90 |
| Out-degree | | |
| – maximum | 31 | 7 |
| – average | 3.60 | 2.90 |
| Path length | | |
| – maximum (diameter | 8 | 6 |
| – average | 3.27 | 2.37 |
| Density | 0.04 | 0.32 |
| Betweenness centrality | | |
| – maximum | 1450.17 | 25.67 |
| – average | 143.13 | 5.40 |

## SOCIAL IDENTIFICATION WITH THE
## ONLINE HATE COMMUNITY

We have seen so far that school shooting fans are apparently from a geo-graphically large area. Although English dominates, German, Spanish, Polish, and Finnish are used as well in the discussions indicating the very internationality of the school shooting fan phenomenon. As noted earlier, YouTube provides the general user with anonymity. Users do not normally reveal their full identities in Facebook, although some users provide links to their other social networking site profiles. Hence, we have a transnational group of people who do not know each other very well and few of them may have actually met offline.

As we have seen, SIDE theory argues that anonymity in online settings enhances conformity to group norms (Postmes and Spears 1998). In other words, when visible cues and other aspects of normal offline interaction are limited, group members have to have some common issue that clues them together. Attraction to the Columbine school shootings is clearly this kind of uniting factor among different actors. We have already seen in table 2.1 that 89 percent of the school shooting fans were Columbine fans. Table 2.3 shows that Columbine is almost the only mentioned school shooting case in the top

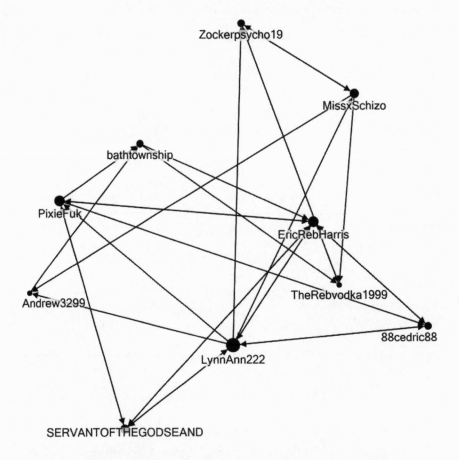

**Figure 2.2.   Network Based on Only Top Ten Profiles. Node sizes are based on the outdegree. Arrows mark in and outdegree. Figure created in NodeXL™.**

ten actor profiles. Only Andrew3299 and EricRebHarris mention other school shootings or similar cases.

**Table 2.3.   Top Ten Nodes in the YouTube School Shooting Fans Network.**

| Node | In/out-degree | Between-ness centrality | Date joined | Nation | Sub-scribers | Views | Profile Photo | Other Acts Cited | Profile active in Aug. 2013 |
|---|---|---|---|---|---|---|---|---|---|
| LynnAnne222 | 13/31 | 1450.17 | 22 Jul 2010 | US | 59 | 248 | Female | Columbine | Active with different profile |
| EricRebHarris | 18/11 | 1294.21 | 11 Jul 2011 | US | 89 | 75,298 | Eric Harris | Columbine, Oklahoma City | Yes |
| PixieFuk | 14/15 | 1105.66 | 15 Jun 2011 | UK | 17 | 0 | Harris and Klebold | Columbine | No |
| TheRebvodka1999 | 14/6 | 915.55 | 25 Feb 2010 | US | 26 | 5,985 | Eric Harris | Columbine | Yes |
| 88cedric88 | 13/13 | 823.69 | 30 Jan 2007 | AUS | 11 | 0 | Male | Columbine | Yes |
| Zockerpsycho19 | 7/9 | 790.93 | 29 Jun 2010 | DEU | 13 | 7,379 | Cat | Columbine | Yes |
| Andrew3299 | 13/6 | 737.49 | 11 Mar 2011 | - | 50 | 80,780 | Eric Harris | Austin, Columbine, Emsdetten, Virginia Tech, Jokela, Winnenden, Oslo/Utøya | Yes |

| Node | In/out-degree | Between-ness centrality | Date joined | Nation | Sub-scribers | Views | Profile Photo | Other Acts Cited | Profile active in Aug. 2013 |
|---|---|---|---|---|---|---|---|---|---|
| Servantof-Thegodseand | 16/10 | 668.07 | 22 Jan 2012 | US | 11 | 0 | - | Columbine | Yes |
| Bathtownship | 7/6 | 640.62 | 17 May 2007 | US | 16 | 0 | Columbine high school | Columbine | Yes |
| MissxSchizo | 5/11 | 549.19 | 27 Dec 2009 | POL | 25 | 0 | Skull with "rebel" | Columbine | Yes |

The Columbine school shooting fans use names and pictures referring to the Columbine tragedy. Certain bands and cultural products are mentioned because school shooters have liked them (Kiilakoski and Oksanen 2011a). Among school shooting fans, cultural references are codes that have to be mentioned to gain access to the group (Paton 2013, 219). They use and repeat these shared codes to keep the group together. For example SERVANTOF-THEGODSEAND states in his main profile: "Proud follower of the immortal Eric Harris and Dylan Klebold!!! They are everything to me!!! IN ERIC AND DYLAN I LIVE!!!!!" Many of them call themselves a family (bearing a decided but uncanny resemblance to the Charles Manson Family). PixieFuk states in her profile main page: "im part of the reb and vodka family and if you dont like it kiss my fucking ass or ill blow your fucking head off." Talking about family and making statements such as "in Eric and Dylan I live" creates a sense of community among these persons who have not necessarily ever met and who are also likely to live long distances from each other.

LynnAnn222 exemplifies a female Columbine fan who claims to be "a supporter for Eric Harris who is the hottest guy ever to have walked the planet." Her profile is the most central in the network as well as the top-ten-only network. Her out-degree is thirty-one, which indicates that she connects to thirty-one other network members by commenting on their profiles. This actor uses a female profile photo and represents herself as a twenty-seven-year-old female from California. LynnAnn222 is a fan of the Columbine school shootings. She joined YouTube with this name in July 2010, yet she has been particularly active in seeking contact with others making statements such as "I love Eric Harris" and "Reb is forever <3."

EricRebHarris has the second highest betweenness centrality in the full network and the highest in-degree (18). He uses Columbine related pictures in his profile. He shows support for the community by statements such as "I Reb n' Vodka I live" or "Eric was like me." His profile includes videos about the Oklahoma City Bombing. EricRebHarris had in total 75,298 video views. Besides him, only Andrew3299 reaches similar video views with his videos related to school shootings and shooting scenes in video games. EricRebHarris and the other three top ten actors use pictures of Columbine shooters as a profile picture. They also disseminate similar angry monolog about humanity. For example, Andrew3299 quotes the Columbine shooters (and Jokela shooter's manifesto) directly: "Hate, I am Full of hate and I love it, I hate people and they better fucking fear me."

Andrew3299 was the only one who listed post-Columbine cases and other recent mass murderers as his heroes, including Anders Behring Breivik. Despite the fact that post-Columbine acts have been equally tragic, they may be too regional to unite people in YouTube. All of them might know Eric Harris or Dylan Klebold from films and documentaries, but for an American teen, identifying with Brazilian, German, or Finnish school shooters might be too far-fetched. Furthermore, most of the post-Columbine school shooters have been Columbine fans themselves (Kiilakoski and Oksanen 2011a; Larkin, 2009; Oksanen et al. 2013). Hence, it is difficult to overstate Columbine's relevance. Columbine is the glue that keeps school shooter fans together.

The group coherence is also maintained by common enemies. First, some school shooting fans openly hate humanity and society in general. Andrew3299, for example, has adopted this line of thinking. In his manifesto-like text, it is associated with his personal problems: "Humanity is my source and main strain of rage. . . . I feel So much fucking emptiness, I Just plain Hate Humanity." Second, school shooters attack the victims of the Columbine tragedy. They troll, for example, the comments sections of the videos dedicated to the victims (e.g., *Rachel Scott's Funeral* video). One of the direct consequences of such attacks is, predictably, that the most active profiles have been deleted. LynnAnn222's profile, for example, has been shut down several times since our data collection began. In autumn 2013 she had another profile with the name Lynn Ann.

Since school shootings are unmerciful cruel murders, it is perhaps not surprising that school shooting fans devote energy justifying these actions. LynnAnnn222 refers to YouTube videos that she claims defends the rights of the Columbine shooters to take their revenge: "Eric and Dylan are the original victims and got some sweet revenge and sweet justice." This is one of the key themes among school shooting fans (Böckler and Seeger 2013). Shootings are seen as justified revenge against bullies or "jocks." Hence, the school shooting fans identify with the shooters and other people expressing similar ideas and calls for revenge. They see their own problems as analogous to those of the shooters. Bullies, jocks, or the entire mainstream society becomes an enemy in this rhetoric. Some express their wish to take action, just like their dead idols did.

## CONCLUSION

In this chapter, we see how easily people group for both good and bad causes. Classic social psychological studies underline that ingroup favoritism can be created even in minimal conditions (Tajfel et al. 1971). This alone, however, does not lead to intergroup conflicts. The conditions enabling intergroup conflict are the existing or perceived social competition and existing real or imaginary threat of other groups. Different culturally existing ideologies and prejudices may also contribute to intergroup conflict. Social identity plays a role in intergroup conflicts as group members seek to define themselves in contrast to other groups. The members may self-stereotype as members of a specific group and depersonalize outgroup members. In anonymous social settings, conformity to social group norms might be even higher and anonymity may intensify attraction to the group.

Hate groups are an extreme example of this kind of intergroup conflict. They target their victims by both speech and violent acts. These groups are united by the very emotion of hate and they flourish in socially and economically turbulent conditions. Historically hate groups have used the newest available technology in the dissemination of the hate propaganda. The current technological developments open new possibilities, and online hate groups have gained popularity since the early 2000s. They actively recruit young people using online technology, and the young may be the most vulnerable to their influence.

Our case study of YouTube school shooting fans shows that similar, rather peculiar and deviant interests, may unite people coming from geographically distant places. These international school shooting fans use a common language and codes that are important for maintaining group solidarity. The school shooting fan group fights for its existence and seeks justifications for school shootings. They see shootings as morally acceptable revenge taken against bullies. School shooting fans are a persistent phenomenon in YouTube and the Columbine case attracts a global following even years after the tragedy. School shooting fans resemble other deviant offline sub-cultures that have relatively stable social rituals, stories and symbols over time (see Sandberg 2013). In transient online cultures, this might mean that the usernames and even users might change, but the fan community remains. Key actors in the network are the ones who actively enforce the shared language and cultural codes.

The current converging of online and offline realities marks a significant challenge to social researchers. We are no longer talking about stable competing groups. Rather the current situation underlines trans-nationality. Not only terrorist groups but also hate groups are formed on looser bases than ever before. These groups are dispersed and they may be the combination of many lone wolves acting independently. Social media unites people from around the globe, but unfortunately it also unites those who are seeking ways of destroying the common good. The excessive material and possibilities of the Internet may especially affect those actively engaged in violent behavior (see "downward spiral model" by Slater et al. 2003). Even the very existence of hate material and hateful people online likely increases the likelihood of actual violence.

## REFERENCES

Agamben, G. 2003. *Stato di eccezione. Homo sacer, II, I.* Torino, Italy: Bollati Boringhieri.
Bartlett, J., J. Birdwell, and M. Littler. 2011. *The New Face of Digital Populism.* London: Demos.

Baumeister, R. F. 1999. *Evil: Inside Human Violence and Cruelty*. New York: Macmillan.

Baumeister, R. F., and M. Leary. 1995. "The Need to Belong: Desire for Interpersonal Attachments as a Fundamental Human Motivation." *Psychological bulletin* 117: 497.

Baym, N. 2000. *Tune In, Log On: Soaps, Fandom, and Online Community*. Thousands Oaks, CA: Erlbaum.

Benjamin, W. (1940) 1974. Über den Begriff der Geschichte. Teoksessa Walter Benjamin: *Gesammelte Schriften* I: 2, 691–704. Frankfurt am Main: Suhrkamp.

Berlet, C., and M. Nemiroff Lyons. 2000. *Right Wing Populism in America: Too Close for Comfort*. Guilford Press.

Billig, M. 2002. "Henri Tajfel's 'Cognitive aspects of prejudice' and the psychology of bigotry." *British Journal of Social Psychology* 41: 171–88.

Blazak, R. 2009. "Toward a Working Definition of Hate Groups." In *Hate Crimes*, edited by B. Perry, B. Levin, P. Iganski, R. Blazak, and F. M. Lawrence, 133–67. Westport, CT: Greenwood Publishing Group.

Böckler, N. and T Seeger. 2013. "Revolution of the Dispossessed: School Shooters and Their Devotees on the Web." In *School Shootings: International Research, Case Studies and Concepts for Prevention*, N. Böckler, T. Seeger, P. Sitzer, and W. Heitmeyer, 309–39. New York: Springer.

Bodenhausen, G., and J. Richeson. 2010. "Prejudice, Stereotyping, and Discrimination." In *Advanced Social Psychoogy: The State of the Science*, edited by R. F. Baumeister and E. J. Finkel, 341–83. New York: Oxford University Press.

Boellstorff, T. 2010. *Coming of Age in Second Life: An Anthropologist Explores the Virtually Human*. Princeton: Princeton University Press.

Bowman-Grieve, L. 2009. "Exploring 'Stormfront': A Virtual Community of the Radical Right." *Studies in Conflict and Terrorism*, 32: 989–1007.

Brewer, M. B. 1999. "The Psychology of Prejudice: Ingroup Love and Outgroup Hate?" *Journal of Social Issues* 55, no. 3: 429–44.

Brewer, M. B. 2010. "Intergroup relations." In *Advanced Social Psychoogy: The State of the Science*, edited by Roy F. Baumeister and Eli J. Finkel, 535–71. New York: Oxford University Press.

Brown, C. 2009. "WWW.HATE.COM: White Supremacist Discourse on the Internet and the Construction of Whiteness Ideology." *The Howard Journal of Communications* 20: 189–208.

Burris, V., E. Smith, and A. Strahm. 2000. "White Supremacist Networks on the Internet." *Sociological Focus* 33: 215–35.

Caiani, M., and L. Parenti. 2013. *European and American Extreme Right Groups and the Internet*. Farnham: Ashgate Publishing.

Chau, M., and J. Xu. 2007. "Mining Communities and Their Relationships in Blogs: A study of Online Hate Groups." *International Journal of Human-Computer Studies* 65: 57–70.

Cherny, L. 1999. *Conversation and Community: Chat in a Virtual World*. Standford: CSLI Publications.

Citron, D. K., and H. Norton. 2011. "Intermediaries and Hate Speech: Fostering Digital Citizenship for Our Information Age." *Boston University Law Review* 91: 1435–84.

Cohen-Almagor R., and S. Haleva-Amir. 2008. "Bloody Wednesday in Dawson College—The Story of Kimveer Gill, or Why Should We Monitor Certain Websites to Prevent Murder." *Studies in Ethics, Law and Technology* 2: 1–37.

Fast, J. 2008. *Ceremonial Violence: A Psychological Explanation of School Shootings*. New York: Overlook Press.

Foxman, A., and C. Wolf. 2013. *Viral Hate: Containing Its Spread on the Internet*. New York: Palgrave MacMillan.

Freeman, L. C. 1978/1979. "Centrality in social networks conceptual clarification." *Social Networks* 1: 215–39.

Gerstenfeld, P. B. 2013. *Hate crimes: Causes, Controls, and Controversies*. London: Sage.

Glick, P. 2005. "Choice of scapegoats." *On the Cature of Prejudice* 50: 244–61.

Green, D. P., and R. L. Seher. 2003. "What Role Does Prejudice Play in Ethnic Conflict?" *Annual Review of Political Science* 6: 509–31.

Haslam, S. Alexander, and Stephen Reicher. 2007. "Beyond the Banality of Evil: Three Dynamics of an Interactionist Social Psychology of Tyranny." *Personality and Social Psychology Bulletin* 33, no. 5: 615–22.

Hawdon, J. 2012. "Applying Differential Association Theory to Online Hate Groups: A Theoretical Statement." *Research on Finnish Society* 5: 39–47.

Haythornthwaite, C. 2007. "Social Networks and Online Community." In *The Oxford handbook of Internet Psychology*, edited by A. Joinson, K. McKenna, T. Postmes, and U. Reips, 121–37: New York: Oxford University Press.

Jones, L. M., K. L. Mitchell, and D. Finkelhor. 2013. "Online Harassment in Context: Trends From Three Youth Internet Safety Surveys (2000, 2005, 2010)." *Psychology of Violence*: 53.

Kiilakoski, T., and A. Oksanen. 2011a. "Soundtrack of the School Shootings: Cultural Script, Music and Male Rage." *Young* 19: 247–69.

Kiilakoski, T., and A. Oksanen. 2011b. "Cultural and Peer Influences on Homicidal Violence: Finnish Perspective." *New Directions for Youth Development* 33 Spring: 31–42.

Lange, P. G. 2007. "Publicly Private and Privately Public: Social Networking on YouTube." *Journal of Computer-Mediated Communication* 13: 361–80.

Larkin, R. W. 2009. "The Columbine Legacy: Rampage Shootings as Political Acts," *American Behavioral Scientist* 52: 1309–26.

Lea, M., R. Spears, and D. de Groot. 2001. "Knowing Me, Knowing You: Anonymity Effects on Social Identity Processes Within Groups." *Personality and Social Psychology Bulletin* 27: 526–37.

Lee, E. and L. Leets. 2002. "Persuasive Storytelling by Hate Groups Online." *American Behavioral Scientist* 45: 927–57.

Lehdonvirta, V., and P. Räsänen. 2011. "How Do Young People Identify with Online and Offline Peer Groups? A comparison between UK, Spain and Japan." *Journal of Youth Studies* 14: 91–108.

Levin, B. 2002. "Cyberhate: A Legal and Historical Analysis of Extremists' Use of Computer Networks in America." *American Behavioral Scientist* 45: 958–86.

Manstead, A. S. R. 2010. "Social Psychology of Emotion." In *Advanced Social Psychoogy: The State of the Science*, edited by Roy F. Baumeister and Eli J. Finkel, 101–37. New York: Oxford University Press.

McKenna, K. Y. A., and J.A. Bargh. 2000. "Plan 9 from Cyberspace: The Implications of the Internet for Personality and Social Psychology." *Personality and Social Psychology Review* 4: 57–75.

Muschert, G. W., and R.W. Larkin. 2007. "The Columbine High School Shootings," in *Crimes and Trials of the Century*, edited by S. Chermak and F. Y. Bailey, 253–66. Westport, CT: Praeger.

Nurmi, J., and A. Oksanen. 2013. "Expressions and Projections of Evil: Coping after a Violent Tragedy." *Deviant Behavior* 34: 859–74.

Näsi, M., P. Räsänen, and V. Lehdonvirta. 2011. "Identification with Online and Offline Communities: Understanding ICT disparities in Finland." *Technology in Society*. 33: 4–11.

Oksanen, A., J. Nurmi, M. Vuori, and P. Räsänen. 2013. "Jokela: The Social Roots of a School Shooting Tragedy in Finland." In *School Shootings: International Research, Case Studies and Concepts for Prevention*, edited by N. Böckler, T. Seeger, P. Sitzer, and W. Heitmeyer, 189–215. New York: Springer.

Paton, N. E. 2013. "Media Participation of School Shooters and Their Fans: Navigating Between Self-distinction and Imitation to Achieve Individuation." In *School Shootings: Mediatized Violence in a Global Age*, edited by. G. Muschert and J. Sumiala, 203–29. Bingley, UK: Emerald Group Publishing Limited.

Postmes, T. and R. Spears. 1998. "Deindividuation and Antinormative Behavior: A Meta-Analysis." *Psychological Bulletin* 123: 238.

Postmes, T., R. Spears, and M. Lea. 1998. "Breaching or Building Social Boundaries? SIDE-effects of Computer-mediated Communication." *Communication Research* 25: 689–715.

Postmes, T., R. Spears, K. Sakhel, and D. de Groot. 2001. "Social influence in computer-mediated communication: The effects of anonymity on group behaviour." *Personality and Social Psychology Bulletin* 27: 1243–54.

Potok, M. 2011. "The Year in Hate and Extremism, 2010." *Intelligence Report*, 141, July 16, 2011. Southern Poverty Law Center. Accessed March 2011, www.splcenter.org/get-informed/intelligence-report/browse-all-issues/2011/spring/the-year-in-hate-extremism-2010.

Prell, C. 2012. *Social Network Analysis: History, Theory and Methodology.* Sage, Los Angeles.

Rheingold, H. 2000. *The Virtual Community. Homesteading on the Electronic Frontier.* Revised edition. Cambridge, MA: The MIT Press.

Ritzer, G., and N. Jurgenson. 2010. "Production, Consumption, Prosumption: The Nature of Capitalism in the Age of the Digital Prosumer." *Journal of Consumer Culture* 10: 13–36.

Sandberg, S. 2013. "Cannabis Culture: A Stable Subculture in a Changing World." *Criminology and Criminal Justice* 13: 63–79.

Sandberg, S., A. Oksanen, L. E. Berntzen, and T. Kiilakoski. "The Stories in Action: The Cultural Influences of School Shootings on the Terrorist Attacks in Norway." Unpublished article manuscript.

Sappho X. 2010. "A New Dawn? Change and Continuity in Political Violence in Greece." *Terrorism and Political Violence* 24: 437–64.

Sherif, M., O. J. Harvey, B. J. White, W. R. Hood, and C. W. Sherif. 1961. *Intergroup Conflict and Cooperation: The Robbers Cave Experiment.* Norman, OK: University Book Exchange.

Simon, B., and B. Klandermans. 2001. "Politicized Collective Identity: A Social Psychological Analysis." *American Psychologist* 56: 319.

Slater, Michael D., Kimberly L. Henry, Randall C. Swaim, and Lori L. Anderson. 2003. "Violent Media Content and Aggressiveness in Adolescents: A Downward Spiral Model." *Communication Research* 30: 713–36.

Southern Poverty Law Center. 2013. "Hate Map." www.splcenter.org/get-informed/hate-Map.

Spears, R., T. Postmes, M. Lea, and A. Wolbert. 2002. "When Are Net Effects Gross Products? Communication." *Journal of Social Issues* 58: 91–107.

Tajfel, H. 1970. "Experiments in Intergroup Discrimination." *Scientific American* 223: 96–102.

———. 1974. "Social Identity and Intergroup Behavior." *Social Science Information* 13: 65–93.

Tajfel, H., M. G. Billig, R. P. Bundy, and C. Flament. 1971. Social Categorization and Behaviour. *European Journal of Social Psychology* 1: 149–78.

Tajfel, H., and J. C. Turner. 1979. "An Integrative Theory of Intergroup Conflict." In *The Social Psychology of Intergroup Relations*, edited by W. G. Austin and S. Worchel, 33–47. Pacific Grove, CA: Brooks/Cole.

Tapscott, D., and A. Williams. 2006. *Wikinomics: How Mass Collaboration Changes Everything.* New York: Portfolio.

Thelwall, M., P. Sud, and F. Vis. 2012. "Commenting on YouTube Videos: From Guatemalan Rock to El Big Bang." *Journal of the American Society for Information Science and Technology* 63: 616–29.

Theweleit, K. 2000. *Männerphantasien 1+2 (Male Fantasies).* München and Zürich: Piper.

Timmermann, W. K. 2005. "The Relationship between Hate Propaganda and Incitement to Genocide: A New Trend in International Law towards Criminalization of Hate Propaganda?" *Leiden Journal of International Law* 18: 257–82.

Turner, J. C. 1982. "Towards a Cognitive Redefinition of the Social Group." In *Social Identity and Intergroup Relations*, edited by H. Tajfel, 15–40. Cambridge, UK: Cambridge University Press.

———. 1985. "Social Categorization and the Self-concept: A Social Cognitive Theory of Group Behavior." In *Advances in Group Processes: Theory and Research*, edited by J. Lawler, 77–122. Greenwich, CT: JAI Press.

Turner, J. C., and K. J. Reynolds. 2010. "The Story of Social Identity." In *Rediscovering Social Identity: Key Readings*, edited by T. Postmes and N. R. Branscombe, 13–32. New York: Psychology Press.

Waldron, J. 2012. *The Harm in the Hate Speech.* Cambridge: Harvard University Press.

Weber, A. 2009. *Manual on hate speech*. Council of Europe publishing. book.coe.int/ftp/3342. pdf.

Williams, D., N. Ducheneaut, L. Xiong, Y. Zhang, N. Yee, and E. Nickell. 2006. "From Tree House to Barracks The Social Life of Guilds in World Of Warcraft." *Games and Culture* 1: 338–61.

Xenakis, Sappho. 2012. "A New Dawn? Change and Continuity in Political Violence in Greece." *Terrorism and Political Violence* 24: 437–64.

Zimbardo. P. 2007. *The Lucifer Effect: Understanding How Good People Turn Evil*. New York: Random House.

*Chapter Three*

# Violence and Street Groups

*Gangs, Groups, and Violence*

## David Kennedy

Research into the connection between groups, especially gangs, and violence is a venerable topic. It has long been recognized that there is a connection, and that it has certain core aspects. Gangs and gang members are disproportionately violent, relative even to other criminal offenders. Gangs draw on those who are already among the most violent and otherwise active offenders, who become more active and violent while they are in gangs. Gang dynamics, such as persistent hostile relationships between gangs, are associated with much of this violence. Gang criminality, such as drug dealing and other illicit economic activity, is closely associated with and often productive of violence (Klein and Maxson 1989).

Beyond those connections and associations—correlations—there have been equally persistent and vexed analytic and empirical problems. One of the most central has been definitional: neither scholars nor practitioners, such as police, have been able to come up with a satisfactory definition of what a "gang" is (Esbensen, Winfree, He, and Taylor 2001). A core issue in this problem is the place of violence in defining gangs and understanding gang behavior: if violence is one of the constituent elements of defining gangs, then assessing the production of violence by gangs is fundamentally compromised, while if violence and other extreme criminality are left out of the definition, framings become so broad as to encompass groups that fall outside common-sense ideas of what a gang is (football teams, the police). Another central problem has been assessing causality. Beyond the clear correlation, do gangs and gang membership as such produce violence, above and beyond the propensities of individual gang offenders? Is there, or should it be considered to be, a difference between offending and violence *committed by* gang members—say, an assault on a domestic partner—and offending and violence *directed by gang members and processes*, such as a murder of a rival gang member "green lighted" by gang leadership? These issues have plagued gang research for generations, without much in the way of conceptual or empirical progress.

This chapter, and much of the research and applied work on which it draws, proceeds in the opposite direction: it begins with violence, particularly homicide and the most serious nonlethal violence, such as nonfatal gun assaults; examines the connection between that violence, gangs, and groups; and then examines the characteristics of those gangs and groups, their members, and their communities. It finds that the connection between violence and groups is strong and that those characteristics are distinctive and of both theoretical and practical import.

Note that this approach resolves none of the issues that have troubled traditional gang scholarship. It does not take on the question of an independent and meaningful definition of "gang," or of the causal factors that drive gang membership and gang violence (it does, as we will see, look at the characteristics of the members of violent groups, and of their violence, but does not, for example, seek to establish why one "at risk" young man becomes a group member while others similarly at risk do not, or why some situations produce violence while other similar situations do not.) And while it finds tremendously strong connections between violence and groups, it does not establish or assert an independent causal connection between gangs and groups and that violence: both theoretically and empirically it allows for the possibility that there are groups and group dynamics exactly like those associated with violence that are *not* associated with violence. Rather, in seeking to understand extreme violence as found in certain communities, it examines that violence; finds the group connection; and examines those groups and group dynamics. This chapter will address that process, those findings, and the applied violence prevention work that they have produced.

## THE ACTION-RESEARCH SETTING AND ASSOCIATED DATA ISSUES

The work on which this paper draws is associated with a particular action-research approach to addressing serious violence. Its development began with the Boston Gun Project of the mid-1990s, an attempt to address youth gun violence at the height of the American crack epidemic. That and subsequent, related work has shared a number of essential elements: a commitment to theoretically and empirically informed practice; research that draws on both qualitative and quantitative data; a close working relationship between researchers and practitioners; and the design and implementation of operational interventions (Kennedy, Braga, and Piehl 2001).

From the beginning of the Boston Gun Project, it became evident that existing formal law enforcement and other data systems were utterly inadequate for meaningful research into the core questions of group-related violence. Jurisdictional (e.g., city-level) gang databases are notoriously compromised by definitional and information/"intelligence" issues (Kennedy 2009). Incident reports and other formal information on violent incidents, such as homicides and shootings, do not routinely contain meaningful information on gang and group connections and dynamics. They can be and in practice are heavily influenced by fundamental and divergent definitional underpinnings, such as whether a given jurisdiction tracks gang incidents by gang involvement or gang motivation (Maxson and Klein 1990). The result is that both formal research and less formal portrayals based on those sources are fundamentally incomplete and misleading. To take one formal example, as the Boston Gun Project research assembled a picture of violence and related group involvement from a variety of sources, a comparison with the picture presented by formal data sources showed that the two had next to nothing in common (Kennedy et al. 1997). To take another, the government of the United States recently reported that in 2011 there were nationally around 1,800 gang homicides (Egley and Howell 2011). This is ludicrous—the real number is probably three or more times higher—and results from a chain of bad reporting that begins with issues identifying and recording gang incidents at the local level; how data are recorded and reported to the FBI; and the categories into which the FBI forces that reporting (the FBI's Supplemental Homicide Report, which capture and convey local data for national aggregation, have only one element for gang homicide—"gangland slaying"—which dates to the Tommy gun era of U.S. gang violence) (Kennedy et al. 1997).

As a result, the Boston Gun Project and subsequent similar research has relied on two methods for gathering information about gangs and groups, and any gang and group connection to violence. The first is the *group audit*, a structured qualitative method for identifying violent groups and group dynamics—such as rivalries and alliances—from frontline practitioners. The second is the *incident review*, a structured qualitative method for assessing group connections to, and the fundamental characteristics of, homicides and nonfatal shootings. Both are frequently supplemented by formal criminal justice and other data (Kennedy et al. 1997). More recently, other methods, particularly social network analysis based on police and other criminal justice data, have been added to those techniques (Papachristos 2006; Radil et al. 2010).

In addition, the embedded partnership role of researchers in these action-research projects provides for sustained exposure to police and other criminal justice agencies, offenders, and communities. That exposure, over time and multiple jurisdictions, sums to a kind of ethnography of, especially, those three elements, and their interactions. Particularly as this work has developed over time from its Boston Gun Project origins, that ethnographic insight has been increasingly important for understanding gang and group dynamics, the violence itself, and how it is produced and can be addressed (Kennedy 2001).

This research approach has been applied primarily in the United States; this chapter draws on findings from—as a distinctly partial list—Boston, Minneapolis, Newark, Cincinnati, Baltimore, Los Angeles, Chicago, Oakland, Stockton, Salinas, New Orleans, High Point, and Philadelphia. In all of these places the same basic patterns were found. It has been formally applied, as well, in a limited number of primarily Commonwealth countries, such as Scotland, England, and Australia, and in Brazil, where the same basic findings were obtained (Bullock and Tilley 2002; Glasgow's Community Initiative to Reduce Violence 2010). Beyond that, the author has had occasion to unpack these issues less formally in conversations with law enforcement personnel, community members, and offenders and ex-offenders in numerous international settings. In each instance, while there are of course meaningful differences across cities and national settings, at a certain level of generality—as set out below—there is so far invariable agreement. It thus begins to appear that at least at that level of generality, what has been found is something approaching a set of basic facts around group-related violence.

## THE CONNECTION BETWEEN VIOLENCE AND GROUPS

The most important finding here is simple—there is a profound and so far invariant connection between serious violence and highly active criminal groups. The typical city-level finding is that groups collectively representing under 0.5 percent of the city population will be connected, as offenders, victims, or both, with between half and three-quarters of all homicides in the city (this is an underestimate and lower bound, since in the research process only those incidents known to be group connected are counted as such; some substantial portion of those not known will in fact also be group connected). The original Boston research, which focused on homicide victimization amongst those age twenty-one and under, found that around sixty-one groups were responsible for at least 60 percent of all such homicides; their collective membership of up to 1,500 represented under 0.3 percent of the city's population. (Kennedy et al. 1996; Kennedy et al. 2001). Recent research from Cincinnati found that three-quarters of homicides were group-involved, with all group members together also representing something less than 0.3 percent of the city. Los Angeles, a very different setting—with a much more active and historically embedded gang scene—showed a slightly different but essentially parallel dynamic; in one police district with a singularly intergenerational Hispanic gang scene, gangs representing around 0.2 percent of the population were involved with about 62 percent of all homicides.

This finding is strongest with respect to homicide. It's unclear whether that is an empirical truth or a data issue; the need to identify group connections to violent incidents via qualitative methods leads in practice to better information on homicides, which get more attention from and are better known to and understood by law enforcement personnel. Similar concentrations, however, are also found with respect to nonfatal shootings; robberies (which are frequently carried out by younger members of street groups), and domestic violence: one examination found group members overrepresented by a factor of seven in domestic homicides (Kennedy 2008), and another found that fully 40 percent of domestic shootings in one city were committed by group members (Braga, forthcoming).

This set of facts—the extremely strong connection between groups, with a relatively small collective number of members, and serious violence—has driven a focus both on understanding the nature of groups and group members; the nature of and the dynamics that produce group-related violence; and methods to address those groups and dynamics.

## THE NATURE OF STREET GROUPS

An equally consistent picture has emerged with respect to the nature of such groups. In distinct contrast to the widespread notion—in law enforcement, the media, and very often in scholarship—that gangs and similar groups are large, organized, hierarchical, and purposeful, groups are in fact typically small, disorganized, and chaotic. Most comprise fewer than fifty members, with the bulk concentrated between about ten and thirty. Apparently larger groups frequently represent a set of smaller sets "claiming" affiliation but having in practice little or no common organization or coordination. Even those smaller sets are frequently unstable, with little real cohesion, and individual members drifting in and out of active membership and sometimes shifting membership to other sets. Formal leadership, meaning any kind of designated executive role, is rare, as is hierarchy and any meaningful division of labor; individuals will have greater and lesser degrees of influence over their peers, but that influence is typically informal and implied rather than formal and explicit. Money-making generally occurs at the individual level—one member sells drugs or does a robbery and keeps whatever he earns—or in fluid subsets of the larger set, in which small groups commit crimes together and share what is earned. Collective accounts, money management, and the like are next to unheard of. Risk and its consequences are similarly individual; a member arrested and prosecuted will be personally responsible for his bail and defense, with no pools for bond and legal fees.

Groups are generally highly territorial, with relatively few that "float" across larger areas; a typical presentation is that members will come exclusively from a small neighborhood area, or an even smaller area such as a housing project. It is not unusual to find such patterns persisting even after residential mobility, with members' residences scattered across a city but members coming back to an original "home" area to hang out and do crime. The essentially local nature of groups is profound and extends to issues of larger gang affiliations, which are present much more in appearance than in fact. Where there are apparent associations with the national gang "supersets," such as Los Angeles's Bloods and Crips and Chicago's People and Folk, such "claiming" is typically in name only, without any lines of reporting or authority, or in fact any connection at all, to the root gangs in Los Angeles and Chicago. Local groups "claiming" Bloods will, for example, fight with other Blood sets and do business with Crip sets without any regard for allegiance and hierarchy (Sullivan 2005). One reason both scholars and law enforcement have missed both the existence and significance of disorganized local groups is because they tend to look for a cohesion that does not in fact exist, and—not finding it—conclude that "gangs" and groups do not exist (McGloin 2005). As senior Los Angeles Crip Aqeela Sherrils puts it, "a lot of people think that there's a level of sophistication within the gang culture like the Mafia. Not at all. There's no organization, there's no nothing" (Duane 2006). Looking instead at what is really there rather than what is expected will reveal the actual dynamic.

Finally, groups and group members spend most of their time doing not much at all—hanging out, drinking and drugging, chasing girls, gambling, and the like—but commit large numbers of both purposive and opportunistic offenses: drug sales, robberies, assaults, domestic and sexual violence, weapon carrying and use, and lesser offenses such as probation and parole violations, drug use, underage drinking and drunk and drugged driving, and the like (some of the earliest gang research identified and labeled such "cafeteria-style" offending (Klein 1995). Serious violent offenses—homicides, nonfatal shootings, edged weapon and other attacks, firing into houses—are relatively rare events in the larger mix of routine chronic offending.

There are exceptions to all of this. There remains relatively organized gangs in Chicago and Los Angeles, though in both cities the idea that there ever were highly disciplined gang hierarchies is much more fiction than reality. In both places, for the most part, what structure and discipline there was has and continues to break down; in Chicago, where the author has been working, coming to grips with current gang violence has meant abandoning the idea of meaningful hierarchy and meticulously mapping and addressing disorganized and highly local gang sets ("factions," in Chicago parlance)

(Papachristos 2012). Movement to the contrary, such as the current shifting of the Mexican Mafia, or "La Eme," in California and the American west and southwest from a street/prison gang into a genuine organized crime hierarchy, is vanishingly rare.

One will sometimes find, on the local level, arms of more organized national gangs, such as the Latin Kings, and even transnational gangs such as MS-13. It is noteworthy that in practice such gangs rarely feature in concerns about local violence: with hierarchy and organization tend to come a certain focus on making money and a commensurate discipline, which weighs against the high levels of more personal and expressive violence that comes with lack of purpose and discipline (Cook et al. 2007). In Los Angeles, for example, law enforcement officials attribute part of the recent striking decrease in gang violence to the influence of La Eme, which disciplines Latino gangs against attention-getting violence and will even "green light" hits against sets that break the rules.

Finally, even though group members are consistently among the highest-rate criminal offenders, there is a division even within these ranks. Where violence is concerned, between 10 percent and 20 percent of group members are what are called by law enforcement, in nomenclature that we have adopted, "impact players": shooters, instigators of conflict, those who will drive vendettas or "beefs" or renew them when they have become dormant. One of the street outreach workers that was part of the original Boston Gun Project action research group said, early in that process, that out of each gang, there were typically one or two who really drove things and would actually pull a trigger (Kennedy 2001). Experience and research have borne out that this is in fact the pattern. It is thus the case that the group setting for violence—0.2 percent of a city's population driving the preponderance of serious violence—in practice distills down to something closer to 0.04 percent, or even less.

## THE NATURE OF GROUP MEMBERS

Members of violent groups are nearly always young minority males, mostly young adults, with typically a small proportion of juvenile males. The typical portrayal of group and gang members as "kids" is inaccurate; juveniles are the exception rather than the rule, with the most active years typically around nineteen to the late twenties. It was once largely the rule that gang/group desistance was normal by, at least, the early thirties, but this is no longer so routinely the case; it is not unusual for members to stay active for some time after this. There are exceptions to this basic picture, as in Glasgow, Scotland, where groups are largely comprised of juvenile whites, but they are very much exceptions.

Group membership, and movement into group membership, is rarely considered and purposive on the part of either the group or potential membership. Gang "recruitment" is mostly a fiction, imposed by law enforcement and other outsiders on what is in fact a loose and largely organic process. Young men typically become gang members because their family or friends are gang members; because they live in an area in which gangs are active and inviting; and because rival gangs treat everyone in their area as members of the local gang or gangs, leading to movement to join for self-protection. Matza's (1964) idea of "drift," originally framed to describe the movement of juveniles into delinquency, remains one of the most accurate: young men slide into group membership (and back out of it) without much calculation, deliberation, or consideration of alternatives.

They frequently do not much like what they find. It is routine, in private conversations with group members, to hear robust and heartfelt protestations against the group life and what comes with it. Pitts's notion of the "reluctant gangster," with one of his English sources saying that "Everybody on the street knows they're going to lose, it's just that we don't know how to win," captures this nicely (Pitts 2007, 2). Group members report living in essentially constant fear; being unable to trust even their friends; being in genuine danger from their enemies; being unable to travel outside very particular areas, and especially being unable to be in or even cross through rivals' areas; knowing large numbers of friends and associates who have been killed and hurt; having been shot, stabbed, and otherwise attacked themselves, often multiple times; being constantly afraid for their families and loved ones; enduring the condemnation that comes from, and the shame they bring on, their families; sometimes (but not always) making large amounts of money, but typically being poor; having no financial reserves or other support such as insurance; constantly fearing, and often being, robbed; and frequently being harassed, stopped, arrested, prosecuted, and imprisoned by law enforcement. Formal data support this high level of contact with law enforcement; a sample of Cincinnati group members, for example, averaged thirty-five prior charges apiece, with about a third exhibiting ten or more felony charges (Engel et al. 2009).

It is particularly important for this discussion to recognize the prevalence of violent victimization in the group population. In our original Boston work, we calculated that group members stood a one in seven chance of being killed, largely by gunshot, over a hypothetical nine-year group membership spell. Since there is typically around a five to one ratio between nonfatal and fatal gunshot wounds, this suggests that most gang members would be shot. Papachristos (2011) identified a core group-involved network in Chicago in which group members—at a time when the U.S. homicide rate stood at around 5:100,000 annually—faced a homicide rate of 3,000:100,000. "[T]he risk of stepping on a landmine in Afghanistan is less than ten out of a one thousand, which means it's safer to walk around a real war zone than it is for the young men in this network to walk around West Garfield Park," he writes.

The fear they feel is thus legitimate. It drives group formation and cohesion, in which members join and stay for self-protection; drives weapon carrying, acquisition, and use; and contributes to the creation and often the escalation of street norms that prescribe unyielding and violent attitudes and conduct as a way of signaling that violence should not be directed at groups and group members, and that violence so directed will be met with retaliation.

Group members frequently hate that violence, even while they and their groups perpetrate it. They frequently report situations in which they were forced into violence against their preferences, as when an enemy would not back down or friends applied pressure they could not feasibly resist. Seasoned group members are often articulate about this—that while there is a very small number of members who thrive on violence, for nearly everybody else it is a response either to an external threat or powerful peer norms. (Similarly, young neighborhood men who do not join these groups often report taking extreme measures to avoid these dynamics, such as not having friends and not leaving the house.) The picture that emerges from group members is of a world in which violence and danger is omnipresent; visited upon individual members by others; cannot be controlled or avoided; and is pressed upon individual members by both enemies and friends.

It is important to recognize that these individual sentiments are generally not expressed in the group or in public. Group members hew to a powerful set of norms, a "street code" governing what it means to be "real," be worthy of respect, and especially how to respond to violence and disrespect and what one owes one's fellow group members. It is widely recognized, in social psychology and many other related disciplines, that group norms and dynamics are not only a simple aggregation of individual norms and preferences but frequently are dramatically out of alignment with those individual norms and preferences. While the street code is informal, it is more or less explicit. Its principal tenets are:

- Disrespect must be met with violence
- The group is my family and we have each other's backs
- I and we are not afraid of the police, prison, or death
- The enemy of my friend is my enemy—if my friend has beef, then I have beef
- I and we are the victims of outside oppression, we have never been given a chance or offered any help, the outside world is more criminal and corrupt than we are—just better at getting away with it—and when we do crime it is justified.

It is entirely possible for every member of a group to reject some or all of these ideas as individuals; for each member of the group to believe the other members in fact support them; and for the group to thus force on itself a continued violence—for example, to commit a drive-by shooting when one member is disrespected by a rival group member—when no member in fact wants to do so. This condition of "pluralistic ignorance" has been found to apply in large numbers of social situations, and it or some close variant of it—the group, and group dynamics, lead members to do things they do not want to do—is a frequent and powerful element in groups and group violence (Matza 1964).

As this suggest, group members are not in fact as alienated from mainstream norms about right and wrong as their conduct would indicate. It is not at all unusual to hear group members express very ordinary and uncompromising views—"killing people is wrong," "shooting that boy was fucked up"—and, for example, behaving meekly when confronted by their elders. They do, however, have a singularly dire view of, and fractured relationship with, actual law enforcement, especially the police. In one assessment of indicators of perceived police legitimacy by gun-involved Chicago parolees (many, but not all, gang members), Meares and Papachristos found that they in fact had higher regard for the law and the duty to obey the law than "ordinary" citizens—they were more likely, for example, to believe that "people should obey the law even when it goes against what they believe is right." (Meares and Papachristos 2009, table 1). But they were significantly less likely to believe that the police were respectful, equitable, and honest (Meares and Papachristos 2009, tables 2, 3, 4). Beyond that, they are likely to understand and express their poor relationship with the police in terms of personal and racial animus—that, as Brunson reports from one of his street informants in St. Louis, "the police don't like black people" (Brunson 2007).

This means that group members will very rarely expect or ask for help from the police. The street code and their own experience and expectations all push for what Black called "self-help"—rather than turning to the law for redress of grievance, they will turn to their own and their group's capacities (Black 1983). The "stop snitching" ethos, generally understood by outsiders as a result of witness intimidation, is in fact more the product of a principled withdrawal from the police and law enforcement. This withdrawal, coupled with the street code and group dynamics, can produce an escalated cascade of reciprocal violence, in which an initial event—a group member's fellow group member is killed—produces a subsequent killing which is seen by the perpetrating group as justice, by the recipient group as an affront requiring payback, and can grow to involve multiple group members on each side and even groups allied with those groups.

## THE NATURE OF GROUP VIOLENCE

This helps begin to explain one of the most significant and generally most unexpected aspects of group violence—that it on balance has very little to do with the illicit economy or, more broadly, any aspect of making money. This is a largely consistent finding in the larger gang literature—that violence is generally "expressive" rather than "instrumental" (see, e.g., Decker 1996; Papachristos, 2009) but has been resolutely rejected by law enforcement and in most policy thinking. It is, however, correct. Boston's group violence was dominated by group-on-group vendettas or "beefs," supplemented by beefs between individual group members. That pattern was to largely hold in subsequent city-level analyses. Strictly economic-related—over drug turf, as repayment for a drug theft, as reprisal for a theft, in the course of a robbery, and the like—is typically under a quarter of all group-related killing. Some substantial portion of that violence, or at least its lethal character, may also be regarded as expressive, in that such disputes often could have been settled non-lethally: it is the street code, and the felt need to adhere to it, that produces the fatalities (alternatives exist even in the group world, as in the Chicago gang practice of administering severe beatings—"pumpkinheads"— for certain violations). The nexus with illicit economic activity is nearly always there, but it is not that nexus that generally drives the violence: it is only a drug-dealing gang member, for the most part, who will kill another for looking at him wrong in a club, but it's the "mean mugging," not the drug market, that precipitates the shooting. Non-U.S. settings, such as Glasgow, clarify the matter; Glasgow's endemic edged-weapon gang violence has nothing to do with any illicit market and is entirely about turf, faction, and "beef."

Such beefs can be started by a wide range of factors—including those involving economic conflict—and then persist for years and decades. The most typical pattern seems to be a conflict between group-involved individuals that then widens to include the individuals' groups and often groups allied with those groups. The precipitating event can be flagrantly trivial on its face; the decades-long war between the Norteño and Sureño Mexican-American gang supersets in the United States is said to have been started by one member stealing shoes from another in prison, while the persistently lethal vendetta between San Francisco's Big Block and West Mob groups, now also decades long, is variously said to have begun over who would rap next at a neighborhood block party or in a dispute over a used car. Those fighting today can often not even explain why. The primacy of the street code, particularly the element that requires violence in return for violence or disrespect; the movement of conflict between individuals into beefs between groups; and the persistence of many groups over time creates the conditions for more or less open-ended vendettas.

Beyond this core violence, group members commit large numbers of crimes that involve violence or the potential for violence. Of these, robberies, especially drug robberies, and home invasions always involve violent confrontations and frequently proceed to more serious and lethal violence. The more active street scenes, especially those involving more or less overt drug trafficking, tend to breed groups and extreme individuals who make their money and their reputations stealing from other groups and criminals ("stick-up boys"). They are not only violent and invite violent responses and reprisals, they keep other groups and offenders on high alert, drive weapon acquisition and carrying, and generally keep the streets on edge. And, as has been noted, group members are disproportionately domestically and sexually violent. This too can have a group and "street code" element to it, as it can be driven by gang rape that emerges from existing violent groups (Bourgois, 2003) and by domestic violence perpetrated by group members seeking to maintain face in the eyes of other group members (Wilkinson 2012).

These individual-, group-, and norm-based factors are real, and real drivers of violence. At the same time, it is critical to recognize that in most situations in which those factors could produce violence, they do not. Most group members will never kill anybody; some groups that are otherwise highly criminally active will never kill anybody; most groups will not kill anybody in any given year; most individual and group conflicts that could give rise to lethal violence will not; most interpersonal situations that could produce, for example, domestic assault will not. The links between groups, group members, street norms, and violence, while concrete, are neither invariant nor, from one perspective—their absolute production of violence—particularly strong. In Los Angeles, for example, there are estimated to be some 450 separate gangs, and some forty thousand gang members (Los Angeles Almanac 2007). In 2012, they collectively produced 152 gang homicides (Kandel, 2013). Even if it is assumed that no gangs and no gang members produced more than one homicide, that year some three hundred gangs and 38,500 gang members killed nobody. The most recent official survey of U.S. jurisdictions on gangs and gang crime reported that gangs and gang membership were up slightly, but that gang homicide was down by a larger proportion (Egley and Howell 2011). These core factors—violent groups and membership in violent groups, intragroup and intergroup dynamics, and the street code—raise the likelihood of, but do not determine, violence.

One thing that becomes glaringly apparent to close observers of the group and street scene is how greatly it in fact departs in this respect from the stereotypes of both law enforcement and group members themselves. It is commonplace for law enforcement to say things such as that in this population "guns have become the preferred method of dispute resolution." In fact, the streets are so riven with disputes between groups and group-involved individuals that were this to be true there would scarcely be anybody left standing. It is closer to the case that guns are very much the *last* resort in dispute resolution—notwithstanding the fact of unconscionably high levels of gun violence. Similarly, groups will express standards such as "you have to hurt anybody who disrespects you," and group members such tenets as "you can't walk away from a fight unless you want to be finished forever," and then routinely not hurt people who disrespect them and routinely walk away from fights. As Garot put it, drawing on his ethnography in an intensely gang-involved southern California school, "In the course of my interviews, I could count on every young man to tell me that anyone who walked away from a fight would be punked for life. I could also count on most young man to tell me of a time when he walked away from a fight." (Garot 2007) Like most risk factors, these predispose without in any way creating inevitability. Group involvement, commitment to the street code, and the like are much more powerful risk factors than the ordinary ones of living in a dangerous neighborhood or early onset of substance abuse, but—also like them, though to a lesser degree—the risk they represent is, more often than not, not realized.

What risk is realized is extremely unevenly distributed even within groups. A relatively small proportion of groups in any given city will be consistently "hot," with another, episodic small proportion "hot" at any given time (an assessment of groups in one police district in Los Angeles found about a third to be "very violent," about half to be "somewhat violent," and the rest to be "not very violent," with not even all the more violent groups being so at any particular moment). Since jurisdictions do not routinely track either street groups or violence by street groups, such "hot groups" are not routinely identified or addressed as such. It is relatively easy to do so, however, and the creation and maintenance of straightforward intelligence and tracking instruments such as "group violence scorecards," which audit homicides and shootings by groups, can identify those groups for a range of interventions (Braga forthcoming).

The same is true at the individual level. When doing street work with violent groups, it's common to run across members who have been shot, stabbed, and otherwise assaulted extraordinarily often, and members who are by common agreement not long for this world. In a recent ride-along by the author in Bermuda, police officers pointed out a young man standing calmly on a city sidewalk and said, "He's about to get killed, and he knows it." As this suggests, street intelligence from police officers, community sources, confidential informants, and specialists such as gang outreach workers can often identify those at such heightened risk. Recent work applying social network analysis to the same problem has shown tremendous promise. Papachristos et al. have found that in networks constructed using existing police data, individuals with social connections to individuals who have been shot show greatly increased risk of being shot themselves, with that risk remaining elevated but attenuating with increased network distance (Papachristos et al. 2012).

Finally, levels of violence in groups and networks of groups vary considerably and, so far, largely unpredictably. The most consistently violent groups will generally be quiet most of the time—in terms of the most serious violence—and then flare up. Groups that are more generally calm will themselves flare up from time to time. At the city level, the network of groups that more or less defines the lethal violence problem can be relatively calm, which will mean that the city's overall violent crime will be down, and then pick up, with a consequent increase in overall violence. Given the heavily reactive and reciprocal nature of group-related violence, the sense one frequently gets is that of a "web" of unstable actors and relationships. That web can be in a state of uneasy but relative calm, which will persist until something perturbs it. That perturbation can come from within, such as the resurgence or collapse of a centrally positioned and violent group, or the reactivation of an influential beef. It can come from without, such as when law enforcement removes central players or central groups from the network, creating instability. Thus perturbed, violence will ripple and re-ripple through the web, until for reasons again both internal and external it can once again stabilize. From the outside, when looking for explanations of such often sudden and dramatic movements in both directions, attention tends to turn to more or less structural factors—demographics, the economy, and the like. From closer to the street, it frequently looks far more immediate and contingent.

## THE COMMUNITY SETTING OF VIOLENT GROUPS

Violent street groups are for all practical purposes found only in generally historically troubled, disenfranchised communities saturated in a broad range of racial, ethnic, economic, family, and community problems. In the U.S. context in which most of the work described herein has been conducted, those communities are primarily deeply disadvantaged and alienated black communities. Communities elsewhere may lack some of the particular facets found in the United States—Glasgow's juvenile white groups have already been mentioned, and UK Afro-Caribbean groups do not have the same experience of structured racial oppression as do U.S. blacks—but it is essentially unheard of to find any meaningful density of or problem with violent street groups outside this broad context of oppression, deprivation, and schism with the rest of local society. Despite perennial fretting by mainstream society that such violence will inevitably leach into other communities and walks of life, such movement is entirely the exception and not the rule (and where it does occur, it seems to move more by the fitful, faddish, faux-romantic embrace of the street code, and not through anything more structural and deterministic).

It is important to note that while such communities and neighborhoods are often regarded by those outside them as "dangerous"—and that, by some objective measures, they are—it is the violent groups that make them so, and that outside the highly patterned violence of those groups, such communities are little or no more dangerous than those around them. Papachristos has found that if one abstracts the group-related violence from the most dangerous neighborhood in Chicago, the remaining population in the neighborhood is at roughly city-level risk (Papachristos 2011). These communities are in a real way two communities—one that of groups and group members, both extraordinarily active and extraordinarily at risk, and one of everybody else, neither particularly active nor particularly at risk, though heavily affected and influenced by the group violence and what flows from it.

Failing to make this differentiation frequently leads to further mistakes, such as a feeling—especially by law enforcement—that at the community level violence is normative, cultural, and generally acceptable. This is profoundly incorrect. Working in these communities shows few things more clearly and strongly than the depth of disapproval of the violence and the prevalence and power of the trauma it brings with it. Parents fear for and too often mourn their children; people are afraid to go outside, and to travel to work and school; religious figures, community activists, and ordinary citizens work tirelessly against the violence. As has been noted, even group members will frequently express intolerance for violence and go to great lengths to avoid it. Research shows that high-violence minority communities in fact have substantially less tolerance for violence than do safer majority communities (Sampson and Bartusch 1998). (This should be common sense; to believe otherwise is to believe that communities like living this way, which while untrue unfortunately is all too credible to all too many.) What field experience also shows is a profound alienation from and distrust toward law enforcement, the state, and the outside world in general. People hate the violence but do not expect the police or the outside to help; are afraid that if they express their concerns about the violence the police and other outsiders will come in and do more damage; and frequently believe that the violence and related issues (such as drug trafficking) are the product of deliberate outside machinations. What reads from the outside as indifference or approval is in fact a profound anger, exhaustion, and alienation.

In this, the communities where group violence thrives seem to be essentially of a piece. The historical nature and present details of that anger, exhaustion, and alienation is clearly different in the United States than it is, for example, in intergenerational white "dole" housing projects in Scotland; relatively recent Afro-Caribbean communities in Manchester and London; and aboriginal reserves in Australia. But the author has experienced essentially identical underlying narratives and dynamics in all of these places: people hate the violence; feel it to be the product of outside neglect and oppression; believe that all or much of that is deliberate; do not expect respect or help from the police or other outsiders; and are unwilling to talk about it in public, except in terms of those outside ills, lest it further impugn their communities and bring more unwanted attention from the outside.

A growing body of work on the "legitimacy" of the police and the law is bringing into steadily sharper focus the idea that this schism between communities and, especially, the police is directly linked to high levels of violence. Where legitimacy—by definition a subjective, perceived quality—is lacking, research shows that people are less likely to obey the law and the police voluntarily; less likely to cooperate with the police and other agents of the law; less likely to express attitudes in conformity with law-abidingness; and less likely to take individual and collective action to prevent and respond to crime (Tyler 2006). In terms of other strong findings in the literature, a lack of legitimacy undermines individual and community capacities to produce informal social control, and diminishes communities' collective efficacy. Angry and mistrustful communities are less likely to speak out against violence when that means standing with police and other outsiders speaking against violence. They are less likely to report crime and otherwise cooperate with those hated and mistrusted authorities. The small numbers of young men most likely to commit serious violence are more likely to do so when the community narrative they hear is about the racist police rather than about how violence is destroying the community. Those same young men are more likely to get a gun and their friends to avenge a fallen peer rather than call police and cooperate with prosecutors.

This process is clearly evident at the ground level in these settings. Group members will frequently say that "nobody cares" about the violence, when nothing is further from the truth. Relatively rare instances of official violence, such as a police officer shooting a young man, will spur vigorous community action, while much more common group-member violence spurs little or none. The core community discourse about the violence majors on the oppression and neglect of outsiders with little or no place for community and individual action and accountability. Group members will explain what they are doing, and why it is justified, in terms of the misdeeds of outsiders ("everybody knows the CIA invented crack," "somebody else is bringing the guns in"). Research is bearing out that in practice these dynamics are in fact productive of violence at the community level (Kane 2005; Kirk and Papachristos, 2011).

Finally, in American settings with high levels of group violence, there is frequently also a high level of aggressive and intrusive policing and arrest, prosecution, and incarceration. It is a normal experience for young men to be stopped and often searched by the police, experiences frequently characterized by rudeness, disrespect, and the use of force. In some communities, or "hot spot" neighborhoods within communities, going to jail and prison is a normal part of the life course, and over time many or most men accumulate criminal records and prison terms. The abusive behavior of police heightens feelings of racism and illegitimacy. It is now well understood that high community rates of incarceration have strong and deeply negative impacts at the individual, family, and neighborhood level: they make affected individuals less likely to earn good livings, undertake education and training, marry, and support their children; increase the likelihood that their children will fail school, be arrested, and be incarcerated; and reduce communities' collective efficacy with regard to crime prevention (Travis 2005; Clear 2007) These are all dynamics that promote the creation and cohesion of violent groups and make it more difficult for those inside and outside these communities to address violent groups. This is a subject that has gotten the most attention in the United States, given that nation's exceptional level of incarceration; whether there are parallels internationally is an important and largely open question.

## THE GROUP VIOLENCE INTERVENTION FRAMEWORK

Attempts to address violent groups have fallen into three main categories: law enforcement, comprehensive community initiatives, and programs aimed at at-risk individuals. None of them have succeeded in any meaningful terms. Law enforcement aimed at groups and group members fails to eliminate those groups or group membership or generally to make any substantial and lasting impact on violence; they can greatly exacerbate schisms between law enforcement and troubled communities (Buntin 2013). Many in law enforcement have long acknowledged this, with the frequent refrain that "we can't arrest our way" out of the problem. Comprehensive community initiatives, such as the U.S. Department of Justice's Office of Juvenile Justice and Delinquency Prevention model gang program, typically involve the coordination of a wide range of law enforcement, other governmental, and nongovernmental organizations (NGOs) to produce systematic prevention, intervention, and enforcement activities around both at-risk and group-involved individuals. They have in general proved difficult to implement; shown small or no impact on overall levels of violence; and little or no impact on overall gang and group involvement (National Gang Center 2010). Similarly inspired interventions, such as Los Angeles' Gang Reduction and Youth Development zones, have shown similarly small and often uncertain impact on violence (Dunworth et al. 2011). Individual-level gang prevention programs, such as the well-funded U.S. Gang Resistance and Education Program (GREAT) have generally been unable to show any or meaningful impact on the more serious outcomes—gang membership and violence—even amongst program participants (Esbensen, 2004), let alone at the city or neighborhood level.

It is important to note that the important question in this respect is not the academic one—did the intervention produce a discernable statistically signif-icant impact—but the more ordinary one: did the intervention make a large and meaningful difference. Where group violence is serious, communities want it greatly reduced. On this metric, traditional approaches have consis-tently failed. The preceding discussion helps understand why this may be true. Law enforcement efforts, even when framed around gang violence, generally address individuals—gangs are not usually legally liable for a giv-en homicide, for example, so the shooter, not the gang, is arrested and prose-cuted. The gang and gang dynamics persist. Where law enforcement does address gangs *qua* gangs, it can never address all the gangs in an area, so the network-of-groups phenomenon that is the real local gang issue, with multi-ple groups influenced by ties of vendetta and alliance, is not addressed. Comprehensive community models rarely break out of this mold: the Office of Juvenile Justice and Delinquency Prevention (OJJDP) model, for example, is designed to create a continuum of care and enforcement aimed at at-risk and gang-involved individuals, and once again misses the core group dynam-ics. Gang prevention programs are once again aimed at individuals, and given the invariably very low rate of group involvement even in the most active areas, nearly inevitably engage primarily with individuals who will not become gang members regardless (and even more primarily with individuals who will never commit serious violence). And none of these frameworks generally recognize or engage with the central issues of the informal street code, law enforcement legitimacy, or the damaging consequences of current law enforcement practice.

In response to this, a different framework has emerged. Growing out of the original youth violence action research in Boston and developed (and continuing to develop) since then, it has the following core features:

- A clear focus on group-involved violence;
- The identification of violent groups, and involved individuals, at the city or neighborhood level;
- The formation of a working partnership consisting of law enforcement, social service providers, and community figures;
- Direct, face-to-face engagement with violent groups in which three core messages are delivered:

  - Violence is unacceptable to the community and will not be tolerated;
  - Group members are important and valued and help is available to them if they want it;

- Continued violence by group members will be met with comprehensive law enforcement attention to the group in question, such that other group members will face legal consequences for such things as drug sales, probation and parole violations, and the like.

- Meticulous and sustained follow-up in which those promises are kept and the face-to-face engagement is repeated as required.

This approach, piloted as "Operation Ceasefire" in Boston (Kennedy et al. 2001) and implemented since in scores of cities in the United States and some foreign settings such as Glasgow (Glasgow's Community Initiative to Reduce Violence 2010) and Rio de Janeiro (Arias and Ungar 2009), has been designed in accordance with the key findings set out in this chapter. It seeks to prevent on the relatively rare occurrence of group-related violence and does not seek to eliminate groups as such, or group membership. It uses figures of natural standing to group members—community elders, surviving parents of murdered children, ex-group members—to articulate community norms against violence and undercut the street code (Kennedy 2010). As part of establishing the core working partnerships, law enforcement is exposed to community partners who loathe the violence and are willing to say so, and community partners are exposed to law enforcement officials who show their commitment to keeping group members alive and out of prison. An explicit process of "reconciliation and truth-telling" between communities and law enforcement surfaces toxic historical and current narratives on both sides and builds on a strong willingness, also on both sides, to move beyond them (Kennedy 2009). These new relationships, practices, and processes are designed to enhance legitimacy and reduce traditional enforcement practices and their unintended consequences for communities (Meares 2009). Variations on these group-focused interventions have been developed and are being deployed specifically for group-involved impact players (Main 2013).

These operations have generally been mounted as customized interventions designed to produce specific, rapid reductions in group-related violence. As the basic framework has become more familiar and more developed, variations have been framed that address open drug markets (Braga and Weisburd 2012), individual violent offenders (who may themselves also be group involved) (Papachristos et al. 2007), and robbery (Ruderman 2013). The same basic principles are even being built into broad police operations in major cities such as Los Angeles, Chicago, and New York, with the prospect of the approach becoming not an adjunct to but the core of law enforcement approaches to this problem (Buntin 2013; Kennedy 2012; Kennedy 2013).

# CONCLUSION

Formal evaluations have consistently shown significant impact—in both the statistical and common-sense meaning of the term—for the framework (Braga and Weisburd 2012). Impacts range from about a one-third reduction in group-related violence to on the order of a 50 percent reduction in lethal violence city-wide. Where individual-level outcomes are available, group members show lessened involvement in violence and lower recidivism rates. The broader police reforms noted above have not yet been subjected to formal evaluation but show considerable promise; in New York City, for example, the shift was associated with about a 25 percent reduction in homicides city-wide at the same time that street stops fell by half. As that example shows, some of the greatest promise here is not just in violence reduction but in reframing how violence, and "violent" neighborhoods, are policed, with broad gains possible in reduced intrusion, reduced arrest and incarceration, and increased legitimacy.

# REFERENCES

Arias, E. D., and M. Ungar. 2009. "Community Policing and Latin America's Citizen Security Crisis." *Comparative Politics* 41: 409–29.

Black, D. 1983. "Crime as Social Control." *American Sociological Review* 48: 34–45.

Bourgois, P. 2003. *In Search of Respect: Selling Crack in El Barrio*. New York: Cambridge University Press.

Braga, A., D. L. Weisburd. 2012. *The Effects of "Pulling Levers" Focused Deterrence Strategies on Crime*. Campbell Systematic Reviews. DOI: 104.4073/csr.2012.6.

Brunson, R. K. 2007. "Police Don't Like Black People: African-American Young Men's Accumulated Police Experiences." *Criminology and Public Policy* 6: 71–101.

Bullock, K., and N. Tilley. 2002. "Shootings, Gangs and Violence Incidents in Manchester: Developing a Crime Reduction Strategy." *Crime Reduction Research Series* Paper 13: 2002.

Buntin, J. 2013. "The LAPD Remade." *City Journal* 23, www.city-journal.org/2013/issue_23_1.html.

Clear, T. R. 2007. *Imprisoning Communities: How Mass Incarceration Makes Disadvantaged Neighborhoods Worse*. New York: Oxford University Press.

Cook, P. J., J. Ludwig, S. A. Venkatesh, and A. A. Braga. 2007. "Underground Gun Markets." *The Economic Journal* 117: F588–F618.

Decker, S. 1996. "Collective and Normative Features of Gang Violence." *Justice Quarterly* 13: 243–64.

Duane, D. 2006. "Straight Outta Boston." *Mother Jones*, January/February, 2006: 61–65; 78–80.

Dunworth, T., D. Hayeslip, and M. Denver. 2011. *Y2 Final Report: Evaluation of the Los Angeles Gang Reduction and Youth Development Program*. Washington, DC: The Urban Institute.

Egley, A., Jr., and J. C. Howell. 2011. *Juvenile Justice Fact Sheet: Highlights of the 2011 National Youth Gang Survey*. Washington, DC: U.S. Department of Justice Office of Juvenile Justice and Delinquency Prevention.

Engel, R. S., G. Baker, M. Skubak Tyllyer, J. R. Dunham, D. Hall, M. Ozer, B. Henson, and T. Godesy. 2009. *Implementation of the Cincinnati Initiative to Reduce Violence (CIRV): Year 2 Report*. Cincinnati: University of Cincinnati Policing Institute.

Esbensen, F. A. 2004. *Evaluating G.R.E.A.T.: A School-Based Gang Prevention Program.* Washington, DC: National Institute of Justice, Office of Justice Program.

Esbensen, F., L. T. Winfree Jr., N. He, T. J. Taylor. 2001. "Youth Gangs and Definitional Issues: When Is a Gang a Gang, and Why Does It Matter?" *Crime and Delinquency* 47: 105–30.

Garot, R. 2007. "Inner-City Teens and Face-Work: Avoiding Violence and Maintaining Honor." In *A Cultural Approach to Interpersonal Communication: Essential Readings*, edited by L. F. Monaghan and J. E. Goodman, 294–317. Oxford: Blackwell.

*Glasgow's Community Initiative to Reduce Violence. 2010. CIRV—First Year Report.* www. actiononviolence.com/sites/default/files/CIRV-year1-report.pdf.

Kandel, J. 2013. "Crime Drops for 10th Year in Los Angeles." NBC Los Angeles. January 7, 2013. www.nbclosangeles.com.

Kane, R. J. 2005. "Compromised Police Legitimacy as a Predictor of Violence Crime in Structurally Disadvantage Communities." *Criminology* 43: 469–98.

Kennedy, D. M. 2001. *Don't Shoot: One Man, a Street Fellowship, and the End of Violence in Inner-City America.* New York: Bloomsbury Press.

———. 2008. *Deterrence and Crime Prevention: Reconsidering The Prospect of Sanction.* London: Routledge.

———. 2009a. "Drugs, Race, and Common Ground: Reflection on the High Point Intervention." *National Institute of Justice Journal* 262: 12–17.

———. 2009b. "Gangs and Public Policy: Constructing and Deconstructing Gang Databases." *Criminology and Public Policy* 8: 711–16.

———. 2010. Practice Brief: *Norms, Narratives, and Community Engagement for Crime Prevention.* New York: John Jay College of Criminal Justice.

———. 2012. "After a Horrific Summer of Murder, Chicago Trying a Bold New Approach." *The Daily Beast.* September 28, 2012, www.thedailybeast.com/articles/2012/09/28/after-a-horrific-summer-of-murder-chicago-trying-a-bold-new-approach.html.

———. 2013. "Getting Beyond Stop-and-Frisk." *New York Daily News.* July 15, 2013.

Kennedy, D., A. Braga, and A. Piehl. 1997. "The (Un)Known Universe: Mapping Gangs and Gang Violence in Boston." In *Crime Mapping and Crime Prevention*, edited by D. Weisburd and J. T. McEwen, 219–62. New York: Criminal Justice Press.

———. 2001. "Developing and Implementing Operation Ceasefire." In *Gun Violence: The Boston Gun Project's Operation Ceasefire*, 5–53. Washington, DC: National Institute of Justice, U.S. Department of Justice.

Kennedy, D., A. M. Piehl, and A. Braga. 1996. "Youth Violence in Boston: Gun Markets, Serious Youth Offender, and a Use-Reduction Strategy." *Law and Contemporary Problems* 59: 147–96.

Kirk, D. S., and A. V. Papachristos. 2011. "Cultural Mechanisms and the Persistence of Neighborhood Violence." *American Journal of Sociology* 166: 1190–1233.

Klein, M. W. 1995. *The American Street Gang: It's Nature, Prevalence and Control.* New York: Oxford University Press.

Klein, M. W., and C. Maxson. 1989. "Street Gang Violence." In *Violent Crimes, Violent Criminals*, edited by N. Weiner, 198–234. Newbury Park, CA: Sage.

*Los Angeles Almanac,* 2007. "Gang Populations—Los Angeles County and City." www. laalmanac.com/crime/cr03v.htm.

Main, F. 2013. "Cops Knocking on Doors of Potential Shooters, Victims." *Chicago Sun-Times*, July 18, 2013, www.suntimes.com/news/crime/21396323-418/cops-knocking-on-doors-of-potential-shooters-victims.html.

Matza, D. 1964. *Delinquency and Drift.* New York: John Wiley and Sons, Inc.

Maxson, C .L., and M. W. Klein. 1990. "Street Gang Violence: Twice as Great, or Half as Great?" In *Gangs in America*, edited by C.R. Huff, 71–100. Thousand Oaks: Sage Publications.

McGloin, J. M. 2005. "Policy Intervention Considerations of a Network Analysis of Street Gangs." *Criminology and Public Policy* 4: 607–35.

Meares, T. L. 2009. "The Legitimacy of Police Among Young African-American Men." *Faculty Scholarship Series.* Paper 528. digitalcommons.law.yale.edu/fss_papers/528.

Meares, T. L., and A. V. Papachristos. 2009. "Policing Gun Crime Without Guns." Available at SSRN 1326932.

National Gang Center. 2010. *Best Practices to Address Community Gang Problems*. Washington, DC: National Institute of Justice, Office of Justice Programs, U.S. Department of Justice.

Papachristos, A. V. 2006. "Social Network Analysis and Gang Research: Theory and Methods." In *Studying Youth Gangs*, edited by J.F. Short and L.A. Hughes, 99-116. Lanham, MD: AltaMira Press.

———. 2009. "Murder By Structure: Dominance Relations and the Social Structure of Gang Homicide." *American Journal of Sociology* 115: 74-128.

———. 2011a. "Murders, Victims Share Local Ties." Chicago Sun-Times, January 17, 2011, www.suntimes.com/news/otherviews/2877760-452/homicide-network-social-risk-victims.html.

———. 2011b. "The Small World of Murder." *Chicago Sun-Times*. January 17, 2011.

———. 2012. "What Is a 'Gang Audit'?" HuffPost Chicago, July 5, 2012, www.huffingtonpost.com/andrew-papachristos/what-is-a-gang-audit_b_1651386.html.

Papachristos, A. V., A. A. Braga, D. M. Hureau. 2012. "Social Networks and the Risk of Gunshot Injury." *Journal of Urban Health* 89: 992–1003.

Papachristos, A. V., T. L. Meares, and J. Fagan. 2007. "Attention Felons: Evaluating Project Safe Neighborhoods in Chicago." *Journal of Empirical Legal Studies* 4: 223–72.

Pitts, J. 2007. *Reluctant Gangsters: Youth Gangs in Waltham Forest*. Bedford, UK: University of Bedfordshire.

Radil, S. M., C. Flint, and G. E. Tita. 2010. "Spatializing Social Networks: Using Social Network Analysis to Investigate Geographies of Gang Rivalry, Territoriality, and Violence in Los Angeles." *Annals of the Associations of American Geographers* 100: 307–26.

Ruderman, W. 2013. "To Stem Juvenile Robberies, Police Trail Youths Before the Crime." *The New York Times*. March 3, 2013.

Sampson, R. J., and D. J. Bartusch. 1998. "Legal Cynicism and (Subcultural?) Tolerance to Deviance: The Neighborhood Context of Racial Differences." *Law and Society Review* 32: 777–804.

Sullivan, M. L. 2005. "Maybe We Shouldn't Study 'Gangs': Does Reification Obscure Youth Violence?" *Journal of Contemporary Criminal Justice* 21: 170–90.

Travis, J. 2005. *But They All Come Back: Facing the Challenges of Prisoner Reentry*. Washington, DC: Urban Institute press.

Tyler, T. 2006. *Why People Obey the Law*. Princeton, NJ: Princeton University Press. U.S. Department of Justice, 2004.

*Chapter Four*

# Intergroup Contact and Genocide

## Wenona Rymond-Richmond

Of the various forms of group violence, genocide represents the most extreme and deadly form. Genocidal violence has affected hundreds of millions of victims who were killed, raped, sexually assaulted, forcibly displaced, kidnapped, robbed, and mutilated. The most severe violations of human rights are committed during genocidal violence. Individuals, families, communities, villages, and cultures are devastated by the atrocities. The expanding research literature on genocide focuses on problems defining genocide (e.g., Chirot and Edwards 2003; Fein 1990), the identification of precursors (e.g., Gurr and Harff 1994; Horowitz 2001), disputes regarding scale (e.g., Hagan, Rymond-Richmond, and Parker 2005; Hagan and Palloni 2006; Heuveline 2001), the creation of typologies (e.g., Chalk and Jonassohn 1990; Chirot and McCauley 2006; Lemkin 1946), and the development of explanatory approaches (e.g., Posen 1993; Kaplan 1993; Diamond 2005; Hardin 1995; Valentino 2004; Kaufman 2001; Oberschall 2000). While many issues have been examined to understand the causes and consequences of genocide, one issue that has been underexplored is the effect of intergroup social contact and geographic proximity between the perpetrators and victims on genocidal violence.

This chapter utilizes the Atrocities Documentation Survey (ADS), which contains 1,136 interviews and surveys with survivors of the genocide in Darfur, residing in refugee camps in Chad to gain insight into racial and ethnic group conflict and cultural intolerance. This analysis is based on 932 genocide survivors originating from twenty-two village clusters (villages) that had at least fifteen respondents included in the survey. In particular, I will examine 1) what if any effect close physical proximity of victim (black Africans) and perpetrator (Arabs) had on total victimization rates including sexual victimization; and 2) the dynamics of racial protection and racial

71

targeting. Questions I seek to answer are: First, is there a connection between racial protection and total victimization? Prior research (Hagan, Rymond-Richmond, and Palloni 2009) found that racial epithets are increased when victims and perpetrators are in close physical proximity, however, we do not yet know if victimization is heighten when this social dynamic exists. Second, there is a more general need to understand how the conditions leading to genocide are similar or different when racial ethnic contact is increased. Understanding the racial, ethnic, and cultural dimensions of the genocide better may lead to greater ability to identify precursors of genocide and provide insight into eliminating or minimizing future group violence.

## DEFINING THE VIOLENCE

### Genocide

Genocide is most often associated with mass killing for the purpose of wiping out an ethnic group in whole or in part. However, the legal definitions, as well as most sociological definitions of genocide, are significantly broader. For example, many people do not associate the crimes of rape and sexual assault with genocide, despite the evidence that rape is used as a tool for wiping out an ethnic group in much the same way as massive killing. The groundbreaking Akayesu judgment by the International Criminal Tribunal for Rwanda, recognizes the similarities in the crimes and states that rape may "constitute genocide in the same way as any other act as long as they were committed with the specific intent."

The term genocide came into existence in 1944 in response to the Holocaust. Raphael Lemkin, a Polish-Jewish lawyer, coined the word genocide by combining the Greek word for race or tribe, *geno-*, with the Latin word for killing, *-cide*. Lemkin's conception of genocide included not only physical, but also psychological destruction:

> Generally speaking, genocide does not necessarily mean the immediate destruction of a nation, except when accomplished by mass killings of all members of a nation. It is intended rather to signify a coordinated plan of different actions aiming at the destruction of essential foundations of the life of national groups, with the aim of annihilating the groups themselves. The objectives of such a plan would be disintegration of the political and social institutions, of culture, language, national feelings, religion, and the economic existence of national groups, and the destruction of the personal security, liberty, health, dignity, and even the lives of the individuals belonging to such groups. Genocide is directed against the national group as an entity, and the actions involved are directed against individuals, not in their individual capacity, but as members of the national group. (1946, 80)

In large part due to Lemkin's efforts, on December 9, 1948, the United Nations approved the Convention on the Prevention and Punishment of the Crime of Genocide (further referred to as the Genocide Convention), thereby establishing genocide as an international crime. Group, rather than individual violence is central. The legal definition of genocide is found in Article II of the Genocide Convention. Article II defines genocide as any of the following five acts committed with intent to destroy, in whole or in part, a national, ethnic, racial, or religious group:

- Killing members of the group;
- Causing serious bodily or mental harm to members of the group;
- Deliberately inflicting on the group conditions of life calculated to bring about its physical destruction in whole or in part;
- Imposing measures intended to prevent births within the group;
- Forcibly transferring children of the group to another group.

For a charge of genocide, only one of the five acts described in Article II, sections a, b, c, d, and e, must be met.

The Genocide Convention represents a historic and momentous advancement in international law by recognizing and defining genocide as criminal. Yet many scholars have critiqued the legal definition of genocide for being too narrow. Examples of narrowness include the omission of political groups and social classes from legal protection. Addressing this deficit, Chirot and Edwards define genocide as "politically motivated mass murder perpetrated by elites or agents of the government" (2003, 15). In her seminal work on genocide, Helen Fein develops a sociological definition of genocide that is more expansive and inclusive than the legal definition. Fein defines genocide as "sustained purposeful action by a perpetrator to physically destroy a collective directly or indirectly, through interdiction of the biological and social reproduction of group members, sustained regardless of the surrender of lack of threat offered by the victim" (1993, 24). Scholars have further altered and expanded upon the legal definition of genocide to include nonlethal acts that threaten the security of members of a group (Lemkin 1946), emphasizing the role of the state (Horowitz 1980), and highlighting one-sided mass killing by the state or other authority (Chalk and Jonassohn 1990).

Tragically, establishing genocide as a crime has not eliminated its occurrence. Millions of individuals have been the victim of genocide since it was legally established. Victims include, but are not limited to approximately 400,000 civilians in the Vietnam War, over one million Bengali in Bangladesh, 100,000 Hutu in Burundi, 1.7 million Cambodians, 200,000 Bosnian Muslims and Croats in the Former Yugoslavia, over 200,000 in Ethiopia, 100,000 Mayan Indians in Guatemala, 50,000 to 200,000 Kurdish in Iraq, 9,000 to 30,000 deaths in what is referred to as the Dirty War in Argentina,

8,000 in the Bosnian genocide, 800,000 Tutsi in Rwanda, and over 400,000 black Africans have been murdered in Darfur.

## Crimes against Humanity

Legal definitions of mass atrocities include genocide and crimes against humanity. Crimes against humanity are defined differently in the Rome Statute and the statutes of the International Tribunals for the Former Yugoslavia (ICTY) and Rwanda (ICTR). Crimes against humanity as defined under the Rome Statute in Article 7.1 must be "part of a widespread or systematic attack directed against any civilian population." Crimes against humanity include murder, torture, rape, enforced prostitution, sexual violence, enslavement, enforced disappearance, crimes of apartheid, and "other inhumane acts of a similar character intentionally causing great suffering, or serious injury to body or to mental or physical health."

While all genocides are by definition crimes against humanity, not all crimes of humanity are elevated to the crime of genocide. Similarly, the term ethnic cleansing may rightfully describe the intentions of the perpetrators, yet this does not carry the same legal meaning and recourse as a determination of genocide. Labeling an atrocity is more than merely semantic as these legal classifications imply different legal and symbolic consequences and can affect the international community's response to the conflict. Other distinctions between the legal definitions include the evidence needed for conviction. The evidence needed for conviction is likely reduced when an atrocity is labeled a crime against humanity rather than genocide.

## GENOCIDE IN DARFUR

The genocidal conflict in Darfur is frequently defined as starting in February 2003. However, group schism and conflict between Arab nomadic herders and black African farmers can be traced back to at least the mid-1980s. Tragically, as of this writing, the genocide is still ongoing. More than 400,000 black African Darfurians have been killed and two to three million have been forcibly displaced (Hagan, Rymond-Richmond, and Parker 2005). The perpetrators are the Sudanese government militia and the Janjaweed, who are almost exclusively Arab. The victims are Darfurians who identify themselves as black African. Most of the reports on the Darfur genocide associate the Arab tribes with a nomadic lifestyle and the African tribes as farmers that have settled on land that was allotted to the tribes. Unlike Southern Sudan, where religious differences are frequently attributed as the cause of conflict, in the Darfur, both Arabs and black Africans practice the Muslim religion.

There is strong agreement that the murders, rapes, and other crimes that have occurred in Darfur are racially motivated (De Waal 2007). Hagan and Rymond-Richmond (2008a; 2008b) argue that the cause of the genocidal conflict in Darfur is racial and ethnic hatred. The testimony of genocide survivors reveals that the predominately Arab perpetrators were yelling racial epithets as they killed, raped, abducted, and destroyed the homes of black African villagers. As demonstrated below, dehumanization was common in the racial epithets:

> You donkey, you slave; we must get rid of you.

> Black prostitute, whore; you are dirty—black.

The documentation of racial epithets used during the attacks provides evidence that the violence was racially motivated. Hagan, Rymond-Richmond, and Parker (2005) further demonstrate that perpetrators use of racial epithets significantly affected the degree of total victimization during the attack.

It is important to recognize that race and ethnicity in Darfur is particularly complex. Elsewhere, I, along with co-authors, have written extensively about this complexity (Hagan and Rymond-Richmond 2008a; 2008b; Hagan, Rymond-Richmond, and Parker 2005). Racial and ethnic identities in Darfur can be confusing because skin tones can overlap between groups, intermarriage was not uncommon in the past, and members of groups can shift in their feelings of being Arab, non-Arab, African, and black African (Hagan and Rymond-Richmond 2008a, xxii). To further understand the complexity of identity in Darfur, it is necessary to examine the role of the state in socially constructing and manipulating racial and ethnic identities. In Darfur, the Sudanese government maliciously exploited differences between Arabic-speaking nomadic herders and non-Arab African farmers with perceived or observed differing racial attributes to organize and mobilize the Janjaweed and militia attacks on black African villages in Darfur (Hagan and Rymond-Richmond 2008a, xxii).

Complexity and confusion regarding race and ethnicity is not a unique factor in the genocide in Darfur. Racial and ethnic complexity have existed in other genocides including the Holocaust and the Rwandan genocide. Chirot and McCauley (2006) describe genocides marked by the particular intricacy of distinguishing victims from perpetrators:

> The Jews were too similar to the Germans, and the Nazis had to begin with measures to identify and separate Jews, to issue identification cards, and to make group membership visible with armbands. Tutsis and Hutus, as we have seen, often could be identified only by their identity cards if they were not denounced by neighbors or others who knew them. The ideal physical types,

tall, thin Tutsi and shorter, rounder Hutus, did not fit a very large proportion of
the population because of centuries of mixing. (89)

Some may dismiss or de-escalate the role of racism in the genocide in Darfur,
instead favoring explanations that prioritize land or civil conflict. Dismissal
of racism as a motivating factor in Darfur because race and ethnicity are
historically complex in the region is a simplistic and flawed critique. It
assumes that scholars and others insisting that the genocide has racial aspects
have deliberately ignored or happen to be ignorant regarding this complexity.
On the contrary, finding that racism is a driving force in the genocidal violence does not mean one is unaware or dismissive of the blurred, complex,
and overlapping issues regarding race, ethnicity, and identity. Omitting considerations of racially motivated violence from situations in which racial and
ethnic distinctions are complex could result in incorrectly failing to label an
atrocity as genocide. Importantly, genocides "involved targeting groups that
were difficult to differentiate on physical or cultural grounds from the perpetrators" have been among "the worst ethnic genocides of the twentieth century" (Chirot and McCauley 2006, 89).

## EXPLANATIONS OF GENOCIDE

The expanding research literature on genocide focuses on problems defining
genocide (e.g., Chirot and Edwards 2003; Fein 1990), the identification of
precursors (e.g., Gurr and Harff 1994; Horowitz 2001), disputes regarding
scale (e.g., Hagan, Rymond-Richmond, and Parker 2005; Hagan and Palloni
2006; Heuveline 2001), the creation of typologies (e.g., Chalk and Jonassohn
1990; Chirot and McCauley 2006; Lemkin 1946), and the development of
explanatory approaches (e.g., Posen 1993; Kaplan 1993; Diamond 2005;
Hardin 1995; Valentino 2004; Kaufman 2001; Oberschall 2000).

Among the established explanations of genocidal victimization are the
following six. First, a state insecurity approach that focuses on justifiable
reactions to insurgent threats (e.g., Posen 1993). Second is a primordial explanation that emphasizes hatreds so long-standing that they are considered
exogenous (e.g., Kaplan 1993). Third, the population-resource perspective,
which emphasizes competition for life-sustaining resources (Diamond 2005).
According to this third point of view, opportunities and incentives are greatest, and resources most strained, in densely settled areas. Fourth is the instrumental perspective, which emphasizes state-based ethnopolitical entrepren-
eurs who advance their interests by cultivating public fear and disrespect of
subordinate groups (Hardin 1995; Valentino 2004). Fifth is the constructionist approach, which focuses on racial symbols and identity manipulation by
elites (e.g., Kaufman 2001). Finally, the sixth approach is a cognitive fram-

ing approach that identifies the shifts that appear during emerging conflicts as ranging from "normal" to "crisis" scripts or frames (Oberschall 2000).

Hagan and Rymond-Richmond (2008a; 2008b) synthesize these six approaches into what they call a critical collective framing approach to explain the atrocities in Darfur. The theory builds on Coleman's (1986) social action theory and draws on criminological theories including Sampson's (2006) and Matsueda's (2007) concepts of collective and social efficacy and Sutherland's (1947) differential social organization theory. The theory helps explain the link between micro-level social actions transforming into macro-level systems leading to organized genocidal victimization.

Social identity theory is particularly germane to understanding how groups divide into "us" and "them." According to social identity theory, group memberships provide a sense of pride and self-esteem (Tajfel and Turner 1979). Self-image within a group can be increased by discriminating against members not included in one's group. As a result, the division between "us" and "them" intensifies, providing a context in which intergroup bias and racism may flourish. Racism in its most extreme form can lead to genocide as it did in Rwanda between the Hutus and the Tutsis, in the former Yugoslavia between the Bosnians and Serbs, in Germany between the Nazis and Jews, and between the Arabs and the black Africans in Darfur.

While many issues have been examined to understand the causes and consequences of genocide, one issue that has been underexplored is the effect of social contact and geographic proximity between the perpetrators and victims on genocidal violence. Does increased social contact and geographic proximity between the victims and perpetrators affect the type or degree of genocidal violence? Intergroup contact theory posits that contact can reduce prejudice between the in-group and out-group under certain conditions (Allport 1954; Watson 1947; Williams 1947). The optimal conditions for contact to result in reduced prejudice are: 1) equal status of the groups, 2) common goals, 3) intergroup cooperation, and 4) the support of authorities, law, or custom (Allport 1954). When these conditions or "positive factors" are present, contact can diminish perceived differences between the groups, resulting in less prejudice and discrimination. Pettigrew and Tropp's (2006) extensive review of the contact literature confirmed that increased contact results in a small but reliable reduction in prejudice. However, some scholars have found that contact increases rather than decreases prejudice (Hewstone 2003; Hodson and Hewstone 2013).

With regard to genocide, evidence suggests that increased contact between groups has negative rather than positive effects for the outgroup. Hagan, Rymond-Richmond, and Palloni (2009) found that in the genocide in Darfur, racial epithets directed at black Africans were increased when nearby Arab villages were spared from harm. In other words, black African victims who lived in close geographic proximity to the Arab perpetrators experienced more racial epithets than victims that did not live in close proximity to the perpetrators. Haagensen and Croes (2012) found that in two out of three genocides examined, increased social contact between perpetrator and victim groups prior to the outbreak of genocide resulted in an increased degree of dehumanization used by the perpetrators against the victims. An explanation provided by the authors is that to kill and rape is difficult when a perpetrator is acquainted with their victim. Therefore, dehumanizing perspectives must be actively cultivated in order for perpetrators to commit crimes against people whom they know and with whom they have had previous social interactions. However, we do not know if total victimization and sexual victimization are increased when there is greater intergroup contact between the victims and perpetrators. These two studies may appear to disprove social contact theory. However, the optimal contact conditions to facilitate reduced prejudice as described by Allport (1954) were not present.

## DATA

The data analyzed comes from the historically unprecedented U.S. State Department Atrocities Documentation Survey (ADS). In the summer of 2004, the Coalition for International Justice (CIJ) conducted 1,136 surveys, open-ended questions, and interviews with Darfur refugees living in twenty refugee camps and settlements in the neighboring country of Chad (see Howard 2006). This remarkable study cost the U.S. government nearly one million dollars to complete, yet aside from a brief summary presentation before Congress by Colin Powell, it remained largely neglected and underutilized (Rymond-Richmond and Hagan 2012). The majority of the refugees fled from one of twenty-two village clusters (villages) in Darfur. Each of the villages had at least fifteen respondents included in this survey. This analysis is based on 932 genocide survivors that fled from one of the twenty-two villages in Darfur.

The descriptive characteristics of this sample are shown in table 4.1. The average refugee was thirty-seven years old. Sixty percent of the sample was female and 40 percent male. Slightly over half (52 percent) were Zaghawa, about one-quarter Masalit (27.5 percent), about one-twentieth Fur (5.5 percent), and the remainder of the sample were from other ethnic groups (14 percent). More than 65 percent (67.2 percent) reported attacks by combined government and Janjaweed forces. Nearly 40 percent (38.3 percent) reported attacks by government forces alone or Janjaweed forces alone.

**Table 4.1.** The Atrocities Documentation Survey of Darfur Refugees Residing in Chad, 2004.

| | Mean | (SD) |
|---|---|---|
| **Respondent Attributes** | | |
| Age | 37.100 | (14.634) |
| Male | 0.400 | (0.491) |
| **African ethnic group membership** | | |
| Zaghawa | 0.527 | (0.550) |
| Fur | 0.055 | (0.288) |
| Masalit | 0.275 | (0.447) |
| Others | 0.143 | (0.330) |
| **Attacking Group(s)** | | |
| GoS or Janjaweed | 0.3828 | (0.345) |
| GoS and Janjaweed | 0.672 | (0.470) |
| Arabs nearby and spared | 0.0719 | (0.258) |
| **Total victimization** | | |
| Racial intention: heard racial epithets | 0.343 | (0.475) |
| **Reported sexual victimization** | | |
| Reported victimization of self | 0.04 | (0.205) |
| Reported victimization of self or other | 0.291 | (0.45) |

Note. GoS refers to the government of Sudan military forces. N = 932. Data are expressed as percentage of respondents unless otherwise indicated.

The ADS data extensively described and measured victimization during the attack that caused the survivors to flee, while en route to the refugee camp in Eastern Chad, and once in the refugee camps. In the interviews, the genocide survivors provide vivid descriptions of the violence, rape, property loss, and torture of self, family, and villagers. In addition, the data includes detailed descriptions of the attackers, previous interactions with nomadic Arabs who, along with the predominately Arabic Sudanese government, became their attackers. Also contained in the interviews are reports of hearing racial epithets, reports of selectively targeting black Africans for harm, and selectively protecting Arabs from harm. These last three experiences are particularly germane to this chapter as well as more broadly to satisfying the legal definition of genocide.

Answers from codes for selectively targeting black Africans for harm and selectively protecting Arabs from harm were cross-validated by reading the interviews and recoding into racial contact. Any reference to Arabs living in or near the respondents' village was recoded as racial contact. References may include statements that the perpetrator and victim resided in the same village, witnessing Arabs selectively not harmed during the genocidal attack, references to black Africans specifically being targeted for harm during the attack, and claims that the victim was well acquainted with the perpetrator (knew their name, were neighbors, worked for, etc.). The vast majority of black African genocide survivors reported that when their village was attacked, there were no groups that were selectively protected from harm. In other words, all the black African villagers became targets of the genocidal violence.

A smaller subset (sixty-seven) reported that Arabs lived in close physical proximity to the black African respondents, occupying either the same village or an area nearby. This group, the Arabs, was selectively protected from harm during the genocidal violence. Respondents report witnessing their Arab neighbors not being attacked while black Africans were violently targeted. Black Africans were subjected to killings, rapes, abductions, torture, bombing, racial epithets, enslavement, and property loss while Arabs residing in the same village or in close physical proximity were systematically unharmed. In some situations the Arab neighbors were not only selectively protected from harm, they also joined the Arab Janjaweed and Sudanese military in the killing and displacing of black Africans.

## KEY DEFINITIONS

The measurement of total victimization was constructed by Hagan and Rymond-Richmond (2008b) to determine the severity of victimization. The measurement relies upon a section of each survey that recorded up to twenty incidents of victimization. Respondents reported attacks on themselves, their families, and their villages involving killing, bombing, rape, abduction, assault, property destruction, and theft leading to displacement (Hagan and Rymond-Richmond 2008b, 883–85). The incidents experienced or witnessed by each respondent were aggregated and assigned the following values: five = reported killings, four = sexual violence or abductions, three = assaults, two = property destruction or theft, and one = displacement. The total victimization scores range from twenty to fifty-six, with an average score for the entire dataset of just over thirty-four.

Sexual victimization as defined in this analysis includes rape, sexual assault, sexual slavery, and acts of sexual molestation such as insertion of foreign objects into the genital opening or anus. Four percent of the interviewees reported personal sexual victimization. Women experienced sexual victimization at a higher rate than men. Seven percent of women reported personal sexual victimization. Rape is highly stigmatized in the Darfur region and personal sexual victimization is very likely underreported to authorities. Reporting of sexual victimization of others occurred with much greater frequency than self-reporting sexual victimization. While 4 percent of respondents reported personal sexual victimization, nearly one third of the respondents (29.1 percent) indicated that other villagers were sexually victimized during the genocidal attack (Hagan, Rymond-Richmond, and Palloni 2009, 1389). Reported sexual victimization of self was coded as 0 if a respondent said they did not experience sexual victimization during the genocidal attacks. Reported sexual victimization of self or others was coded as 0 if respondent reported no sexual victimization of self or of other villagers, and 1 if a respondent reported sexual victimization of self or others.

Racial intention is measured in a binary report of whether a respondent heard the perpetrators shouting racial epithets during the attack on their village which preceded flight to the refugee camp. Examples of racial epithets include:

"Nuba" (a derogatory term for black Africans)

Kill the blacks.

Black people, today is the day you are going to die.

You are not citizens, you are blacks, you must leave.

## FINDINGS

### Distancing of Arabs from Black African Villagers

Interview data contained in ADS includes accounts of increased ethnic tensions during the years leading up to the genocide. Prior to the genocidal violence, black Africans and Arabs frequently resided within close proximity to one another and sometimes within the same village. Further, the relational closeness, such as "the scope, frequency, and length of interaction between people, the age of their relationship, and the nature and number of links between them in a social network" (Black 1976, 41; Campbell 2009) existed prior to the genocidal violence. Intermarriage, an indicator of relational closeness, was not uncommon between black Africans and Arabs (Chirot and McCauley 2006). Markets were used by both groups thereby offering another place of group contact. Some genocide survivors struggled with understanding why the relationship with their Arab neighborhoods changed. Miriam states, "I know nothing of their reason. They just came and attacked our people just like that. There were no quarrels with neighbors before."

One of the results of the heightening ethnic tensions was increased relational distance between black Africans and Arabs. Markets where the groups used to interact became increasingly segregated. Villages that include both black African and Arab residents became rarer. In the time leading up to the genocide, when racial and ethnic tensions were mounting between the two groups, many interviewees reported that Arabs who had long been their neighbors, began to move away from the black African villages. Contact between the groups diminished, and their relationship changed. A male from west Darfur region reports, "There were Arabs in our area. We grew up with them but when the problems started they went far away." Several other genocide survivors in the ADS report a similar pattern of Arabs moving out of black African villages or villages in proximity to black African villages:

> There had been Arab settlements before the attacks, but months earlier the Arabs were warned and they left the area. They came either to Chad or to the large towns to stay. They are now going back to Darfur. They are dividing the land among the Arab leaders.

> There used to be Arabs in the area, but they left when the problems started a year and a half ago.

> There were Arabs living outside our village before. They all moved to Beida about 6 months before the attack.

> No nearby villages with Arabs. Arabs use to live in Karnoi—they left months before the attack.

There were Arabs in our village. When the Arabs left about 8 months ago, the problems started.

There were Arabs in our area. We grew up with them but when the problems started they went far away.

## Varied Degrees of Contact

While the overall pattern across Darfur indicated a state of increased racial tension and increased segregation between blacks and Arabs, the degree of interaction and contact between the black African villagers and the Arabs varied according to location at the time of the genocidal attacks. The village clusters of Garsila, Al Genuina, and Bendesi reported more contact between groups, and while Koulbous, Tine, Umm Bourou, Adar, Tandubayah, Near Tine, and Girgira reported less contact. With the exception of Koulbous, each village reporting less contact with Arabs was predominately Zaghawa, and these villages were all in the northern region of Darfur. The black African villages in closer proximity to Arabs were predominately Fur and Masalit, and located in the southern region of Darfur.

A subset (sixty-seven) of the respondents reported that during the genocidal attacks, Arabs occupying the same village as black Africans or in close physical proximity to black African villages were systematically unharmed during the attack. The following examples of Arabs systematically being protected from harm demonstrate intentional selectivity regarding which particular ethnic groups were to be destroyed, in whole or in part:

Yes Arabs exempted; only blacks were targets. There are no Arabs in town except civil servants, and they all live in a separate part of town. That part of town was not attacked.

No one entered the Arab village which I could see from my village. In fact, they came together with the Sudan military to attack our village."

This is Omar Bashir's policy to eliminate the black race. He knows this in part because the Arab settlement, a five-hour walk away, and the Guimer tribe, were not hurt at all.

They were not targeted.

All the black villages were attacked. Only village of Arabs are not attacked.

While the degree of racial ethnic contact varied village by village, what the villages shared in common was residing in a region that was dominated by state-led Arabization ideology. This Arabization ideology manifested itself in many ways, including limited and unequal services. In the words of one genocide survivor, "we don't have schools, hospitals, or other things. The government said we don't deserve things." Efforts by black Africans to assert their rights failed. Haroun, a genocide survivor residing in a refugee camp in Chad states, "Africans from the area told the Sudanese government, we want our rights [development, education]. So the Sudanese government decided to kill everyone [black Africans] to get rid of the headache." Further demonstrating the racial ethnic discrimination, Haroun said that when his village was attacked the Janjaweed were "yelling and calling people 'slaves.'" Policies and a culture of Arab supremacy laid the foundation for the genocidal violence inflicted upon black African villagers by Arab Janjaweed and the predominately Arab Sudanese military. Personal reports of the effects of Arabization include the following:

> In 1986 a discriminatory regime came to power. There was even discrimination where we went to university.

> For about thirteen years the government has had a policy of arming Arabs and giving them horses to attack the villages of Darfur.

> The government of Sudan wants to kill Darfurians and replace them with Arabs. The president wants to clean the blacks in Darfur.

> The government have been saying for three years that they want to throw all the black people off the land.

## Total Victimization

An independent sample $t$-test comparison of the severity of victimization mean scores between the groups that experienced increased racial contact with the group that did not report racial contact was performed. Comparison of $t$ tests shows a significant different between the two groups in degree of total victimization. Living in close physical proximity to Arabs (racial contact) resulted in significantly higher degree of total victimization mean score (0.36 compared to 0.34). Total victimization is significant at 0.003 (see table 4.2). Total victimization is greater when Arabs lived in or near the black African villages compared to if they did not. In other words, respondents who reported that nearby Arab villages were spared were more likely to report higher degrees of total victimization.

Incidents of torture (measure included amputation, skinning the flesh of the victim and gang rape) also occurred with greater frequency when Arabs lived nearby and were selectively protected from harm during the genocidal attack. Approximately 5 percent (45 out of 865) of the genocidal attacks included torture when the perpetrators did not live in close physical proximity, compared to almost 21 percent (14 out of 67) when the perpetrators lived

| | Arabs Nearby N=67 | | Arabs not Nearby N=865 | | |
|---|---|---|---|---|---|
| | M | SD | M | SD | |
| Total victimization | 36.403 | 6.318 | 34.064 | 6.289 | * |
| Racial intention: heard racial epithets | .612 | .491 | .323 | .468 | ** |
| Reported sexual victimization | | | | | |
| Reported victimization of self | .09 | .288 | .04 | .197 | |
| Reported victimization of self or others | .4179 | .497 | .2809 | .450 | * |

$* p \leq .05; ** p \leq .01$

Note: Significant differences between intergroup contact and no intergroup contact are denoted with asterisks. Significance tests are based on independent sample *t*-tests.

**Table 4.2. Descriptive Statistics for Study Variables by Arabs Nearby and Spared from Harm.**

in close physical proximity. In other words, torture was four times greater when there was social contact between the groups than when social contact was reduced. Amir, a male Masalit from western Darfur, reported that in addition to killing, looting, and bombing his village, the Janjaweed and Sudanese militia amputated the limbs of six men. They also forced mothers to watch their children being killed before the mothers were themselves shot. In addition, "Ten babies were killed by throwing them into the fire. The attackers split open ten children's heads." In a separate incident of torture, ten newborn babies were "killed by boiling them in water."

## Racial epithets

Approximately one-third (34 percent) of the Darfurian survivors reported that the perpetrators yelled or shouted a racial epithet when they attacked. Many reported that they were unable to hear what the Janjaweed and GoS militia were shouting because of loud bombing. Some were unable to repeat what their attackers said because they did not understand the Arabic language spoken by the perpetrators.

The mean rate of a black African hearing a racial epithet significantly increased when Arabs resided nearby and were spared from harm during the genocidal violence. The mean incidence of hearing epithets for the black African group that lived near Arabs who were spared from harm is 0.612 compared to 0.323—the rate of black Africans reporting hearing racial slurs from their attackers if Arabs did not reside nearby. In other words, nearly twice as many racial epithets were reported during the genocidal violence when Arabs lived in or nearby black African villagers, than if they did not. Examples of racial epithets include the following:

We kill our cows when they have black calves—we will kill you too.

All the people in the village are slaves, you make this area dirty, we are here to clean the area.

Kill the nuba slaves.

Kill the blacks.

We hate the blacks. We will kill the blacks.

Racial epithets were also reported by black African rape victims. Fatima was gang raped by ten men and she quotes them as yelling, "You are black people's wives and you bear black children, but now you have to bear white people's children." Near the village of Seleya, the perpetrators told their victims, "We will kill all men and rape the women. We want to change the color. Every woman will deliver red. Arabs are the husbands of those women."

## Sexual Victimization

Hagan, Rymond-Richmond, and Palloni (2009) found that sexual victimization was not increased in locations where nearby Arab villages were spared from harm. Despite the minor variation between Hagan, Rymond-Richmond, and Palloni's measures of racial contact used in this analysis, finding that sexual victimization was not affected by the geographical proximity of victims and perpetrators is supported, with one exception.[1] The ADS data contains various measures of rape, sexual assault, and sexual humiliation. Hagan, Rymond-Richmond, and Palloni (2009) measured sexual victimization of others as the count of the number of other persons in the village to have been sexually attacked (coded from 1 to 10) as reported by each respondent. The current analysis expands this code as well as the other sexual victimization codes, including self-reported rapes; witnessing the rape of others; total number of rapes reported; and a dichotomous variable for respondent reporting the rape of self or others. Each measure of rape and sexual violence was found not to be significantly related to racial contact with the exception of the dichotomous variable for respondent reporting the rape of self or others. The mean for sexual victimization of self or others for the group that reported Arabs lived nearby and were spared from harm was significantly higher (significant at 0.032 assuming variance is not equal) than the mean for the group that reported Arabs did not reside nearby (0.42 compared to 0.28). In other words, reports of rape (self or others) are greater in locations where intergroup contact between the victim and perpetrator exists.

# CONCLUSION

Long after a genocidal attack is over, targeted groups continue to be affected by the violence. Entering a refugee or internally displaced people (IDP) camp does not end the pain and suffering of genocide survivors. Chronic mental health problems, including depression, anxiety, and posttraumatic stress disorder affect a significant proportion of refugees in the aftermath of genocide and racial and ethnic violence (De Jong et al. 2001; Fazel, Wheller, and Danesh 2005). For Darfurian refugees in Cairo depressive symptoms include "hopelessness, tearfulness, apathy, decreased concentration, decreased or increased sleep, low appetite, weight loss, low mood, decreased energy, and guilt" (Meffert and Marmar 2009, 1841). Darfurian refugees in Chad described their mental state as "fatigue," "shock," and "nervous shakes" (Rymond-Richmond and Hagan 2012, 147).

Physical and sexual violence, deaths of family members and fellow villagers, and the loss of property continue to impact genocide survivors. In addition, new forms of victimization emerge in the camps that include stigmatization, ostracism, and family disruptions. For example, rape victims continue to be victimized in the camps. The impact of sexual violence can result in reproductive trauma, pregnancy, and sexually transmitted diseases. Psychological consequences include profound feelings of helplessness and despair that may persist as posttraumatic stress disorder. Frequently in the camps, raped women suffer from stigma or ostracism. Their likelihood of marriage is reduced. Intergroup rape affects not only individuals, but also the entire community. Intergroup rape can be a means of controlling the reproduction of the targeted group and is a powerful weapon for the destruction of social groups. In Serbia, Kosovo, Darfur, and some other conflict-affected areas, perpetrators rape with the intention of instilling terror, dehumanizing the victims, and as a means of population extermination (see Diken and Laustsen 2005; Hagan, Rymond-Richmond, and Palloni 2009; Mullins and Rothe 2008; Mullins 2009; Rymond-Richmond and Hagan 2012; Salzman 1998; Wood 2006).

In societies in which lineage is determined by patrilineal parentage, rape can alter the ethnic lineage of female rape victims children. A cohort of children born from rape occurred in former Yugoslavia, post-war Bangladesh, and Darfur produced mixed ethnic children. Intergroup rape is a means of controlling biological and cultural reproduction and is a powerful weapon of destruction. Included within the definition of genocide in the Genocide Convention are "measures intended to present births within the group." In addition to rape altering the children's ethnic lineage, children symbolize the genocide and the subsequent derogation of the victims (Mullins 2009, 722).

Understanding the racial, ethnic, and cultural dimensions of genocide may lead to the greater ability to identify precursors of genocide and provide insight into eliminating or minimizing future group violence. There is a general need to understand how conditions leading to genocide are similar or different when racial ethnic contact is present. Intergroup contact could facilitate peace and tolerance as is predicted by Allport's social contact theory. Conversely, intergroup contact could create or augment racial cleavages and inequality. Findings from this study suggest that in Darfur, when the victims and perpetrators lived in close physical proximity, victimization, including sexual victimization and torture, and the use of racially derogatory language was increased. The challenge is to find ways to reduce group conflict, discrimination, inequality, and genocidal violence.

## NOTE

1. Hagan, Rymond-Richmond, and Palloni (2009) used the code Ethnic exception: Arab villages spared. In this analysis the same code was used and then cross-validated by reading the interviews and recoding into racial contact.

## REFERENCES

Allport, G. W. 1954. *The Nature of Prejudice*. Reading, MA: Addison-Wesley.
Black, Donald. 1976. *The Behavior of Law*. San Diego, CA: Academic Press.
Campbell, Bradley. 2009. "Genocide as Social Control." *Sociological Theory* 27: 150–73.
Chalk, Frank, and Kurt Jonassohn. 1990. *The History and Sociology of Genocide: Analyses and Case Studies*. New Haven, CT: Yale University Press.
Chirot, Daniel, and Jennifer Edwards. 2003. "Making Sense of the Senseless: Understanding Genocide." *Context* 2: 12–19.
Chirot, Daniel, and Clark McCauley. 2006. *Why Not Kill Them All? The Logic and Prevention of Mass Political Murder*. Princeton, NJ: Princeton University Press.
Coleman, James S. 1986. "Social Theory, Social Research, and a Theory of Action." *American Journal of Sociology* 91: 1309–35.
De Jong, J. T., I. H. Komproe, M. Van Ommeren, M. El Masri, M. Araya, N. Khaled, et al. 2001. "Lifetime Events and Posttraumatic Stress Disorder in Four Postconflict Settings." *Journal of the American Medical Association* 286: 555–62.
De Waal, Alex. 2007. "Reflections on the Difficulties of Defining Darfur's Crisis as Genocide." *Harvard Human Rights Journal* 20: 25–33.
Diamond, Jared. 2005. *Collapse: How Societies Choose to Fail or Succeed*. New York: Penguin.
Diken, B., and C. B. Laustsen. 2005. "Becoming Abject: Rape as a Weapon of War." *Body and Society* 11: 111–28.
Fazel, Mina, Jeremy Wheeler, and John Danesh. 2005. "Prevalence of Serious Mental Disorder in 7,000 Refugees Resettled in Western Countries: A Systematic Review." *The Lancet* 365: 1309–14.
Fein, Helen. 1990. "Social Recognition and Criminalization of Genocide." *Current Sociology* 38: 1–7.
———. 1993. *Genocide: A sociological Perspective*. London: Sage.
Gurr, Ted Robert, and Barbara Harff. 1994. *Ethnic Conflict in World Politics*. Boulder, CO: Westview Press.
Haagensen, Lisa, and Marnix Croes. 2012. "Thy Brother's Keeper?: The Relationship between Social Distance and Intensity of Dehumanization During Genocide." *Genocide Studies and Prevention* 7: 223–50.

Hagan, John, and Alberto Palloni. 2006. "Death in Darfur." *Science* 313: 1578–79.

Hagan, John, and Wenona Rymond-Richmond. 2008a. *Darfur and the Criminology of Genocide*. Cambridge: Cambridge University Press.

———. 2008b. "The Collective Dynamics of Race and Genocidal Victimization in Darfur." *American Sociological Review* 73: 875–902.

Hagan, John, Wenona Rymond-Richmond, and Alberto Palloni. 2009. "Racial Targeting of Sexual Violence in Darfur." *American Journal of Public Health* 99: 1386–92.

Hagan, John, Wenona Rymond-Richmond, and Patricia Parker. 2005. "The Criminology of Genocide: The Death and Rape of Darfur." *Criminology* 43: 525–61.

Hardin, Russell. 1995. *One For All: The Logic of Group Conflict*. Princeton, NJ: Princeton University Press.

Heuveline, Patrick. 2001. "Approaches to Measuring Genocide: Excess Morality during the Khmer Rouge Period." In *Ethnopolitical Warfare: Causes, Consequences, and Possible Solutions,* edited by D. Chirot and M. Seligman, 93–108. Washington, DC: American Psychological Association.

Hewstone, M. 2003. "Intergroup Contact: Panacea for Prejudice?" *Psychologist* 16: 352–55.

Hodson, G., and M. Hewstone, editors. 2013. *Advances in Intergroup Contact*. London, UK: Psychology Press.

Horowitz, Donald. 2001. *The Deadly Ethnic Riot*. Berkeley, CA: University of California Press.

Horowitz, Irving Louis. 1980. *Taking Lives: Genocide and State Power*. New Brunswick, NJ: Transaction Books.

Howard, Jonathan P. 2006. "Survey Methodology and the Darfur Genocide." In *Genocide in Darfur: Investigating the Atrocities in the Sudan*. Edited by Samuel Totten and Eric Markusen. 59–74. New York: Routledge.

Kaplan, Robert. 1993. *Balkan Ghosts: A Journey through History*. New York: St. Martin's Press.

Kaufman, Stuart. 2001. *Modern Hatreds: The Symbolic Politics of Ethnic War*. Ithaca, NY: Cornell University Press.

Lemkin, Ralph. 1946. "Genocide." *American Scholar* 15: 227–30.

———. 1994. *Axis Rule in Occupied Europe*. Washington, DC: Carnegie Endowment for International Peace.

Matsueda, Ross. 2007. "Differential Social Organization, Collective Action, and Crime." *Crime, Law and Social Change* 46: 33.

Meffert, Susan M., and Charles R. Marmar. 2009. "Darfur Refugees in Cairo: Mental Health and Interpersonal Conflict in the Aftermath of Genocide." *Journal of Interpersonal Violence* 24: 1835–48.

Mullins, Christopher W. 2009. "We are Going to Rape you and Taste Tutsi Women." *British Journal of Criminology* 49: 719–35.

Mullins, Christopher W., and D. L. Rothe. 2008. *Blood, Power and Bedlam: Violations of International Criminal Law in Post-Colonial Africa*. New York: Peter Lang.

Oberschall, Anthony. 2000. "The Manipulation of Ethnicity: From Ethnic Cooperation to Violence and War in Yugoslavia." *Ethnic and Racial Studies* 23: 982–1001.

Pettigrew, T. F., and L. R. Tropp. 2006. "A Meta-Analytic Test of Intergroup Contact Theory." *Journal of Personality and Social Psychology* 90: 791–83.

Posen, Barry. 1993. "The Security Dilemma and Ethnic Conflict." *Survival* 35: 27–47.

Rymond-Richmond, Wenona, and John Hagan. 2012. "Race, Land, and Forced Migration in Darfur." In *Punishing Immigrants: Policy, Politics, and Injustice*, edited by Kubrin, Zatz, and Martinez, 138–56. New York: New York University Press.

Salzman, Todd A. 1998. "Rape Camps as a Means of Ethnic Cleansing: Religious, Cultural and Ethnic Responses to Rape Victims in the Former Yugoslavia." *Human Rights Quarterly* 20: 348–78.

Sampson, Robert. 2006. "How Does Community Context Matter? Social Mechanisms and the Explanation of Crime Rates." In *The Explanation of Crime: Crime, Mechanisms, and Development*, edited by P. H. Wikstrom and R. Sampson, 31–60. Cambridge, UK: Cambridge University Press.

Savelsberg, Joachim, and Ryan King. 2011. *American Memories: Atrocities and the Law*. New York: Russell Sage Foundation.

Sutherland, E. H. 1947. *Principles of Criminology*, 8th edition. Philadelphia: Lippincott.

Tajfel, H., and J. C. Turner. 1979. "An Integrative Theory of Group Conflict." In *The Social Psychology of Intergroup Relations*, edited by W. G. Austin, S. Worchel, 33–47. Monterey, CA: Brooks/Cole.

United Nations. 1948. *Convention on the Prevention and Punishment of the Crime of Genocide*.

United Nations Judgment Report. 1998. The Prosecutor v. Jean-Paul Akayesu, Case No. ICTR-96-4-T, 1998, International Criminal Tribunal for Rwanda, Office of the Prosecutor at 7.8.

Valentino, Benjamin A. 2004. *Final Solutions: Mass Killing and Genocide in the 20th Century*. New York: Cornell University Press.

Watson, Goodwin. 1947. *Action for Unity*. New York: Harper.

Williams, R. M., Jr. 1947. *The Reduction of Intergroup Tensions*. New York: Social Science Research Council.

Wood, Elisabeth Jean. 2006. "Variation in Sexual Violence during War." *Politics and Society* 34: 307–41.

*Chapter Five*

# Group Violence Against the State

*The Hindsight Story of the Thirty-Year War in Sri Lanka*

Tharindi Udalagama and Premakumara de Silva

In January 2008, the U.S. Federal Bureau of Investigation (FBI) said that "the Tamil Tigers are among the most dangerous and deadly extremists in the world." The United States branded the Liberation Tigers of Tamil Elam (LTTE) a "terrorist organization" in October 1997. The FBI held the group responsible for perfecting the "use of suicide bombers," inventing the suicide belt, pioneering "the use of women in suicide attacks," and murdering nearly 4,000 persons in 2006–2007 in Sri Lanka.

—DeVotta 2009, 1021

The terms "conflict" and "violence" should by no means be confused. Violence is to harm and hurt someone, by physical and/or verbal means. Although conflict may lead to violence, conflict and violence are different conceptually.

—Galtung 2003

Violence has taken many shapes and forms in the world in many contexts between diverse groups within and between countries. Social scientists have attempted to find reasons why humans form groups and why different groups resort to violence against each other.

In Marx's view, humans are a threat to themselves because they attempt to change systems and societies through conflict. Humans form groups to fulfill their need to belong. For this reason, we seek "group membership" and may belong to more than one group based on factors such as race, ethnicity, religion, class, and occupation. Some of the groups we belong to may be ascribed to us at birth. For instance, religion in most South Asian countries is decided at birth: you belong to the religion of your parents. Attempts to change one's religion could amount to social exclusion as it is seen as an act against one's predetermined group membership.

In a functionalist perspective, groups are an essential stitch in the fabric of society, as they provide order to chaos. If we had no groups to belong to, we would be indecisive as to what our cultural values and beliefs might be. As a group, we can identify what we value and what we believe. We identify ourselves with a certain culture because we belong to a group and thus we abide by the values and beliefs of that culture. For instance, it is unacceptable for a Muslim to eat pork and it is similarly unacceptable for a Hindu to eat beef. Group members accept these values by default. This contributes to the order of an Islamic society or a Hindu society as there will be no selling of pork in an Islamic society and there will be no beef stalls in a Hindu society. The social fabric organizes itself by the cultural values and beliefs of the group. However, questions arise when there is more than one group and more than one value system. How should the social fabric arrange itself? This question and the inability to find a justifiable answer to the question contribute to the violence among groups that we see today.

Until relatively recently few anthropologists examined violence and conflict between groups and the state, especially violence among groups within states, which is often rooted in ethnicities, nationalism, bids for autonomy and self-determination, and political demands for fundamental change of the existing nation-state. Some research has looked primarily at the invention and reinvention of categorical differences inflicted by language, culture, and history in colonial and postcolonial societies (Kapferer 1988; Spencer, 1990; Tambiah 1986).

In this new age where globalization has marred national borders and technologies have challenged relations based on time and space, we see an escalation of group violence around the world. From the many violent conflicts around the globe, we have chosen to revisit the civil war that transpired in Sri Lanka for over three decades and understand the nature of violence that the terrorizing separatist group, Liberation Tigers of Tamil Elam (LTTE), had against the state.

The violent war waged against the state by the LTTE is seen as a classic case study in "separatism." With the increased emphasis on "one state for one nation," the LTTE became a prime force to create a separate state for the Tamil population across the world. The Tamils were one ethnic group amongst many in the world that had no "state" to represent them internationally. The Tamils are a dispersed population, in diaspora around the world, with no legitimate homeland. The LTTE propagated this ideology throughout their efforts to win over their own state by separating the North and East of Sri Lanka under a flag called "Elam." Such rationalization for violence defined LTTE as a separatist group. They believed that integrating with the dominant group would compromise their identity. Hence, the separatist ideology that found justification for the existence of LTTE was actually based on identity politics.

We contemplate this conflict as "group violence" in the sense of political groupings rather than ethnic groupings. Though the literature written on the Sri Lankan civil war largely portrays the Sinhala-Tamil ethnic groups as the two groups in conflict, here we look at the formation of a terrorist group against the state that resulted in violence for decades. How did a ragtag group that numbered less than fifty members before the civil war began in 1983 become "among the most dangerous and deadly extremists in the world?" We seek not to take sides and interpret the motives behind the actions of the LTTE in relation to an ethnic minority mentality, but to understand the intense violence that both parties resorted to and endured throughout the war, and the scars it has left behind.

The LTTE however was not the first large-scale attacker against the Sri Lankan state. In 1971,[1] and again in the late 1980s,[2] a generation of young Marxist Sinhalese called the JVP (*Janata Vimukti Preramuna* or People's Liberation Front) revolted against the state and its ruling elites. In both occasions, the JVP's group violence against the state was repelled by counterattacks by the government and paramilitary forces killing off many young people, including the JVP leadership.[3]

## HISTORICAL BACKDROP

Sri Lanka, though not as diverse as India, is still diverse with respect to ethnicity, caste and religion. The island country is predominantly Sinhala Buddhist with minorities of Tamil Hindus, Muslims, and Christians. Though the island has married the Sinhala Buddhist and Tamil Hindu cultures through various historical treaties and alliances, frictions between the two groups have marked the nation's history.

The civil war that raged from 1976 to 2009 marks the bloodiest battles ever fought on the soil of this island. The causes of the war are deeply rooted in the construct of ethnic identities (Spencer 1990; Roberts 1997; 1998). If we are to take a historical view on the matter, Sinhala kings married princesses from India, who were of a different ethnicity but of royal blood. Such marriages were also political alliances to hinder any invasions from Indian powers. These alliances led to the assimilation of aspects of Hinduism into Buddhism and created a hybrid culture that served both ethnicities. But, with colonization, the building of a nation-state dismantled the existing social structure and replaced it with a power structure that illuminated the divisions within Sri Lankan society.

Identity as it was displaced before colonization changed during the colonial state. It is said that the last four kings of the Kandyan kingdom were recast as members of the "Malabar race" of South Indian origin, implying the old "enemies of the Sinhala race" (Davy 1821, in Gunawardena 1994). Toward the end of the nineteenth century, the national movement was raising its head, with pioneers from diverse ethnicities contributing to the growth of a national and religious consciousness among the masses (Gunawardena 2008; Obeyesekere 1997). As the Indian subcontinent gained independence and the British lost interest in retaining an empire, Sri Lanka gained independence in 1948. The historical moment of independence also brought about a period that entailed a search for identity (Gunawardena 2008). The constitutional arrangements of the postcolonial state refashioned the relations among the diverse ethnic, religious, and social groups that affected the stability of the newly born nation-state (Gunawardena 2008).

Failure to arrive at a collective identity common to all ethnicities is seen as one main reason for the outbreak of violence in Sri Lanka. Tensions are inevitable, especially in a country where rich ethnic diversity is present that creates minority and majority groups (Scott 1999). The Tamil minority became quite self-conscious from the initial stages of a postcolonial state and began to organize themselves politically in hope of integrating themselves into the power structures of the country. The establishment of these political organizations itself illustrates the failure to arrive at a collective national identity.

The majority of Sinhalese, on the other hand, were blind to the minority insecurities emerging in the country. With independence gained, the colonial elite were busy with establishing a nation-state. As Hettige (2008) points out, the state was deeply divided in many ways after colonization, and ethnic division was just one among many. The nationalistic wave that arose after independence was more about an imagined community that the majority had in their head rather than a suppression of a minority. The foregone prestige of the era of the kings was to be re-awakened in the modern postcolonial state. In that sense, the Sinhalese being in power by virtue of being the majority engaged in policy making that further dismantled any hope of a collective identity.

As a result, tension between the minority Tamils and the majority Sinhala manifested itself in the form of "riots," in 1956 and 1958, and again in 1977, 1981, and most traumatically of all in July 1983. Since then there has been no major outbreak of anti-Tamil violence in the Sinhala-dominated southern region of the country, but the conflict has conjoined around the separatist LTTE's war against the Sri Lankan state. The Tamil minority rights movement can be legitimately viewed as the product of the state's repression of earlier nonviolent protest. As Hettige (2008) states, the policies that came to be after independence did not consider the needs and wants of the minorities. This caused much grievance and frustration among minorities, ultimately resulting in violent warfare.

## THE WAR AGAINST THE STATE

The civil war against the state in Sri Lanka exploded on 23 July 1983. The Liberation Tigers of Tamil Elam, popularly known as the LTTE, initiated the war on the premise of a separate, independent state for the Tamils within the island of Sri Lanka. The violent conflict in Sri Lanka was brutal, dirty, and deadly. Human rights abuses were widespread; suicide bombings and terror against civilians became integral parts of "living with violence." The LTTE is the only militant group in the world that once possessed its own "military": Tigers (infantry), Sea Tigers, Women's brigade, and Air Tigers. With these forces, the LTTE, began its armed campaign in Sri Lanka for a separate Tamil homeland.

The first attacks by the LTTE were against the police, implying a campaign of violence against the state. This campaign also targeted Tamil politicians who were in dialogue with the government. For example Alfred Duraiappah, mayor of Jaffna, was murdered by the LTTE leader, Prabakaran, in 1975. In 1977, the leader of LTTE once again carried out the killing of a Tamil member of parliament, M. Canagaratnam. Later, in 2005, the LTTE killed Lakshman Kadiragamar, a Tamil diplomat and politician who was at the time of his death the minister for foreign affairs of Sri Lanka. Such incidents illuminate the exclusive nature of this war in the context of group violence: the LTTE did not consider the ethnicity of those they killed, it was the relationship the victim had with the state that was considered in all the political killings that occurred during the civil war. The LTTE ruthlessly eliminated Tamil opponents in its goal of becoming the sole voice of Tamils. It was also widely criticized for its forced use of child soldiers[4] and the UN panel of experts reports strongly criticized the LTTE for multiple human rights abuses.

Literature on "group violence" suggests that because we identify as groups and construct a mentality of "us and the other" we build cohesion within our own group to stand against the other. When looking at the group violence in Sri Lanka it clearly shows that the LTTE killed members of their own group for their cause. For more than a decade, the thirty-odd disparate Tamil militant groups merged, split, scattered and re-formed in an exhausting cycle of squabbling and jostling for power and prominence. Such violence internalized towards the group membership explains that a "threat perception" is not only against other groups but also against members of their own group who seemed to deviate from groupthink and establish contacts with the so-called "other group." This nature of the conflict can be emphasized with retributive murders and the killings of perceived opponents, and moderate Tamil politicians such as Alfred Duraiappah, M. Canagaratnam, Neelan Thiruchelvam, and Lakshman Kadiragamar, among others. Although the LTTE has been a source of terror within the Tamil population, it has nevertheless directed most of its energy, most of its violence, and expended most of its martyrs in the struggle against forces that are clearly "external": the Sinhala-dominated Sri Lankan state and security forces and the Indian Peace Keeping Force (IPKF) sent by Prime Minister Rajiv Gandhi between 1987 and 1990.

"Black July" in 1983 is perceived as the outbreak of the war. The LTTE launched a deadly ambush on Sri Lankan Army checkpoint "Four Four Bravo" outside the town of Thirunelveli in Jaffna peninsula, killing an officer and twelve soldiers (Rajasingham 2002). Using the nationalistic sentiments sown throughout the nation by nationalistic movements to their advantage, the Jayawardena government organized a week of violence in the south, resulting in entire residential areas of Tamil housing being destroyed, Tamil businesses looted, and up to an estimated three thousand Tamils killed (Harrison 2003). Many of the Tamils fled Sinhalese-majority areas. Some migrated under refugee status to countries that sympathized with the Tamils and their cause for separatism.

As a result, the LTTE was able to operate and maintain representative offices in at least forty countries. The expatriate Tamil community in Canada, the United Kingdom, Switzerland, and a dozen other countries created new transnational networks that included legitimate and illegitimate business and investments through front companies, offshore accounts, pseudonymous charitable institutions, and the exponential explosion of nongovernmental organizations (NGOs). These organizations provided an endless sequence of filters and decoys through which funds for the purchase of arms could be disguised and channeled to the LTTE to strengthen their military capabilities against the state's resistance. The closed nature of the international Sri Lankan Tamil community provided carte blanche for LTTE control, which was exerted through intimidation, blackmail, beatings, threats against opponents' family members both abroad and in Sri Lanka, and a number of killings of Tamils who did not support separatist ideology.

## VIOLENCE AGAINST UNARMED CIVILIANS

The LTTE launched their first attack on Sinhalese civilians on 30 November 1984 in two tiny farming villages in the district of Mullaitivu in the northeast of Sri Lanka. The two villages known as "The Kent and Dollar farms" were located near "Manal Aru," a divisional Secretariat in the Tamil district of Mullaitivu. Manal Aru was of immense importance since it was situated on the border of three districts: Mullaitivu, Trincomalee and Anuradhapura. More importantly, it was the sole gateway between the northern and the eastern parts of the island where Tamils were the majority. Realizing its strategic importance and in a bid to quell the rising threat of Tamil nationalism, the government renamed "Manal Aru" as Weli Oya,[5] and attempted to colonize the area. A total of 13,288 Tamil families living in forty-two villages were asked to vacate their homes and farmlands within forty-eight hours, or else they would be forcibly evicted by the army. This threat and act of eviction by the Sinhalese army led to a bloody retaliation by the LTTE. About fifty LTTE cadres travelled by night in two buses armed with rifles, machine guns, and grenades. One of the buses sped to Dollar Farm and the other to Kent Farm. The attacks were timed to start simultaneously in the early hours of the morning. The LTTE fighters shot and hacked the guards, the prisoners, and the male members of the families. Eighty-two Sinhalese, including civilians, home guards, and military personnel, were reported dead.

The massacre in Anuradhapura in 1985 is remembered as the largest attack on Sinhalese civilians by the LTTE and the first major operation carried out by the LTTE in a non-Tamil area. The LTTE hijacked a bus on May 14, 1985, and entered Anuradhapura. As the LTTE cadres entered the main bus station, they opened fire indiscriminately with automatic weapons, killing and wounding many civilians who were waiting for buses (Gunaratna 1998). LTTE cadres then drove to the Buddhist Sri Maha Bodhi shrine and gunned down nuns, monks, and civilians as they were worshipping inside the shrine (Gunaratna 1987). Before they withdrew, the LTTE strike force entered the national park of Wilpattu and killed eighteen Sinhalese in the forest reserve. The LTTE cadres massacred 146 Sinhalese men, women, and children in Anuradhapura that day.

The state either condemned or responded to these attacks. The Kent and Dollar Farm massacre was the LTTE's response to the threat carried out by the Sinhalese army, namely, the murder of Tamil villagers settled in Manal Aru in order to colonize the area with Sinhala people. The Government answered the Anuradhapura massacre by massacring twenty-three Tamils sailing from the island of Delft to the island of Nainathievu allegedly by deploying Sri Lankan Navy personnel. These accounts illuminate how violence was answered with violence, according to the "eye for eye" norm by both parties.

In 1987, LTTE cadres stopped a bus and butchered thirty-four Buddhist monks, the majority of them young boys training to be monks. In 1990, a platoon of LTTE killed 147 men and boys as they worshipped in a mosque. The following year, they killed 109 Muslim men, women, and children in the village of Palliyagodella. The LTTE appear to have slaughtered captured soldiers and policemen with especially terrifying ferocity. In 1990, LTTE cadres forced the surrender of dozens of police stations in eastern Sri Lanka and executed six hundred police officers in and around the town of Kalmunai. In 1996, when they overran a military camp in Mullaitive in the north, more than 1,200 soldiers were killed, executed, or "disappeared."

Another wave of brutal attacks on civilians happened in 2006 amidst the peace process mediated by Norway. The LTTE began to focus on civilian targets by planting attacks on commuter trains and buses around the country, as well as in Colombo and her suburbs (Harrison 2008). For instance, six Sinhalese rice farmers were massacred in their paddy fields by suspected LTTE cadres (Sunday Observer, 2006) and thirteen Tamil civilians were killed in the islet of Kayts (Luthra, 2006). Even during the last stand at the war front the LTTE is said to have used Tamil civilians as a human shield to protect themselves (Reuters 2009). Such claims were later backed by the accounts of civilians who told reporters that they were held by force by the Tamil Tigers (*International Herald Tribune*, 2009). For more than two decades, the LTTE raided Muslim and Sinhalese villages throughout Tamil-majority areas, in an effort to drive both communities out. They hacked, clubbed, shot, burned, and hanged civilians in a long series of massacres. The majority of those killed were Sinhalese, but a disproportionate number were Muslim. Children were slaughtered alongside the men and women in dozens of small-scale incidents.

The LTTE also planted bombs on trains, aircraft, and buses. As early as 1986, they planted a bomb that exploded prematurely on an Air Lanka national carrier plane as it sat on the tarmac in Colombo Airport, killing twenty-one people, including thirteen foreigners. In 1987, a car bomb exploded in Colombo's Pettah market, killing 113 civilians. In 1996, four briefcase bombs exploded simultaneously on a train, killing sixty-four passengers and wounding more than four hundred others. In 2006 a roadside blast killed sixty civilians on a bus in Kebithigollewa. The long list of LTTE atrocities sowed terror throughout the country. It is alleged that between the 1983 riots and May 2009, there were around two hundred individual LTTE attacks on civilian targets, in which between 3,700 and 4,100 civilians were killed. In relative terms, and in the course of a long and bloody civil war, the number of civilians killed by terrorist acts attributed to the LTTE was somewhat modest compared with estimates of the overall civilian death toll.

## SUICIDE ATTACKS

As the war between the government and the LTTE intensified in the late 1980s, the LTTE converted Tamil helplessness into a potent military force characterized by the will to die. In the conscious manufacture of a tradition of heroic self-sacrifice, reckless death in the cause of Elam was achieved. The use of suicidal attackers is an efficient deployment of resources, the LTTE's tactical weapon or smart bomb.

In July 1987, the LTTE carried out their first suicide attack. "Captain Miller" of the Black Tigers drove a small truck carrying explosives through the wall of a fortified Sri Lankan army camp, reportedly killing forty soldiers. They carried out over 378 suicide attacks, more than any other terrorist organization in the world, and the suicide attack became a trademark of the LTTE and a characteristic of the civil war. Suicide attackers were used to hit infrastructure, military hardware and personnel, and high-impact civilian targets. Forty-seven of the attackers were women, whose gender assisted them in reaching guarded spaces. The youngest is believed to have been eighteen years old. The aim of the attackers was not simply to commit suicide, but rather to achieve a political or military gain.

Suicide bombers were used by the LTTE to reach heavily guarded political and military leaders. In 1991, it was a female Black Tiger who killed former Indian Prime Minister Rajiv Gandhi in Tamil Nadu, South India. In 1992, another bomber rammed his motorbike into the staff car of Sri Lanka's senior naval officer, Vice Admiral Clancy Fernando, killing him and four other officers. The following year, Sri Lanka's president, Ranasinghe Premadasa, became the first and only sitting president in the world to be killed by a suicide bomber. In 1999, twenty-three people were killed when a suicide bomber attempted to kill President Chandrika Kumaratunga. She survived, but lost an eye in the attack. In 2006, a pregnant LTTE Black Tiger suicide bomber named Anoja Kugenthirasah blew herself up at the Sri Lankan Army headquarters in Colombo, attempting to assassinate the commander of the Sri Lanka Army, Lieutenant General Sarath Fonseka. A few months later, Secretary of Defense Gotabaya Rajapaksa's motorcade was almost rammed by an autorickshaw of Black Tigers that exploded, killing some of his escort. Successful suicide attacks killed dozens of politicians, functionaries, and senior security personnel, while other assassinations, such as that of Tamil politician and Sri Lankan Foreign Minister, Lakshman Kadiragamar, were carried out by sniper rifles or remotely detonated roadside bombs.

Such attacks by the LTTE were not only carried out against politically important personnel. Some suicide attacks were orchestrated to terrorize civilians or to disrupt the infrastructure of the country. For instance, in 1995, Black Tigers struck oil storage complexes, blowing themselves up along with twenty-two soldiers, vital storage tanks and oil products worth an estimated ten million dollars. On New Year's Eve 1996, a three-man Black Tiger team drove a truck laden with 200 kilograms of high explosives into the seaside high-rise building housing the Central Bank in Colombo, killing ninety-one people, wounding a further 1,400 and causing extensive damage to nine downtown buildings. In 1998, eight Sea Tiger boats laden with explosives ploughed into two navy ships on the Point Pedro coastline of northern Sri Lanka, killing fifty-one troops as well as twenty-eight civilians. A few months later, the LTTE carried out an attack on the World Heritage Site, the "Dalada Maligawa" (Temple of Tooth Relic), in Kandy, killing eight civilians who had come to worship at this Buddhist shrine. Then in 2001, a fourteen-man Black Tigers raid on Colombo International Airport destroyed twenty-five aircraft, crippled the tourist industry and cost the country hundreds of millions of dollars in hardware and lost tourist revenue. Such attacks were purely to implant fear and threat in the minds of the government. They were also encrypted messages of the power the LTTE had and how much it had grown since the beginning in 1983.

Suicide attacks were also directed at non-Sri Lankans, for example, as previously mentioned, Rajiv Gandhi in 1991. The LTTE directed Thenmozhi Rajaratnam to blow herself up at a campaign rally for Gandhi, killing him and fourteen other bystanders, making LTTE the first terrorist organization to kill a world leader (*India Today* 2010). The death of Rajiv Gandhi tainted the image of the LTTE in the eyes of India as well as the international community. Though the Indian Supreme Court sentenced the Leader of LTTE, Velupillai Prabhakaran, as responsible for the death, the Tigers have not claimed responsibility to date.

Throughout the thirty years of civil war, Sri Lanka's human capital has taken severe losses. Many civilians, other than the security personnel and the LTTE cadres who were at the warfront lost their lives. Table 5.1 illuminates how expensive the war has been to the country during the last thirteen years. Of the total death toll, the majority has been LTTE cadres; this is approximately 54.6 percent. Hence, we could assume that towards the end of the war the LTTE had faced much destruction by the state-armed forces. Comparatively the state armed forces have lost 12.7 percent of lives from the total. During the years of the peace talks the deaths were reduced drastically; but they have equally risen in the years after the breakdown of the peace talks. It is important to note that the last year of the war, 2009, marked the highest loss of lives compared to the rest of the years. Significantly the loss of lives affected civilians more heavily than armed forces or LTTE cadres in the year 2009. Civilian deaths comprised approximately 71.3 percent of the total deaths in the year 2009. By observing this pattern one could infer that the ending of the war cost more innocent civilian lives than the lives of those who were actually in the battlefield.

## THE STATE'S RESPONSE TO PEACE

The government of Sri Lanka did attempt to come to a settlement with the LTTE through peaceful means throughout the warring years. The first attempt at peace talks began in 1985 in Thimpu, but soon failed, initiating a wave of violence in 1987. In 1995, the newly elected president, SLFP leader Chanrika Kumaratunga, returned to peace talks with the LTTE. The president's offer of peace included an extensive devolution package and a fundamental reform of government that would have amounted to the end of unitary

Table 5.1.  **Loss of Lives during the Civil War from 2000–2013.**

| Year | Civilians | Security Force Personnel | LTTE Cadres | Total |
|---|---|---|---|---|
| 2000* | 162 | 784 | 2845 | 3791 |
| 2001 | 89 | 412 | 1321 | 1822 |
| 2002 | 14 | 1 | 0 | 15 |
| 2003 | 31 | 2 | 26 | 59 |
| 2004 | 33 | 7 | 69 | 109 |
| 2005 | 153 | 90 | 87 | 330 |
| 2006 | 981 | 826 | 2319 | 4126 |
| 2007 | 525 | 500 | 3352 | 4377 |
| 2008 | 404 | 1314 | 9426 | 11144 |
| 2009 | 11111 | 1315 | 3139 | 15565 |
| 2010 | 0 | 0 | 0 | 0 |
| 2011 | 0 | 0 | 0 | 0 |
| 2012 | 0 | 0 | 0 | 0 |
| 2013 | 0 | 0 | 0 | 0 |
| Total** | 13503 | 5251 | 22584 | 41338 |

*Data since March 14, 2000. **Data till July 28, 2013. Source: Numbers are compiled from news reports and are provisional: www.satp.org/satporgtp/countries/shrilanka/database/annual_casualties.htm, accessed on July 24, 2013.

and centralized government. But, without a majority in parliament, her proposal fell afoul of the same political brinkmanship that parties in opposition had assumed since the 1950s. The United National Party (UNP) joined forces with hardline Sinhala nationalist parties to oppose the proposals, while, for their part, the LTTE rejected anything short of a separate state. After a short peace, the new government resolved to bring the Tigers back to the negotiating table by force, and war resumed.

The need to arrive at a solution by peaceful means died down for over a decade and resurfaced only in the mid-2000s. In February 2000, both parties requested Norway to be a mediator in the peace talks between the government and the LTTE. The unilateral ceasefire declared by the LTTE in December 2000 was cancelled by April 2001 as the group resorted to violent means against the state again. The cancellation was marked on July 2001 when the LTTE carried out a suicide mission on the only international airport in Sri Lanka, the Bandaraniake International Airport. The attack destroyed eight Air Force planes and four Sri Lankan Airlines planes. Some suggest that the attack was to commemorate Black July in 1984 where thousands of Tamils were killed.

In 2002, the peace process was refueled, seemingly with some influence from the "9/11" attacks in the United States. The peace process was allegedly a negotiation between the United National Party and the LTTE. The other political parties and the Muslim community were excluded from the process. This exclusion is seen as an influential factor for the failure of the peace process. Neither party appeared to have a clear idea about what they could negotiate as middle ground; however, the LTTE leadership would not give up the idea of separatism. The UNP government agreed to an interim administration of the north and east, but they could not succumb to the intended separate state demanded by the LTTE. The Sinhalese nationalist groups, including Buddhist monks in the south, were vehemently against the idea of giving administrative powers to the LTTE. The backlash that hit the UNP government led President Chandrika Kumaratunga to call for fresh parliament elections that paved the way for Mahinda Rajapakse to become prime minister.

The ceasefire agreement was marked by many infractions from both parties, more from the LTTE and less from the government troops, as reported by the Sri Lanka Monitoring Mission. Both parties accused each other of continuing covert operations of warfare. In addition to all these tensions, the LTTE faced factionalism among their troops, with Vinayagamoorthy Muralitharan (alias Colonel Karuna), the Eastern commander of the LTTE, pulling out more than five thousand cadres, claiming unequal distribution of power in the east among the Tamils themselves. Only with the damage of the tsunami in 2004 was there a marked decrease in violence: this directly influenced the ending of the war.

After a wave of violence in 2006, the peace talks continued with the mediation of Norway. In April 2006, the LTTE officially withdrew from the peace process giving way to more violence. The presidential elections in 2005 were decisive in ending the war. The United Nations Party candidate, Ranil Wickramasinghe, advocated the reopening of peace talks, while the United People's Freedom Alliance (UPFA) candidate Mahinda Rajapakse called for tougher negotiations with the LTTE to redraft the ceasefire agreement. The LTTE pushed the Tamil community to boycott the elections, and openly stated their intention to escalate violence if the government failed to take serious steps towards peace. Violence continued with an increase of guerrilla warfare in the north as well as clashes between the Sea Tigers and the Sri Lankan Navy. By 2008, the state also officially pulled out of the peace process and resorted to violence.

## INTERNATIONAL RESPONSE TO THE WAR

A considerable amount of international attention was gained throughout the war and a growing sympathy for the Tamils and the LTTE from the international community was apparent. Many Tamils were welcomed under refugee status to developed countries such as Canada, the United States, Britain, and other European countries. However, the assassination of Foreign Minister Lakshaman Kadiragama cost the LTTE much of the sympathy it had enjoyed from the international community. There was a long drawn silence by the international community regarding the attacks carried out by the government against the LTTE after the assassination. The European Union decided to proscribe the LTTE as a terrorist organization on 19 May 2006. This resulted in the freezing of LTTE assets in all twenty-seven EU member nations. In a statement, the European Parliament said that the LTTE did not represent all Tamils and called on the organization to "allow for political pluralism and alternate democratic voices in the northern and eastern parts of Sri Lanka" (Baruah 2006).

With the international recognition of LTTE as a terrorist group, the Sri Lankan state gained the upper hand in May 2009. State troops declared victory on the 16 May 2009 and Prabakaran, the leader of the LTTE, was claimed dead on 18 May 2009. Sri Lanka is experienced at dealing with counterinsurgency, having brutally put down JVP attempts to overthrow governments in 1971 and 1988–1990. Yet, numerous Sri Lankan military debacles, due to malfeasance, flaccid strategy, and LTTE tenacity and ingenuity, and the massive economic and human costs of defeating the rebels, all thwarted successive governments from doing what the Rajapaksa administration did so aggressively between 2006 and 2009. The Rajapaksa regime's approach differed from previous governments by giving the military carte blanche to fight the LTTE to the end, regardless of the economic, human, and diplomatic costs (De Votta 2009, 1041–42).

At a 2009 press conference in Geneva, United Nations Secretary General Ban Ki-moon (United Nations 2009) said:

> I am relieved by the conclusion of the military operation, but I am deeply troubled by the loss of so many civilian lives. The task now facing the people of Sri Lanka is immense and requires all hands. It is most important that every effort be undertaken to begin a process of healing and national reconciliation. I listened very carefully to what President Rajapaksa said in his address to parliament today. The legitimate concerns and aspirations of the Tamil people and other minorities must be fully addressed.

This statement led to the appointment of the Lessons Learnt and Reconciliation Commission (LLRC) to investigate the facts and circumstances that led to the failure of the ceasefire agreement made operational on 27 February

2002; the lessons that should be learned from those events; and the institutional, administrative and legislative measures that need to be taken to prevent any recurrence of such concerns in the future and to promote further national unity and reconciliation among all communities (*Sunday Leader* 2011). The report by the Lessons Learnt and Reconciliation Commission became the basis for the discussion on Sri Lanka at the United Nations Human Rights Council's nineteenth session in March 2012. The council adopted a resolution for promoting reconciliation and accountability in Sri Lanka, urging the Sri Lankan government to implement constructive recommendations made in the LLRC report (United Nations 2012). These recommendations are yet to be fully implemented by the Sri Lankan state. As Jayatilake (2013, 263) argues, what we must prevent is "the breakup of the country based on monopolistic ethnic ownership of the northeast . . . we cannot deny the Tamils right to co-ownership, and such recognition is the only means to prevent separate ownership" and future violence against the state. It is necessary to have a Sri Lanka "which remains unitary but contains an irreducible autonomous political space for the Tamil people of the north and east" (Jayatilake 2013, 265).

## CONCLUSION

This chapter has attempted to map the nature of violence during the civil war in Sri Lanka. We defined "group formation" in this context in the form of political groups: the LTTE and the state rather than the ethnic groups of Sinhala and Tamil. Sri Lanka has paid a horrendous price for its civil war. The conflict slowed development, exacerbated "brain drain" from the country, contributed to anomie and political decay, militarized and brutalized society, displaced about one million people, and killed over 100,000 people, including 23,000 government troops. Government figures indicate that 6,261 soldiers and 22,000 LTTE cadres were killed and 21,551 soldiers wounded in July 2006–May 2009 alone. This means the LTTE lost over 40,000 cadres during the conflict, considering its own reported casualty figures up to 2006. A study by Harvard Medical School and the University of Washington asserts that at least 220,000 people perished in Sri Lanka's civil war from 1975 to 2002.

Though the formation of the LTTE against the state can be emphasized as a formation of political groups based on separatism, we cannot ignore the ethnic tensions that underlined the civil war. The historical baggage that failed to construct a common identity for all ethnicities in the postcolonial nation state seems to be the root cause of the tensions. The majority-minority relations that were established giving Tamils a minority status and the Sinhalese the majority status depending on the head count of the population further intensified the tensions. Policies and allocation of resources in the post-colonial state seemed to have had an ethnic bias, which disadvantaged the minority. These intense tensions led many Tamil youth to organize political-ly as the LTTE. The conflict that began to gain equality for Tamils expanded to separatist ideals, on the premise that one nation-state should represent one ethnicity. For this reason, the LTTE waged war with the Sri Lankan state for nearly three decades.

The violent forms the war took were unique in the world, winning inter-national attention. The LTTE made history for being the first terrorist organ-ization to kill a world leader by suicide mission and for attempting the highest number of suicide attacks on political leaders and civilians. This war tactic was considered the most brutal and unique to the LTTE.

The LTTE's use of civilians as a shield to protect themselves in the final hour gave the Sri Lankan army the challenge of implementing a "humanitar-ian mission" within an operational mission so that as many civilians as pos-sible could be saved. Ending the war with most international states agreeing that LTTE was a terrorist organization and by implementing the recommen-dations of the LLRC, the root courses of violence against the Sri Lankan state can be seriously addressed. Hopefully, this will bring long lasting peace to post-conflict Sri Lankan society.

## NOTES

1. In 1971 the JVP launched an insurrection, which has been described as the first of its nature in modern Sri Lankan history (Uyangoda 2003, 38). This insurrection was short lived—spanning a few weeks, and has been portrayed by some as lacking adequate planning and preparation (see Gunaratna 1987).

2. The second phase of the JVP also saw a high level of militarization, and the creation of its military wing—the dreaded DJV (Deshapremi Janatha Vyaparanaya/Patriotic People's Or-ganization). This allowed the JVP leadership to distance itself from, and deny responsibility for, much of the grisly violence that it carried out.

3. Estimates of those who died vary from around forty thousand to 100,000, while thou-sands were "disappeared." It is this era that is commonly known as the *Bheeshanaya* or era of terror (see Wadugodapitiya 2010).

4. Serious recruitment of children (and women) into the LTTE began after the LTTE decided to take on the Indian Peace Keeping Force, which was sent to the Island in 1987 as part of an agreement between Sri Lanka and India.

5. Sinhalese translation of a Tamil name.

## REFERENCES

Baruah, Amit. 2006. "European Union bans LTTE." *The Hindu Online,* May 31, 2006, ac-cessed July 21, 2013, www.hindu.com/2006/05/31/stories/2006053117200100.htm.
DeVotta, Neil. 2009. "The Liberation Tigers of Tamil Elam and the Lost Quest for Separatism in Sri Lanka." *Asian Survey* 49, no. 6: 1021–51.

Galtung, Johan. 2003. "Rethinking Conflict: The Cultural Approach." Speech delivered at the informal meeting of the European ministers responsible for cultural affairs. Council of Europe, Strasbourg, February 17–18 2003, www.coe.int/ T/E/Cultural_Co-operation.

Gunaratna, Rohan. 1987. *War and Peace in Sri Lanka: With a Post-Accord Report from Jaffna.* 1st ed. Institute of Fundamental Studies: Sri Lanka.

————. 1998. *International and Regional Implications of the Sri Lankan Tamil Insurgency.* December 2, 1998, accessed July 21, 2013, 212.150.54.123/articles/articledet.cfm?articleid= 57.

Gunawardana, R. A. L. H. 1994. "Colonialism, Ethnicity and the Construction of the Past: The Changing 'Ethnic Identity' of the Last Four Kings of the Kandyan Kingdom." In *Pivot Politics: Changing Cultural Identities in Early State Formation Processes*, edited by Martin van Bakel, Renee Hagestijin, and Pieter van de Velde, 197–221. Amsterdam: Het Spinhuis.

————. 2008. *Periodization in Sri Lankan History: Some Reflections with Special Emphasis on the Development of the State.* Social Scientists' Association: Sri Lanka.

Harrison, Frances. 2003. "Twenty years on—Riots That Led to War." *BBC News,* July 23, 2003, accessed on July 20, 2013, news.bbc.co.uk/2/hi/south_asia/3090111.stm.

————. 2008. "Sri Lanka's War Turns on Civilians." *BBC News*, June 6, 2008, accessed July 20, 2013, news.bbc.co.uk/2/hi/south_asia/7440183.stm.

Hettige, Siri T. 2008. "Public Policies and Ethnic Relations in Sri Lanka." In *The State, Development and Identity in Multi-Ethnic Societies: Ethnicity, Equity and the Nation*, edited by Nicholas Tarling and Edmund Terence Gomez, 205–15. Oxon, Canada: Routledge.

*International Herald Tribune.* 18 December 2006. "Fleeing Tamil Refugees Describe Being Held by Separatists as Sri Lanka Shelled Camps." Retrieved June 23, 2014 from www.iht. com/articles/ap/2006/12/18/asia/AS_GEN_Sri_Lanka_Refugees.php.

Jayatilake, Dayan. 2013. *Long War, Cold Peace: Conflict and Crisis in Sri Lanka.* Colombo: Vijitha Yapa.

Kapferer, Bruce. 1998. *Legends of People, Myths of State: Violence, Intolerance and Political Culture in Sri Lanka and Australia.* Washington, DC: Smithsonian Institution Press.

Luthra, Dumeetha. 2006. "Sri Lanka Villagers Flee Massacre." *BBC News*, May 20, 2006, accessed on July 21, 2013, news.bbc.co.uk/2/hi/south_asia/5000920.stm.

Obeyesekere, Gananath. 1997. "The Vicissitudes of the Sinhala-Buddhist Identity through Time Change." In *Sri Lanka: Collective Identities Revisited*, edited by Michael Roberts, 355–84. Colombo: Marga Institute.

Rajasingham, K. T. 2002. "Sri Lanka: The Untold Story. Chapter 30: Whirlpool of violence." *Asia Times, Online*, March 9, 2002, accessed on July 26, 2013, www.atimes.com/ind-pak/ DC09Df04.html.

Roberts, Michael, editor. 1997. *Sri Lanka: Collective Identities Revisited.* Colombo: Marga Publications.

Reuters. April 21, 2009. "Tamil Tigers Vow no Surrender to Sri Lanka Military." Retrieved June 23, 2013 from mobile.reuters.com/article/worldNews/idUSTRE53K1WJ20090421.

Scott, David. 1999. *Refashioning Futures: Criticism after Postcoloniality.* Princeton: Princeton University Press.

Spencer, Jonathan. 1990. "The Power of the Past." In *Sri Lanka: History and the Roots of Conflict*, edited by Jonathan Spencer. London: Routledge.

*Sunday Observer.* April 30, 2006. "LTTE Carnage at Gomarankadawala." Retrieved June 20 2013. www.sundayobserver.lk/2006/04/30/fea13.html.

Swamy, M. R. Narayan. 2006. *Tigers of Lanka: From Boys to Guerrillas.* Colombo: Vijitha Yapa Publications.

Tambiah, Stanley Jayaraj. 1986. *Sri Lanka: Ethnic Fratricide and the Dismantling of Democracy.* Chicago: University of Chicago Press.

"President Releases LLRC Report To Parliament, The UN And Public." *The Sunday Leader*, December 18, 2011, accessed on July 21, 2013, www.thesundayleader.lk/2011/12/18/ president-releases-llrc-report-to-parliament-the-un-and-public/.

United Nations. May 19, 2009. "Joint Press Conference held by UN Secretary-General and World Health Organization Director-General, Margaret Chan." Retrieved June 19, 2013. www.un.org/sg/offthecuff/?nid=1291.

Uyangoda, Jayadeva. 2003. "Social Conflict, Radical Resistance and Projects of State Power in Southern Sri Lanka: The Case of the JVP." In *Building Local Capacities for Peace: Rethinking Conflict and Development in Sri Lanka*, edited by M. Mayer, D. Rajasingham-Senanayake, and Y. Thangarajah, 37–64. New Delhi, India: MacMillan India LTD.

Wadugodapitiya, Menaka Dhananjali. 2010. "Fragments of Terror: Memories and Narratives of Former Insurgents in Southern Sri Lanka." Edinburgh Research Archive. Retrieved June 20, 2013 from hdl.handle.net/1842/4.

Vaitheespara, Ravi. 2007. *Theorizing the National Crisis: Sanmugathasan, the Left, and the Ethnic Conflict in Sri Lanka*. Colombo: Social Scientist's Association.

Van den Berghe, Pierre L. 1967. *Race and Racism: A Comparative Perspective.* New York: John Wiley and Sons.

*Chapter Six*

# (Non)Violence and Conflict

*A Theoretical Assessment of Civil Resistance and the Syrian Conflict*

## Jeanne Chang and Alec Clott

Nonviolent actions against a state actor often contrast with popular notions of rebellion, revolution, and even terrorism. While nonviolent action undoubtedly can be a part of rebellious and revolutionary acts, the very notion traditionally tends to conjure images of justified group resistance against a state actor. As the conflict in Syria continues, the lines demarcating different groups, as well as the line between justified and illegitimate forms of violence, seem to become less clear over time. With allegations of chemical warfare, human rights violations, and an ever growing refugee crisis, the Syrian conflict endures as one of the most violent conflicts on the current global stage with no apparent end in sight. In this chapter, we shall use the Syrian conflict as a test case enabling us to reflect upon the strengths and limitations of two recent analyses of the conditions for effective nonviolent resistance campaigns.

In March 2011, protests began in Damascus and Deraa with the stated goal of bringing about the release of political prisoners (BBC, "Syria Profile: A Chronology of Key Events," Oct. 8, 2013). Although several prisoners were released and Bashar Assad's regime initiated a discourse of reform, anti-regime sentiment persisted. As opposition protesters continued to organize, violent regime repression increased. Resistance that began as mass demonstrations and protests in several key cities over the next two years developed into a full-scale conflict with numerous factions, groups, and actors involved. Currently, the opposition may encompass upwards of one thousand distinct groups totaling 100,000 combatants. The Supreme Military

Council of the Free Syrian Army networks many of the major forces in Syria, such as the Syrian Islamic Liberation Front. Yet even the extent to which this network constitutes a unified or coherent opposition force is unclear and continues to be a matter for debate (BBC, "Syria Crisis: Guide to Armed and Political Opposition," Oct. 17, 2013). The geopolitical nature of the conflict has involved various levels of military and non-military support flowing from foreign powers both near and far, such as the United States, Russia, Turkey, Iran, and Israel.

While the causes of the prolonged crisis continue to be debated on the international political stage, the extent of the violence is increasingly visible. Justified or unjustified, fatalities among all parties are growing in number. An increasing number of civilians have fled Syria. Yet with clear instances of peaceful civil mass demonstrations beginning in 2011, why did nonviolent resistance strategies fail to endure throughout the course of the conflict? What are the reasons for the transformation of what began as a peaceful protest movement into one of our century's most violent conflicts? In the context of group violence against a state, we examine theoretical approaches to understanding the efficacy of nonviolent resistance, using the Syrian Civil War as a case study. We analyze Erica Chenoweth and Maria J. Stephan's book, *Why Civil Resistance Works*, and Peter Ackerman and Berel Rodal's article, "The Strategic Dimensions of Civil Resistance." In the latter article, Ackerman and Rodal argue that three specific criteria are necessary for non-violent civil resistance to be successful. We analyze the extent to which these criteria are applicable and identifiable in the context of the Syrian Civil War. Regarding *Why Civil Resistance Works,* our concern is to understand and utilize Chenoweth and Stephen's six mechanisms of leverage as a set of defining characteristics of nonviolent movements and apply these mechanisms to the Syrian Civil War to better understand the reasons why violence has come to characterize the conflict and to assess the adequacy of the theoretical approach.

The results of this theoretical analysis of the Syrian conflict demonstrate that the opposition forces fail to meet several of the criteria and mechanisms of leverage as articulated by Chenoweth and Stephan, and Ackerman and Rodal. This conclusion is not surprising given the violent nature of the conflict. However, failure to meet these criteria is not necessarily the sole cause for the emergence of civil violence. It is possible that even if a movement meets all the criteria and mechanisms of leverage outlined by these two works, a movement may still be susceptible to violent modes of resistance. This is because there is a relatively limited amount of literature on proposed theories for nonviolent movements and therefore they may not encompass all criteria for nonviolent resistance. In addition, there is a lack of distinction between critical moments in political movements, such as their inception or resolution. These limitations suggest that further research and discourse on the criteria and characteristics of nonviolent resistance is needed.

## REVIEW OF LITERATURE

### Hawdon's Typology of Violence

Violence, as a concept, encompasses actions ranging from muggings between individuals to warfare between states. In order to explore the conditions for possible success and failure of nonviolent civil resistance movements, it is necessary to define violence: that is, that which would not be present given the existence of such a movement. For the purpose of this research, we define violence following Hawdon who, in turn, adapts Donald Black's definition given earlier in this book: "the use of physical force against people or property, including threats and attempts." Furthermore, Hawdon's typology of violence categorizes individuals, groups, and states as the three main perpetrators and victims of violence. Our analysis focuses on group violence against the state, which manifests in the forms of rebellion, revolution, sabotage, and terrorism. While the various groups and factions opposing the Syrian government have been labeled as both revolutionary and terrorist actors, depending upon the political stance of the labeler, this research will simply represent the conflict in Syria as including group violence against the state and the state's violent response.

The definition and typology of violence provided allows for a clear assessment of theoretical approaches to nonviolence. By choosing a clear instance of group violence against the state, that is, the resistance to the Syrian government, we can assess the applicability of theoretical characteristics and criteria for nonviolent movements. Especially helpful is the fact that civil resistance in Syria began as nonviolent and later transformed into a violent conflict. What factors in Syria contributed to the conflict's degenerating into violence, as opposed to continuing as nonviolent conflict?

Specifically, our research adopts the characteristics of nonviolent conflict outlined by Erica Chenoweth and Maria J. Stephan in *Why Civil Resistance Works*, and the criteria developed by Peter Ackerman and Berel Rodal in "The Strategic Dimensions of Civil Resistance." Ackerman and Rodal provide clear and concise conditions for success of nonviolent resistance. Chenoweth and Stephan articulate the mechanisms of leverage of successful nonviolent movements, and show how they can be more effective than violent opposition. The authors discuss the advantages and drawbacks of large scale participation including specific reasons why people may not participate, compromising the efficacy of the movement, and specific methods of gaining power over the opponent.

## Ackerman and Rodal's Criteria for Nonviolent Movements

Peter Ackerman and Berel Rodal were the chair and vice chair, respectively, of the International Center on Nonviolent Conflict, at the time of their publication "The Strategic Dimensions of Civil Resistance." The authors outline the history of nonviolent movements of the early twentieth century beginning in 1904 with the mass protest in St. Petersburg and ending with the Serbian Otpor at the turn of the century (Ackerman and Rodal 2008). A handful of events in the twenty-first century are mentioned as well.

Ackerman and Rodal argue that contrary to the claims made by other theoretical approaches, "structural and geopolitical factors" are not determining factors when analyzing the potential success or failure of civil resistance movements (2008, 116). While acknowledging that such factors may be important, Ackerman and Rodal propose instead that by analyzing past instances of successful nonviolent movements, three different criteria for success may be identified. The first is that:

> a movement must unite behind leadership that represents the breadth of the nation, not just certain parties and classes. That leadership must also agree on a set of achievable goals. (117)

The first criterion indicates the importance of solidarity within a nonviolent movement, specifically, a solidarity that extends throughout and unites the whole nation. The movement's leadership must not be factionalized, but must be motivated by a shared commitment to the same realistic goals. The second criterion elaborates upon the first:

> successful civil resistance is the fruit of systematic planning, able to attract and mobilise the participation of people of diverse backgrounds by engaging the manifold elements of civil society: old and young, male and female, rich and poor. (118)

This requirement seemingly elaborates upon the first by explicitly stating that not only must the solidarity extend to the whole nation, but to the diversity of its parties and peoples. Ackerman and Rodal also argue that this can bring strength in numbers, which is necessary since a far reaching movement will have increased avenues which to apply counter-pressure against the state. Emphasis is placed too upon the "systematic planning" beyond protests (118). The last criterion is that:

> the movement must adhere to nonviolent discipline, because violence brings with it serious costs. With the eruption of violence on the part of the resistance, citizen participation evaporates. (118)

The last requirement elaborates upon the effectiveness of dedicated non-violent movements. The authors argue that violence will decrease the likelihood of defection of key state actors and groups who might otherwise be swayed by civil movements. Thus, for instance, the police are less likely to join protestors if those protestors are shooting at them.

## Chenoweth and Stephan: *Why Civil Resistance Works*

Erica Chenoweth and Maria J. Stephan collaboratively wrote *Why Civil Resistance Works* in 2011. Currently Chenoweth is an associate professor at the University of Denver's Josef Korbel School of International Studies and while working on the book, had been an assistant professor of government at Wesleyan University. Stephan works for the U.S. State Department as a strategic planner and was previously the director of policy and research at the International Center on Nonviolent Conflict. Using statistical analysis as well as various case studies of specific countries, territories, and events, Chenoweth and Stephan detail specific mechanisms of leverage needed for a nonviolent campaign to succeed and indicate why some of these factors may cause a campaign to fail.

Chenoweth and Stephan (2011) advance two main theses: 1) nonviolent resistance attracts higher levels of participation than does violent resistance and is therefore more successful; and 2) high levels of participation in nonviolent campaigns "activate various mechanisms of leverage to improve the odds of success" (30). They support their first claim by explaining that nonviolent campaigns have lower barriers to participation and thus are able to attract more participants. Specific types of barriers that might hinder participation include physical barriers, informational difficulties, moral barriers, and the ability to commit to the campaign. Chenoweth and Stephan emphasize the importance of high rates of participation because their statistical analysis of a large number of nonviolent conflicts shows that increased participation leads to increased probability of success.

Chenoweth and Stephan also argue that the success of nonviolent campaigns is augmented by mass participation because it increases the ability to apply critical mechanisms of leverage over the regime. Leverage is the ability to impose costs on the adversary's attempts to maintain the status quo or retaliate against the resistance. Such costs to the regime may include failure to perform basic functions, declining GDP, loss of power, and a general breakdown of the normal order of society. Chenoweth and Stephan argue that maximizing leverage is critical to the success of resistance campaigns. According to the authors, there are six major mechanisms of leverage: coercion, loyalty shifts, backfiring, international sanctions and external support, tactical diversity and innovation, and finally, evasion and resilience. Each of these mechanisms is amplified in efficacy by both increasing the number of participants in the campaign and expanding the diversity of recruits in the campaign.

The first mechanism of leverage, coercion, aims to gain public support by systematically breaking down and removing the adversary's key sources of power, such as economic revenue, support of military elites, supporting organizations, and public loyalty (Chenoweth and Stephan 2011). While it is difficult to defeat a unified adversary, isolating the adversary from its economic and institutional support may increase the probability of campaign success. Leverage is achieved when the adversary's most important power sources are taken away through mass noncooperation and protest. Nonviolent coercion systematically breaks down an adversary's funding sources through sustained pressure by mobilizing mass broad-based tactics of noncooperation such as protests, strikes, boycotts, and labor stoppages. Chenoweth and Stephan conclude that, "states may be more susceptible to internal fissures in the face of massive nonviolent action than to limited, violent opposition" (46).

Second, effective resistance campaigns shift public loyalties from the regime to the resistance to further divide the regime's unity. Chenoweth and Stephan argue that the chances of successfully shifting loyalties increase with the number of participants in the resistance, the diversity of participants, and the number of connections between the resistance and regime. The more loyalties that are shifted from the regime to the resistance, the more likely it is that the campaign will succeed. If the number of diverse participants in the resistance is large, then there is a greater chance that personal connections, such as kin ties, exist between the resistance and regime. A high number of interpersonal connections increases the likelihood of loyalty shifts. Presumably, leverage over the adversary is increased by shifting loyalties because removing support from the regime means that human capital has now been taken away and has likely been transferred to the resistance. If citizens initially loyal to the regime (such as soldiers, policemen, and other authority figures who "question the viability, risks, and potential costs of military action against the nonviolent campaign"), have relationships with those in the resistance, it is all the more likely that they would be willing to switch loyalties (Hathaway, cited in Chenoweth and Stephan 2011, 47). An overall rise in loyalty shifts increases the probability of campaign success. Chenoweth and Stephan tested defection rates of state security forces by campaign and correlated those rates with the campaigns' violence or nonviolence. They found that large nonviolent campaigns are most likely to "produce defections within security forces," and thus provide the most leverage for the campaign (48).

Third, Chenoweth and Stephan explain that the concept of backfiring of regime actions is more likely to occur in nonviolent campaigns rather than violent campaigns. Backfiring is a result of the regime attempting to retaliate against the resistance, but it miscalculates and underestimates the results of its actions resulting in loss of allies and support both domestically and internationally. The authors' main emphasis for this mechanism of leverage is that it is simply more likely to occur as a response to nonviolent than violent campaigns. Backfire is more likely to happen when local populations and international actors sympathize with the resistance but take a passive role in the conflict. People are more likely to sympathize with a nonviolent resistance movement violently suppressed, for instance, than with a violent movement violently attacked. If backfire occurs, resistance campaigns must be able to identify and take advantage of the situation to gain leverage. Chenoweth and Stephan do not articulate specific methods for utilizing this leverage in taking advantage and turning lost regime support into resistance support. They do however allude to the utilization of other mechanisms of leverage such as loyalty shifts and coercion to take advantage of the situation.

Fourth, Chenoweth and Stephan discuss the use of international sanctions and external support as a mechanism for leverage. They argue that diplomatic pressure and international sanctions are 70 percent more likely to be granted in support of large, nonviolent resistances rather than violent resistances (53). However, their data also show that foreign governments are more likely to give material support to violent campaigns compared to nonviolent ones. They also emphasize the unreliability of external state support: "external state support may also undermine insurgents' odds of success," because, "state support is unreliable, inconsistently applied to opposition groups around the world, and sometimes ineffective in helping campaigns" (54). The authors even go as far to say that in the eyes of the local populations, external state support can delegitimize the movement, provoke people to think that the movement is corrupt, and distance the local populace from the resistance—which is risky for the campaign. Overall Chenoweth and Stephan state that "state support may be a double edged sword, rife with trade-offs for insurgency groups," but that civil resistance movements are financially autonomous 90 percent of the time (55). These sanctions and external support act as mechanisms of leverage in multiple ways, but mainly help by funding campaigns and intimidating the regime.

Fifth, Chenoweth and Stephan argue that tactical diversity and innovation are influenced by the size and the diversity of the population. The more people involved, and the more people from diverse backgrounds, the greater is the chance of novel ideas for effective resistance. They note once again that nonviolent campaigns attract more participants because they have lower barriers to participation than do violent campaigns.

Sixth, evasion and resilience tactics are described as the final leverage mechanism. They explain that the resilience of a campaign is crucial for success because it demonstrates the ability of the opposition to maintain the advantage over the regime in spite of oppression and superior power. Resilience encompasses how well a campaign can "maintain a significant number of participants, recruit new members, and continue to confront the adversary in the face of repression" (57). Chenoweth and Stephan also note that successful campaigns are capable of progressing towards their goals while still enduring the costs of regime repression. The authors state that, "to achieve success, a campaign must go beyond persistence and achieve a shift in power between the opposition and the adversary" (58).

## ANALYSIS

The first criterion for a successful resistance campaign, as outlined by Ackerman and Rodal, is that an opposition must stand in solidarity under a unified leadership; furthermore, the goals and aspirations of the opposition must be made clear and must be realistic. An essential point to be made is about the complexity of the Syrian resistance. The Supreme Military Council (SMC) of the Free Syrian Army (FSA) is a large opposition network. The SMC reportedly contains thirty members, "six representing each of five 'fronts' in Syria—Northern (Aleppo and Idlib), Eastern (Raqqa, Deir al-Zour and Hassaka), Western (Hama, Latakia and Tartus), Central (Homs and Rastan) and Southern (Damascus, Deraa and Suwaida)," (BBC, "Syria Crisis: Guide to Armed and Political Opposition," Oct. 17, 2013). Each front delegates power in a similar way, culminating at the Chief-of-Staff, General Idris. While the structure of this opposition may seem unified, critics question not only Idris's willingness to institute standardized orders but the solidarity of its subgroups (BBC, Oct. 17, 2013).

The affiliates, or subgroups of the FSA, seem to have different goals. Many of the groups suffer from internal splits, thereby creating new groups pursuing new goals or joining with others (BBC, Oct. 17, 2013). The widely recognized multi-actor and party nature of the opposition stands as evidence that Ackerman's first criterion is not applicable in Syria. What is more, considering the violent nature of the Free Syrian Army, the point may be moot anyway. However, this illustration served to demonstrate that a "first step" of unification, which potentially could sustain or even lead to nonviolent methods, has not been met. There does seem to be nonviolent movement, the Syrian Opposition Coalition (SOC), but the SOC recently has faced problems of coherence as well. In September 2013, eleven key Islamist combatant forces simultaneously and publicly rejected the SOC. While this rejection resulted from a range of factors, some arguably external (such as the U.S.–Russian agreement on the handling of chemical weapons), it is a clear manifestation of the internal struggle over long term goals regarding political direction for a post-Assad Syria (*Economist*, "Syria's War: Their Own Men," Sept. 28, 2013).

Ackerman and Rodal's second criterion emphasizes two key points: incorporation of a diverse populace and strategic implementation of goal acquisition. It is difficult to argue that the first point applies to Syria. The conflict is often referred to as a sectarian conflict, embodying religious, ethnic, and political divisions. The frequently cited example of the sectarian nature of the conflict is the tension between Alawites and Sunni Muslims. The Alawites have had a disproportionate amount of political control and influence over Syria during the past decades (BBC, "The 'Secretive Sect' in Charge of Syria," May 17, 2012). The split between Sunnis and Alawites is not the only divide shaping the conflict. Some speculate that there is a trend among the Christian population (roughly 10 percent of the overall population) to "support President Assad, particularly as sectarian violence has increased and jihadist militant groups calling for an Islamic state in Syria have grown in strength." Support for Assad may resort from a fear of a hypothetical post-Assadi targeting of Christians in the face of strengthening Islamist political and social groups (BBC, "Syria's Beleaguered Christians," Apr. 23, 2013). On the other hand, many Christians seem to support the opposition. A specific example is George Sabra, the Christian leader of the Syrian National Council—a prominent opposition group within the Syrian National Coalition (Al Arabiya News, "Syrian Opposition Group Refuses to Attend Geneva Peace Talks," 2013). It is also argued by some that the regime is purposely fueling the sectarian divide to gain support of minority groups (BBC, Apr. 23, 2013).

It is not only religious affiliation that determines whether a group of people will support or oppose the regime. Politically, it is evident that the Baath Party not only holds control of Syrian politics but supports Assad's government. Despite some defections after the repression of peaceful mass demonstrations, it is now surmised, "the Baath Party officials involved were appeared [sic] to be relatively minor." Potentially the Baath party members, many from other minority groups, benefit the most from the status quo, which may not hold true if the regime is to fall (BBC, "Profile: Syria's Ruling Baath Party," Jul. 9, 2012).

The last criterion noted by Ackerman and Rodal is that to maintain widespread support, resistance movements must maintain nonviolent methods of opposition. Syria serves as a prime example of a context where initially resistance to a regime was primarily nonviolent but transitioned into a violent opposition. Again, the legitimacy of violence is not in question here—the theoretical framework for nonviolence is. In this context, one might argue that the Syrian conflict is an example of an initial nonviolent movement that turned towards violent methods for obtaining goals. And, as violence arguably does beget violence, this transition is indicative of the great difficulty of holding to a commitment to nonviolent resistance.

Arguably this criterion speaks not only to a characteristic of a successful nonviolent movement, but to the likelihood that any opposition could potentially turn, or return, to nonviolent means of protest. Potentially the introduction of violence presents itself as an irreversible social or political event. By adopting violent means of protest, the Syrian opposition may arguably be validating the use of violence by the regime. It is more difficult to cast doubt on or sow suspicion of the opposition by employing allegations of terrorism, and human rights violations if that same opposition is publicly known for its nonviolent methods of protest.

Finally, it is important to note the strategic implementation of goal acquisition in the context of these diverse groups. While it is clear there are publicly recognized opposition groups with stated goals and arguably strong strategies to overcome the regime—the differences in goals and planning are falling on group lines. That is to reiterate the previous criterion—there is a lack of cohesion on planning, and therefore goals, due to the inherent multigroup and multi-party nature of the conflict.

## Chenoweth and Stephan: *Why Civil Resistance Works*

As previously stated, our goal is to analyze Chenoweth's and Stephan's six main mechanisms of leverage for a resistance campaign in relation to the Syrian conflict since 2011. We want to determine the extent to which these critical mechanisms of leverage were effectively implemented by the resistance campaigns, and if in fact they had been implemented, why the campaigns have not experienced more success. By identifying instances in the Syrian conflict where each of these mechanisms may have played a role, we aim to shed light on why nonviolent movements have not succeeded in the Syrian conflict.

Chenoweth's and Stephan's first mechanism of leverage is coercion, where the campaign attempts to gain leverage by breaking down and or removing sources of power and support from the regime. Specific instances of the resistance boycotting or actively trying to coerce the state, which then resulted in the breakdown of sources of power, are difficult to find. Arguably, it is harder to implement strategies for coercion given a divided opposition. Perhaps the only coercive efforts that were effective were from external international entities rather than being mobilized by the resistance. The initial nonviolent resistance movement in Damascus arguably had short term coercive effects that resulted in the release of political prisoners in addition to the regime's promises of reform. However, the introduction of violent means of repression at the hands of the state indicated that the opposition may not have been able to continue with nonviolent means (BBC, "Syria Profile: A Chronology of Key Events," Oct. 8, 2013). It is clear that these coercive effects were not longstanding, though it is unclear whether or not this is due to the introduction of violence, the stubbornness or intractability of the Assad government, or any other social or political factors.

Loyalty shifts in the Syrian conflict include instances where figures from the Assad regime have defected and shifted support to the resistance. By early January 2013, Assad still had a firm core of military support, but "a good number of senior Sunni officers ha[d] defected, leaving Alawites, the minority Muslim sect to which the Assad family belongs, ever more dominant," (*Economist*, "Syria's Conflict: No End in Sight," Jan. 12, 2013). Over time, there were clear examples of defection from the state. For instance, Baath officials such as Abdo Hussameddin defected from the party as a result of the government's retaliation against the opposition (BBC, "Profile: Syria's Ruling Baath Party," Jul. 9, 2012). It may be that loyalty shifts are hurting the opposition too, because internal shifts between opposition groups lead to a lack of cohesion (BBC, Oct. 17, 2013).

The shifts among opposition groups are representative of the groups' varying values and goals. Internal loyalty shifts due to lack of cohesion may have undermined the value of loyalties gained from the regime. There is still a strong military that feels justified in its actions against the opposition, perhaps as a result of the opposition's turn to violence.

There have been various instances of backfire in the Syrian conflict. Specifically, Assad has violently retaliated against the opposition, including against nonviolent protesters. Specifically, in May 2012, Assad forces attempted to arrest "prominent peace activists" attempting to subdue the resistance. These actions have only encouraged "more support for international isolation of Assad and his top supporters," such as increased sanctions by the European Union against the regime (The Monitor's Editorial Board, "Nonviolent Tactics may be Syria's Only Path to Freedom," May 14, 2012). The regime's actions also backfired in an attempt to stifle demonstrators at the University of Aleppo by shooting and killing protestors. The events were video recorded by various activists, who were able to use their footage to reinforce the commitment of current supporters and inspire others to join the uprising. For example, student activist Ahmed Saad is quoted as saying: "We started with fifty people, but now 1,000 protesters come out, in many neighborhoods, so we are optimistic," (Peterson, 2012). These instances are evidence of the Syrian resistance campaigns taking advantage of regime backfire to gain support and leverage. While potentially effective, however, there may not be the desired frequency of backfire response.

Among the most complicated dimensions of the Syrian conflict are international sanctions and external support, which figure into the fourth of Chenoweth and Stephan's mechanisms. There have been various examples of external support for the resistance. On the other side, Russia and Iran continue to support President Assad, and fighters from the militant group Hezbollah bolster Assad troops (BBC, "Syria Profile—Leaders," Sept. 4, 2013).

Although foreign governments and external militant groups have shown varying degrees of support, together they have not conclusively helped or hindered the resistance. With suspicion, speculation, ideologies, and motivations politicizing every foreign country's move in relation to the conflict, any mention of this mechanism is guaranteed to stir debate. The external pressures that resulted in the chemical arms deal seem to be indicative of Chenoweth and Stephan's mechanism of leverage (BBC, "Q&A: Syria Chemical Weapons Disarmament Deal," Oct. 31, 2013; Weir, "Russia: Chemical Weapons Deal a Good Start, but Syria Peace is Still Far Off," Oct. 1, 2013). However, given the heated geopolitical discourse over the conflict and hesitation over providing direct military support, the mechanism is called into question. Potentially, the violent nature of the opposition (as well as its including groups associated with violent terrorists), is detrimental to gaining wider support from the international political stage—the violent methods of the opposition allow other political actors to question their legitimacy and therefore support the regime or simply remain neutral in regards to the conflict.

Many of the instances of nonviolent protests in Syria were fueled by emotionally charged tactics, but there seem to have been fewer tactical innovations and variations than Chenoweth and Stephan would consider necessary to make significant contributions to an effective campaign. The dearth of clever oppositional tactics may be the result of the Syrian opposition's not being well organized. The few instances of tactical surprise seem to be on the side of the state. For example, the alleged use of chemical weapons was a tactical surprise. Alternatively, the regime claims the opposition conducts violent operations such as terrorist acts (BBC, Sept. 4, 2013). This accusation potentially demonstrates that some instances of effective tactical innovation have been violent by nature and therefore are irrelevant to Chenoweth and Stephan's mechanism of leverage. However, this is not to say there are no creative, nonviolent methods of protest. A few tactical innovations of nonviolent resistance have been mobilized by groups in Damascus; for example, letting loose donkeys with pictures of al-Assad or releasing "freedom balloons" filled with confetti (the *Monitor*'s Editorial Board, Feb. 29, 2012). Yet, perhaps these instances of creative nonviolent methods are overshadowed or rendered irrelevant by the severity of the ongoing violent conflict.

Chenoweth's and Stephan's final mechanism of leverage is evasion and resilience. This is a difficult mechanism to assess due to the often contradictory or limited information coming from the state. For example, it is hard to question the resilience of the violent opposition due to the fact the conflict is ongoing after two years. Alternatively, the resilience of a nonviolent opposition is harder to discern due to the dearth of public examples of nonviolent protests at the level witnessed at the beginning of the conflict. There are a few examples of nonviolent tactics such as protests at Aleppo University (the

*Monitor*'s Editorial Board, May 14, 2012), there does not seem to be a number sufficient to reach an optimal level as characterized by Chenoweth and Stephan. Evasion is a difficult concept to analyze given that it is inherently tied to resilience. On one hand, the opposition continues to resist the state; on the other hand, there is a growing refugee crisis, making manifest the self-removal of a vast amount of citizens (*Economist*, "Syria's Refugees: Drowning in the Flood," Feb. 2, 2013). Perhaps one could conjecture that many of the refugees would otherwise be participants in a nonviolent resistance (Chenoweth and Stephan 2011).

## CONCLUSION

While the labels of terrorism, revolution, and rebellion are employed to pursue distinct goals, all are forms of group violence against the state and commonly are applied to similar social phenomena. With respect to Syria, the sort of violence that is defined as direct assertions of lethal force is unarguably applicable. Yet this was not always the case: the beginning of the conflict between the regime and what would become an opposition began in a nonviolent manner through mass protests and demonstrations. Without attributing direct causation, it is still possible to analyze the Syrian conflict to test differing theoretical criteria and frameworks of nonviolent movements. A test of these theories in the context of a violent conflict allows us to assess their applicability.

Ackerman and Rodal list three major conditions for the efficacy of a nonviolent movement. They argue that these criteria constitute a successful nonviolent movement: solidarity under unified leadership, strategic planning for a diverse population, and a dedication to nonviolent means of opposition. Syria has not met any of these. For example, there seems to be no unified opposition. Chenoweth and Stephan's mechanisms of leverage highlight that the Syrian opposition had long-term difficulties coercing the state, has suffered from loyalty shifts more than they have benefitted, and may not fully be taking advantage of the state's missteps. Furthermore, it is not experiencing overt or sufficiently supportive assistance from external actors, and is arguably failing to innovate effectively. The violent nature of the conflict, in addition to the refugee crisis, further complicates the nature of evasion and resilience beyond the scope of Chenoweth and Stephan's explanation.

Given that the Syrian opposition fails to satisfy the criteria or characteristics given in each theoretical framework, the validity of the frameworks is arguably strengthened. A lack of solidarity, clear goals, and a clear continued dedication to nonviolent means of protest by the majority of the opposition hinders a nonviolent movement. Furthermore, these social and political phenomena continue to work against a potential return to nonviolence. As individual frameworks, Ackerman and Rodal compared to Chenoweth and Stephan's differ in purpose and scope. While Ackerman and Rodal's criteria were pulled from an article briefly summarizing and concluding trends in nonviolent resistance movements, Chenoweth and Stephan's characteristics are part of a comprehensive argument rooted in data about a large number of nonviolent movements beginning in the twentieth century. Ackerman and Rodal present their criteria in a manner that suggests that they are necessary conditions for an opposition to be nonviolent. Alternatively, Chenoweth and Stephan's mechanisms are presented such as to be more advantageous for and likely to occur in nonviolent civil resistance than in violent means of opposition. Therefore, our analysis leans towards testing a theoretical set of general requirements and a comprehensive argument that lists effective characteristics of civil resistance.

Alternatively, the Syrian opposition's failing to satisfy the criteria or characteristics given in each theoretical framework can be interpreted as unrelated to their validity. There are certain areas of discussion regarding violent conflict that are not directly addressed or elaborated on by either framework. For example, it is debatable whether theoretical perspectives of nonviolent movements are applicable only at the inception of resistance, or if they can continually be applied after the introduction of violent conflict. It is unclear whether or not attempts by the opposition to address or meet these criteria and characteristics would allow for, or even encourage, an effective return from violent conflict to civil resistance. The introduction of sustained violence may fundamentally alter the social and political environment to the detriment of civil resistance. Yet, that is not to argue that a return to nonviolence is impossible. The lack of clear discussion on "critical moments" in phases of resistance, such as their inception or solution, would be a topic worthy of future research.

An analysis of various phases or critical moments of resistance movements would also aid their application. Chenoweth and Stephen's work is the first empirically based research of its kind on nonviolent resistance movements. The groundbreaking research presented in *Why Civil Resistance Works* lends itself not only to a strong applicable theoretical framework, but an argument for the effectiveness of nonviolent protest over violent resistance. Additional quantitative research can only prove beneficial to further understanding the characteristics, criteria, and effectiveness of civil resistance. In sum, the theoretical approaches outlined in Chenoweth and Stephan's work and Ackerman and Rodal's work shed some light on the reasons for the transformation of Syria's nonviolent resistance movement into violent conflict. However, this chapter has argued that there are also explanatory limitations given the limited amount of extant research. Therefore, the analysis of the reasons for the transition of Syria's conflict cannot be taken as definitive. Venezuela, Bosnia, Ukraine, and others are experiencing varying degrees of violent and nonviolent conflict. While theoretical frameworks may not neatly fit with all of the conflicts of today, further attention and future research can only continue to shed light on the successful application of civil resistance as a means of achieving political and social goals.

## REFERENCES

Ackerman, Peter, and Berel Rodal. 2008. "The Strategic Dimensions of Civil Resistance." *Survival* 50: 111–26.

Al Arabiya News. 2013. "Syrian Opposition Group Refuses to Attend Geneva Peace Talks," accessed November 14, 2013, english.alarabiya.net/en/News/middle-east/2013/10/13/Key-Syrian-opposition-group-rejects-peace-talks-.html.

BBC. 2012. "Profile: Syria's Ruling Baath Party." Last modified July 9, 2012. Accessed November 14, 2013, www.bbc.co.uk/news/world-middle-east-18582755.

———. 2012. "The 'Secretive Sect' in Charge of Syria." Last modified May 17, 2012. Accessed November 14, 2013, www.bbc.co.uk/news/world-middle-east-18084964.

———. 2013. "Syria's Beleaguered Christians." Last modified April 23, 2013. Accessed November 14, 2013, www.bbc.co.uk/news/world-middle-east-22270455.

———. 2013. "Syria Crisis: Guide to Armed and Political Opposition." Last modified October 17, 2013. Accessed November 14, 2013, www.bbc.co.uk/news/world-middle-east-24403003.

———. 2013. "Syria Profile: A Chronology of Key Events." Last modified October 08, 2013. Accessed November 14, 2013, www.bbc.co.uk/news/world-middle-east-14703995.

BBC News. 2013. "Q&A: Syria Chemical Weapons Disarmament Deal." Last modified October 31, 2013. Accessed November 15, 2013, www.bbc.co.uk/news/world-middle-east-23876085.

———. 2013. "Syria Profile: Leaders." Last modified September 4, 2013. Accessed November 15, 2013, www.bbc.co.uk/news/world-middle-east-14703912.

Chenoweth, Erica. 2013. "Erica Chenoweth International Relations, Political Violence and Civil Resistance." Accessed November 15, 2013, www.ericachenoweth.com/.

Chenoweth, Erica, and Maria Stephan. 2011. *Why Civil Resistance Works: The Strategic Logic of Nonviolent Conflict*. New York: Columbia University Press.

*Economist*. 2013. "Syria's Conflict: No End in Sight." Last modified January 12, 2013. Accessed November 15, 2013, www.economist.com/news/middle-east-and-africa/21569424-president-bashar-assad-sounds-another-death-knell-diplomacy-no-end-sight.

———. 2013. "Syria's Refugees: Drowning in the Flood." Last modified February 2, 2013. Accessed November 15, 2013, www.economist.com/news/middle-east-and-africa/2157 1143-foreign-governments-and-agencies-are-failing-syrias-refugees-drowning-flood.

———. 2013. "Syria's War: Their Own Men." Last modified September 28, 2013. Accessed November 15, 2013, www.economist.com/news/middle-east-and-africa/2158 6879-islamist-rebels-sever-ties-political-opposition-their-own-men.

Peterson, Scott. 2012. "How 'Pro-regime' Aleppo Became one of Syria's Biggest Battlegrounds." *The Christian Science Monitor*, Last modified August 3, 2012. Accessed November 15, 2013, www.csmonitor.com/World/Middle-East/2012/0803/How-pro-regime-Aleppo-became-one-of-Syria-s-biggest-battlegrounds.

The *Monitor*'s Editorial Board. 2012. "Nonviolent Tactics may be Syria's Only Path to Freedom." Last modified May 14, 2012. Accessed November 15, 2013, www.csmonitor.com/Commentary/the-monitors-view/2012/0514/Nonviolent-tactics-may-be-Syria-s-only-path-to-freedom.

———. 2012. "Syria Protests Must Stick to Nonviolence." Last modified February 29, 2012. Accessed November 15, 2013, www.csmonitor.com/Commentary/the-monitors-view/2012/0229/Syria-protests-must-stick-to-nonviolence.

Weir, Fred. 2013. *The Christian Science Monitor*. "Russia: Chemical Weapons Deal a Good Start, but Syria Peace is Still Far Off." Last modified October 1, 2013. Accessed November 15, 2013, www.csmonitor.com/World/Europe/2013/1001/Russia-chemical-weapons-deal-a-good-start-but-Syria-peace-is-still-far-off-video.

*Chapter Seven*

# Killing Before an Audience

*Terrorism and Group Violence*

Mark Juergensmeyer

Are "lone wolf" terrorists really lone wolves? Some of the most striking terrorist attacks in recent years have been perpetrated by one or two individuals who do not appear, at first glance, to be part of an organized group. Yet, as I will explain in this chapter, in each case there is an audience in mind and a larger network of imagined supporters for whom the act is meant to impress. Even lone-wolf terrorist acts, I believe, are examples of group violence.

On April 15, 2013, during the Boston Marathon, two backpacks were casually placed along the curbside near the finish line. When they were ignited in a pair of horrific blasts, three innocent bystanders were killed and 264 others were injured. In the days that followed, surveillance camera photographs identified the culprits, who turned out to be not agents of some foreign terrorist force, but two local young athletes: twenty-six-year-old Tamerlan Tsarnaev and his nineteen-year-old brother, Dzhokhar.

The Boston case appears to be similar to many of the other lone-wolf terrorist attacks in the United States in recent years. Before Boston, there was the December 2012 Newtown massacre by Adam Lanza in Sandy Hook Elementary School; the July 2012 movie theater shootings by James Holmes in Aurora, Colorado; the August 2012 attack on the Milwaukee Sikh Gurdwara by Wade Michael Page; the 2010 Times Square bombing attempt by Faisal Shahzad; the 2007 Virginia Tech shootings by Seung-Hui Cho; the 1996 Atlanta Olympic Park bombing by Eric Robert Rudolph; and most dramatic of all, the 1995 Oklahoma City Federal Building bombing carried out by Timothy McVeigh.

Some of these were committed by Christians, some by Muslims, and some by those with no particular religious affiliation at all. In almost all cases, though, these have been instances where lonely, alienated individuals have raged against a society that they thought had abandoned them. These lone-wolf events are different from other instances in recent years where organized radical religious groups such as the Christian militia or Muslim jihadi organizations have plotted attacks and recruited participants to be involved in them. In the lone-wolf cases, religious ideas, when they appeared at all, seemed to be more of an excuse than a reason for the violence. Yet in each of these cases the perpetrators had a larger audience in mind, and an imagined community of supporters to encourage them.

The Boston incident is a case in point. Though at first the motives of the Tsarnaev brothers were not clear, Jihadi extremist ideology and a Chechen ethnic community of supporters were in the background of what appears to be a complicated web of motivations. Like the other cases in recent years, their actions were on one level simply expressions of the rage of angry young men. Or, in the case of the Tsarnaev brothers, the bombing was the expression of the rage of one angry young man assisted by his younger brother.

It is true that the surviving Tsarnaev, nineteen-year-old Dzhokar, did not appear to be either a loser or a loner. He was a likeable, skateboarding, high school athlete who seemed to harbor little rage against anyone, much less toward society. But it's also clear that he worshipped his older brother, Tamerlan. Some describe Dzhokar as following Tamerlan around "like a puppy." So Dzhokar's participation may have been due less to personal rage or religious ideology than to sibling pressure from Tamerlan, seven years his elder.

Then what about Tamerlan Tsarnaev? He was clearly a troubled young man. He had dropped out of college, was arrested for assaulting a previous girlfriend, had strained relations with his wife, could not receive U.S. citizenship because of the assault record, and had to abandon his dream of becoming an Olympic boxer because he was not an American citizen. Worse, he did not have a social support network. He told one colleague, "I don't have a single American friend," and then added, "I don't understand them." And then he began to be more deeply involved in radical religious and political ideas related to the family's war-torn homeland, Chechnya.

The details of his connections to the separatist organizations and jihadi ideology that accompanies some aspects of the rebellious movement are still unclear. Jihadi literature was found in the brothers' apartment, and Dzhokar scrawled anti-American jihadi slogans on the inside of the boat where he was found during the manhunt that brought him to justice. They seemed to think that their actions would promote the cause of Chechen independence. But at least one Chechen rebel leader proclaimed that Tamarlan had nothing to do with the rebel movement, and that he was a product of America. For Tamarlan, however, the notion of being a part of a great holy battle seemed appealing.

For such people, wars are exciting, and the imagined wars of great religious conflict are more than exhilarating. They offer the promise of opportunity, the hope of victory and triumph, and they provide an ennobling role as a soldier within that cosmic war. Perhaps most directly, such imagined wars provide a justification for violence, including violent revenge against the society that they think has shunned them.

Hence the defense of religion provides a cover for violence. It gives moral license to something horrible that the perpetrators had longed to do, to show the world how powerful they really could be, and to demonstrate their importance in one terminal moment of violent glory. Religion doesn't cause violence, but it often provides the legitimization for it.

One does not need religion to do this, of course. After all, Adam Lanza shot up the Newtown school and James Holmes attacked the Aurora movie theater crowd without a nod toward religion. But in the cases of Atlanta Olympic Park bomber Eric Robert Rudolph and the Sikh Gurdwara attacker, Wade Michael Page, motivations appear to have included the defense of Christian society. Times Square attempted bomber, Faisal Shahzad, and the Boston bomber, Tamerlan Tsarnaev, justified their acts of rage as defending Islamic society.

The most devastating acts of terrorism perpetrated by lone-wolf killers in recent years were both conducted for reasons related to religion—to the defense of an imagined Christian civilization that was under attack by forces of secularism and what they regarded as alien religion. These were the 1995 bombing of the Oklahoma City Federal Building by Timothy McVeigh and the 2011 attack on the youth camp near Oslo by Anders Breivik. The similarities between Norway's mass killer Anders Breivik and Oklahoma City bomber Timothy McVeigh are striking. Both were good-looking young Caucasians who imagined themselves soldiers in a cosmic war to save Christendom. Both thought their acts of mass destruction would trigger a great battle to rescue society from liberal forces of multiculturalism that allowed non-Christians and non-whites positions of acceptability. Both regretted the loss of life but thought their actions were "necessary." For that they were staunchly unapologetic. Their similarities even extend to the kind of explosive used in their actions. Both used a mixture of fuel oil and ammonium nitrate fertilizer which Breivik said he needed for his farm operations. The farm, it turned out, was rented largely because it was a convenient place to test his car bombs.

And then there is the matter of dates. McVeigh was fixed on the day of April 19, the anniversary of the Waco siege. Breivik chose July 22, which was the day in 1099 that the Kingdom of Jerusalem was established during the First Crusade. The title of Breivik's manifesto, which was posted on the

Internet on that day, is *2083*, the date that Breivik suggested would be the culmination of a seventy-year war that began with his action. Yet seventy years from 2011 would be 2081—why did he date the final purge of Muslims from Norway to be two years later, in 2083? I found the answer on page 242 of Breivik's manifesto, where he explains that on 1683 at the Battle of Vienna, the Ottoman Empire military was defeated in a protracted struggle, thereby insuring that most of Europe would not become part of the Muslim empire. The date in Breivik's title is the four hundredth anniversary of that decisive battle, and in Breivik's mind he was recreating the historic efforts to save Europe from what he imagined to be the evils of Islam. The threat of Islam is a dominant motif of his 1,500-page manifesto, *2083: A European Declaration of Independence*.

The writing of a manifesto is a major difference between Breivik and McVeigh, who was not a writer; instead McVeigh copied and quoted from his favorite book, the novel, *The Turner Diaries* written by neo-Nazi William Pierce under the pseudonym Andrew Macdonald. But the novel McVeigh loved explains his motives in a matter eerily similar to the writings of Breivik in his book, *2083*: he thought that liberal politicians had given in to the forces of globalization and multiculturalism, and that the "mudpeople" who were non-white, non-Christian, non-heterosexual, non-patriarchal males were trying to take over the country. To save the country for Christendom the righteous white, straight, non-feminist Christian males had to be shocked into reality by the force of an explosion that would signal to them that the war had begun. These were McVeigh's ideas from *The Turner Diaries*, but they were also Breivik's.

"The time for dialogue is over," Breivik writes on page 811 of his manifesto. "The time for armed resistance has come." The enemy of Breivik's imagined war were "the cultural Marxist/multiculturalist elites" whom he regarded as the "Nazis of our time," intent on "leading us [i.e., white Europeans] to the cultural slaughterhouse by selling us into Muslim slavery." Breivik says, threateningly, to the "multiculturalist elite" that "we know who you are, where you live and we are coming for you."

Breivik's manifesto is an interesting and eclectic document, something of a scrapbook of everything from his instructions for small-scale farming to a syllabus for a course on revolution that he'd love to see taught (complete with extensive bibliography that includes authors such as Immanuel Wallerstein, Theda Skocpol, and Eric Hobsbawm, and recommends as a textbook the book, *Theorizing Revolution,* written by my colleague at Santa Barbara, John Foran). It also includes theoretical and historical overviews of European history and political ideas, and an attempt to explain Muslim ideas and Islamic history, skewed in such a way to make it appear as if this major religious tradition was an ideology intent on controlling the world. The manifesto also includes a manual of how to make terrorist devices and conduct acts of terrorism—a manual not unlike the "Army of God" handbook created by Christian anti-abortion activists, most likely penned by Lutheran pastor Michael Bray in Bowie, Maryland. It advises on costumes that might be worn, such as a policeman's uniform, and how to avoid detection.

Perhaps the most interesting section is Breivik's chronology, day by day, of the weeks preceding his bombing and massacre on July 22. It ends the chronology with this matter-of-fact statement: "I believe this will be my last entry. It is now Fri July 22nd, 12.51." Moments later he posted the 1,500-page book on the Web site. Then, presumably, he drove to downtown Oslo to detonate the bomb that killed seven and shattered buildings housing offices of the ruling political party. Afterwards he donned his policeman's uniform to gain entrance to the liberal party's youth camp where he coldly murdered over seventy young people in a rampage that lasted more than an hour.

Like McVeigh, he thought that this horrible dramatic action would bring a hidden war into the open. Like many modern terrorists, his violent act was a form of performance violence, a symbolic attempt at empowerment to show the world that for the moment he was in charge. The terrorist act was a wake-up call, and a signal that the war had begun. Behind the earthly conflict was a cosmic war, a battle for Christendom. As the title of Breivik's manifesto indicates, he thought he was recreating that historical moment in which Christianity was defended against the hordes, and Islam was purged from what he imagined to be the purity of European society.

Breivik meticulously detailed what he expected to be the historical trajectory of this war through four stages, culminating in 2083. He expected that the forces of multiculturalism would be tough, and would resist the efforts to combat it. "It will take us up to seventy years to win," Breivik writes on page 811 of his manifesto, but adds that "there is no doubt in our minds that we will eventually succeed." In the final phase of the great cosmic war, the civil war between the evil multiculturalists and the righteous few, a series of coup d'etats throughout Europe will overthrow the liberal forces. Then, finally "the deportation of Muslims" will begin, and European Christendom will be restored.

Is this a religious vision, or is religion simply used to justify Breivik's racist ideology? It is true that Breivik—and McVeigh, for that matter—were much more concerned about politics and history than about scripture and religious belief. But much the same can be said about Osama Bin Laden, Ayman al-Zawahiri, and many other Islamist activists. Bin Laden was a businessman and engineer, and Zawahiri was a medical doctor; neither were theologians or clergy. Their writings show that they were much more interested in Islamic history than theology or scripture, and imagined themselves as recreating glorious moments in Islamic history in their own imagined wars. Tellingly, Breivik writes of al Qaeda with admiration, as if he would love to create a Christian version of their religious cadre. If bin Laden is a

Muslim terrorist, Breivik and McVeigh are surely Christian ones. Breivik was fascinated with the Crusades and imagined himself to be a member of the Knights Templar, the crusader army of a thousand years ago. But in an imagined, cosmic war, time is suspended, and history is transcended as the activists imagine themselves to be acting out timeless roles in a sacred drama. The tragedy is that these religious fantasies are played out in real time, with real and cruel consequences.

## PERFORMANCE VIOLENCE

How do we make sense of such theatrical forms of violence? What were the perpetrators trying to accomplish? These are questions that I have pondered in my book, *Terror in the Mind of God,* from which many of the following insights have been taken (Juergensmeyer). The traditional way of answering these questions is to view dramatic violence as part of a strategic plan. This viewpoint assumes that terrorism is always part of a political strategy—and, in fact, some social scientists have defined terrorism in just this way: "the use of covert violence by a group for political ends" (Laqueur, 73). In some cases this definition is indeed appropriate, for an act of violence can fulfill political ends and have a direct impact on public policy.

Yet the situation is more complicated than that. The Israeli elections following the assassination of Prime Minister Yitzhak Rabin in 1996 provide a case in point. Shortly after Rabin was killed, his successor, Shimon Peres, held a 20 percent lead in the polls over his rival, Benjamin Netanyahu, but this lead vanished following a series of Hamas suicide attacks on Jerusalem buses. Netanyahu narrowly edged out Peres in the May elections. Many observers concluded that Netanyahu—no friend of Islamic radicals—had the terrorists of Hamas to thank for his victory. When the Hamas operative who planned the 1996 attacks was later caught and imprisoned, he was asked whether he had intended to affect the outcome of the elections. "No," he responded, explaining that the internal affairs of Israelis did not matter much to him. This operative was a fairly low-level figure, however, and one might conjecture that his superiors had a more specific goal in mind. But when I put the same question to the political leader of Hamas, Dr. Abdul Aziz Rantisi, his answer was almost precisely the same: these attacks were not aimed at Israeli internal politics, since Hamas did not differentiate between Peres and Netanyahu (Rantisi). In the Hamas view, the two Israeli leaders were equally opposed to Islam. "Maybe God wanted it," the Hamas operative said of Netanyahu's election victory. Even if the Hamas leaders were being disingenuous, the fact remains that most of their suicide bombings have served no direct political purpose.

Other examples of religious terrorism have also shown little strategic value. The release of nerve gas in the Tokyo subways and the attacks on the World Trade Center did not provide any immediate political benefits to those who caused them. Although the financial costs of the September 11, 2001, attacks were staggering, there is no evidence that Osama bin Ladin and other members of the al Qaida network launched the attacks solely to cripple the U.S. economy. Mahmud Abouhalima, convicted for his part in the 1993 World Trade Center bombing, told me that assaults on public buildings did have a different kind of strategic value in that they helped to "identify the government as enemy." In general, however, the political and economic ends for which these acts were committed were distant indeed (Abouhalima).

A political scientist, Martha Crenshaw, has shown that the notion of "strategic" thinking can be construed in a broad sense to cover not just immediate political achievements but also the internal logic that propels a group into perpetrating terrorist acts (Crenshaw). As Abouhalima said, many of those who committed them felt they were justified by the broad, long-range benefits to be gained. My investigations indicate that Crenshaw is right—acts of terrorism are usually the products of an internal logic and not of random or crazy thinking—but I hesitate to use the term strategy for all rationales for terrorist actions. Strategy implies a degree of calculation and an expectation of accomplishing a clear objective that does not jibe with such dramatic displays of power as the destruction of the World Trade Center towers. These creations of terror are done not to achieve a strategic goal but to make a symbolic statement.

By calling acts of religious terrorism "symbolic," I mean that they are intended to illustrate or refer to something beyond their immediate target: a grander conquest, for instance, or a struggle more awesome than meets the eye. As Abouhalima said, the bombing of a public building may dramatically indicate to the populace that the government or the economic forces behind the building were seen as enemies, to show the world that they were targeted as satanic foes. The point of the attack, then, was to produce a graphic and easily understandable object lesson. Such explosive scenarios are not tactics directed toward an immediate, earthly, or strategic goal, but dramatic events intended to impress for their symbolic significance. As such, they can be analyzed as one would any other symbol, ritual, or sacred drama.

I can imagine a line with "strategic" on the one side and "symbolic" on the other, with various acts of terrorism located in between. The hostage taking in the Japanese embassy by the Tupac Amaru in Peru—clearly an attempt to leverage power in order to win the release of members of the movement held prisoner by the Peruvian government—might be placed closer to the political, strategic side. The Aum Shinrikyo nerve gas attack might be closer to the symbolic, religious side. Each was the product of logical thought, and each had an internal rationale. In cases such as the Tokyo nerve gas attack that were more symbolic than strategic, however, the logic was focused not on an immediate political acquisition, but at a larger, less tangible goal.

The very adjectives used to describe acts of religious terrorism—symbolic, dramatic, theatrical—suggest that we look at them not as tactics but as performance violence. The spectacular assaults of September 11, 2001, were not only tragic acts of violence; they were also spectacular theater. In speaking of terrorism as "performance," however, I am not suggesting that such acts are undertaken lightly or capriciously. Rather, like religious ritual or street theater, they are dramas designed to have an impact on the several audiences that they affect. Those who witness the violence—even at a distance, via the news media—are therefore a part of what occurs. Moreover, like other forms of public ritual, the symbolic significance of such events is multifaceted; they mean different things to different observers.

This suggests that it is possible to analyze comparatively the performance of acts of religious terrorism. There is already a growing literature of studies based on the notion that civic acts and cultural performances are closely related. The controversial parades undertaken each year by the Protestant Orangemen in Catholic neighborhoods of Northern Ireland, for instance, have been studied not only as cultural events but also as political statements. So it is not unreasonable to view public violence as performances as well.

In addition to referring to drama, the term performance also implies the notion of "performative"—as in the concept of "performative acts." This is an idea developed by language philosophers regarding certain kinds of speech that are able to perform social functions: their very utterance has a transformative impact (Austin). Like vows recited during marriage rites, certain words not only represent reality but also shape it: they contain a certain power of their own. The same is true of some nonverbal symbolic actions, such as the gunshot that begins a race, the raising of a white flag to show defeat, or acts of terrorism.

Terrorist acts, then, can be both performance events, in that they make a symbolic statement, and performative acts, insofar as they try to change things. When Mohammad Attah piloted an American passenger plane directly into the World Trade Center towers; when Yigal Amir aimed his pistol at Israel's prime minister, Yitzhak Rabin; and when Sikh activists targeted Punjab's chief minister with a car bomb in front of the state's office buildings, the activists were aware that they were creating enormous spectacles. They probably also hoped that their actions would make a difference—if not in a direct, strategic sense, then in an indirect way as a dramatic show so powerful as to change people's perceptions of the world.

But the fact that the al Qaida pilots and the assassins of Prime Minister Rabin and Chief Minister Beant Singh hoped that their acts would make such a statement does not mean that they in fact did. As I noted, public symbols mean different things to different people, and a symbolic performance may not achieve its intended effect. The way the act is perceived—by both the perpetrators and those who are affected by it—makes all the difference. In fact, the same is true of performative speech. One of the leading language philosophers, J. L. Austin, has qualified the notion that some speech acts are performative by observing that the power of the act is related to the perception of it. Children, for example, playing at marriage are not wedded by merely reciting the vows and going through the motions, nor is a ship christened by just anyone who gives it a name (Austin).

The French sociologist Pierre Bourdieu, carrying further the idea that statements are given credibility by their social context, has insisted that the power of performative speech—vows and christenings—is rooted in social reality and is given currency by the laws and social customs that stand behind it (Bourdieu 117). Similarly, an act of terrorism usually implies an underlying power and legitimizing ideology. But whether the power and legitimacy implicit in acts of terrorism are like play-acted marriage vows or are the real thing depends in part on how the acts are perceived. It depends, in part, on whether their significance is believed.

This brings us back to the realm of faith. Public ritual has traditionally been the province of religion, and this is one of the reasons that performance violence comes so naturally to activists from a religious background. In a collection of essays on the connection between religion and terrorism published some years ago, one of the editors, David C. Rapoport, observed—accurately, I think—that the two topics fit together not only because there is a violent streak in the history of religion, but also because terrorist acts have a symbolic side and in that sense mimic religious rites. The victims of terrorism are targeted not because they are threatening to the perpetrators, he said, but because they are "symbols, tools, animals or corrupt beings" that tie into "a special picture of the world, a specific consciousness" that the activist possesses (Rapoport, xiii).

The street theater of performance violence forces those who witness it directly or indirectly into that "consciousness"—that alternative view of the world. This gives the perpetrators of terrorism a kind of celebrity status and their actions an illusion of importance. The novelist Don DeLillo goes so far as to say that "only the lethal believer, the person who kills and dies for faith," is taken seriously in modern society (DeLillo, 157). When we who observe these acts take them seriously—are disgusted and repelled by them, and begin to distrust the peacefulness of the world around us—the purposes of this theater are achieved.

## KILLING FOR AN AUDIENCE

As DeLillo once said, terrorism is "the language of being noticed" (157). Without being noticed, in fact, terrorism would not exist. The sheer act of killing does not create a terrorist act: murders and willful assaults occur with such frequency in most societies that they are scarcely reported in the news media. What makes an act terrorism is that someone is terrified by it. The acts to which we assign that label are deliberate events, bombings and attacks performed at such places and times that they are calculated to be observed. Terrorism without its horrified witnesses would be as pointless as a play without an audience.

Perhaps the most enduring image from the tragic bombing of the Oklahoma City Federal Building on April 19, 1995, was the photograph of the bloody, mangled body of an infant carried in the arms of a rescue worker who attempted—futilely, as it turned out—to save the small child's life. Perhaps no other picture could have portrayed as poignantly the pathos of innocence defiled or evoked so strongly the righteous anger of many over what appeared to be a hideous and senseless act. The perpetrators of the bombing were not the photographers of this picture, of course, nor were they the ones who distributed it on the front pages of newspapers around the world. Yet this picture, its wide circulation, and the public revulsion it produced were an intrinsic part of the terrorist event, magnifying its horror far beyond the number of people immediately affected by the blast.

For many who have been involved in plotting terrorist attacks, the ability to seize the attention of the public through the news media is precisely the point. When I asked Mahmud Abouhalima what he felt to be the greatest threat to Islam, he gave a surprising answer: media misrepresentation (Abouhalima). He told me that secularism held a virtual lock on media control and that Islam did not have news sources to present its side of contemporary history. By implication, acts of terrorism such as the one for which he was convicted—the 1993 bombing of the World Trade Center—laid claim to the images and headlines of the world's media, at least for a moment. Abouhalima himself was very media conscious. He carefully read news accounts about himself and his group, indicating which ones he felt were fair (*Time* magazine, for example), and which ones he thought were scurrilous (*New York Times* and *Newsday*, for instance). Abouhalima was particularly incensed over a book written by *Newsday* reporters, *Two Seconds under the World*, in which he was characterized as the master conspirator behind the World Trade Center bombing. On the other hand, he proudly kept in his cell the copy of *Time* magazine in which his picture appeared on the cover and the account of his life was the lead story. In this case, he felt that the facts about him were portrayed fairly and nonjudgmentally.

In my own attempts to interview activists supporting or involved in terrorist acts, I found individuals fairly receptive to meeting with me and telling their stories. My initial contacts with them were through academic colleagues or journalists. Many of them were more open to the possibility of my interviewing them if the contacts came through news media connections. The more international the media network, the better. In Japan, for instance, I was told by officials in Aum Shinrikyo that they would speak with me as long as I was not accompanied by Japanese journalists or scholars. I had the impression that they were concerned not only with objectivity—suggesting that non-Japanese could judge their situation more honestly—but also with the breadth of their audience. In talking with an American scholar they hoped to get their message to the wider world.

Moreover, there was not much more the Japanese media could have discovered about the Aum Shinrikyo movement: the media coverage of the group in Japan was already at saturation level. The March 20, 1995, nerve gas incident marked the beginning of an extraordinary media frenzy that lasted most of that year and much of the next, encompassing hundreds of hours of television time and thousands of articles and books. One of the journalists reporting the story herself became a celebrity as a result of her reportage, and other journalists clamored to interview her. Just as the American public was drawn into the events following the bombing of the U.S. embassies in Africa, the World Trade Center, and the Oklahoma Federal Building, and as the news media of the Middle East have been dominated by the terrorist acts of Muslim and Jewish activists, the Japanese came to look on terrorism as a kind of national drama.

The *New York Times*, in considering whether to publish the Unabomber's 35,000-word manifesto in 1995, agonized over the role that the news media was being coerced into playing, and questioned whether the newspaper's coverage—especially its willingness to publish the bomber's writings—would alleviate terrorism by helping to solve the mystery of the bomber's identity or add to terrorism's suffering by inadvertently encouraging other activists to seek the exposure that the newspaper seemed willing to offer. The publisher of the *Times*, Arthur Sulzberger, Jr., lamented the idea of "turning our pages over to a man who has murdered people." But he added that he was "convinced" that they were "making the right choice between bad options." The fact that the publication of the manifesto eventually led to the identification of Theodore Kaczynski as the bomber by his brother David would seem to vindicate the decision of the *Times* publishers. It brought to an end a seventeen-year string of violence involving sixteen letter bombings that wounded twenty-three and left three others dead. Still, it is unclear whether other activists might have been spurred on by the newspaper's capitulation to a terrorist's media demands. In the case of the visual medium of television, however, there is little that terrorists need to demand, since the highly sensational nature of their activities captures television's attention immediately and completely.

In a collection of essays on contemporary culture, Jean Baudrillard described the terrorism of the late twentieth century as "a peculiarly modern form" because of the impact that it has on public consciousness through electronic media. According to Baudrillard, terrorist acts have emerged "less from passion than from the screen: a violence in the nature of the image" (Baudrillard, 75). Baudrillard went so far as to advise his readers "not to be in a public place where television is operating, considering the high probability that its very presence will precipitate a violent event." His advice was hyperbolic, of course, but it does point to the reality that terrorist events are aimed at attracting news media exposure and perhaps would not happen as frequently, or in the same way, if the enormous resources of the news media were not readily at hand to promote them.

The worldwide media coverage of the attacks on the World Trade Center, the U.S. embassies in Africa, and the Oklahoma City Federal Building illustrates a new development in terrorism: the extraordinary widening of terror's audience. Throughout most of history the audiences for acts of terrorism have been limited largely to government officials and their supporters, or members of rival groups. What makes the terrorism of recent years significant is the breadth of its audience, a scope that is in many cases virtually global.

When television does not adequately report the ideas and motivations behind their actions, many activist groups have found the Internet and the World Wide Web to be effective alternatives. Movements such as Hamas and Aryan Nations have well-established Web sites. An anti-abortion site, "The Nuremberg Files," which advocated the killing of abortion clinic doctors and maintained a list of potential targets, was removed by its Internet service provider in February 1999, after a red line was drawn through the name of Dr. Barnett Slepian on the day after he was killed by an assassin. The creator of the site, Neal Horsley, said that the move was "a temporary setback" and vowed to return to the World Wide Web. Other groups, including Christian Identity and militia activists, have protected their sites with passwords that allow only their members to gain access. Thus, even when the audience is selective, the message has been projected through a public medium.

In some cases an act of violence sends two messages at the same time: a broad message aimed at the general public and a specific communication targeted at a narrower audience. In cases of Islamic violence in Palestine and Sikh terrorism in India, for instance, one of the purposes of the assaults was to prove to movement members that the leadership was still strong enough to engender the life-and-death dedication of their commandos. In other cases, the point was to intimidate followers of the movement and to force them to follow a hard-line position rather than a conciliatory one. In the case of

Andres Brievik, his manifesto was aimed at an imagined community of supporters who shared his vision of violently defending Christendom against the forces of multiculturalism.

Motives such as these help to explain one of the most puzzling forms of contemporary violence: silent terror. These intriguing acts of terrorism are ones in which the audience is not immediately apparent. The public is often mystified by an explosion accompanied only by an eerie silence, with no group claiming responsibility or explaining the purpose of its act. As days passed after bombs ripped through the American embassies in Kenya and Tanzania on August 7, 1998, and no person or group took credit for the actions, questions arose as to why no group had owned up to the attacks in order to publicize its cause. Similarly, no one, including members of Osama bin Ladin's al Qaida network, claimed responsibility for the spectacular assault on September 11, 2001. If one assumes that the attack was conducted, in part, to advertise the group's cause, why would members of the group not take credit for it?

This question has also been posed after other, similarly unexplained terrorist events. The 1985 bombing of the Air India jetliner, the 1994 truck bomb that destroyed a Jewish center in Buenos Aires, and the 1996 explosion of a U.S. military housing complex in Dhahran, Saudi Arabia, were all followed with silence. In cases where the anonymous perpetrators have been identified, such as the Pan Am 103 bombing over Lockerbie, Scotland, in which Libyan government officials were accused, acknowledgment of the crime by the perpetrators still has not been forthcoming.

Even in the cases where the accused were brought to trial and convicted—such as the 1993 World Trade Center assault, the Oklahoma City bombing, and the Tokyo subway attack—the guilty have still denied their complicity. Mahmud Abouhalima, even after being convicted of participation in the World Trade Center bombing, told me that he was "nowhere near" the building at the time of the blast and that he had no relationship with Sheik Omar Abdul Rahman, the spiritual leader of the group convicted of the bombing (Abouhalima). Assuming for the moment that the government case against him was strong and that he was in fact involved in the crime for which he was convicted, why would he or any other activist involved in a violent incident deny it?

When he discussed the Oklahoma City bombing, Abouhalima said that it made no difference who the perpetrators of that event were, as long as the event made the point that the American government was an enemy. This was significant, Abouhalima said, since one of the things that frustrated him was the American public's complacency, its inability to recognize that great struggles were going on in the world, and its denial that the U.S. government was deeply involved in them. Bombing a public building demonstrated the reality of that hidden war. Since terrorism is theater, the catastrophes at the

World Trade Center, the Oklahoma City Federal Building, and the U.S. embassies in Africa broadcast that message to the world. From the point of view of the perpetrators, this was enough; the message was successfully sent, and they did not need to brag about their ability to convey it.

In a world in which information is a form of power, public demonstrations of violence have conveyed potent messages indeed. When groups are able to demonstrate their capacity for destruction simultaneously in different parts of the world, as in the case of the U.S. embassy bombings in 1998, this is an even more impressive display than single-target events. It is no less so if the only audiences who know who did it, who can appreciate the perpetrators' accomplishment, and who can admire their command over life and death are within the group itself. The act demonstrates their ability to perform a powerful event with virtually global impact.

The forms of religious terrorism that have emerged in the last decade of the twentieth century have been global in at least two senses. Both the choices of their targets and the character of their conspiratorial networks have often been transnational. The very name of the World Trade Center indicates its role in transnational global commerce, and citizens of eighty-six different countries were among its victims. The members of the al Qaida network of perpetrators of these and other attacks were multinational—ethnically originating in Saudi Arabia, Egypt, Sudan, Afghanistan, Pakistan, Algeria, and elsewhere—and they plotted their attacks in such diverse locales as Germany, Spain, Sudan, Morocco, and the United States. These incidents have also been global in their impact, in large part because of the worldwide, instantaneous coverage by transnational news media. This has been terrorism meant not just for television but for CNN. In the case of the al Qaida attacks on the World Trade Center and elsewhere, these have also been events meant for al Jezeera television, the news station in Qatar that broadcasts throughout the Middle East.

Increasingly, terrorism has been performed for a television audience around the world. This means that a single individual—a "lone wolf" terrorist—can make as much of a public spectacle as an organized cadre. Thus Andres Breivik, Timothy McVeigh, and the Tsarnaev brothers were able to accomplish an impact on public life that few organized movements have been able to do. Yet their actions were intended for a hidden audience of their imagined admirers as much as they were for the supporters of the status quo. In this peculiar way, therefore, lone acts of terrorism have been collective events, events that have drawn people together by the power of performance.

This global dimension of terrorism's audience, and the transnational responses to it, gives special significance to the understanding of terrorism as a public performance of violence—as a social event with both real and symbolic aspects. As Bourdieu has observed, our public life is shaped as much by symbols as by institutions. For this reason, symbolic acts—the "rites of institution"—help to demarcate public space and indicate what is meaningful in the social world (Bourdieu, 117). In a striking imitation of such rites, terrorism has provided its own dramatic events—whether by organized movements or by lone individuals who imagine themeselves as part of a larger group. These rites of violence have brought an alternative view of public reality—not just a single society in transition, but a world challenged by strident visions of transforming change.

## REFERENCES

Abouhalima, Mahmud. 1997. Convicted co-conspirator of World Trade Center Bombing, 1993. Interview with the author, Lompoc Federal Penitentiary, September 30, 1997.

Austin, J. L. 1962. *How to Do Things With Words.* Oxford: Clarendon Press.

Baudrillard, Jean. 1993. *The Transparency of Evil.* London: Verso.

Bourdieu, Pierre. 1991. *Language and Symbolic Power.* Cambridge, MA: Harvard University Press.

Crenshaw, Martha. 1990. "The Logic of Terrorism: Terrorist Behavior as Strategic Choice." In Walter Reich, ed., *Origins of Terrorism.* Cambridge UK: Cambridge University Press and Woodrow Wilson Center Press.

DeLillo, Don. 1991. *Mao II.* New York: Penguin.

Juergensmeyer, Mark. 2003. *Terror in the Mind of God.* Berkeley: University of California Press.

Laqueur, Walter. 1987. *The Age of Terrorism.* Boston: Little, Brown.

Rantisi, Abdul Aziz. 1998. Political head of Hamas. Interview with the author, Khan Yunis, Gaza, March 2, 1998.

Rapoport, David. 1982. "Introduction." In David Rapoport and Yonah Alexander, eds., *The Morality of Terrorism.* New York: Pergamon Press.

*II*

# The Victims of Group Violence

*Chapter Eight*

# Gender, Weight, and Inequality Associated with School Bullying

Anthony A. Peguero and Lindsay Kahle

The social problem of bullying among youth is gaining increasing attention because of long-lasting detrimental consequences for health, educational, and well-being outcomes for bullying victims and offenders. In turn, routine activity and lifestyle theories are often utilized to understand the correlates associated with school bullying. Within school bullying research and this theoretical framework, physical characteristics (i.e., gender and weight) are important factors toward understanding school bullying. Although limited research has established weight in relationship to being bullied, little is known about how the intersection of gender and weight are characteristics contributing to bullying victimization and perpetration. This study utilizes the 2005/2006 Health Behavior in School-Aged Children (HBSC) data to investigate how gender and weight may contribute to bullying victimization and perpetration within U.S. schools. Drawing from the 2005/2006 HBSC sample that consists of 7,143 youth, findings indeed indicate that the intersection of gender and weight are associated with bullying victimization and perpetration at school. This study discusses the importance of understanding how gender and weight are relevant in school bullying.

Routine activity and lifestyle are often utilized in criminological theories to explain patterns in youth violence. The theories' main theses are that in order for violence to occur, the convergence of a motivated offender, lack of a capable guardian, and a suitable target, as well as individual behavior and lifestyle contribute to his or her experiences with youth violence (Cohen and Felson 1979; Cohen, Kluegel, and Land 1981; Hindelang, Gottfredson, and Garofalo 1978). Although there has been an abundance of research investigating, testing, and confirming the routine activity and lifestyle hypotheses predicting youth violence, Finkelhor and Asdigian (1996) began an inquiry that questioned the conceptualization of individuals being a "suitable target." Finkelhor and Asdigian (1996) argued the factors that contribute to making an individual a suitable target for violence and the motivation for offending are complex, especially for youth. In light of the growing educational and social concern about school bullying, there is a growing amount of research investigating the correlates that contribute to school bullying.

Bullying is a serious problem within the U.S. school system and is receiving increasing attention. This problem is more than simple teasing or just "kids being kids." Although some teachers, educational policymakers, school administrators, parents, and community stakeholders sometimes refer to school bullying as "minor" infractions, this is not intended to minimize the magnitude or the effects of these experiences. It is evident that there are serious and lifelong consequences from being bullied at school; victims often suffer from lower self-esteem, chronic absenteeism, school avoidance, feeling unsafe and insecure in the school setting. Bullying derails educational progress and success, and in rare situations even leads to suicide (Espelage and Swearer 2010; Finkelhor 2008; Olweus 1993). Bullying is particularly problematic because schools are institutions of socialization (Espelage and Swearer 2010; Finkelhor 2008; Olweus 1993); therefore, understanding and addressing bullying that occurs in schools is essential for establishing a safe and healthy learning environment for all youth (Espelage and Swearer 2010; Olweus 1993; Muschert and Peguero 2010; Muschert, Henry, Bracy, and Peguero 2013). Although research demonstrates that physical characteristics (e.g., gender and weight) conditionally determine the likelihood of being bullied at school, it remains unknown if the intersection of gender and weight contributes to school bullying.

This research seeks to determine if the intersection of gender and weight contributes to school bullying victimization and perpetration. First, a conceptual argument that depicts the importance of gender and weight in the relationship between routine activity, lifestyle, and school bullying will be presented. Next, data from a nationally representative sample of students aged eleven to seventeen years ($N = 7,143$) who participated in the 2005/2006 Health Behaviors in School-Aged Children (HBSC) survey were utilized for this research that explores the question of whether the intersection of gender and weight are physical characteristics that contribute to school bullying. Findings indicate, in general, that the intersection of gender and weight indeed moderates the relationship between routine activity, lifestyle, and bullying and youth violence; however, there are important nuances presented and examined. Finally, this study discusses the implications for future youth violence research and policy implementation that focuses on addressing inequality and school bullying.

## ROUTINE ACTIVITY, LIFESTYLE, AND THE SIGNIFICANCE OF GENDER AND WEIGHT

Routine activity and lifestyle theories propose that individual violence stems from the recurrent and prevalent activities that individuals are involved in their daily lives (Cohen and Felson 1979; Hindelang, Gottfredson, and Garofalo 1978; Felson 1986; 1998). It is an individual's routine activity and lifestyle that influences his or her experiences with violence (Cohen and Felson 1979; Hindelang, Gottfredson, and Garofalo 1978; Felson 1986; 1998). Routine activity and lifestyle theories suggest that key spatial and temporal elements must be present for violence to occur: a motivated offender, in the absence of a capable guardian, and with a suitable victim as well as involvement in particular group or social activities that may contribute to an individual's experiences with violence. Hence, the presence of any one of these factors increases the likelihood of violence to occur. It is also apparent, however, that demographics are also important characteristics in the relationship between routine activity, lifestyle, and violence. Cohen, Kluegel, and Land (1981) also stressed the importance of "socio-demographic characteristics, because the resulting lifestyle similarity is likely to bring potential offenders and potential victims into direct contact more often than when such characteristics are not shared" (509). Because socio-demographic characteristics are an important aspect of routine activity and lifestyle for youth, examining whether gender and weight moderate the relationship between routine activity, lifestyle, and violence is reasonable. Indeed, research has demonstrated that gender and weight may matter for the link between routine activity, lifestyle, and violence.

For males and females, routine activity and lifestyle reflect the differences in cultural expectations, gender-specific, and gender group collective experience within society (Dugan and Apel 2003; Popp and Peguero 2011; Wilcox, Tillyer, and Fisher 2009). Gender plays a major role in the routine activity and lifestyle of an individual and risk of violence. Jensen and Brownfield (1986) critique routine activity and lifestyle theories research for its failure to address gender, "the most persistent and prominent correlate of victimization" (88). Jensen and Brownfield (1986) found that gender is strongly associated with different types of experiences of violence. Thus, routine activity and lifestyle researchers acknowledge that gender matters in the victim's experiences with violence (Dugan and Apel 2003; Hindelang, Gottfredson, and Garofalo 1978; Miethe and Meier 1994). It is also argued that physical characteristics may also be linked to the gender disparities between routine activity, lifestyle, and violence.

Finkelhor and Asdigian (1996) argue that personal traits put individuals at risk, not necessarily through any routine activity or lifestyle mechanism, but by congruent needs, motives, or re-activities with potential offenders. Finkelhor and Asdigian (1996) suggest that physical characteristics such as gender and weight can contribute to a potential target's experiences with violence. For instance, Finkelhor and Asdigian (1996) categorize three ways in which physical characteristics can matter in the relationship between routine activity, lifestyle, and violence: *target vulnerability* (e.g., physical weakness or psychological distress), *target gratifiability* (e.g., female gender for the crime of sexual assault), or *target antagonism* (e.g., behaviors or ethnic or group identities that may spark hostility or resentment). Therefore, individual physical characteristics, such as gender and weight, can moderate the link between routine activity, lifestyle, and youth violence. Building on the Finkelhor and Asdigian (1996) work, Augustine, Wilcox, Ousey, and Clayton (2002) argued gender is a risk factor because it is a proxy for physical characteristics such as size and strength. Therefore, gender is related to being a suitable victim, and females are more vulnerable to victimization because of their size and strength and independent of their routine activities and level of guardianship (Augustine et al. 2002).

Within a routine activity and lifestyle approach, there is a symbiotic relationship between victimization and offending. Routine activity and lifestyle theorists argue that once youth participate in deviance, this behavior increases the exposure to situations that are primed for victimization (Mustaine and Tewksbury 1998; Schreck, Fisher, and Miller 2004; Schreck, Wright, and Miller 2002). Deviant youth are often victimized because their relationships as well as their routines and activities involve interacting with other delinquents and adult criminals (Mustaine and Tewksbury 1998; Schreck, Fisher, and Miller 2004; Schreck, Wright, and Miller 2002). Furthermore, as youth become more involved in a deviant lifestyle, the line between offender and victim becomes difficult to distinguish. It is also apparent that researchers have highlighted gender distinctions in this victim/offender overlap. Henson and colleagues (2010) did find that gender moderated the link between deviance and victimization. They argue that females appear less vulnerable to victimization because they are less likely to be exposed to and involved in delinquency as part of their routine activities. At this point, it appears that the links between routine activity, lifestyle, and adolescent violence and victimization can be moderated by gender and physical characteristics. What remains unclear is if these relationships are mirrored in school bullying.

## SCHOOL BULLYING, ROUTINE ACTIVITY, LIFESTYLE AND THE SIGNIFICANCE OF GENDER AND WEIGHT

Because there has been an increasing focus on ameliorating violence and bullying since the 1999 Columbine shootings (Muschert and Peguero 2010; Muschert et al. 2013), a number of theoretical paradigms have been utilized to understand the factors associated with violence and bullying at school. Routine activity and lifestyles theories have often guided research on violence and bullying at school. Researchers have argued that applying routine activity and lifestyle theories to research youth violence and bullying at school is appropriate because, as in communities, school participants (i.e., students, faculty, staff, and administrators) engage in common activities and symbiotic interactions that influence one another and connect all school participants (Nofziger 2009; Schreck, Miller, and Gibson 2003; Tillyer, Wilcox, and Gialopsos 2010). According to the researchers who have applied routine activity and lifestyle theories within a school setting, a student's experiences with violence are determined by his or her routines and behavioral patterns.

It is also known that gender matters in the relationship between routine activity, lifestyle, and youth violence and bullying that occurs within schools. Although both boys and girls must attend school, this does not make schools gender neutral places. In fact, there is substantial research to suggest that schools reinforce traditional gender roles and gender differences in terms of the likelihood and types of violence and bullying youth experience while at school (Popp and Peguero 2011; Tillyer, Wilcox, and Gialopsos 2010; Wilcox, Tillyer, and Fisher 2009; Young, Boye, and Nelson 2006). In essence, because researchers argue that the educational treatment and experiences, interpersonal relationships and friendships, routines and activities, and engagement in deviance between girls and boys are significantly distinct, it is logical that the links between routine activity and lifestyle theories with school violence and bullying would also differ by gender (Popp and Peguero 2011; Tillyer, Wilcox, and Gialopsos 2010; Wilcox, Tillyer, and Fisher 2009). Research has also highlighted gender distinctions in the relationship between physical characteristics, violence, and bullying at school.

As noted, from a routine activity perspective, physical characteristics matter in terms of a "suitable target." There is evidence that indicates that being overweight can contribute to being bullied at school. Schwimmer, Burwinkle, and Varni (2003) argue that obesity is considered to be "one of the most stigmatizing and least socially acceptable conditions in childhood" (1818). Youth who are overweight or obese are at an increased risk for being stigmatized for their weight. A number of studies have shown a positive relationship between weight and bullying victimization for youth at school (Farhat, Iannotti, and Simons-Morton 2010; Griffiths et al., 2006; Schwimmer, Burwinkle, and Varni 2003; Taylor 2011). Moreover, some have also indicated that even after controlling for race/ethnicity, socioeconomic status, social skills, and academic achievement, being overweight or obese is a strong predictor for bullying (Farhat, Iannotti, and Simons-Morton 2010; Griffiths et al. 2006; Schwimmer, Burwinkle, and Varni 2003; Taylor 2011). As for gender distinctions, Taylor (2011) reports that overweight girls were most frequently teased and bullied. Although prior research denotes that girls' bullying victimization is often indirect or verbal while boys' bullying victimization is often direct or physical as well as being intragender (Espelage and Swearer 2010; Finkelhor 2008; Young, Boye, and Nelson 2006), Taylor (2011) finds that overweight girls experience increased indirect and direct bullying from boys and girls. Although it appears that being overweight or obese is linked to increased odds of being bullied at school, the role of being underweight to victimization, as well as how weight is linked to being a bullying perpetrator, by gender remain uncertain.

## Current Study

The Centers for Disease Control and Prevention stresses that violence and bullying at school is a top public health concern because of the harmful effects on youth. School violence and bullying are known to have detrimental consequences on physical health, emotional well-being, and educational progress (Espelage and Swearer 2010; Finkelhor 2008; Olweus 1993). Bullying, specifically, within U.S. schools is a growing concern among parents, school officials, and policymakers. In early 2011, the first-ever White House Conference on Bullying Prevention was held in hope of addressing bullying within U.S. schools. Although the social, political, and media attention is increasing, it is important to consider the complexities and disparities associated with school bullying. Thus, this study draws from routine activity and lifestyle frameworks to explore the intersection of gender and weight in relationship to the occurrence of bullying.

In terms of examining the significance of the intersection of gender and weight with the relationship between routine activity, lifestyle, and bullying, there are three primary questions that this study seeks to explore. First, does the intersection of gender and weight moderate bullying victimization? Second, does the intersection of gender and weight moderate bullying perpetration? Third, does the intersection of gender and weight moderate the distinct types of bullying victimization and perpetration? In sum, using a nationally representative sample of 7,143 students from the 2005/2006 Health Behavior in School-Aged Children (HBSC), this research explores the role that the intersection of gender and weight has on being a suitable target or motivated perpetrator for bullying at school. This study extends the previous research by (a) confirming routine activity and lifestyle theories, (b) confirming the importance of the intersection of gender and weights in understanding bullying, and (c) exploring if the intersection of gender and weight matters in the different types of bullying.

METHOD

## Data

The U.S. 2005/2006 Health Behavior in School-Aged Children (HBSC) survey is conducted every four years on a nationally representative, school-based sample. The survey is part of a collaboration between more than forty countries coordinated by the World Health Organization. More information on methods and procedures can be found at www.hbsc.org. A three-stage stratified clustered sampling, with classes as the sampling units, was used to select a nationally representative sample of students in grades six through ten during the 2005/2006 school year. Racial/ethnic minority students were oversampled to provide better population estimates. Data were collected through self-report questionnaires distributed in the classrooms; respondents' anonymity was ensured throughout the data collection process. The sample for these analyses included 3,464 male and 3,679 female public school students.

## Bullying: Victimization and Perpetration

Experiences in bullying were measured by two questions asking the frequency with which respondents bullied others or were bullied at school in the past couple of months. Response items ranged from *I haven't been bullied (or I haven't bullied another student) at school the past couple of months* to *several times a week*. As measured in other HSBC bullying research (Farhat, Iannotti, and Simons-Morton 2010; Luk, Wang, and Simons-Morton 2010; Wang, Iannotti, and Luk 2010), school bullying is operationalized as two distinct types: victimization and perpetration. To measure these, students were asked to specify if they have been exposed to these forms of school bullying in the past couple of months: (1) I was called mean names, was made fun of, or teased in a hurtful way; (2) other students left me out of things on purpose, excluded me from their group of friends, or completely ignored me; (3) I was hit, kicked, pushed, shoved around, or locked indoors; (4) other students told lies or spread false rumors about me and tried to make others dislike me; (5) I was bullied with mean names and comments about my race or color; (6) I was bullied with mean names and comments about my religion; (7) other students made sexual jokes, comments, or gestures to me; (8) I was bullied using a computer or e-mail messages or pictures; and, (9) I was bullied using a cell phone. For school bullying perpetration, students were asked to specify if they have engaged in these forms of school bullying in the past couple of months: (1) I called another student(s) mean names, made fun of, or teased him or her in a hurtful way; (2) I kept another student(s) out of things on purpose, excluded him or her from my group of friends, or completely ignored him or her; (3) I hit, kicked, pushed, shoved around, or locked another student(s) indoors; (4) I spread false rumors about another student(s) and tried to make others dislike him or her; (5) I bullied another student(s) with mean names and comments about his or her race or color; (6) I bullied another student(s) with mean names and comments about his or her religion; (7) I made sexual jokes, comments, or gestures to another student(s); (8) I bullied another student(s) using a computer or e-mail messages or pictures; and, (9) I bullied another student(s) using a cell phone. Each of the measurements of school bullying (i.e., victim and perpetrator) are dichotomized to indicate whether or not the student experienced or engaged in bullying at school. A scale was then constructed adding each form of bullying that resulted in a measure that ranged from 0–9 for bullying victimization and perpetration.

Gender is coded male or female based on the student's self-report of their biological sex. Male students serve as the reference group.

Body mass index (BMI) was computed from youths' self-reported height and weight, which HSBC studies (Farhat, Iannotti, and Simons-Morton 2010; Mikolajczyk, Iannotti, Farhat, and Thomas 2012; Al Sabbah et al. 2009) have shown to be adequate estimates for actual height and weight. For each gender, the BMI-for-age percentiles were derived using the CDC 2000 growth chart. In addition, BMI-for-age weight status categories and the corresponding percentiles were as follows: (1) underweight indicates that the student is in the less than fifth percentile; (2) healthy weight indicates the student is in between the fifth and eighty-fifth percentile; (3) at risk of overweight indicates the student is in between the eighty-fith and ninety-fifth percentile; or, (4) overweight indicates the student is in the greater than ninety-fifth percentile. Students who are in the healthy weight category serve as the reference group.

Students self-reported their age at the time of the survey, which ranged from eleven to seventeen. As measured in previous HSBC research (Mikolajczyk et al. 2012; Wang, Iannotti, and Luk 2010), academic adjustment was measured by two items, with four response options for each: (1) in your opinion, what does your class teacher(s) think about your school performance compared to your classmates'? The response options ranged from "below average" to "very good"; and, (2) how do you feel about school at present? The response options ranged from "I don't like it at all" to "I like it a lot." Thus, the academic adjustment scale ranged from 0–6.

As measured in previous HSBC research (Danielsen, Wiium, Wilhelmsen, and Wold 2010; Wang, Iannotti, and Luk 2010), students were asked about their perceptions of their classmates' support with three items: (1) most of the students in my classes are kind and helpful; (2) other students accept me as I am; and, (3) the students in my class(es) enjoy being together. Response options ranged from strongly disagree (0) to strongly agree (4). Thus, the perceived classmate support scale ranged from 0–12.

As measured in previous HSBC research (Currie et al. 2008; Farhat, Iannotti, and Simons-Morton 2010; Wang, Iannotti, and Luk 2010), the family affluence scale was developed especially for the HBSC, as the proxy for socioeconomic status. It consists of four items assessing family material wealth (i.e., having own bedroom, number of times on a traveling vacation in a year, number of home computers, and number of cars owned). This scale has been shown to have desirable reliability and validity. The four items were combined to produce a linear composite score, with a range from 0 (lowest affluence) to 9 (highest affluence).

Students self-reported their race/ethnicity; five racial/ethnic groups were considered: African American, Latino/a American, Asian American, other race/ethnicity American, and White American (the reference category).

## Analysis Strategy

Because HBSC is designed as a cluster sample in which schools are sampled with unequal probability and then students are sampled or "nested" within these selected schools, the subsample of the HBSC data violates the assumption of independent observations. Stata offers procedures designed to control for the nesting of observations within aggregate units and formulated specifically for design-based survey analysis. This study accounts for this non-independence by using survey estimation techniques. These survey estimators effectively adjust for clustering of observations within schools. As presented in table 8.1, because the dependent variables, bullying victimization and perpetration, is skewed and violates the normality assumption underlying the linear model with a mean of 1.61 for boys and 1.75 for girls in a nine-point index, it is appropriate to estimate an overdispersed Poisson-based regression modeling. This analytical approach recognizes that individuals within a particular school may be more similar to one another than individuals in another school and, therefore, may not provide independent observations. Poisson-based regression models the log of the expected count as a function of the predictor variables, thus for a one-unit change in the predictor or independent variable, the difference in the logs of expected counts is expected to change by the respective regression coefficient with the other predictor/independent variables in the model held constant (Long 1997).

Table 8.2 presents the Poisson-based regression modeling results of the relationships and interactions between routine activity, lifestyle, gender, BMI, other pertinent student factors, and school bullying victimization. In the baseline model of table 8.2, bullying victimization is regressed on the categories of BMI (i.e., being underweight, at risk of being overweight, and being overweight) with healthy weight youth as the reference. In model 2, gender and other student characteristics controlled for in this study are then included in the analysis.

In model 3, the interaction of BMI and gender are considered in relationship to school bullying victimization. Similar analyses are presented in table 8.3, respectively, for school bullying perpetration. Table 8.4 highlights logistic regression analysis of each classification of bullying victim and perpetrator. Only the significant odds ratios are presented in the table.

## RESULTS

### Descriptive Statistics

As presented in table 8.1, the average level of school bullying for boys is higher than that for girls. It appears that the distinctions between boys and girls experiences with bullying are significant. On average, boys have a 1.61, and girls have a 1.75, rate of bullying victimization on a nine-point scale. On average, boys have a 1.41, and girls have a 1.06, rate of bullying perpetration on a nine-point scale. There are also significant gender distinctions in rela-

| | Range | Boys (N = 3,464) | | Girls (N = 3,679) | | |
|---|---|---|---|---|---|---|
| | | M | SD | M | SD | |
| Bullying | | | | | | |
| Victimization | 0 – 9 | 1.61 | 2.24 | 1.75 | 1.97 | * |
| Perpetration | 0 – 9 | 1.41 | 2.16 | 1.06 | 1.66 | * |
| Body Mass Index | | | | | | |
| Underweight | 0 – 1 | .03 | .17 | .03 | .16 | |
| At Risk | 0 – 1 | .19 | .39 | .17 | .37 | * |
| Overweight | 0 – 1 | .16 | .36 | .12 | .32 | * |
| Healthy | 0 – 1 | .62 | .48 | .68 | .46 | * |
| Student Characteristics | | | | | | |
| Age | 11 – 17 | 13.79 | 1.47 | 13.69 | 1.43 | |
| Academic Adjustment | 0 – 6 | 2.43 | 1.44 | 2.18 | 1.42 | * |
| Perceived Classmate Support | 0 – 12 | 4.37 | 2.50 | 4.54 | 2.49 | * |
| Family Affluence Scale | 0 – 9 | 5.44 | 1.70 | 5.34 | 1.76 | |
| African American | 0 – 1 | .19 | .39 | .21 | .40 | |
| Latino/a American | 0 – 1 | .22 | .43 | .23 | .40 | |
| Asian American | 0 – 1 | .05 | .20 | .04 | .20 | |
| Other Race/Ethnicity American | 0 – 1 | .12 | .33 | .13 | .33 | |
| White American | 0 – 1 | .42 | .45 | .42 | .45 | |

\* $p \leq .05$

*Notes:* Significant differences between males and females are denoted with asterisks. Significance tests are based on chi-square tests (for dummy variables) and Welch's *t*-tests (for continuous variables), and verified with nonparametric Wilcoxon-Mann-Whitney tests.

**Table 8.1. Descriptive Statistics for Study Variables by Gender.**

tionship to BMI. Boys are more at risk of being overweight (*M* = .19, *SD* = .39) and being overweight (*M* = .16, *SD* = .36) than their female counterparts. On the other hand, girls are at healthier weights (*M* = .68, *SD* = .46) than their male counterparts. Academic adjustment and perceived classmate support are the other student characteristics that are significantly distinct between boys and girls in this study. Boys report having higher levels of academic adjustment (*M* = 2.43, *SD* = 1.43) than girls (*M* = 2.18, *SD* = 1.42) on a six-point scale. Boys report having lower levels of perceived classmate support (*M* = 4.37, *SD* = 2.50) than girls (*M* = 4.54, *SD* = 2.49) on a twelve-point scale.

## Bullying Victimization

Table 8.2 presents the Poisson-based regression analysis of school bullying victimization. The baseline model establishes the role that BMI has with bullying victimization. Youth who are at risk of being overweight ($\beta$ = .101, $p \leq .001$) and who are overweight ($\beta$ = .140, $p \leq .001$) experience increased school bullying.

Model 2 explores the roles of student characteristics on the likelihood of school bullying victimization. At this stage of the analysis, BMI still matters.

| | Model 1 $\beta$ | SE | Model 2 $\beta$ | SE | Model 3 $\beta$ | SE |
|---|---|---|---|---|---|---|
| Body Mass Index | | | | | | |
| Underweight | .065 | .055 | -.010 | .055 | .186 ** | .075 |
| Girls | | | | | -.397 *** | .111 |
| At Risk | .101 *** | .024 | .036 † | .025 | .089 ** | .035 |
| Girls | | | | | -.100 * | .050 |
| Overweight | .140 *** | .027 | .056 * | .027 | .061 * | .038 |
| Girls | | | | | -.004 | .054 |
| Student Characteristics | | | | | | |
| Girls | | | .048 ** | .019 | .080 ** | .024 |
| Age | | | -.087 *** | .006 | -.088 *** | .006 |
| Academic Adjustment | | | .068 *** | .006 | .068 *** | .006 |
| Perceived Classmate Support | | | .108 *** | .003 | .109 *** | .003 |
| Family Affluence Scale | | | .006 | .005 | .006 | .005 |
| African American | | | -.029 | .024 | -.028 | .024 |
| Latina/o American | | | -.001 | .005 | -.001 | .005 |
| Asian American | | | .126 ** | .045 | .124 ** | .045 |
| Other Race/Ethnicity American | | | .053 ** | .022 | .054 ** | .022 |
| Constant | .465 *** | .012 | .415 *** | .118 | .405 *** | .119 |
| R2 | .002 *** | | .051 *** | | .052 *** | |
| Log Likelihood | -13799.609 | | -13100.360 | | -13092.455 | |

† $p \leq .1$; * $p \leq .05$; ** $p \leq .01$; *** $p \leq .001$
The omitted categories are healthy weight youth, males, and White Americans

**Table 8.2. Poisson Regression Coefficients and Standard for Bullying Victimization.**

Youth who are at risk of being overweight ($\beta$ = .036, $p \leq$ .1) and who are overweight ($\beta$ = .056, $p \leq$ .05) experience increased school bullying. While controlling for other factors considered in this study, girls also report increased school bullying victimization ($\beta$ = .048, $p \leq$ .01). For other student characteristics, age, academic adjustment, perceived classmate support, and race/ethnicity are related with the likelihood of school bullying victimization for youth. As students get older, their experiences with bullying decrease ($\beta$ = -.087, $p \leq$ .001). As students' academic adjustment increase, their experiences with bullying increase ($\beta$ = .068, $p \leq$ .001). As students' perceived classmate support increase, their experiences with bullying decrease ($\beta$ = -.108, $p \leq$ .001). Asian American ($\beta$ = .126, $p \leq$ .01) and other race/ethnicity American ($\beta$ = .053, $p \leq$ .01) youth have higher reported incidents of school bullying victimization in comparison to their white American peers. In general, these student characteristics remain consistent throughout the analysis of school bullying victimization.

Interactions between BMI and gender in relation to school bullying victimization are included in the analysis and presented in model 3. At this stage of the analysis, boys who are underweight have increased experiences with being bullied at school ($\beta$ = .186, $p \leq$ .01). On the other hand, girls who are underweight have decreased experiences with being bullied at school ($\beta$ = -.211, $p \leq$ .001). Boys who are at risk of being overweight have increased experiences with being bullied at school ($\beta$ = .089, $p \leq$ .01). Girls who are at risk of being overweight, however, have decreased experiences with being bullied at school ($\beta$ = -.011, $p \leq$ .05). The main effect for boys suggests that being overweight is a risk factor for being bullied at school ($\beta$ = .061, $p \leq$ .05). Because the interaction terms for girls and being overweight are non-significant, this suggests that there is no significant difference from the main effect. In other words, being overweight is also a risk factor for being bullied at school for girls.

## Bullying Perpetration

Table 8.3 presents the Poisson-based regression analysis of school bullying perpetration. The baseline model 4 establishes the role that BMI has with bullying perpetration. Youth who are underweight ($\beta$ = -.212, $p \leq$ .01) have fewer incidences of being a bully at school. Youth who are at risk of being overweight ($\beta$ = .128, $p \leq$ .001) and who are overweight ($\beta$ = .129, $p \leq$ .001) have more incidences of being a bully at school.

Model 5 explores the roles of student characteristics on the likelihood of school bullying perpetration. At this stage of the analysis, BMI still matters. Youth who are underweight ($\beta$ = -.202, $p \leq$ .01) have fewer incidences of being a bully at school. Youth who are at risk of being overweight ($\beta$ = .066, $p \leq$ .05) and who are overweight ($\beta$ = .043, $p \leq$ .1) have more incidences of

| | Model 4 | | | Model 5 | | | Model 6 | | |
|---|---|---|---|---|---|---|---|---|---|
| | β | SE | | β | SE | | β | | SE |
| **Body Mass Index** | | | | | | | | | |
| Underweight | -.212 | ** | .073 | -.202 | ** | .073 | -.301 | ** | .101 |
| Girls | | | | | | | .217 | † | .147 |
| | | | | | | | | | |
| At Risk | .128 | *** | .028 | .066 | * | .028 | .078 | * | .038 |
| Girls | | | | | | | -.030 | | .058 |
| | | | | | | | | | |
| Overweight | .129 | *** | .031 | .043 | † | .032 | -.011 | | .042 |
| Girls | | | | | | | .128 | * | .064 |
| | | | | | | | | | |
| **Student Characteristics** | | | | | | | | | |
| Girls | | | | -.248 | *** | .022 | -.266 | *** | .028 |
| Age | | | | -.010 | † | .007 | -.009 | † | .007 |
| Academic Adjustment | | | | .160 | *** | .007 | .160 | *** | .007 |
| Perceived Classmate Support | | | | .048 | *** | .004 | .048 | *** | .004 |
| Family Affluence Scale | | | | .033 | *** | .006 | .033 | *** | .006 |
| African American | | | | .248 | *** | .026 | .246 | *** | .026 |
| Latina/o American | | | | .004 | | .007 | .004 | | .007 |
| Asian American | | | | -.073 | | .059 | -.070 | | .059 |
| Other Race/Ethnicity American | | | | .044 | † | .027 | .046 | † | .027 |
| | | | | | | | | | |
| Constant | .166 | *** | .013 | -1.037 | *** | .140 | .004 | *** | .140 |
| R2 | .002 | *** | | .040 | *** | | .040 | *** | |
| Log Likelihood | -12324.343 | | | -11844.445 | | | -11841.019 | | |

† $p \leq .1$; * $p \leq .05$; ** $p \leq .01$; *** $p \leq .001$
The omitted categories are healthy weight youth, males, and White Americans

**Table 8.3. Poisson Regression Coefficients and Standard for Bullying Perpetrator.**

being a bully at school. While controlling for other factors considered in this study, girls also report decreased school bullying perpetration ($\beta$ = -.248, $p \leq$ .01). For other student characteristics, age, academic adjustment, perceived classmate support, family affluence scale, and race/ethnicity are related with the likelihood of school bullying perpetration for youth. As students get older, their engagement with bullying perpetration decreases ($\beta$ = -.010, $p \leq$ .1). As students' academic adjustment increases, their engagement with bullying perpetration increases ($\beta$ = .160, $p \leq$ .001). As students' perceived classmate support increases, their engagement with bullying perpetration increases ($\beta$ = .048, $p \leq$ .001). As students' family affluence scale increases, their engagement with bullying perpetration increases ($\beta$ = .033, $p \leq$ .001). African American ($\beta$ = .248, $p \leq$ .001) and other race/ethnicity American ($\beta$ = .044, $p \leq$ .1) youth have increased engagement with school bullying perpetration in comparison to their White American peers. In general, these student characteristics remain consistent throughout the analysis of school bullying perpetration.

Interactions between BMI and gender in relation to school bullying perpetration are included in the analysis and presented in model 6. At this stage of the analysis, boys who are underweight have decreased experiences with bullying others at school ($\beta$ = -.301, $p \leq$ .01). On the other hand, girls who are underweight have increased experiences with bullying others at school ($\beta$ = .084, $p \leq$ .1). Boys who are at risk of being overweight have increased experiences with bullying others at school ($\beta$ = .078, $p \leq$ .05). Because the interaction terms for girls who are at risk of being overweight is non-significant, this suggests that there is no significant difference from the main effect. In other words, being at risk of being overweight is also linked to girls bullying others at school. Girls who are overweight have increased experiences with bullying others at school ($\beta$ = .128, $p \leq$ .05).

## Categories of Bullying Victimization and Perpetration

Table 8.4 presents the logistic regression analysis for the distinct types of bullying. For bullying victimization, there are clear gender distinctions between the relationship between BMI and being bullied at school. Only the significant odds ratios for the interaction of BMI and gender with bullying victimization are presented in table 8.4. Underweight girls are 52.3 percent less likely to be called names at school ($p \leq$ .05). Underweight boys are 47.5 percent and overweight girls are 41.4 percent more likely to be excluded by others at school ($p \leq$ .1). Underweight boys are 58.2 percent more likely to be physically attacked at school ($p \leq$ .1). Underweight girls are 61.9 percent less likely to be physically attacked at school ($p \leq$ .05). Boys who are at risk of being overweight are 28.2 percent more likely to have others lie or make slanderous comments about them at school ($p \leq$ .05). Boys who are underweight are twice as likely to be bullied about their race/ethnicity at school ($p \leq$ .05). Girls who are underweight are 88.3 percent less likely to be bullied about their race/ethnicity at school ($p \leq$ .001). Girls who are at risk of being overweight are 29.8 percent less likely to be bullied about their race/ethnicity at school ($p \leq$ .1). Boys who are overweight are 32.7 percent more likely to be bullied about their religion at school ($p \leq$ .1). Boys who are underweight are 80.1 percent more likely to have had others made sexual jokes, comments, or gestures to them at school ($p \leq$ .05). Girls who are underweight are 67.6 percent less likely to have had others made sexual jokes, comments, or gestures to them at school ($p \leq$ .05). Boys who are overweight are 44.2 percent more likely to be bullied via e-mail messages or pictures at school ($p \leq$ .05). Girls who are underweight are 72.3 percent less likely to be bullied via e-mail messages or pictures at school ($p \leq$ .1). Girls who are overweight are 49.4 percent less likely to be bullied via e-mail messages or pictures at school ($p \leq$ .05). Girls who are at risk of being overweight are 37 percent less likely to be bullied via cell phone at school ($p \leq$ .05).

For bullying perpetration, there are clear gender distinctions between the relationship between BMI and bullying others at school. Only the significant odds ratios for the interaction of BMI and gender with bullying perpetration are presented in table 8.4. Overweight boys are 14.9 percent less likely to call

|  | Victimization | | Perpetrator | |
|---|---|---|---|---|
|  | Boys | Girls | Boys | Girls |
| Name Calling |  |  |  |  |
| Underweight | --- | .477 (*) | --- | --- |
| At Risk | --- | --- | --- | --- |
| Overweight | --- | --- | .851 (†) | 1.822 (**) |
| Exclusion |  |  |  |  |
| Underweight | 1.475 (†) | --- | .584 (†) | 2.238 (*) |
| At Risk | --- | --- | --- | .652 (†) |
| Overweight | --- | 1.414 (†) | --- | --- |
| Physical |  |  |  |  |
| Underweight | 1.582 (†) | .381 (*) | --- | --- |
| At Risk | --- | --- | --- | --- |
| Overweight | --- | --- | --- | --- |
| Slander |  |  |  |  |
| Underweight | --- | --- | --- | --- |
| At Risk | 1.282 (*) | --- | 1.421 (†) | .611 (*) |
| Overweight | --- | --- | --- | --- |
| Race/Ethnicity |  |  |  |  |
| Underweight | 2.057 (*) | .117 (***) | --- | --- |
| At Risk | --- | .702 (†) | 1.447 (*) | --- |
| Overweight | --- | --- | --- | --- |
| Religion |  |  |  |  |
| Underweight | --- | --- | --- | --- |
| At Risk | --- | --- | 1.395 (*) | .552 (*) |
| Overweight | 1.327 (†) | --- | 1.420 (†) | --- |
| Sexual Jokes |  |  |  |  |
| Underweight | 1.801 (*) | .424 (*) | .375 (*) | --- |
| At Risk | --- | --- | 1.546 (**) | --- |
| Overweight | --- | --- | --- | --- |
| Computer/Email |  |  |  |  |
| Underweight | --- | .277 (†) | --- | .226 (†) |
| At Risk | --- | --- | 1.760 (**) | --- |
| Overweight | 1.442 (*) | .506 (*) | 1.829 (*) | --- |
| Cell Phone |  |  |  |  |
| Underweight | --- | --- | --- | --- |
| At Risk | --- | .630 (*) | 1.619 (*) | .604 (†) |
| Overweight | --- | --- | 1.699 (†) | .619 (†) |

$†\ p \leq .1;\ *\ p \leq .05;\ **\ p \leq .01;\ ***\ p \leq .001$

**Table 8.4. Logistic Regression Odds Ratio for Bullying Victimization and Perpetrator by Gender.**

others names at school ($p \leq .1$). Overweight girls are 82.2 percent more likely to call others names at school ($p \leq .01$). Underweight boys are 41.6 percent less likely to exclude others at school ($p \leq .1$). Underweight girls are over twice as likely to exclude others at school ($p \leq .05$). Girls who are at risk of being overweight are 34.8 percent less likely to exclude others at school ($p \leq .1$). Boys who are at risk of being overweight are 42.1 percent more likely to lie or make slanderous comments about others at school ($p \leq .1$). Girls who are at risk of being overweight are 38.9 percent more likely to lie or make slanderous comments about others at school ($p \leq .05$). Boys who are at risk of being overweight are 44.7 percent more likely to bully others for their race/ethnicity at school ($p \leq .05$). Boys who are at risk of being overweight are 39.5 percent more likely to bully others about their religion at school ($p \leq .05$). Boys who are overweight are 42 percent more likely to bully others about their religion at school ($p \leq .1$). Girls who are at risk of being overweight are 44.8 percent less likely to bully others about their religion at school ($p \leq .05$). Boys who are underweight are 62.5 percent less likely to have made sexual jokes, comments, or gestures to others at school ($p \leq .05$). Boys who are at risk of being overweight are 54.6 percent more likely to have made sexual jokes, comments, or gestures to others at school ($p \leq .01$). Boys who are at risk of being overweight are 76 percent more likely to bully others via e-mail messages or pictures at school ($p \leq .01$). Boys who are overweight are 82.9 percent more likely to bully others via e-mail messages or pictures at school ($p \leq .05$). Girls who are underweight are 77.4 percent less likely to bully others via e-mail messages or pictures at school ($p \leq .1$). Boys who are at risk of being overweight are 61.9 percent more likely to bully others via cell phone at school ($p \leq .05$). Boys who are overweight are 69.9 percent more likely to bully others via cell phone at school ($p \leq .1$). Girls who are at risk of being overweight are 39.6 percent less likely to bully others via cell phone at school ($p \leq .1$). Girls who are overweight are 38.1 percent less likely to bully others via cell phone at school ($p \leq .1$).

## DISCUSSION

Routine activity and lifestyle theories argue that in order for violence to occur, the convergence of a motivated offender, lack of a capable guardian, and a suitable target, as well as individual behavior and lifestyles contribute to his or her experiences with youth violence. But, what makes youth a "suitable target" for their victimization, or a motivated perpetrator for victimizing others? This study confirms that certain characteristics, like gender and weight, moderate what makes youth a "suitable target" or motivated perpetrator for bullying; therefore, serving as the link between routine activities, lifestyle, and youth violence. The following section discusses this in three primary ways: (1) how the intersection of gender and weight moderate bullying victimization, (2) how the intersection of gender and weight moderate bullying perpetration, and (3) how the intersection of gender and weight moderate the distinct types of bullying victimization and perpetration.

### The Intersection of Gender and Weight and Bullying Victimization

This study finds that girls have higher rates of bullying victimization than their male counterparts, and that students who are overweight or at risk of being overweight experience increased school bullying. These results cannot confirm nor deny that females might be considered more vulnerable to bully victimization "because of their sheer size and strength," as outlined by Augustine and colleagues (2002); however, it joins numerous studies (Farhat, Iannotti, and Simons-Morton 2010; Griffiths et al. 2006; Schwimmer, Burwinkle, and Varni 2003; Taylor 2011), by confirming that overweight youth are at an increased risk of bully victimization at school.

According to Finkelhor and Asdigian certain personal characteristics, appear to increase vulnerability to victimization because certain offenders "are drawn to or react to certain types of victims or certain characteristics in victims" (6). This process, also known as "target congruence" increases the risk of victimization, because the students are considered vulnerable targets. Finkelhor and Asdigian (1996) state that some of the attributes contributing to *target vulnerability* include small size and physical weakness; in which case, a youth's gender or weight affects their capacity to resist or deter their victimization, and thus the youth becomes an easier target. This study extends further, drawing out specific gender distinctions among *target vulnerability*.

While girls report higher prevalence of bullying victimization, how weight is associated with bullying victimization differs by gender. Overall, weight has more effect on increased victimization for boys than it does girls. Boys who are underweight and at risk for being overweight have increased experiences with bullying victimization, while girls who are underweight, and at risk for being overweight have decreased experiences of bullying victimization. This suggests, not only that weight may play a greater role in the victimization of boys, but also draws into question cultural expectations of gender and weight (or body size). Our results are consistent with research suggesting that schools reinforce traditional gender roles and gender differences in terms of the likelihood and types of violence and bullying youth experience while at school (Popp and Peguero 2011; Tillyer, Wilcox, and Gialopsos 2010; Wilcox, Tillyer, and Fisher 2009; Young, Boye, and Nelson 2006). However, it also illustrates that a more complex picture of how weight operates differentially within genders, making youth suitable targets for bully victimization, exists and warrants further investigation.

## The Intersection of Gender and Weight and Bullying Perpetration

Within the routine activity and lifestyles theoretical framework, distinguishing which characteristics contribute to being a "suitable target" bullying victimization is more commonly researched than distinguishing which characteristics contribute to being a motivated offender for bullying perpetration. Few studies have outlined the roles gender and weight play in bullying perpetration, but this study yields significant evidence that physical characteristics, such as gender and weight, also moderate bullying perpetration. Overall, boys are more likely to bully others than their female counterparts. Students who are underweight have fewer incidences of being a bully at school, while students who are at risk of being overweight and overweight, have more incidences of being a bully at school.

Gendered nuances also exist within these findings. When personal characteristics are taken into account, underweight girls actually report more instances of bullying perpetration, while their male counterparts report fewer instances of bullying perpetration. Again, our results allude to the possibility of differences in cultural expectations of gender and weight and how they in turn, moderate a youth's likelihood of being a motivated offender for bullying perpetration. Further research may provide a more in-depth look at the differences in cultural expectations of gender, weight, and bullying perpetration.

While a significant amount of empirical evidence is limited regarding the influence of gender and weight on bullying perpetration, a plausible assumption for the influence of gender and weight on bullying perpetration may be found within routine activity and lifestyle approaches. Within these frameworks, a symbiotic relationship between victimization and offending exists. Routine activity and lifestyle theorists argue that once youth participate in deviance, they are in turn exposed to situations that are primed for victimization (Mustaine and Tewksbury 1998; Schreck, Fisher, and Miller 2004; Schreck, Wright, and Miller 2002). Hence, at this point, the explanation diverges from explaining how certain characteristics contribute to bullying perpetration, and focuses more on how the line between victim and perpetrator becomes more difficult to distinguish the more involved in a deviant lifestyle a youth becomes.

## The Intersection of Gender and Weight and Types of Bullying

When examining the intersection of gender and weight on types of bullying behaviors, this study finds that, overall, boys are more likely to have increased bully victimization and perpetration, than their female counterparts. Types of bully victimization are gendered as well. Prior research finds that girls' bullying victimization is often indirect or verbal while boys' bullying victimization is often direct or physical (Espelage and Swearer 2010; Finkelhor 2008; Young, Boye, and Nelson 2006). This study confirms this finding, because girls are significantly more likely to be excluded from things (indirect bullying) if they are overweight. On the other hand, boys reported increased likelihood of victimization for every type of bullying behavior, except name calling (verbal direct bullying) and being bullied by a cell phone (verbal direct/cyber bullying).

Gender differences also exist among types of bullying perpetration. While boys were actually less likely to call others names if they were overweight, and exclude others and make sexual jokes about others if they were underweight, girls were actually more likely to call others names if they were overweight, and over twice as likely to exclude others if they were considered underweight. These opposite findings between boys and girls lend additional evidence to the possibility of the important role that cultural expectations of gender and weight play in bullying behavior.

This study provides additional support that routine activity, lifestyle, and adolescent violence and victimization can be moderated by gender and physical characteristics, and that these relationships are mirrored in school bullying. This study extends prior research within the routine activity and lifestyle theories frameworks by focusing more directly on specific elements within that framework (i.e., how the intersection of gender and weight moderate what makes youth a "suitable target" and motivated perpetrator).

## LIMITATIONS AND FUTURE DIRECTION

Within this study, it was clear that intersections of weight and gender moderated bullying victimization and perpetration; however, this study is not without any limitations. First, the cross-sectional analysis limited the ability to establish a causal relationship between gender, weight, routine activity, lifestyle, and youth violence at school. Thus, this research could not establish the causal relationship between gender, weight, routine activity, lifestyle, and youth violence at school. Ideally, future research would utilize longitudinal data to develop a causal model linking gender and weight to school bullying victimization and perpetration. Second, qualitative research could better illuminate our understanding of the school factors that influence this study's quantitative examination of routine activity, lifestyle, and youth violence across various school contexts. There are social nuances with friendships, tensions, and conflict across various school contexts—especially when considering gender and weight. Third, future research should investigate how cultural expectations, or socialization, of gender and weight (i.e., feminine and masculine gender roles), influence the likelihood and types of bullying victimization and perpetration. Individual sexuality must also not be overlooked, and be taken into consideration in addition to gender role socialization. Despite the limitations associated with this analysis, this study's findings provide avenues for future research on routine activity, lifestyle, and youth violence across various school contexts.

## CONCLUSION

Bullying is a pervasive problem within the United States and worldwide. Bullying is no longer considered a "minor" infraction, because of the slew of consequences that emerged as a result of bullying behaviors. What is drawn into constant question among parents, researchers, and policymakers alike is: which youth are targeted for bullying victimization and why, and which youth are perpetrating the bullying behavior. This study contributes to a long line of research that addresses this issue. Understanding and addressing bullying that occurs within schools is essential to reducing and eliminating many of the negative effects brought on by these experiences. However, a deeper motive for addressing these issues lies within sheer power relations and how they essentially perpetuate numerous inequalities that are not just limited to adolescent development.

Bullying behaviors represent an asymmetric power relationship (Olweus 1993), in which the student has difficulty defending him or herself to the individual (or individuals) who hold a sense of power or domination over them. It is unhealthy to socialize youth in environments that foster behaviors that reproduce inequalities based on an array of socio-demographic characteristics. Gender and weight are only two of many characteristics (among others like: class, race/ethnicity, sexuality, etc.), that research suggests contribute to bullying behavior. Inequalities embedded in these characteristics are reinforced through bullying behavior and can have lasting, lifelong detrimental impacts. Broadening the scope to recognize that behaviors, like bullying, influence youth by perpetuating inequalities is important. In the long run, policies addressing these issues have both immediate and long-term effects. Research that seeks to understand which characteristics, like gender and weight, contribute to youth violence and bullying is important and must be ongoing in order make progress towards a healthier learning environment for youth, as well as a society as a whole.

## REFERENCES

Al Sabbah, Haleama, Carine A. Vereecken, Frank J. Elgar, Tonja Nansel, Katrin Aasvee, Ziad Abdeen, Kristiina Ojala, Namanjeet Ahluwalia, and Lea Maes. 2009. "Body Weight Dissatisfaction and Communication with Parents Among Adolescents in 24 Countries: International Cross-Sectional Survey." *BioMed Central Public Health* 9: 52–62.

Augustine, M. C., P. Wilcox, G. C. Ousey, and R. R. Clayton. 2002. "Opportunity Theory and Adolescent School-based Victimization." *Violence and Victims* 17: 233–53.

Cohen, L. E., J. R. Kluegel, and K. C. Land. 1981. "Social Inequality and Predatory Criminal Victimization: An Exposition and Test of a Formal Theory." *American Sociological Review*, 46: 505–24.

Cohen, Lawrence E., and Marcus Felson. 1979. "Social Change and Crime Rate Trends." *American Sociological Review* 52: 170–83.

Currie, C., M. Molcho, W. Boyce, B. Holstein, T. Torsheim, and M. Richter. 2008. "Researching Health Inequalities in Adolescents: The Development of the 'Health Behavior in School-Aged Children' (HBSC) Family Affluence Scale." *Social Science and Medicine* 66: 1429–36.

Danielsen, A. G., N. Wiium, B. U. Wilhelmsen, and B. Wold. 2010. "Perceived Support Provided by Teachers and Classmates and Students' Self-reported Academic Initiative." *Journal of School Psychology* 48: 247–67.

Dugan, Laura, and Robert Apel. 2003. "An Exploratory Study of the Violent Victimization of Women: Race/ethnicity and Situational Context." *Criminology* 41: 959–80.

Espelage, D. L., and S. M. Swearer. 2010. *Bullying in North American Schools: A Social–Ecological Perspective on Prevention and Intervention*. New York: Routledge.

Farhat, Tilda, Ronald J. Iannotti, and Bruce Simons-Morton. 2010. "Overweight, Obesity, Youth, and Health-risk Behaviors." *American Journal of Preventive Medicine* 38: 258–67.

Felson, Marcus. 1994. *Crime and Everyday Life: Impact and Implications for Society*. Thousand Oaks, CA: Sage Publishers.

———. 1986. "Linking Criminal Choices, Routine Activities, Informal Control and Criminal Outcomes." In *The Reasoning Criminal*, edited by D. B. Cornish and R. V. Clarke, 119–28. New York: Springer-Verlag.

Finkelhor, David. 2008. *Childhood Victimization: Violence, Crime and Abuse in the Lives of Young People*. Oxford, UK: Oxford University Press.

Finkelhor, David, and Nancy L. Asdigian, 1996. "Risk Factors for Youth Victimization: Beyond a Lifestyles Theoretical Approach." *Violence and Victims* 11: 3–20.

Griffiths, L. J., D. Wolke, A. S. Page, and J. P. Horwood. 2006. "Obesity and Bullying: Different Effects for Boys and Girls." *Archives of Disease in Childhood* 91: 121–25.

Henson, B., P. Wilcox, B. W. Reyns, and F. T. Cullen. 2010. "Gender, Adolescent Lifestyles, and Violent Victimization: Implications for Routine Activity Theory." *Victims and Offenders* 5: 303–28.

Hindelang, M. S., M. Gottfredson, and J. Garofalo. 1978. *Victims of personal crime*. Cambridge, MA: Ballinger Press.

Jensen, G. F., and D. Brownfield. 1986. "Gender, Lifestyles, and Victimization: Beyond Routine Activities." *Violence and Victims* 1: 85–99.

Long, J. S. 1997. *Regression Models for Categorical and Limited Dependent Variables*. Thousand Oaks, CA: Sage.

Luk, Jeremy W., Jing Wang, and Bruce G. Simons-Morton. 2010. "Bullying Victimization and Substance Use Among U.S. Adolescents: Mediation by Depression." *Prevention Science* 11: 355–59.

Miethe, Terance D., and Robert F. Meier. 1994. *Crime and Its Social Context: Toward an Integrated Theory of Offenders, Victims, and Situations*. Albany: State University of New York Press.

Mikolajczyk, Rafael T., Ronald J. Iannotti, Tilda Farhat, and Vijaya Thomas. 2012. "Ethnic Differences in Perceptions of Body Satisfaction and Body Appearance Among U.S. School Children: A Cross-Sectional Study." *BioMed Central Public Health* 12: 425.

Muschert, Glenn W., Stuart Henry, Nicole L. Bracy, and Anthony A. Peguero. 2013. *Responses to School Violence: Confronting the Columbine Effect*. Boulder, CO: Lynne Reinner Publishers.

Muschert, Glenn W., and Anthony A. Peguero. 2010. "The Columbine Effect and School Antiviolence Policy." *Research in Social Problems and Public Policy* 17: 117–48.

Mustaine, Elizabeth E., and Richard A. Tewksbury. 1998. "Predicting Risks of Larceny Theft Victimization: A Routine Activity Analysis Using Refined Lifestyle Measures. *Criminology* 36: 829–58.

Nofziger, Stacey. 2009. "Deviant Lifestyles and Violent Victimization at School." *Journal of Interpersonal Violence* 24: 1494–1517.

Olweus, Dan. 1993. *Bullying at School: What We Know and What We Can Do*. Malden, MA: Wiley-Blackwell Publishing.

Popp, Ann Marie, and Anthony A. Peguero. 2011. "Routine Activities and Victimization at School: The Significance of Gender." *Journal of Interpersonal Violence* 26: 2413–36.

Schreck, Christopher J., Bonnie S. Fisher, and J. Mitchell Miller. 2004. "The Social Context of Violent Victimization: A Study of the Delinquent Peer Effect." *Justice Quarterly* 21: 23–48.

Schreck, C. J., J. M. Miller, and Chris L. Gibson. 2003. "Trouble in the School Yard: A Study of the Risk Factors of Victimization at School. *Crime and Delinquency* 49: 460–84.

Schreck, C. J., Richard A. Wright, and J. Mitchell Miller. 2002. "A Study of Individual and Situational Antecedents of Violent Victimization." *Justice Quarterly* 19: 159–80.

Schwimmer, J. B., T. M. Burwinkle, and J. W. Varni. 2003. "Health-Related Quality of Life of Severely Obese Children and Adolescents. *Journal of the American Medical Association* 289: 1813–19.

Taylor, Nicole L. 2011. "'Guys, She's Humongous!': Gender and Weight-Based Teasing in Adolescence." *Journal of Adolescent Research* 26: 178–99.

Tillyer, Marie S., Pamela Wilcox, and Brooke M. Gialopsos. 2010. "Adolescent School-Based Sexual Victimization: Exploring the Role of Opportunity in a Gender-Specific Multilevel Analysis." *Journal of Criminal Justice* 38: 1071–81.

Wang, J., R. J. Iannotti, and J. W. Luk. 2010. "Peer Victimization and Academic Adjustment Among Early Adolescents: Moderation by Gender and Mediation by Perceived Classmate Support." *Journal of School Health* 81: 386–92.

Wilcox, Pamela, Marie S. Tillyer, and Bonnie S. Fisher. 2009. "Gendered Opportunity? School-Based Adolescent Victimization." *Journal of Research in Crime and Delinquency* 46: 245–69.

Young, Ellie L., America E. Boye, and David A.Nelson. 2006. "Relational Aggression: Understanding, Identifying, and Responding in Schools." *Psychology in the Schools* 43: 297–312.

*Chapter Nine*

# Victims of Online Hate Groups

*American Youth's Exposure to Online Hate Speech*

James Hawdon, Atte Oksanen, and Pekka Räsänen

The Internet revolutionized social relations by providing tools for instantaneous communication and organization. Penetrating every social institution, it has changed virtually everything that requires human communication, from how we do business to how we meet our potential spouses. Since over 90 percent of American teens and young adults regularly going online (Lenhart et al. 2010; also see European Travel Commission 2013), it is important to understand the role of information and communication technologies (ICTs) in their lives. As with most social innovations, ICTs present both opportunities and risks. As a space for open communication, youth use the Internet to develop and maintain friendships and educate themselves about the world (Uslaner 2004; Oksman and Turtiainen 2004; Valkenburg and Peter 2007; Yahoo Finance 2003). However, the Internet also provides youth a gateway to online hate communities (Livingstone et al. 2011; ADL 2001) and a dizzying array of sites containing hateful speech or hateful materials (Foxman and Wolf 2013; ADL 2001). Despite the potential threat these groups and speech acts pose (see Hawdon 2012; Foxman and Wolf 2013; Waldron 2012), we lack critical information about the extent to which America's youth are exposed to them and the consequences of being exposed to hate-filled messages. We aim to address this gap in the literature.

Using data from 1,032 young people between the ages of fifteen and thirty, we investigate the extent to which American youth are exposed to online hate speech and other types of hate material. We also report on specific aspects of the experiences youth have with online hate speech such as the targets of the hate speech, the site or service on which the messages were seen, how the youth found the site, and how disturbing they found the material. Finally, we consider how the exposure to online hate varies by basic demographic characteristics.

We begin by reviewing the literature about online hate groups and hate speech. We discuss the rise of such groups on the Internet and the spread of hate speech on the Web. We then report the results of our survey of youth regarding their exposure to online hate speech. Finally, we discuss the potential threat online hate poses in light of our findings.

## LITERATURE REVIEW

Online hate is spread by both organized groups and by those acting independently. Defining hate groups, hate speech, and hate material is a tricky, sensitive, and complex task (for detailed discussion of this issue, see Blazak 2009; or Wall 2001); however, we use a relatively simple definition that focuses on *the expressed hatred of some collective*. Hate groups are obvious sources of hate speech and hate material; however, individuals maintain many online sites and services that express hate. Given our focus on Web sites, it is extremely difficult to determine the formality of the group maintaining the site. Moreover, given the data used (self-reported exposure to hate speech), much of the material to which the respondents refer is likely not the result of formally organized hate groups. Nevertheless, the sites the respondents visit all express hatred toward some collective; and, we maintain that is the essence of online hate speech: the use of ICT to "advocate violence against, separation from, defamation of, deception about or hostility towards others" (Franklin 2010:2). Those expressing hate—be they members of a group or a lone individual—profess attitudes that devalue others because of their religion, race, ethnicity, gender, sexual orientation, national origin, or some other characteristic that defines a group.

There is a tendency for researchers to discuss "hate speech." While most messages advocating the hatred of some group are formally speech acts (for a discussion and definition of speech acts, see Searle 1969), the multimedia nature of the Internet permits the use of other forms of communication to convey hatred. Visual materials, including artwork, photos, and on-line games can also express derogatory attitudes and norms about some group. We include such "hate material" in the analysis and discussion and use the terms hate speech and hate material interchangeably. While some form of communication may be more effective at conveying hate than others, the issue of effective messaging is beyond the scope of this chapter. For us, any form of communication that conveys the hatred of some collective is hate speech or hate material and therefore appropriate for our study.

## The Spread of Hate Groups and Other Sources of Online Hate

Hate groups began using the Internet in the mid-1990s, almost immediately after it was developed (Amster 2009; Gerstenfeld et al. 2003; Levin 2002). Their main objectives are to recruit and connect like-minded people in support of their cause (Douglas 2007; Douglas et al. 2005; Gerstenfeld et al. 2003; McNamee et al. 2010). Their messages revolve around educating members and the public about their group and cause, promoting association with the group, encouraging participation in affairs related to their cause, invoking the "natural right" of the group, and indicting other groups for causing or perpetuating their group's negative public image (McNamee et al. 2010; also see Duffy 2003). They use a variety of methods to spread their ideology, including Web sites, file archives, blogs, listservers, news groups, Internet relay chats, clubs and groups in Internet communities, online video games, and Web rings (see Amster 2009; Douglas 2007; Franklin 2010).

While online hate groups are as old as the Internet itself, the expansion of social media allowed large numbers of hate groups to establish an online presence. For example, the number of active hate groups operating in the United States increased by 66 percent between 2000 and 2010, and by 2010 there were over one thousand active hate groups online (Potok 2011). The growth of hate groups from the political right has been especially pronounced (Brown 2009; Cooper 2010; Chen et al. 2008; Potok 2011) as there was a substantial increase in rightwing hate group formation and activity after the 2008 election of Barak Obama (see Southern Poverty Law Center 2013). The targets of these groups' hate are most typically blacks, Jews, Muslims, gays, women, and immigrants (Cooper 2010; Gerstenfeld et al. 2003; Tynes 2006). These groups have been pioneers in using the Internet to reframe their groups' image, maintain and disseminate their principles, and educate or reeducate others. They have been relatively successful at recruiting members, and other online hate groups copy their tactics (Amster 2009; Lee and Leets 2002).

Although rightwing hate groups are the most prominent online, the Web offers a place for any brand of extremism. Leftwing hate groups were more active in the United States and Europe in the 1960s and 1970s (Fletcher 2008), and their overall numbers declined beginning in the 1980s (Qi et al. 2010); nevertheless, leftwing hate groups are present and active online. Similar to their rightwing counterparts, these groups—be they eco-terrorist, extreme leftist, radical animal rights, or other groups with violent goals—promote an ideology of hate towards some group with whom they ideologically disagree. U.S. authorities currently consider leftwing hate groups to be a relatively minor, yet potentially significant, threat (Fletcher 2008). Of course, the relative threat of rightwing and leftwing groups could change should the political climate change.

Social media allows online hate groups to be increasingly visible and successful at reaching and recruiting significant numbers of Internet users. For example, Stormfront, thought to be the first hate group with a Web presence, boasts of 159,000 members and is one of the most frequently visited hate groups on the Internet (see Bowman-Grieve 2009; Brown 2009). The Stormfront homepage encourages visitors to "browse our other nine million posts" (www.stormfront.org/forum/). Although based in the United States, it operates in numerous nations and maintains a separate page for children (kids.stormfront.org)—although it has not been updated for some time (see Amster 2009).

In addition to growing membership, Chau and Xu (2007) document that hate groups gained popularity in blogs since the early 2000s, and it is very likely that scholars underestimate their activity because many hate groups remain hidden in the "dark web" that is not indexed by standard search engines (Chen et al. 2008; Fu et al. 2010). Some of this popularity is among youth and young adults. Several studies reveal that hate groups actively, creatively, and effectively recruit young people (Douglas et al. 2005; Lee and Leets 2002; Lennings et al. 2010). Shafer (2002), for example, reports that of 132 Internet hate sites, 4.5 percent target pre-adolescent children with bright colors, animation, and references to popular cartoon characters.

While hate groups seem to be here to stay, these organizations comprise only a fraction of the demeaning messages aimed at various groups on the Internet. Indeed, the number of hate sites on the Internet has grown even more substantially than the number of hate groups. While there were approximately 150 active online hate sites in 1996, by 2009, there were at least 11,500 Web sites, including pages on social networking sites (SNS), discussion forums, and blogs that focus on spreading intolerance, recruiting members, and instructing people on how to commit violence (Cooper 2010). Moreover, technology has made it easy for even amateur hate sites to be attractive, rhetorically sophisticated, and technologically slick.

*Potential Risks of Exposure to Online Hate Material*

Online hate speech is potentially dangerous. First, there is evidence that exposure to online hate speech harms those who experience it (Leets 2001; Leets and Giles 1997; Lee and Leets 2002; Subrahmanyam and Šmahel 2011). Members of the targeted groups can suffer short-term emotional effects such as mood swings, a sense of anger, loneliness, and fear (Tynes et al. 2004; Tynes 2006). Long-term effects of exposure to online hate speech can include reinforcing discrimination against vulnerable groups (Cowan and Mettrick 2002; Foxman and Wolf 2013). Exposure can also lead victims to develop defensive and vigilant attitudes, which can last for months and potentially years (Leets 2002).

Second, research reveals that online communities offer important sources of social identification for youth, and many youth do not distinguish between people they meet online from those they meet offline (Lehdonvirta and Räsänen 2010). Thus, online hate groups can become important socializing agents in the lives of youth. As a result, exposure to online hate speech can encourage youth to perpetuate online hate speech (Foxman and Wolf 2013). Research indicates that children are increasingly posting online hate material (Gerstenfeld et al. 2003; Tynes et al. 2004), and this intergenerational perpetuation of hateful ideologies strengthens hate groups and their causes (Perry 2000; Tynes 2006). Indeed, the Internet promotes the creation of an international extremist community (Burris et al. 2000).

Third, while hate groups and sites do not always advocate violence (see Douglas et al. 2005; Glaser et al. 2002; Gerstenfeld et al. 2003; McNamee et al. 2010; Zickmund 2000), they nevertheless have been linked to violent acts, including acts of mass violence and terror (Daniels 2008; Foxman and Wolf 2013; Kiilakoski and Oksanen 2011; Ybarra et al. 2008). For example, youth who report that many of the Web sites they visit depict real people being violent are five times more likely to report engaging in serious violent behaviors than are their peers who do not visit such Web sites (Ybarra et al. 2008). While exposure to online hate material does not inevitably lead to acting on these ideas, there is reason to believe these forces will increase the likelihood of some people engaging in hate-inspired actions (Hawdon 2012).

It is therefore important to consider the extent to which youth are exposed to hate speech online. It is also important to begin understanding the effects exposure to this speech has on them. Unfortunately, only a few empirical studies address these important questions (e.g., Bossler and Holt 2009; Bossler et al. 2012; Holt and Bossler 2008; Marcum, Higgins, and Ricketts 2010; Marcum, Ricketts, and Higgins 2010; Navarro and Jasinski 2012; Ngo and Paternoster 2011; Pratt et al. 2010; Reyns 2013; van Wilsem 2013a; 2013b). Generally, these studies are theoretically routed in routine activity theory, which argues that victimization occurs when a motivated offender and a suitable target converge in an environment that lacks capable guardianship (Cohen and Felson 1979). There are undoubtedly motivated offenders on the Internet, and unless their parents or guardians intensely supervise youth, the Internet largely lacks capable guardianship. Thus, "suitable targets" will likely be victimized online, and one's lifestyle may determine if one is a suitable target.

In terms of suitable targets, existing studies indicate that a variety of behaviors and demographic characteristics are related to online victimization. For example, individuals whose lifestyles place them in risky online situations have the highest probabilities of exposure to online hate material.

One of the lifestyle activities that would increase exposure to dangerous situations is general technology use. Indeed, general technology use is a predictive factor for almost all technology-based violent experiences and exposures (Ybarra et al. 2011; also see Marcum, Higgins, and Ricketts 2010; Marcum, Ricketts, and Higgins 2010). Similarly, having many online friends should decrease the likelihood of exposure to online hate material since being embedded in a strong social network generally provides protection from victimization, at least in the offline world. In terms of psycho-social characteristics, high levels of sensation seeking or risk taking appear to be positively correlated with accessing hate sites (Slater 2003). Finally, age and being male appear to increase the likelihood of exposure to hate material, while being an ethnic minority appears to be a protective factor against exposure and victimization (Ybarra et al. 2011).

We now turn to our data to begin addressing this gap in our research. Our research is exploratory in nature, but in terms of research questions we aim to document the following:

1. The extent to which American teens and young adults are exposed to online hate speech, images, or other material;
2. The targets of the hate material;
3. The site or service on which the hate material is seen or heard;
4. How they found the site;
5. How disturbing they found the material.

We then offer a basic exploratory analysis relating several demographic characteristics and the youths' online behavior to exposure to hate material.

## METHODS

Our data are from 1,032 youth ages fifteen to thirty. Internet users were recruited from a demographically balanced panel of Americans who voluntarily agreed to participate in research surveys. The panel is administered by Survey Sample International (SSI), and it includes over one million unique member households. Potential panel participants are recruited through random digit dialing, banner ads, and other permission-based techniques. E-mail invitations were sent to a sample of panel members stratified to mirror the U.S. population on age, gender, education level, and income. Our sample quota was calculated to be nationally representative on age and gender and to have appropriate regional coverage.

Demographically balanced online panels are recommended to protect against bias in online surveys because screening can help target respondents and panelists have already agreed to participate in the online surveys and been screened for online activities (Evans and Mathur 2005; Wansink 2001). Moreover, the recruitment and selection processes, the use of pre-panel interviews, and incentives increase the seriousness and validity of those who ultimately become part of the panel (see Wansink 2001). Comparing our sample to Census data (U.S. Census Bureau 2013), it becomes clear that our sample matches the general population of American youth and young adults on key demographic factors. Table 9.1 compares our sample to the general population of fifteen to twenty-nine year olds on several characteristics. As can be seen, the sample is within the expected margin of error of approximately (+/-) 3.2 percent with respect to percent of African American, sex, native born, and educational level. Hispanics are slightly underrepresented (15.1 percent of the sample compared to 18.6 percent of the population); however, this difference is close to the expected margin of error and we do not consider the difference large enough to justify weighting the data. We therefore consider the sample as accurately reflecting the diversity of the American youth population.

## Descriptive Analyses: Exposure to Online Hate

Our primary focus is to determine the extent to which American teens and young adults are exposed to online hate speech. To measure exposure, respondents were asked, "In the past three months, have you seen hateful or degrading writings or speech online, which inappropriately attacked certain groups of people or individuals?" Of the 1,032 surveyed young people, 551 (53.4 percent) responded "yes" to that question. Among those who had been exposed to hate material, 163 (15.8 percent of the total sample, 30.0 percent of those exposed) said they had personally been the target of hateful or degrading online material, and 210 respondents (38.6 percent of those exposed) say they worry about being targeted for hateful or degrading online material.

We also asked those respondents who had seen hate material online to indicate the target of the hateful material. Respondents were given a list of

**Table 9.1.  Sample Comparison with Population.**

|                                  | Sample | Population |
|----------------------------------|--------|-----------|
| Percent Female                   | 50.3   | 51.1      |
| Percent Native Born              | 90.9   | 91.0      |
| Percent African American         | 13.8   | 15.1      |
| Percent Hispanic                 | 15.1   | 18.6      |
| Percent with High School Degree  | 89.4   | 87.1      |

several potential targets and asked to mark all that applied. Table 9.2 reports the percentage of respondents who had seen hate messages about each targeted group. As seen in the table, the hateful material most commonly focused on sexual orientation (60.6 percent) or ethnicity/nationality (60.1 percent); however, respondents also noted that political views (47.9 percent), religious conviction (45.4 percent), gender (43.6 percent) and physical appearance (41.2 percent) were common targets of hate.

Respondents were also asked about the site or Web service on which they saw the hateful or degrading material. Again, respondents were provided a list of several Web sites and asked to indicate all of those on which they saw hateful or degrading material. Table 9.3 reports the percentage of respondents who saw hate material on each site. Not surprising, the most popular sites and services were the most common sources of hate material. Facebook clearly led the way and YouTube was a distant second.

We also asked respondents how they ended up on the Web site on which they most recently saw or heard hateful or degrading material. They were provided with the answers "I deliberately found my way there," "I got the link to the site from a friend or acquaintance," and "I got there by accident." Recall that 482 respondents (46.7 percent) had not been exposed to hate material. Of the 545 who had been exposed and provided valid answers to this question, 200 (36.7 percent of those exposed) ended up on the site deliberately, 117 (21.5 percent) received a link to the site from a friend or

**Table 9.2.   Target of hate content seen by fifteen to thirty-year-olds exposed to hate material (n = 551).**

| Group or Characteristic Targeted for Hate | Number Respondents Seeing Material Targeting Group | Percent Seeing Material |
|---|---|---|
| Sexual Orientation | 334 | 60.6 |
| Ethnicity | 331 | 60.1 |
| Political Views | 264 | 47.9 |
| Religious Conviction/Belief | 250 | 45.4 |
| Gender | 240 | 43.6 |
| Physical Appearance | 227 | 41.2 |
| Terrorism | 120 | 21.8 |
| School Shootings | 117 | 21.2 |
| Misanthropy or General Hatred of People | 97 | 17.6 |
| Physical Disability | 74 | 13.3 |

acquaintance, and 228 (41.8 percent) ended up on the site accidently. Thus, it appears that most youth and young adults are exposed to online hate material by accidentally finding the page.

It is interesting to note that those who saw the material by accident were more likely to consider it to be disturbing. Respondents were asked to rank how disturbing they found the hateful material on a scale from 1 to 5 (1 = not at all disturbing and 5 = extremely disturbing), and 23.2 percent of those seeing the material by accident considered it to be extremely disturbing. By

**Table 9.3.  Social media sites/services where hate material was seen by those exposed to hate material (n = 551).**

| Site or Service | Number of Respondents Seeing Hate Material On Site | Percent Seeing Material On Site |
|---|---|---|
| Facebook | 346 | 62.8 |
| YouTube | 116 | 21.1 |
| General message boards | 106 | 19.2 |
| Tumblr | 78 | 14.2 |
| Blogs | 73 | 13.2 |
| Image boards (e.g., 4chan) | 59 | 10.7 |
| Photo-sharing sites | 36 | 6.5 |
| Newspaper message boards | 35 | 6.4 |
| Online role-playing games | 35 | 6.4 |
| Google+ | 32 | 5.6 |
| Pop-up sites | 31 | 5.6 |
| Home pages | 30 | 5.4 |
| Email | 27 | 4.9 |
| Skype | 25 | 4.5 |
| Anonymous network (e.g., Tor) | 25 | 4.5 |
| Wikipedia | 25 | 4.5 |
| Instant Messangers | 23 | 4.2 |
| Myspace | 12 | 2.2 |
| Mylife | 11 | 2.0 |
| Livejournal | 8 | 1.5 |
| Habbo | 7 | 1.3 |
| Ning | 3 | 0.5 |

comparison, 19.7 percent of those who saw the material through a link provided to them by a friend and 16.5 percent of those who deliberately searched for it said they found the material to be extremely disturbing. Finally, respondents were also asked, "In the past three months, have you produced online material that other people interpreted as hateful or degrading"? Of the 543 respondents who answered the question, 42 (7.7 percent) admitted to producing online hate material.

### Predictive Analysis: Exposure to Online Hate Material

We conduct two predictive analyses. The first predicts if in the past three months respondents saw hateful or degrading writings or speech online, and the second predicts if respondents produced online material that other people interpreted as hateful or degrading. Given the exploratory nature of our research, we began fitting a model with several general demographic factors and variables that others suggest are related to exposure to online hate speech (e.g., Perry 2000; Slater 2003). We investigate if race (white vs. nonwhite), ethnicity (Hispanic or not Hispanic), being native born or not, gender, age (measured continuously), and education (high school degree or less, some college, college degree or more) are related to our variables of interest.

In addition to these demographic factors, we include measures of online activity and if they are risk takers. We measure online activity in two ways. First, respondents were asked how many friends they had on Facebook, the most popular social networking site. Second, respondents were asked about the different social networking sites or applications they used. We created a SNS activity variable by summing the services respondents said they used during the past three months (range 1–21). The variable was dichotomized at the median number of services used (six services): "Passive users" had used one to six and "active users" more than six SNSs or online applications during the past three months. Slightly over 40 percent (43.3 percent) of the sample were passive users, and 57.7 percent were active users. Finally, since high level risk taking appears to be positively correlated with accessing hate sites and engaging in verbal attacks online (Slater 2003), we included a variable that measures risk-taking behavior. Respondents were asked to indicate on a scale from 1 to 10 if they enjoyed taking risks (high scores equal risk takers).

We first fit a model that includes all of the predictor variables, and then we eliminate those that were not statistically significant. Due to space considerations, we present only the trimmed models; however, complete models are available from the authors. Table 9.4 reports the results of the model predicting exposure to online hate material. The effects of the predictors are presented with the odds ratios (OR). We use the odds ratios to compare the relative significance of the independent variables. In addition, we also report standardized linear estimates (B) for each variable.

As for the exposure to online hate material (see table 9.4), the adjusted effects show that all variables except "White" are significantly related to exposure to online hate material. Despite this, however, ethnicity appears to matter, since Hispanic respondents are almost 1.7 times as likely as others to witness online hate material. When examining the other findings, we see that the younger the respondent the more likely he or she is exposed to hate material online. Males and those born in the United States are more likely to be exposed to hate material as compared to females and respondents born outside the country. As predicted, active SNS users are considerably more likely to report exposure to hate material. Compared to passive users, active users are 2.74 times more likely to report being exposed to online hate material. It is noteworthy that the differences between educational categories are relatively strong. The predicted probabilities of witnessing hate material online for those with a college degree are over twice those with only a high school degree. In addition, those with some college background are nearly 1.5 times more likely to report exposure to online material compared to those with a college degree. This model accounts for 15 percent of the total variance in exposure to online hate material.

## DISCUSSION

Online hate material has become a major concern in many Western societies (e.g., Foxman and Wolf 2013; Waldron 2012), yet there are very few studies focused on young people's exposure to hateful or threatening online material. Our study fills this gap with an original survey of American youth ages fifteen to thirty. We explored both exposure to and the creation of hate speech and hate material. We also investigated the targets of hate speech and the sites or services where such material was seen or heard. Our results show that over half of the respondents were exposed to hate speech. Almost half (41.8 percent) of the respondents exposed to such material saw it accidently, and these respondents were the most likely to say they found the material extremely disturbing. Only a small proportion of respondents (7.7 percent) admitted to producing online hate material.

Not surprising, the hate material was most frequently seen on the most popular social networking sites. The hateful material most commonly focused on sexual orientation (60.6 percent) or ethnicity/nationality (60.1 percent); however, respondents also noted that political views (47.9 percent), religious conviction (45.4 percent), gender (43.6 percent), and physical appearance (41.2 percent) were common targets of hate. Our findings, which confirm the findings of other researchers, point to the fact that online hate

|                      | B(SE)          | OR        |
|----------------------|----------------|-----------|
| Age (years)          | -.100 (0.020)  | 0.905***  |
| Male                 | .304 (0.137)   | 1.356*    |
| Born in the U.S.     | .475 (0.236)   | 1.608*    |
| White                | .134 (0.162)   | 1.144     |
| Active SNS-user      | 1.009 (0.137)  | 2.743***  |
| Education (BA)        |               |           |
|     High school    | -.883 (0.197)  | 0.414***  |
|     Some college   | -.400 (0.176)  | 0.670*    |
| Hispanic             | .510 (0.220)   | 1.665*    |
| -2 Log likelihood    | 783.658        | .         |
| Nagelkerke Pseudo $R^2$ | .154        | .         |

*Note:* N = 1,023. *$p \leq .05$ **$p \leq .01$ ***$p \leq .001$
Reference categories: Female, Foreign Born, non-White, Passive SNS-user, College degree or more, and non-Hispanic.

**Table 9.4. Logistic Regression for Exposure to Online Hate Material.**

material comes in many forms and online users can encounter it in a number of ways. It also demonstrates that many young people find this material accidently and, when they do, they find it offensive and disturbing.

Based on our predictive analysis, age, gender, education, national origin, and ethnicity are associated with exposure to hate material online. Specifically, young, relatively educated, males who were born in the United States are the most likely to be exposed. Furthermore, Hispanic respondents were more likely to be exposed to online hate material than were other ethnic groups. Perhaps not surprisingly, those who were active SNS users were significantly more often exposed to hate speech. We found no variation in exposure by the number of online friends the respondents reported having, or the respondents' self-reported risk taking.

It has already been noted in the literature that political views and religious convictions are often targeted for online hate material (see Foxman and Wolf 2013; Cooper 2010). Race, ethnicity, and nationality can provide a similar target for hate speech or other forms of hate-related material, and much of this material relates to broader notions of racism (Brown 2009; Gerstenfeld et al. 2003). Our findings show that hate speech also concerns personal characteristics such as sexual orientation, gender, and physical appearance. These identity-related issues are especially important for impressionable young people using social media to explore and forge their own identities (see Boyd 2007).

Different reports show that the numbers of hate groups have increased online and, with this growth, there is a higher chance of exposing to such material (Cooper 2010; Potok 2011). Our study confirms these findings. Social media has revolutionized social interaction, but it has also made its users more vulnerable to harassment, bullying, and threats. Those willing to share deviant opinions or aggression and hatred towards others find willing partners more easily than before, and they possibly share their opinions openly without hiding their identity. It is notable that in our study the hate material was concentrated on the most popular SNS such as Facebook (62.8 percent) and YouTube (47.9 percent), but much less so on Twitter (21.1 percent), which is also among the most popular and followed social media in the United States.

It is worrisome how high of a proportion of America's youth and young adults are exposed to hate speech. Hate groups are known to use carefully designed strategies to attract young respondents (Lee and Leets 2002; Amster 2009). Social media sites such as Facebook and YouTube provide them tools to disseminate their message. On social media sites, small groups of people may have a highly visible presence. Expression of open hatred towards others may have become more commonplace, and those who practice it are likely to be highly active online.

Our research has important limitations that readers should consider when interpreting our findings. First, we are unsure of the nature of the hate material the respondents report seeing. The question simply asked if they had seen inappropriate hateful or degrading material. While we believe this item is aptly broad enough to capture the various forms of hate speech that floods the Internet, it lacks specificity. That is, we are not sure if this material was meant to be hateful or if the respondent simply interpreted it as such. While the respondents' interpretations of material are obviously important, the intent of the material's author is also important. Our data do not permit us to glean any information about the author of the material.

Second, we do not know the specific type of material that was seen or heard. We cannot say if the respondent read text, saw a video, viewed an image, played a game, or encountered the hateful material in some other way. The manner by which the material is consumed is potentially important, but we are unable to address this issue.

Next, our study was primarily descriptive and there is an obvious need for additional investigations and theorizing. Future researchers need to investigate more fully what leads to variation in exposure to and the production of online hate material. Moreover, researchers need to theorize the nature of online hate. Is it the same as other forms of expression or does new ICT make online hate material a different phenomenon? Finally, our analysis is limited to American youth, and we strongly encourage future scholars to conduct cross-national research.

## CONCLUSION

The Internet revolutionized social interaction, and increasing numbers of youth now spend a considerable amount of time online. While the online world has opened countless opportunities to expand our minds, experiences, and social networks, it also creates new risks and threats. Online hate material is one such threat. Our research contributes to a growing literature about online, or viral, hate. While a number of researchers have documented the growth of hate groups and hate material online, few have tracked if these groups and this material is actually seen, read, or heard. Using a unique sample of young Americans ages fifteen to thirty, we attempt to answer that question. Our results are somewhat shocking as over half of our sample have been exposed to online hate material in the past three months.

As others have noted (e.g., Foxman and Wolf 2013), online hate is difficult to contain. Laws are likely to be ineffective. Not only do producers of online hate material invoke their right to free speech, laws banning viral hate are extremely difficult to enforce. While consideration of the possibilities for containing the spread of Internet hate is beyond the scope of our data and this chapter, our findings about the extent to which youth are exposed to this material should serve as a warning for those who are concerned about the potential threat online hate poses. In addition, our research shows that a minority of youth and young people are also involved in producing online hate material. These people admit to creating and posting hateful messages; it is likely that others in our sample also engaged in these activities but did not admit to it. This finding, too, should serve as a warning. *Hate is a part of the online experience.* While the hateful material these youth are exposed to is in the virtual world, it has real world consequences. As Foxman and Wolf (2013, 37) note about the old nursery rhyme that claims "words can never hurt me," that comforting notion has been "sadly discredited in the Internet age."

While we found that most participants consider the hateful material they saw to be disturbing, and most reactions to extreme acts of hate continue to be overwhelming negative (see, e.g., Lindgren 2011), the possibility of online hate groups to foster intolerance and promote violence should not be ignored. Our research clearly reveals there is a population that believes expressing hateful and intolerant attitudes is acceptable and even desirable, and our research also demonstrates that America's youth are exposed to this material. Future researchers need to consider the consequence of this widespread and widely accessed form of hate.

## REFERENCES

Amster, S-E. 2009. "From Birth of a Nation to Stormfront: A Century of Communicating Hate." In *Hate Crimes*, edited by B. Perry, B. Levin, P. Iganski, R. Blazak, and F. Lawrence, 221–47. Westport, CT: Greenwood Publishing Group.

Anti-Defamation League. 2001. *Poisoning the Web: Hatred Online Internet Bigotry, Extremism and Violence*. archive.adl.org/poisoning_web/introduction.asp.

———. 2006. *National Socialist Movement Raises Profile to become America's Largest Neo-Nazi Group*. archive.adl.org/PresRele/Extremism_72/4837_72.htm.

Blazak, R. 2009. "Toward a Working Definition of Hate Groups." In *Hate Crimes*, edited by B. Perry, B. Levin, P. Iganski, R. Blazak, and F. Lawrence , 133–67. Westport, CT: Greenwood Publishing Group.

Bossler, A., and T. Holt. 2009. "On-line Activities, Guardianship, and Malware Infection: An Examination of Routine Activities Theory." *International Journal of Cyber Criminology* 3: 400–20.

Bossler, A., T. Holt, and D. May. 2012. "Predicting Online Harassment Victimization among a Juvenile Population." *Youth and Society* 44: 500–23.

Bowman-Grieve, L. 2009. "Exploring 'Stormfront': A Virtual Community of the Radical Right." *Studies in Conflict and Terrorism* 32: 989–1007.

Boyd, D. 2007. *Why Youth (Heart) Social Network Sites: The Role of Networked Publics in Teenage Social Life*. MacArthur Foundation Series on Digital Learning—Youth, Identity, and Digital Media Volume (Ed. David Buckingham). Cambridge, MA: MIT Press.

Brown, C. 2009. "WWW.HATE.COM: White Supremacist Discourse on the Internet and the Construction of Whiteness Ideology." *The Howard Journal of Communications* 20: 189–208.

Burris, V., E. Smith, and A. Strahm. 2000. "White Supremacist Network on the Internet." *Sociological Focus* 33: 215–34.

Chau, M., and J. Xu. 2007. "Mining Communities and Their Relationships in Blogs: A Study of Hate Groups." *International Journal of Human-Computer Studies* 65: 57–70.

Chen, H., W. Chung, J. Qin , E. Reid, M. Sageman, and G. Weimann. 2008. "Uncovering the Dark Web: A Case Study of Jihad on the Web." *Journal of the American Society for Information Science and Technology* 59: 1347–59.

Cooper, A. 2010. *Facebook, Youtube+: How Social Media Outlets Impact Digital Terrorism and Hate*. Los Angeles: Simon Wiesenthal Center.

Cowan, G. and Mettrick, J. 2002. "The Effects of Target Variables and Setting on Perceptions of Hate Speech." *Journal of Applied Social Psychology* 32: 277–99.

Daniels, J. 2008. "Race, Civil Rights, and Hate Speech in the Digital Era." In *Learning Race and Ethnicity: Youth and Digital Media*, edited by A. Everett, 129–54. Cambridge, MA: The MIT Press.

Dey, R., Z. Jelveh, and K. Ross. 2012. Facebook Users Have Become Much More Private: A Large-Scale Study. 4th IEEE International Workshop on Security and Social Networking (SESOC), Lugano, Switzerland. Access June 15, 2012 www.cis.poly.edu/~ross/papers/FacebookPrivacy.pdf.

Douglas, K. 2007. "Psychology, Discrimination and Hate Groups Online." In *The Oxford Handbook of Internet Psychology*, edited by A. Joinson, K. McKenna, T. Postmes, and U. D. Reips, 155–64. Oxford: Oxford University Press.

Douglas, K., C. Mcgarty, A. M. Bliuc, and G. Lala. 2005. "Understanding Cyberhate: Social Competition and Social Creativity in Online White Supremacist Groups." *Social Science Computer Review* 23: 68–76.

Duffy, M. 2003. "Web of Hate: A Fantasy Theme Analysis of the Rhetorical Vision of Hate Groups Online." *Journal of Communication Inquiry* 27: 291–312.

European Travel Commission. 2013. *New Media Trend Watch: US Usage Patterns.* www.newmediatrendwatch.com/markets-by-country/17-usa/123-demographics.

Evans, J. R., and A. Mathur. 2005. "The Value of Online Surveys." *Internet Research* 15: 195–219.

Fletcher, H. 2008. "Militant Extremists in the United States." *Council on Foreign Relations Backgrounder.* Available at: smargus.com/wp-content/uploads/2009/06/cfr_militant_extrem ists_in-the_usa.pdf.

Foxman, A., and Wolf, C. 2013. *Viral Hate: Containing Its Spread on the Internet.* New York: Palgrave MacMillan.

Franklin, R. 2010. *The Hate Directory.* www.hatedirectory.com/hatedir.pdf.

Fu, T., A. Abbasi, and H. Chen. 2010. "A Focused Crawler for Dark Web Forums." *Journal of the American Society for Information Science and Technology* 61: 1213–31.

Gerstenfeld, P., D. Grant, and C. P. Chiang. 2003. "Hate online: A Content Analysis of Extremist Internet Sites." *Analysis of Social Issues and Public Policy* 3: 29–44.

Glaser, J., J. Dixit, and D. P. Green. 2002. "Studying Hate Crime with the Internet: What Makes Racists Advocate Racial Violence?" *Journal of Social Issues* 58: 177–93.

Hawdon, J. 2012. "Applying Differential Association Theory to Online Hate Groups: A Theoretical Statement." *Journal of Research on Finnish Society* 5: 39–47.

Holt, T., and A. Bossler. 2008. "Examining the Applicability of Lifestyle-Routine Activities Theory for Cybercrime Victimization." *Deviant Behavior* 30: 1–25.

Hunter, C. 2012. "Number of Facebook users could reach 1 billion by 2012." *The Exponent Online.* Accessed January 23, 2012 www.purdueexponent.org/features/article_8815d757-8b7c-566f-8fbe-49528d4d8037.html.

Lee, E., and L. Leets. 2002. "Persuasive Storytelling by Hate Groups Online." *American Behavioral Scientist* 45: 927–57.

Leets, L. 2001. "Response to Internet Hate Sites: Is Speech Too Free in Cyberspace?" *Communication and Law Policy* 6: 287–317.

———. 2002. "Experiencing Hate Speech: Perceptions and Responses to Anti-Semitism and Antigay Speech." *Journal of Social Issues* 58: 341–61.

Leets, L., and H. Giles. 1997. "Words as Weapons: When Do They Wound? Investigations of Racist Speech." *Human Communication Research* 24: 260–301.

Lehdonvirta, V., and P. Räsänen. 2010. "How do Young People Identify with Online and Offline Peer Groups? A Comparison between UK, Spain and Japan." *Journal of Youth Studies* 13: 1–18.

Lenhart, A., K. Purcell, A. Smith, and K. Zickuhr. 2010. "Social Media and Mobile Internet Use among Teens and Young Adults." *Pew Internet and American Life Project.* Accessed December 18, 2012, pewinternet.org/.

Lennings, C., Amon, K., Brummert, H., and Lennings, N. 2010. "Grooming for terror: The Internet and young people." *Psychiatry, Psychology and Law* 17: 424–37.

Levin, B. 2002. "Cyberhate: A Legal and Historical Analysis of Extremists' Use of Computer Networks in America." *American Behavioral Scientist* 45: 958–86.

Livingstone, S., L. Haddon, A. Görzig, and K. Ólafsson. 2011. *Risks and Safety on the Internet: The Perspective of European Children. Full Findings.* LSE, London: EU Kids Online.

Lindgren, S. 2011. "YouTube gunmen? Mapping Participatory Media Discourse on School Shooting Videos." *Media, Culture and Society* 33: 123–36.

Marcum, C., G. Higgins, and M. Ricketts. 2010. "Potential Factors of Online Victimization of Youth: An Examination of Adolescent Online Behaviors Utilizing Routine Activity Theory." *Deviant Behavior* 31: 381–410.

Marcum, C., M. Ricketts, and G. Higgins. 2010. "Assessing Sex Experiences of Online Victimization: An Examination of Adolescent Online Behaviors Using Routine Activity Theory." *Criminal Justice Review* 35: 412–37.

McNamee, L. G., B. L. Peterson, and J. Peña. 2010. "A Call to Educate, Participate, Invoke and Indict: Understanding the Communication of Online Hate Groups." *Communication Monographs* 77: 257–80.

Navarro, J., and J. Jasinski. 2012. "Going Cyber: Using Routine Activities Theory to Predict Cyberbullying Experiences." *Sociological Spectrum* 32: 81–94.

Ngo, F., and R. Paternoster. 2011. "Cybercrime Victimization: An Examination of Individual and Situational Level Factors." *International Journal of Cyber Criminology* 5: 773–93.

Oksman, V., and J. Turtiainen. 2004. "Mobile Communication as a Social Stage." *New Media and Society* 6: 319–39.

Perry, B. 2000. "Button-Down terror": The Metamorphosis of the Hate Movement." *Sociological Focus* 33:113–31.

Potok, M. 2011. *The Year in Hate and Extremism, 2010. Intelligence Report*, 141. Southern Poverty Law Center. www.splcenter.org/get-informed/intelligence-report/browse-all-issues/2011/spring/the-year-in-hate-extremism-2010.

Pratt, T., K. Holtfreter, and M. Reisig. 2010. "Routine Online Activity and Internet Fraud Targeting: Extending the Generality of Routine Activity Theory." *Journal of Research in Crime and Delinquency* 47: 267–96.

Qi, X., K. Christensen, R. Duval, E. Fuller, A. Spahiu, Q. Wu, and C-Q Zhang. "2010. A Hierarchical Algorithm for Clustering Extremist Web Pages." *ASONAM, IEEE Computer Society*: 458–63.

Reyns, B. 2013. "Online Routines and Identity Theft Victimization: Further Expanding Routine Activity Theory beyond Direct-Contact Offenses." *Journal of Research in Crime and Delinquency* 50: 216–38.

Rideout, V., U. Foehr, and D. Roberts. 2010. *Generation M²: Media in the Lives of 8- to 18-year-olds*. Menlo Park, CA.: Henry J. Kaiser Family Foundation.

Schafer, J. 2002. "Spinning the Web of Hate: Web-based Hate Propagation by Extremist Organisations." *Journal of Criminal Justice and Popular Culture* 9: 69–88.

Searle, J. 1969. *Speech Acts*. Cambridge: Cambridge University Press.

Slater, M. D. 2003. "Alienation, Aggression, and Sensation Seeking as Predictors of Adolescent Use of Violent Film, Computer, and Website Content." *Journal of Communication* 53: 105–21.

The Southern Poverty Law Center. 2013. *Active U.S. Hate Groups*. Access June 14, 2013. www.splcenter.org/get-informed/hate-map.

Subrahmanyam, K. and D. Šmahel. 2011. *Digital Youth: The Role of Media in Development*. New York: Springer.

Turpin-Petrosino, C. 2002. "Hateful Sirens: Who Hears Their Song? An Examination of Student Attitudes toward Hate Groups and Affiliation Potential." *Journal of Social Issues* 58: 281–301.

Tynes, B. 2006. "Children, Adolescents, and the Culture of Online Hate." In *Handbook of Children, Culture, and Violence* edited by N. Dowd, D. Singer, and R. F. Wilson, 267–89. Thousand Oaks, CA: Sage.

Tynes, B., L. Reynolds, and P. M. Greenfield. 2004. "Adolescence, Race and Ethnicity on the Internet: A Comparison of Discourse in Monitored and Unmonitored Chat Rooms." *Journal of Applied Developmental Psychology* 25: 667–84.

Uslaner, E. M. 2004. "Trust, Civic Engagement, and the Internet." *Political Communication* 21: 223–42.

Vahlberg, Vivian. 2010. *Fitting into their Lives: A Survey of Three Studies about Youth Media Usage*. Newspaper Association of America Foundation. www.americanpressinstitute.org/docs/foundation/research/fitting_into_their_lives.pdf.

Valkenburg, P., and J. Peter. 2007. "Online Communication and Adolescent Well-Being: Testing the Stimulation versus the Displacement Hypothesis." *Journal of Computer-Mediated Communication* 12: 1169–82.

van Wilsem, J. 2013a. "Bought It, but Never Got It: Assessing Risk Factors for Online Consumer Fraud Victimization." *European Sociological Review* 29: 168–78.

————. 2013b. "Hacking and Harassment: Do They Have Something in Common? Comparing Risk Factors for Online Victimization." *Journal of Contemporary Criminal Justice,* 29: 437–53.

Waldron, J. 2012. *The Harm in the Hate Speech.* Cambridge, MA, and London: Harvard University Press.

Wansink, B. 2001. "Editorial: the Power of Panels." *Journal of Database Marketing* 8: 190–94.

Wolak, J., K. Mitchell, and D. Finkelhor. 2006. *Online Victimization of Youth: Five Years Later.* New York: National Center for Missing and Exploited Children.

Yabarra, M., Mitchell, K., and Korchmaros, J. 2011. "National Trends in Exposure to and Experiences of Violence on the Internet among children." *Pediatrics* 128: e1376–e1386.

Yahoo Finance. 2003. *Born to Be Wired: The Role of New Media for a Digital Generation.* Accessed December 18, 2012 us.yimg.com/i/promo/btbw_2003/btbw_execsum.pdf.

Zickmund, S. 2000. "Approaching the Radical Other: The Discursive Culture of Cyberhate." In *The Cybercultures Reader,* edited by D. Bell and B. M. Kennedy, 237–53. New York: Routledge.

*Chapter Ten*

# Selecting Targets

*The Influence of Judgments, Mobility, and Gender on Intragroup Violence Among Tamil Refugees*

## Christian Matheis, Virginia Roach, Michelle Sutherland, and James Hawdon

Scholars and peace activists who seek to intervene against group *vs.* group violence may find it beneficial to consider *target selection* in addition to research on causal and explanatory factors. Various individual and environmental elements influence the way members of groups select targets of violence. In this chapter, we consider factors influencing the selection of targets in the context of Sri Lankan Tamils living in diaspora. Through a meta-analysis of research and discourse on epistemic evaluations of group identity, mobility and immobility, and sexual assault during wartime, we emphasize the complexity of circumstances that contribute to violence between groups.

The task of giving a general picture of group violence poses difficulties, and yet it remains important to offer compelling insight into such events. Often, intragroup violence—violence among groups of people acting collectively—results from conditions that, predictably, foster and exacerbate tensions. Desperate circumstances and living in a culture of extreme violence can undoubtedly lead to violence; yet, not all people act violently when in dire situations. Moreover, desperation can result from a multitude of factors, yet no single variable or set of variables correlate in ways that predict violence perfectly. Further complications arise when we consider the complexity of the effects of sex, gender, or other demographic factors on group-to-group violence. While offering a general theory of violence is beyond the scope of the chapter, we argue that existing theories of intragroup violence either ignore or rely on an underdeveloped theory of target selection. Recognizing why some targets are deemed worthy of contempt and violence while others are not can help scholars understand the root causes of group violence. This chapter offers insights into target selection during incidents of intra-group violence in hopes of illustrating the importance of this understudied dimension of violence.

We develop our understanding of target selection through secondary research on violence among the Tamil. We illustrate some of the key factors that contribute to target selection, as well as factors that limit or mitigate incidents of violence among groups. We begin with a brief overview of the conflict in Sri Lanka that led to the Tamil diaspora. We then consider how the epistemic judgments for violence shape target selection in three situations. We then discuss the relationship between mobility, epistemic judgments, violence, and target selection.

The specific cases we consider are Tamil refugees who remained in Sri Lanka and Tamil youths who immigrated to London. We then consider incidents of rape and sexual assault perpetrated by Tamil men against Tamil women and girls. We conclude by discussing how studies of target selection in cases of intragroup violence, and perhaps in broader cases as well, can elucidate opportunities to propose interventions against future violence.

## HISTORICAL OVERVIEW: SRI LANKAN TAMILS IN DIASPORA

Later chapters in this volume provide additional details about the Sri Lankan civil war; however, we provide a brief historical overview to provide context for our discussion of target selection. Sri Lanka is home to two main ethnic and religious groups: the Sinhalese and the Tamils. The Sinhalese are Buddhists; most Tamils are Hindu, with a significant number of Christians and Muslims. These two main groups had a long history of relative peace (Rajas-ingham-Senanayake 2001); however, British colonial rule fostered divisions among them. Under British colonial rule, English-educated Tamils dominated Sri Lankan society. With independence in 1948, the Buddhist Sinhalese majority asserted their dominance and their identity. Shortly after independence, the Sinhalese began to exercise their power and attempted to eliminate the Tamil culture (Brubaker and Laitin 1998; Stone 2011). The Ceylon Citizenship Act, passed in 1948, made it virtually impossible for Tamils to become citizens and severely disenfranchised the Tamil migrants who had moved to Sri Lanka from India to work on tea plantations. Buddhism became the official religion. In 1956, the Sinhala Only Act declared Sinhala the country's sole official language, and many Tamil-speaking civil servants were forced to resign because they were not fluent in Sinhala (Raychaudhuri

2009). Sinhalese educators refused to teach Tamil youths, and Tamils were restricted in the universities.

This created resentment among the largely Hindu Tamil minority and tensions between Buddhist Sinhalese and Hindu Tamils grew steadily. The Tamils responded to growing oppression by forming numerous pro-Tamil militant groups. Feuding between several pro-Tamil paramilitaries occurred, and eventually the Liberation Tigers of Tamil Eelam (LTTE) emerged as the sole oppositional group (Brubaker and Laitin; also see Balasunderam 2009; Stone 2011). The LTTE won supremacy among the rival Tamil groups largely because they harnessed the "aesthetic character of violence," becoming outrageously brutal in their methods (Balasunderam 2009).

By 1983, conflict between government forces and the LTTE erupted as the LTTE fought to create an independent Tamil state in northern and eastern Sri Lanka. While the LTTE fought the Sri Lankan government, violence erupted between the various other pro-Tamil militias as they fought to control traditional Tamil areas and to represent the Tamil people to both Tamil and Sinhalese constituencies (see Udalagama and de Silva in this volume; also see Bush 2003). This intra-ethnic conflict among Tamils in Sri Lanka contributed to dissention and mistrust among the Tamil communities, leading to more violence. Thus, violence engulfed the small island nation.

Although the government declared victory in May 2009, the 26 years of intermittent fighting killed between 80,000 and 100,000 people (jama. jamanetwork.com/article.aspx?articleid=1104178). Over 13,000 civilians lost their lives in the last decade of the conflict alone. In addition to those killed or wounded, the conflict also resulted in massive numbers of refugees. Researchers estimate that the civil war displaced over 800,000 Sri Lankans (see Udalagama and de Silva in this volume) (Husain, et al. 2011). For many of those displaced, the violence of the war followed them to their refugee camps or new neighborhoods.

## Tamil Internal Displacement, Immobility, and Violence

By July 2009, two percent of Sri Lankans were internally displaced persons (IDPs). In Jaffna District, this estimated number reached 23 percent (see Husain et al. 2011). Over three-fourths of the displaced were Tamils. The Tamil IDP camps perpetuated poverty and refugee-like situations, mainly at the will of politicians: the longer the refugees suffered, the longer the aid money would flow (Muggah 2008, 105). In 2009, Minick Farm, located in Northern Sri Lanka, had conditions so poor that toilets designed to handle a maximum of twenty people were being used by more than one hundred (United Nations Office for the Coordination of Humanitarian Affairs 2009). The structure of the camps made it difficult for the IDPs living there to create a sustainable existence because there were insufficient resources to support the overcrowding population and the camp residents were not permitted to work (Muggah, 106). Despite the deplorable conditions, residents were rarely, if ever, allowed to leave (Amnesty International 2009). The circumstances within the camps became progressively worse as the conflict continued.

In addition to lacking sufficient resources, the IDP camps were extremely violent. As various pro-Tamil paramilitary groups fought among themselves and allied with the Sri Lankan government against the LTTE, Tamils were pitted against Tamils. The Sri Lankan government capitalized on this intragroup conflict. They often used pro-government Tamil paramilitary groups to administer the camps, and these groups did so oppressively (Bush 1993). For example, the pro-Tamil paramilitary group EPDP policed many of the IDP camps, and they maintained control through kidnapping and murder (Bush 1993; Bush 2003). They claimed they needed tight control to facilitate screening for Tamil Tigers among the refugees because of the LTTE's tendency to hide in the camps and use the refugees as human shields. The practice of ruthlessly searching for rebels hiding in camps and then violently eliminating anyone deemed dangerous fostered high levels of suspicion among the camps' residents. Almost anyone was a potential rebel and a potential threat.

Even when the refugees could leave the camps, it was often too dangerous to do so (see Bush 2003). During the conflict, many roads in the border region were controlled by the Army during the day and the LTTE at night. Both sides used roadblocks to dissuade travel, and kidnappings and murders were frequent even on roads controlled exclusively by one side were subject to frequent kidnappings and murders. Undeniably, violence was common because perpetrators could commit violent acts and then easily flee to the protection of their own group (Hyndman 2004). This inability to travel had devastating effects on civilians and their communities. In essence, the refugees became trapped and powerless, and refugee communities became ethnic enclaves where everyone was a potential security threat (see Rajasingham-Senanayake 2001; 2011). Thus, the reality of the camps and refugee communities was that residents were frequently victims of violence, and Tamils perpetrated much of this violence against fellow Tamils.

## The Tamil Diaspora, Immobility, and Violence

In addition to the internally displaced, thousands fled the island. As recently as 2009, roughly 60,000 Tamils resettled in London as part of the worldwide Tamil diaspora related to the civil war (Balasunderam 2009; Zunzer 2004). Although Sri Lankans had immigrated to the United Kingdom ever since independence, after the escalation of violence in the early 1980s, a new wave of immigrants came. Unlike prior immigrants who were highly educated and professionally connected, this wave of immigrants were disproportionately poorer people fleeing the hostilities at home (van Hear, Pieke, and Vertovec 2004).

This most recent wave of Sri Lankan immigrants to the United Kingdom fled their homes seeking a more peaceful and prosperous life; but instead the Tamils in London faced poor living conditions, very low social standing due to their refugee status, and socio-economic factors that gave them little hope for improvement. Poverty largely confined them to neighborhoods with their fellow Tamil refugees. Indeed, like those who remained in Sri Lanka, these refugees faced the many problems associated with poverty. Recent research by Wayland (2004), Young (2007), and Balasunderam (2009) document the social exclusion faced by Tamil immigrants. Specifically, compared with citizens of the United Kingdom who were not part of the Tamil diaspora, education and employment opportunities for these immigrants are severely lacking.

The result of this hyper-segregation and lack of social mobility was violence. Researchers have documented ongoing intragroup violence among Tamils who have resettled in London, including acts of extreme brutality (Balasunderam 2009). These acts have resulted in long-term injuries and death among victims, as well as life-sentence imprisonment among perpetrators (Balasunderam 2009). Among London's Tamil population, youths who join or form gangs perpetuate the majority of Tamil-Tamil violence. The London Metropolitan Police Authority (2004) attributes the high rate of youth participation in criminal activities to "deprivation, poor parenting, under achievement at school and lack of aspiration" (43). In response, the LMPA recommends diversionary activities as a possible solution to youth participation in violence, justified on the assertion that the aforementioned *individuated* factors comprise the dominant variables in youth criminal activities.

Yet, there is abundant evidence that the intragroup violence among the Tamils is rooted in structural, macro-level, factors. This holds true both in the refugee camps during the war and in London since the mass wave of immigration there because of the war. Macro-level factors such as the lack of long-term educational and employment opportunities contribute to criminal activities among Tamil youth in London as well as refugees in Sri Lanka. Considering these macro-level factors undermines the legitimacy of individuating the causes of intragroup violence. To an important extent, macro-level factors, broadly explained in terms of inclusion in public affairs and opportunities in labor markets, provide the strongest corollary explanations for the reasons many Tamils engage in violence.

According to recent studies (Wayland 2004; Young 2007; Balasunderam 2009), structural factors such as limited educational and employment opportunities and lack of legitimate avenues for mobility decrease social cohesion and increase social conflict. Indeed, exclusion from public affairs and labor activities erodes social solidarity (Helly, Barsky, and Foxen 2003). These institutionalized aspects of exclusion from public affairs and participation in labor markets degrade the practical and ideological relevance of national and citizen identity among resettled Tamils and Tamil youth whose parents reset-tled in London. Conversely, identifying with and maintaining loyalty to smaller social groups, such as gangs in the case of London's Tamil youth or various pro-Tamil paramilitaries in Sri Lanka, does present opportunities for gaining self-esteem and status otherwise unavailable through other means. Thus, the conditions in which resettled Tamils endure social denigration and immobility result in extreme measures as systematically marginalized groups act on what little means they have for gaining self-esteem (Balasunderam 2009, 40). As Balasunderam (2009, 38) notes:

> it seems that gang involvement is more closely associated with lack of access to education and employment, continuing exposure to extreme violence, terri-torial disputes stemming from Sri Lanka, London turf wars and the need to retain respect on the street and achieve the degree of protection that such respect affords. The Tamil gangs tend to have a loose structure, a fairly flat hierarchy and are described as being unsophisticated.

Thus, hyper-segregation and lack of social mobility has resulted in violence in both Sri Lanka and London. This is a common and well-documented result of poverty and insufficient opportunities to pull oneself from it. Yet, there is another common, but less documented, consequence of immobility: the vio-lence suffered by the group is largely inflicted by the group. That is, fellow Tamils committed most of the violence experienced by the Tamil refugees. What can explain this aspect of target selection? While consideration of macro-level factors can help explain why some Tamils committed or commit violence, they do not explain how individuals justify intragroup violence by selecting certain people as targets. We now aim to show that micro-level factors, specifically the localized identification with and loyalty to specific subgroups (Tamil gangs in this case), function as epistemic justifications for target selection, culminating in intragroup violence.

## Toward a Theory of Target Selection: Social Mobility, Local Identities and Group Loyalties

Lacking educational and employment opportunities, resettled Tamils likely experience little solidarity with larger groups such as Sri Lankans in general or long-time citizens of the United Kingdom who, comparatively, enjoy greater participation in public affairs and opportunities in labor markets. If, as Hardin (1997) shows, individuals cannot plausibly predict that the achievement of national interests include and advance the achievement of their individual interests then individuals have little or no practical motive to prioritize national identities (Hardin 1997, 55). Further, loyalty to nations or larger social groupings (e.g.. Sri Lankans, Londoners, citizens, etc.) holds little practical benefits and, therefore, tends to represent minimal ideological worth (Hardin 1997).

This research suggests the role of group identity and loyalty are important epistemic factors in rationalizing violent acts during social conflicts. Broad social factors such as educational and employment opportunities and other forms of social mobility influence rational decision making and pattern levels of conflict among Tamils broadly; yet, the reasons Tamil youths feel no loyalty on the basis of nationalistic or metropolitan identities cannot account for how they *differentiate* among one another in selecting targets of violence. Instead, both macro-level social trends and micro-level epistemic factors prefigure the correlations between the variables: 1) acts of violence carried out by individuals, and 2) group memberships of those who perpetuate acts of violence. Recognizing this makes it possible to explain how people within the same broader social group—Tamil youths in London, for example— differentiate other Tamils in London, selecting some as targets of violence while leaving others alone.

To identify with and maintain loyalty to gangs or small groups results in a form of respect that individuals cannot attain through educational and employment opportunities, nor from participation in broader cultural and social activities (Balasunderam 2009, 38). More than merely categories of association, these identities and loyalties have an epistemic function in the justification of actions people otherwise would not take. As Hardin (1997) explains, people acting on the basis of identities and loyalties do so through what he deems *a-rational drives*. As opposed to acting on *rational drives*, those who act on a-rational drives do not have to contemplate or explicate reasons for actions they take. When a-rational drives such as group identity and group loyalty supplant or subordinate rational drives, no further reasons warrant consideration. In this way, loyalties and identities function epistemically to replace contemplative consideration ("rationality"). This has implications for the ways in which people acting on a-rational drives respond to conflict in terms of risk taking, weighing the relative consequences and benefits of engaging in conflicts, and evaluating the relative worth of themselves and others.

If group members a-rationally privilege particular identities and loyalties over broader social obligations they may also tend to take actions of an increasingly costly nature to themselves as individuals (Hardin 1997, 47). Believing in, predicting, and desiring the overall benefits to their small group, such as a gang or a paramilitary group, an individual may engage in risky actions even when doing so risks individual consequences (such as injury, imprisonment, or death). To that end, Hardin's work can help explain the motives for intragroup conflict and, potentially, violence. Depending on the importance that individuals place on group identity and group loyalty, those factors serve as epistemic justifications for engaging in violence toward members of one's larger subgroup. *Differentiation* within a group, the evaluation of members of one's own subgroup with one's own identity, and the loyalty to that identity, functions at an epistemic level to justify intragroup violence. Namely, those who enact intragroup violence: 1) rank the circumstances facing them as members of larger social groups as less important than membership in smaller, close-knit groups, and 2) accept group loyalties as de facto justifications for engaging in violence against targets selected through a process of differentiation.

Loyalties tend to be confined to small, close-knit groups when social mobility is limited because social mobility weakens the social or physical barriers that hinder interaction among differing social positions. When social mobility is restricted, intergroup contacts decrease, thereby decreasing the group's heterogeneity. This decreased heterogeneity reduces pluralism and heightens differences among those "insiders" and "outsiders." That is, when mobility is low, prejudice against the "out-group" increases (see Hawdon 1996). In addition, when mobility is limited, there are limited groups available for membership. As a result, the exit costs associated with leaving or being ousted from any specific group increase, thereby amplifying the group's ability to demand conformity to its norms and goals (see Hawdon 1996; 2005).

When mobility is limited, as in the case of the Tamil refugees, the importance of their small group is heightened since their ability to join others is severely curtailed. Their primary loyalties are to the small, close-knit group in which they belong, and increased prejudice against "outsiders" leads to greater differentiation within the group. Suspicions are aroused not only among people of different groups, but also among those within the same groups. Even those once considered insiders or who share membership in some larger group are eligible for exclusion from the smaller group. In this way, the smaller group is "purified" and the rewards of membership heightened. In addition, the group's heightened control over its members forces members to accept group loyalties as *de facto* justifications for engaging in violence. If the group decides violence is necessary, the members must enact it because the protection and promotion of group interests are paramount and the costs for being exiled from the group are so high, including possible violent victimization by rivals.

This process can lead to what has been called "ethnic outbinding." Ethnic outbinding is when opposing factions within groups form, resulting in violent confrontations between groups that are supposedly working for the same cause, and ethnic outbinding was "classically and tragically" prevalent in Sri Lanka among the Tamils (Balasunderam 2009). Numerous observers note how this ethnic outbinding resulted in escalated violence in Sri Lanka as different factions of "Tamil Patriotism" clashed. Refugees also carried these intra-ethnic conflicts with them as they fled to various countries around the world. Indeed, Tamil youths who engage in violence tend to act as members of gangs with identities that reference and derive from particular geographical areas of London, as well as to genealogical origins, such as towns and villages in Sri Lanka prior to resettlement (Balasunderam 2009; Ratnapalan 2012).

Consequently, social immobility, by heightening the importance of local identities and loyalties, leads to apparent intragroup violence; however, the violence is, in fact, intergroup. Because the larger group is subdivided into factions, members of rival factions are suitable targets. Often, these rivals are the preferred target because of the perceived need to demarcate group boundaries. This tendency is elevated further when this social immobility is coupled with physical immobility: the result is heightened violence among those rival groups (see a similar discussion in Kennedy's chapter of this volume). That is, when physical immobility limits interactions to those in immediate physical proximity, those closest are the easiest targets for violence.

These insights help explain how the violence that plagued Sri Lanka was frequently intra-Tamil. These insights should also apply to other situations where violence appears to be intragroup. For example, gang members who share similar structural positions yet are members of rival gangs commit a large percentage of homicides in the United States (see, e.g., Kennedy et al. 2001). Yet, can these insights also help explain when potential targets *are not selected*? We believe they can, and the Sri Lankan civil war again provides an excellent case study.

## MOBILITY AND RAPE AS A WEAPON OF WAR

In civil wars and refugee camps, one of the most prominent forms of violence is sexual violence. Indeed, "Major-General Patrick Cammaert, former commander of United Nations peacekeeping forces in the Democratic Republic of Congo, notes that 'It has probably become more dangerous to be a woman than a soldier in armed conflict,'" with sexual violence causing more death or disability among women aged fifteen to forty-four than cancer, malaria, traffic injuries, and general welfare combined (George 2009). During the Rwanda genocide, for example, the estimated number of rapes is between 250,000 and 500,000, many of which are extreme rapes (which include permanent visible scarring, dismemberment, or mutilation of genitals), gang rapes, or forced prostitution and enslavement. Roughly 75 percent of the female population during Liberia's civil war (1989–2003) was raped, often gang raped (George 2009).

There are two prevailing theories concerning the cause of widespread wartime rape committed by soldiers and rebels: opportunity and strategy (Cacic-Kumpes 1992; Farr 2009; George 2009; Hughes and Foster 1996; Schott 2001; 2011; Wood 2009). War can obviously increase the opportunity for rape as the resulting chaos decreases normal forms of social control. In fact, some military officials appear to assume that "recreational rape" occurs when soldiers lack sexual partners. This explains why Japanese military authorities supported the proliferation of military brothels after the widespread rape of civilians in Nanjing (Farr 2009).

In addition to wars providing opportunity for rape, rape can be a wartime strategy. Using rape as a weapon is common during genocides to facilitate ethnic cleansing, when women are raped repeatedly and forced to give birth (Schott 2011; Wood 2009). The use of rape as a tool of genocide occured in the Darfur conflict, where Arab men raped African women because the biracial children were considered Arab in that society. Another strategic use of rape is to build cohesion among soldiers and foster group identity.

Alternatively, the strategy can be used to cause shame. For example, impregnated women may be forced to undergo abortions to induce psychological torment. Alternately, when women are raped and visibly scarred, everyone knows what happened to them, which can lead to abandonment by the community and "social death" (Schott 2011). Another tactic is to force family members to rape each other (Farr 2009). Regardless of the specific tactic, rape is an effective weapon against individuals and communities. As Melanne Verveer, the U.S. State Department's ambassador-at-large for global women's issues, testified, rape "destroys the fabric of society from within and does so more effectively than do guns or bombs."

Often, rape is so widespread during conflict that it is seen as an inevitable part of war (Wood 2009). However, it was conspicuously absent among the LTTE, with fewer than ten rapes reported or discovered during the entire conflict (Wood 2009). Though patriarchal in nature, the LTTE was effective at curtailing violence against women within their divisions and against non-LTTE members. This context is interesting because rape was widespread throughout the war in general, particularly on the side of the government and the Indian peace-building interveners (Wang 2011). Farr (2009) argues these were crimes of opportunity more than strategy. Yet, among the most brutal Tamil militant group, that abuse was almost never committed. Why was this the case?

Although ethnic in its origins, the Sri Lankan conflict was never genocidal, and this eliminated the possibility of rape as a tool for ethnic cleansing. As for rape as a tool for humiliation and shame, this was something that simply was not part of the Tamil strategy; in fact, their stance was quite the opposite. One explanation for the LTTE's restraint is that the members were often deeply religious (see Roberts 2005). While often casted as a secular militant Tamil group, in reality, the LTTE were deeply religious, and their leaders frequently used religion to form their methods and religious symbols to motivate their members (Roberts 2005; Wang 2011). Since many LTTEs were extremely religious and their religions prohibit pre-marital and extra-marital sex, the LTTE did not use rape as a strategy of war.

Another factor that limited the LTTE's use of rape is that Tamil society was very patriarchal, and women were viewed as subordinate to men. A woman was bound to her father until marriage, then to her husband, and then to her son if her husband died (Wang 2011). Women had few opportunities for self-sufficiency, and the division of labor along gender lines left them little autonomy. Yet, they were fiercely protected and men were not allowed to touch women (Wang 2011). In addition, as the war raged on, women were increasingly integral combatants. It is estimated that women comprised between 30 and 40 percent of LTTE militants in the late 1980s and 1990s (Wang 2011). These conditions immediately eliminated using rape as a strategy by forbidding the selection of women as targets of sexual violence. It set the stage for the protection of Tamil women's bodies from intragroup violation, and the constant emphasis on chastity apparently protected non-LTTE women as well.

While these factors can account for why the LTTE leadership did not promote rape as a weapon of war, they do not necessarily explain why rape was used so infrequently by the LTTE members. Most religions forbid rape and many religious men have fought wars; most societies are patriarchal and call for the protection of women, and yet many patriarchs have fought in wars and raped the women of their enemy. While the dominant norms of the LTTE are important, it must be recognized that the LTTE leadership used its strict, hierarchical organization to prevent sexual harassment of women.

The structure of the LTTE was extremely hierarchical and well disciplined, and this made it effective at maintaining these cultural norms. When joining the LTTE, recruits were required to take an oath to uphold the mission of the LTTE, and part of it included eschewing extramarital sexual relations with women (Wood 2009). Pre-marital sex was not tolerated and chastity and loyalty were promoted. To enforce these norms when women became integral combatants, the sexes were separated and dress codes were required (Wang 2011). Intermarriage of members was encouraged by leaders, but all relations had to be approved (Wang 2011; 2009). Thus, the strict hierarchical organization allowed leaders to forbid the option of selecting women as targets of sexual violence.

As explained above, the lack of mobility among the Tamils and among the LTTE would help maintain the leaderships' rigid authority and control. Former LTTE members were most frequently reprimanded with imprisonment or death; therefore, as the war raged on and social mobility slowed to a virtual halt, the exit costs for LTTE members became increasingly high.

Therefore, deviating from group norms became dangerous. Thus, the LTTE leadership gained even greater control over the members, and they could more effectively enforce their religious and patriarchal norms that limited the use of rape as a weapon of war.

## CONCLUSION

Intragroup violence results from a combination of social, psychological, and geographical factors. We have demonstrated the complexity of various causes and effects that may help explain how and when intragroup violence arises, and some of the factors involved in selecting the targets of such violence. Though we offer by no means an exhaustive set of causal factors, we highlight the importance of macro- and micro-level variables. Specifically, we note how social immobility creates a situation where identities and group loyalties become localized and tied to small, tightly knit groups. Then, under conditions of limited opportunities for mobility, these tightly knit groups often find motives for violence that targets what outside observers might consider fellow group members. In reality, we argue, the lack of opportunity to succeed in the larger group leads to the marginalized groups dividing into subgroups. In the case of Sri Lanka and many other struggles, this process led to ethnic outbinding. What appeared to be intra-Tamil violence, in both Sri Lankan refugee camps and the slums of London, was, in fact, inter-Tamil violence.

Even though the variables discussed herein are of limited explanatory power, this analysis may help identify various opportunities for broadening our understanding of intragroup violence. Scholars and peace activists who seek to understand intragroup violence must avoid individuating the causes of such actions to personality or psychological factors, a noncontroversial course of thought already adopted by many social scientists. Revealing macro-level factors helps illustrate the circumstances in which individuals in certain social groups with relatively limited or diminished life prospects carry out criminal activities as a coping mechanism. However, the over-emphasis on broad social circumstances as causal of intragroup violence may obfuscate the epistemic constructs individual actors use in selecting targets of violence.

Realizing the role of social mobility and its effects on social identities and group loyalties may also have implications for those attempting or advocating intervention to prevent or ameliorate intragroup violence. Our discussion suggests that when mobility is restricted, be it through social or physical conditions, people suffer. This suffering leads to desperation that in turn often results in violence. It is therefore of the utmost importance that everyone is free to maintain a bearable quality of life. This suggests that an effective strategy to prevent intragroup violence is to expand opportunities for cultural, political, and economic inclusion. Increased mobility would allow greater educational and employment opportunities, thereby providing for a life that is at least sustainable.

While macro-level desperation and injustice may need to be eliminated or mitigated to foster peace or at least a halt to outright hostilities in many cases, we must realize that while broader social circumstances may lead groups to act violently, aspects of association with groups may ameliorate these broader social influences. That is, group identity and group membership may alter the ways in which people respond to social circumstances, and people rely on their intimate groups as sources of epistemic justifications for different courses of action. Therefore, while addressing issues of social mobility is important for combating violence, we must also find means of disrupting or otherwise altering the role of group identity and group loyalty in decision-making processes. By more carefully considering mobility and epistemic facets of intragroup violence, researchers, practitioners, and activists may find nuanced means of proactive and responsive intervention.

In conclusion, we suggest that a nuanced understanding of target selection may assist scholars and activists in proposing interventions that can prevent or mitigate intragroup violence.

## REFERENCES

Amnesty International. 2009. "Unlock the camps in Sri Lanka: Safety and Dignity for the Displaced Now—A Briefing Paper." London: Amnesty International Publications. ASA 37/016/2009, August 10, 2009, www.amnesty.org/en/library/info/ASA37/016/2009/en.

Balasunderam, Ahalya. 2009. "Gang-related Violence Among Young People of the Tamil Refugee Diaspora in London." *Safer Communities* 8: 34–41.

Brubaker, R., and D. D. Laitin. 1998. "Ethnic and Nationalist Violence." *Annual Review of Sociology* 24: 423–52.

Bush, Kenneth D. 1993. "Reading Between the Lines: Intra-Group Heterogeneity and Conflict in Sri Lanka." *Refuge: Canada's Journal on Refugees* 13: 15–22.

———. 2003. *The Intra-Group Dimensions of Ethnic Conflict in Sri Lanka*. New York: Palgrave Macmillan.

Cacic-Kumpes, Jadranka. 1992. "Ethnicity, War and Rape." *Migracijske teme* 8: 95–104.

Farr, Kathryn. 2009. "Armed Conflict, War Rape, and the Commercial Trade in Women and Children's Labour." *Pakistan Journal of Women's Studies: Alam-e-Niswan* 16: 1–31.

George, J. Bryjak. 2009. "War and Rape." *Peace Magazine* 25: 6.

Hardin, Russell. 1997. *One for All: The Logic of Group Conflict*. Princeton: Princeton University Press.

Hawdon, James. 1996. "Cycles of Deviance: Structural Change, Moral Boundaries, and Drug Use, 1880–1990." *Sociological Spectrum* 16: 183–207.

———. 2005. *Drugs and Alcohol Consumption as a Function of Social Structure: A Cross-cultural Sociology*. Lewistown, NY: Mellen Press.

Helly, Denise, Robert F. Barsky, and Patricia Foxen. 2003. "Social Cohesion and Cultural Plurality." *Canadian Journal of Sociology /Cahiers Canadiens de Sociologie*: 19–42.

Hughes, Donna M., and Kathleen Foster. 1996. "War, Nationalism, and Rape." *Women's Studies International Forum* 19: 183–84.

Husain, Farah, Mark Anderson, Barbara Lopes Cardozo, Kristin Becknell, Curtis Blanton, Diane Araki, and Eeshara Kottegoda Vithana. 2011. "Prevalence of War-Related Mental Health Conditions and Association with Displacement Status in Postwar Jaffna District, Sri Lanka." *JAMA* 306: 522–31.

Hyndman, Jennifer, and Malathi De Alwis. 2004. "Bodies, Shrines, and Roads: Violence, (Im)mobility and Displacement in Sri Lanka." *Gender, Place and Culture: A Journal of Feminist Geography* 1: 535–57.

Kennedy, David, Anothony Braga and Anne Piehl. 2001. "Developing and Implementing Operation Ceasefire." *In Gun Violence: The Boston Gun Project's Operation Ceasefire*, 5–53. Washington, DC: National Institute of Justice, U.S. Department of Justice.

London Metropolitan Police Authority. 2004. Metropolitan Police Authority Website Archive. United Kingdom: *London Metropolitan Police Service and Metropolitan Police Authority Joint Annual Report, 2003–2004*, accessed April 2013, policeauthority.org/metropolitan/downloads/committees/cop/cop-040206-04-appendix01.pdf.

Manasse, Michelle Eileen, and Natasha Morgan Ganem. 2009. "Victimization as a Cause of Delinquency: The Role of Depression and Gender. *Journal of Criminal Justice* 37: 371–78.

Muggah, R. 2008. *Relocation Failures in Sri Lanka*. New York: Zed Books.

Rajasingham-Senanayake, Darini. 2001. "Transformation of Legitimate Violence and Civil Military Relations." In *Coercion and Governance: The Declining Political Role of the Military in Asi*a, edited by Mutiah Alagapa, 294–315. Stanford, CA: Stanford University Press.

———. 2011. "Identity on the Borderline: Modernity, New Ethnicities, and the Unmaking of Multiculturalism in Sri Lanka." In *Perspectives on Modern South Asia: A Reader in Culture, History, and Representation,* edited by Kamala Visweswaran, 199–208. Chichester, United Kingdom: Wiley-Blackwell.

Ratnapalan, Laavanyan M. 2012. "Memories of Ethnic Violence in Sri Lanka among Immigrant Tamils in the UK." *Ethnic and Racial Studies* 35: 1539–57.

Raychaudhuri, Sumana. 2009. "Will Sri Lanka Drive the Tigers to Extinction?" *The Nation*, February 23, 2009. Accessed September 18, 2013 from www.thenation.com/article/will-sri-lanka-drive-tigers-extinction.

Roberts, Michael. 2005. "Saivite Symbols, Sacrifice, and Tamil Tiger Rites." *Social Analysis*: 67–93.

Schott, Robin May. 2001. "War Rape, Social Death and Political Evil." *Development Dialogue* 55: 47–62.

———. 2011. "War Rape, Natality and Genocide." *Journal of Genocide Research* 13: 5–21.

Stone, David R. 2011. "Sri Lankan Civil War." *The Encyclopedia of War*. New York: Wiley.

United Nations High Commission on Refugees. 2012. *The State of the World's Refugees 2012: In Search of Solidarity.* Edited by Judith Kumin and Andrew Lawday. Oxford: Oxford University Press.

United Nations Office for the Coordination of Humanitarian Affairs. 2009. "Sri Lanka: 'Too Many People' at Huge IDP Camp." *IRIN Asia*, Access September 11, 2013, www.irinnews.org/Report/84805/SRI-LANKA-Too-many-people-at-huge-IDP-mp-UN.

van Hear, Nicholas, Frank Pieke, and Steven Vertovec. 2004. "The contribution of UK-based diasporas to development and poverty reduction." *COMPAS* (Centre on Migration, Policy and Society), University of Oxford.

Wang, Peng. 2011. "Women in the LTTE: Birds of Freedom or Cogs in the Wheel?" *Journal of Politics and Law* 4: 100–8.

Warner, Barbara D., and Shannon K. Fowler. 2003. "Strain and Violence: Testing a General Strain Theory Model of Community Violence." *Journal of Criminal Justice* 31: 511–21.

Wayland, S. 2004. "Ethnonationalist Network and Transnational Opportunities in the Sri Lankan Tamil Diaspora." *Review of International Studies* 30: 405–26.

Wood, Elisabeth Jean. 2009. "Armed Groups and Sexual Violence: When Is Wartime Rape Rare?" *Politics and Society* 37: 131–61.

Young, J. 2007. *The Vertigo of Late Modernity*. London: Sage.

Zunzer, W. 2004. *Diaspora Communities and Civil Conflict Transformation.* Berlin: Berghof Research Centre for Constructive Conflict Management.

*III*

# Consequences of Group Violence

*Chapter Eleven*

# Consequences of Group Violence Involving Youth in Sri Lanka

## Siri Hettige

Group violence as a social phenomenon has been explored by behavioral scientists with diverse disciplinary persuasions such as psychology, social psychology, psychoanalysis, critical social theory, sociology, and anthropology. Many of these explorations have focused attention on how groups engaged in violent acts are formed and why they direct collective violence against rival groups. As far as group violence involving youth is concerned, two theoretical concepts seem to be important, namely convergence and identity. While convergence refers to the process of individuals with shared values, ideas, and interests coming together, identity pertains to internally homogenized groups with a common identity *vis-a-vis* other groups. The social and political landscapes of many societies today are populated by a number of distinct identity groups. In this regard, Sri Lanka is not an exception.

This chapter explores the rise of distinct identity groups among post-independence Sri Lankan youth, their tendency to engage in group violence and its diverse consequences.

### IDENTITY FORMATION IN COLONIAL AND POSTCOLONIAL SRI LANKA

Ethno-religious violence is not entirely a postcolonial phenomenon in Sri Lanka. Historians have examined several incidents of ethno-religious violence during the colonial period, in particular during British rule from the late 1700s to the mid-twentieth century. These incidents contributed to the crystallization of emergent ethno-religious identities in the country. On the other hand, colonial rule itself set in motion a range of social, economic, and political processes, many of which facilitated the formation of distinct social, cultural, and political identities among people. The formation of social classes, as well as occupational, linguistic, and political groups, was evident throughout the colonial period. What is noteworthy is that some pre-existing identities were also reinforced during the colonial period. So much so that by the time Sri Lanka achieved political independence in 1948, Sri Lankan society was comprised of a number of distinct ethno-linguistic, class and ideological groupings. These divisions were further articulated through so-cial and political processes in the decades following political independence to the point that class and ethnic identity politics came to dominate the political landscape during this period. A steadily expanding younger popula-tion (due to a high rate of population growth) came under the influence of social and political discourses that emphasized class and ethnic identities through modernization and the spread of modern education. Changes in eco-nomic and educational policies after independence reinforced the above ten-dencies. For instance, the change of the medium of instruction in secondary schools and universities from English to native languages led to a *de facto* re-segregation of schools along ethno-linguistic lines throughout the country. This also led to a strong monolingual tendency in education. Most youths in the process became monolingual and could not communicate across ethno-linguistic divisions in society. In other words, the younger population be-came increasingly divided into almost exclusive ethno-linguistic groups. Even though young people, in particular the educated ones, shared broadly similar aspirations and life goals, their exclusive ethnic identities persuaded them to treat the competition for scarce public resources such as state sector employment as a zero-sum game. This tendency became stronger over time, as the Sri Lankan state became increasingly identified with the majority Sinhalese Buddhist community and the country's economy fell increasingly under the control of the state.

Sri Lankan youth became increasingly politically active, especially after the 1960s. Expansion of university education created space for youth politi-cal activism. In fact, universities became focal points for radical youth poli-tics in the country. Though youth initially became active members of already established political parties, both Marxist as well as nationalist, more and more youth began to rally around new, militant political parties established and led by youth leaders belonging to different ethnic groups. The most significant among these have been the People's Liberation Front (JVP) and the Liberation Tigers of Tamil Elam (LTTE). The former was led by a Marxist Sinhalese youth leader who broke away from the Sri Lankan com-munist party in the late 1960s. The latter was led by V. Prabakaran, a Tamil youth leader who initially belonged to the Tamil United Liberation Front, an active, long-established political party in the north of Sri Lanka. Both parties became increasingly radical and militant and led anti-state rebellions starting in the early 1970s. Both parties harbored marginalized youth constituencies from Sinhalese and Tamil communities, respectively, though their membership had often been broadened.

Colonial economic and social policies created a highly unequal class society, polarized between a privileged, urban upper class and a mass of rural peasants, who either tilled small plots owned by new and traditional land owners or else worked as laborers on commercial plantations, again owned by urban propertied classes. The country's education system at this time also remained polarized between privileged urban schools that imparted an English education to the children in urban elite families, and vernacular rural elementary schools that catered to underprivileged rural children. Such an education system provided almost no opportunity to rural underprivileged children for upward social mobility. Both the private sector and the colonial state recruited English-educated youth graduating from urban schools. Vernacular-educated rural youth, if they migrated to the city, could become casual laborers or informal sector workers. White-collar jobs largely remained the prerogative of the privileged urban class.

It is against the above background that postcolonial language and educational policy shifts should be understood. With increasing democratization of the Sri Lankan polity, elected representatives came under increasing pressure from the rural masses to introduce more equitable economic and social policies. Introduction of universal, free education in the early 1940s would have been at least partly due to the growing social demand for education, while the change of instruction from English to the vernacular facilitated the spread of education throughout the country. The change of the official language from English to Sinhala in 1956 and the subsequent amendment of legislation in 1958 to allow the use of Tamil in the north and east for official purposes enabled vernacular-educated youth to have access to state sector employment, previously reserved for the English-educated minority.

The expansion of educational opportunities, increased opportunities for upward social mobility through public sector employment, and the improvement of life chances for youth, in particular underprivileged youth, did not necessarily keep up with the steadily increasing demand for such opportunities due to rapid population growth after independence, in particular the expansion of the educated youth population in the country. The socialist, central planning model of development that favored state-led development, often at the expense of private enterprise, did not generate employment, in particular the white-collar employment in highest demand by youth. So, by the early 1970s, unemployment rates in general and youth employment in particular reached crisis proportions. Increasing unrest among youth with secondary and tertiary education due to the lack of employment opportunities prepared an environment conducive for the first JVP- led uprising in 1971.

The militant youth political movement led by the JVP was inspired not only by the socialist movement at home but also by revolutionary political movements elsewhere. In fact, the movement came to be referred to as the Che Guevara movement.

Given that the JVP attracted mostly rural Sinhalese youth, equally disaffected Tamil youth in the north and east of the country did not have any significant engagement with the JVP. Given their minority status within the Sri Lankan polity, their attitudes toward the Sri Lankan state were quite different. While the JVP's aspiration was to capture state powers, the militant Tamil youths began to dream about political autonomy for the Tamil community in the Tamil dominated regions. As is well known, the LTTE, around which these disaffected Tamil youths rallied, aspired to establish a separate state in the north and east. The armed struggle they waged against the Sri Lankan state intensified after 1983 when anti-Tamil riots in that year spearheaded by Sinhalese nationalist groups led to further radicalization of Tamil nationalist politics. The intensification of the conflict between the Sri Lankan state and the LTTE led to a widening of the ideological divide between the two ethnic communities. The involvement of the Indian government in the Sri Lankan conflict as an external stakeholder in the mid-1980s led to agitations by Sinhalese nationalist groups, including the JVP, against the Indian intervention in the internal conflict in Sri Lanka. The second JVP-led, anti-state uprising in the late 1980s was as much concerned with the grievances of disaffected Sri Lankan youth as with the increasing significance of Tamil nationalism in the country. So, the post-1983 group violence in the country involved the Sri Lankan state as well as Sinhalese nationalist groups and Tamil nationalist groups. Sinhalese youth were highly involved in this triangular conflict in a highly complex manner. While many Sinhalese youth were involved in the conflict as both civil political activists and armed combatants, a significant proportion of Tamil youth were engaged in armed combat against the Sri Lankan security forces in the north and the east.

## CONSEQUENCES OF GROUP VIOLENCE

The above conflict ended in 2009 with the military defeat of the LTTE. Yet, the consequences of the conflict are long lasting. In the remaining part of this chapter, an effort is made to examine these consequences under several sub themes: state-society relations; erosion of liberal democracy; insecurity and vulnerability of youth; migration of youth; identity segregation and marginalization; and the future prospects of youth.

## State-Society Relations

Group violence involving different groups of youth has had a significant impact on state-society relations in the country. Increasing militarization of society due to the intensification of conflict, both in the north as well as in the south, led to many deaths among youth across the ethnic divide resulting in a hardening of attitudes; yet, it also created opportunities for employment, particularly among underprivileged Sinhalese youth. The increasing sense of insecurity created by the war, in particular random terrorist attacks on civilian targets, raised the profile of the security forces in the country. The members of the combat troops were elevated to the level of war heroes entitled to the praise, admiration, and support of the civilian population. Propaganda machines of both the government and the LTTE mobilized uncritical popular support for the combatants.

During these almost three decades of war, there were times when diverse views as to how to end the war were discussed and debated. There were several attempts by the Sri Lankan government, with or without the involvement of international actors, to find a negotiated political settlement to the conflict. Civil society organizations, the business community, intellectuals, and the media played a significant part in these efforts. In other words, the conflict was not entirely a matter for the conflicting parties. The issues were discussed freely involving various stakeholders in a broadly democratic environment.

In other words, despite a contentious ideological environment, the war did not curtail liberal democratic movements, at least in the first two decades since its beginning. The leftist and liberally oriented political parties openly advocated a peaceful, negotiated settlement to the conflict. Yet, when peace initiatives and political negotiations failed to produce any tangible results, hardline nationalist groups gained the upper hand. Many Sinhalese youth rallied around nationalist parties and groups during the period leading to the 2005 presidential elections. The leading Sinhalese nationalist candidate, Mahinda Rajapaksha, promised to annul the existing peace accord between the government and the LTTE, signaling an all-out war against the LTTE after the elections. Rajapaksha brought other Sinhalese nationalist groups and parties into his fold and built a broad ethno-nationalist coalition to spearhead his election campaign. Having won the presidential election, the newly elected president took various measures to prepare the country for an all-out war against the LTTE. These measures included strengthening of the military in terms of human and material sources; creating a supportive environment for military efforts; and restricting media freedom to prevent critical discussions of war-related matters.

The war ended in mid-2009 with the defeat of the LTTE. Yet, the developments since then point to a further weakening of the institutions of liberal government (see Hettige 2013b). It is necessary to identify the key factors that have reinforced this post-war trend.

## Erosion of Liberal Democracy

Postcolonial Sri Lanka was hailed as a model democracy in Asia in the immediate aftermath of her independence. The establishment of modern institutions in diverse sectors, and their smooth functioning in line with the secular democratic values that were absorbed and adhered to by the members of the colonial elite that came into being during the colonial period, reinforced the liberal democratic form of government in the country. The clear affinity that the country developed over time with the colonial center and the direct and indirect impact that British institutions had on the local elites no doubt played a major part in the propagation of secular democratic values in Sri Lanka. In this regard, the education system was a major influence on younger generations. Initially, exposure to British educational institutions would have shaped the attitudes and world view of young Sri Lankans in a certain fashion (Jayasuriya 1977). Yet, the transformation of local education systems under the influence of nativistic forms was a significant development with implications for identity formation, value orientation, and political ideology (Jayaweera 1986). For instance, many educational institutions became nationalist in their orientation and this trend no doubt began to have a significant impact on youth. Ethno-linguistic divisions among youth became more pronounced and these in turn began to shape their political ideologies and practices.

The increasingly ethno-nationalist orientation of many Sri Lankan youth led to the formation of virtually exclusive political movements among them. These movements advocated political goals that were in conflict with each other. For instance, the JVP's preference for a unitary state of Sri Lanka naturally contradicted with the LTTE idea of a separate state for Tamils in the north and east of Sri Lanka. Jathika Hela Urumaya, an extremist Sinhalese Buddhist party, also attracted many Sinhalese youth into its fold over the most recent decade. This party became a constituent part of the post-2005 coalition government led by President Mahinda Rajapakshe.

The rise of ethno-nationalism in politics has been accompanied by an increasing intolerance of liberal democratic values. The rise to power of a Sinhalese nationalist regime in 2005 signaled the beginning of a reactionary turn in national politics. While the escalation of the war after 2005 resulted in a further curtailment of civil liberties in general, the trend continued even after the end of the war in 2009, indicating a more persistently anti-liberal tendency in national politics.

As mentioned before, the dominant political divisions among youth in the country fall along ethno-nationalist lines, and there is no overwhelming tendency among youth to embrace liberal democratic values, particularly in rural areas. This trend appears to reflect the difficulties that youth experience in transcending ethno-religious divisions to form a political movement based on secular democratic values. This problem in turn tends to reinforce the illiberal tendencies in mainstream politics.

## Increasing Insecurity and Vulnerability of Youth

Increasing violence in society naturally creates an insecure environment for almost everybody, in particular for those who are engaged in the acts of violence. Group violence involving youth in recent years has posed grave risks to the lives of youth activists and the members of the security forces of the government. Thousands of youths were killed over the past three decades of intense conflict and violence. It is estimated that over 60,000 Sinhalese youth were killed during the second JVP-led anti-state uprising in the late 1980s. While over 100,000 persons have been killed in the north and the east during the ethnic conflict over the last three decades, a majority of these persons have been youth, though detailed statistics do not exist on the actual numbers involved.

The increasing risks faced by youth engaged in group violence have led to several outcomes. First, many youths who were not combatants have fled the conflict zone and even left the country as refugees/asylum seekers to protect their lives or avoid persecution by security forces. Second, in many areas, early marriages for young children have been arranged to prevent youth conscription into militant groups or security forces. And finally, the normal activities of youth have been disrupted by violence. These include education, vocational training, and employment, not to mention social and cultural activities.

## Exodus of Youth

An exodus of youth has been a major outcome of group violence in Sri Lanka. As mentioned above, it has been a natural response on the part of youth faced with grave risks and uncertainty to find their way out of the country in search of a secure and stable environment. Hundreds of thousands of youth left the country over the last three decades due to group violence. Many of these youth were not active participants in violence; yet, the widespread sense of insecurity and uncertainty persuaded them to leave the country.

The impact of mass migration of youth belonging to all communities is felt in diverse spheres such as the labor market, civil society organizations, and even national politics. These impacts need careful investigation, both empirically and theoretically. For instance, the shrinking of the labor force, in particular of younger workers, has driven wages up, in addition to creating severe shortages of labor in specific vital sectors such as tea plantations, export industries, and agriculture. Another consequence of the exodus of youth is the formation of a politically active diaspora outside the country, exerting considerable pressure on domestic politics.

## Identity, Segregation, and Marginalization

Group conflicts involving Sri Lankan youth during the last several decades have reinforced pre-existing ethnic identities, exacerbating segregation and marginalization. Though there have been several isolated attempts by civil society organizations to help youth transcend these pre-existing divisions, their impact on mainstream youth society has been marginal. For instance, school-twinning programs implemented by such organizations as the United Nations Development Programme (UNDP) have enabled schoolchildren belonging to different ethno-linguistic groups to interact, develop mutual understanding and establish long-lasting personal relationships, but only a small number of schoolchildren have benefited from such programs. The vast majority of schoolchildren remain segregated and do not have opportunities to establish meaningful contact across various divisions. Furthermore, many underprivileged youth remain marginalized due to poor education and a lack of desirable employment opportunities. Given this state of affairs, the vast majority of youth in the country are unlikely to develop an overreaching national identity and form a social citizenship on the basis of secular democratic values. While the underprivileged youth will continue to depend on the state, which is widely perceived by minorities as biased towards the Sinhalese-Buddhist community, the group violence that characterized the recent past is unlikely to subside unless major policy shifts take place at a national level.

## Future Prospects of Youth

The three decades of group violence that Sri Lankan youth have been exposed to in diverse ways have decisively shaped their future prospects in society. This is a vast theme that deserves detailed discussion and analysis but the limited space available here precludes such a detailed treatment. So, what is attempted here is to provide a brief sketch that could be elaborated in an article in the near future.

Group violence has altered the lives of diverse groups of surviving youth in a decisive fashion. These populations include migrant youth, disabled youth, youth whose education and training were disrupted due to conflict, and those who were deprived of other socioeconomic opportunities as children and youth. The future prospects of these different groups vary widely.

There are considerable efforts on the part of the government to facilitate the reintegration of surviving members of the security forces and the families of those who died in action. Though there are also efforts to support some of the surviving combatants of militant groups, there is little evidence to show how these efforts impact the lives of those survivors and their families.

What is noteworthy is that the divisions that led to the formation of different youth constituencies that helped foment group violence continues to be perpetuated through social, political, and cultural processes. Therefore, the younger children today appear to go through more or less the same processes that their older counterparts went through in their youth. Therefore, what is of considerable concern here is not just the future prospects of youth who were participants in past group violence, but also the future prospects of younger children today.

## CONCLUSION

This chapter has explored the phenomenon of group violence involving youth in Sri Lanka and generally addressed some of the consequences of this type of group violence. While some of these consequences pertain to youths themselves, others relate to the wider social and political context of the country. In this regard, the weakening of the liberal democratic tradition is significant as it has a bearing on governance, development and reconciliation among conflicting groups in society. Though some of the past social and political conflicts have subsided in recent years, there are clear signs today of new group conflicts developing in the country. As in the past, these conflicts are more likely to draw in marginalized and otherwise segregated youth from diverse groups, doubtlessly affecting their present and future well-being and prospects, and effectively perpetuating an ongoing historical cycle.

## REFERENCES

Berk, Richard A. 1974. *Collective Behavior.* Dubuque, IA: W.C. Brown.
Gellner, David N., editor. 2010. *Varieties of Activist Experience.* New Delhi: Sage Publications.
Gould, Roger V. 1999. "Collective Violence and Group Solidarity: Evidence from a Feuding Society." *American Sociological Review* 64: 256–380.
Hettige, Siri T. 1989. *Wealth, Power and Prestige: Emerging Patterns of Inequality in a Peasant Context.* Colombo: Ministry of Higher Education of Sri Lanka.
———. 2004. "Economic Policy, Changing Opportunities for Youth and the Ethnic Conflict in Sri Lanka." In *Economy, Culture, and Civil War in Sri Lanka*, edited by Michael D. Woost and Deborah Winslow, 115–32. Bloomington: Indiana University Press.
———. 2010. "Youth and Political Engagement in Sri Lanka." in Gellner, *Varieties of Activist Experience*, 81–102. New Delhi: Sage India.
———. 2013. "Neo-liberal reforms, The Ethnic Conflicts and the Decline of Liberal Democracy in Sri Lanka." Unpublished paper, 2013.

Jayasuriya, J. E. 1976. *Educational Policies and Progress During British Rule in Ceylon (Sri Lanka), 1796–1948*. Colombo: Associated Educational Publishers.

Jayaweera, Swarna. 1986. *Educational Policies and Change From the Mid-Nineteenth Century to 1977*. Maharagama: National Institute of Education.

Little, Angela W., and Siri T. Hettige. 2013. *Globalization, Employment and Education in Sri Lanka*. London: Routledge.

Russell, Jane. 1982. *Communal Politics under the Donoughmore Constitution 1931–1947*. Colombo: Tissara Publishers.

Staub, Ervin R. 1996. "Cultural Roots of Violence: the Example of Genocide and Contemporary Youth Violence in the United States." *American Psychologist* 51: 117–32.

van Ginneken, Jaap. 1992. *Crowds, Psychology and Politics, 1871–1899*. New York: Cambridge University Press.

White, Robert D. (2006). "Swarming and the social dynamics of group violence." *Trends and Issues in Crime and Criminal Justice* 326: 1–6.

*Chapter Twelve*

# Gender Dimensions of Group Violence

## Donna Pankhurst

Group violence is most often committed by young men against other men. This self-evident fact is not often brought into analyses of the causes and consequences of group, or indeed other forms of, violence. In analyses of the specifically gendered dimensions of violence, there are a range of theoretical positions on the significance of different types of masculinities, but these are of varying rigor. This chapter attempts to import such insights into more general analyses of violent conflict. Using the lens of gender equips us with more than a binary understanding of male versus female behavior, and is able to provoke questions (and some answers) as to the differential behaviors of men per se, where some men actively choose to participate in particular types of violence, whereas others choose to resist. The chapter goes on to explore the highly gendered and varied impacts of group violence.

This analysis is explored against the background of an emerging debate amongst some writers and activists that a) intensely unequal gender relations actually cause wars and b) specific types of masculinities are themselves therefore behind the conditions that lead to mass violence, and we are doomed to continue to face these kinds of violence unless we address gender inequality and specifically what we expect from men.

### GROUP VIOLENCE

The word violence has had a huge range of meanings within specific disciplinary perspectives for a very long time, as described by Hawdon in this volume. Nonetheless it remains the norm for these different approaches to remain largely distinct (in their use, research, and publication) and at the same time for the word to be used in a loose, colloquial way without reference to scholarly work at all. In this chapter I shall focus on contexts of (nonstate) war and the "civil violence" which occurs after wars (which often includes "gang-based" violence). In such contexts violence is often narrowly defined to include certain types of bodily harm (also as described by Hawdon in this volume) directly caused by deliberate acts.

There are several reasons why we do not usually have anything like accurate data for war-related deaths. Even when this narrow definition is used, data are contentious, as was demonstrated in international disputes about deaths in Iraq (e.g., Davies 2006). Sometimes in the context of war and conflict, this tight definition is extended to include illness and death caused by deliberate acts, such as the removal and prevention of access to food, water and, medical treatment, in which the timescale may be considerably longer than the strict definition of the period of "conflict." Furthermore, it is often the case that casualty numbers are reported without making these distinctions clear, or indeed making clear whether casualty refers to death or injury, and so the confusion is compounded. These definitional problems present scholars with serious challenges when considering large scale data sets of group violence, and also sometimes obfuscate communication between scholars aiming to identify causes of the same phenomena.

These very broad types of violence have of course been the focus of commentaries for the whole of human history. Before I launch into my main contribution—that of what a gender analysis can give—I here summarize briefly how I see the very broad disciplinary approaches which are in current use. To be clear, if we take quite a broad definition of violence then we are generally talking about deliberately causing bodily harm. At its simplest, social science scholars have sought to explore the meanings of individual acts to both the perpetrator and victim-survivor,[1] with some investigation and theorizing of the motivations of the perpetrators, and this approach has often led to analyses of emotions that cause aggression. Within social science there is a huge range of approaches, and researchers from different traditions often do not "talk to" each other. Such approaches include consideration of the sociological context (childhood and even baby experiences—attachment theory, etc.), socialization, and culture (and the approval of some types of violence as culturally defined), and the politics of violence (e.g., Galtung's [1969] specification of cultural or structural violence).

In addition there has been much research and analysis in the membership of groups which commit such violence—whether by conscious choice or due to having similar characteristics. Most of this literature is based in social science and covers such topics as: responses to social factors (such as the denial of basic needs); the power of leaders over followers; various processes of stigmatizing or even demonizing "the other" by individuals and groups, and expressing the sense of belonging through the medium of violence (especially with gangs, but also in revolutionary groups of many types).

From the natural sciences there is a long history of work that focuses on the impact of particular genes, parts of the brain and hormonal balances, and in recent decades in particular how hormonal responses may change during life experiences, to consider for instance how well-adapted aggressive behavior can become socially inappropriate violence. Scientists nowadays rarely argue that there are simple biological explanations for such behaviors or changes, but are more focused on the interactions between these and social/ environmental factors. No "violence gene" has been discovered, or a particular place in the brain where such impulses reside, although some parts of the brain—particularly the hippocampus and amygdala—are receiving more attention, particularly in the study of psychopathy and absence of empathy.

The type of violence that I have been most interested in is that which takes place during, and immediately after, wars/conflicts since the Cold War, which have tended to be fought by civilian based groups, sometimes against each other or state-backed forces. In these types of conflicts young men continue to be the majority perpetrators and also often the majority victims of violence. My own work has focused on the experiences of women in these contexts, as they were once hidden and ignored, and the types of violence committed by men against women were not subject to much rigorous research or analysis. Over time I came to recognize the limitations of analyses which only look at women's points of view as they cannot give us a very deep understanding of the motivations and actions of the male perpetrators (or male victim-survivors).

## MEN AND WOMEN, MALE AND FEMALE, MASCULINE AND FEMININE

For whatever reason aggressive behavior leading to violence—however defined—is more common, cross-culturally, in men than in women, and more common in men under thirty than over. This self-evident fact sits alongside the fact that not all people with the same neuro-biological features and sociocultural environments develop the same levels of aggression, antisocial behavior or proclivity to violence. So, although our understanding of violence has increased considerably in recent decades, we are left with many questions.

Similarly we need to keep in mind various complexities regarding the definitions of gender and even sex. There is a very large literature on these terms and how they can be used, but here I summarize briefly:

- *Sex* refers to the distinguishable biological differences between male and female. We tend to discuss these in binary terms but there are a minority of people for whom this is not straightforward, and much of what we think of as biological is also socially constructed.
- *Gender* refers to the socially constructed elements of what it is to be a man and a woman, which are different in different societies (and groups within societies) and often change over time. They are therefore not natural in any sense.
- A gender-aware analysis therefore asks the question, "Is this phenomenon we are studying/planning different for women and men in this location at this moment, and if so why, and with what implications?" This involves looking at *both* genders, using interdisciplinary tools.
- Masculinities and femininities are terms that are used to describe many aspects of each gender in a specific time and location. In recent times the former has received considerable attention, especially but not only in relation to explaining violence, whereas the latter has become rather unfashionable.

In order to attempt to keep a balanced approach in this chapter I consider men and women both as perpetrators and victim-survivors, with a view to identifying what is useful about a gendered analysis in the study of group violence.

## MEN AS PERPETRATORS OF VIOLENCE

Our volume title may be read to infer that terrorists tend to have a history of bullying (perhaps as survivors as well as perpetrators). I do not think we all necessarily mean this but for me there is a connection in common "explanations" for violence committed by men as being the experience of violence in the broadest sense as children and young men. Many analysts draw on "common-sense" explanations, seen as "self-evident," as to why men commit violent acts during and after wars, such as a history of being brutalized during their prolonged exposure to violence during wars. Not all wars are the same in the type or degrees of violence, however, indicating that this is not a straightforward causal relationship which is predictable. Furthermore there is considerable variation in the amount of specifically sexual violence committed by men against women during and after wars, and there is even less of a neat explanation for this than for other forms of violence. It is extremely rare for writers to comment on the variations, and far more common for people to assume that all wars are similar in the amount and causes of interpersonal violence, and that the phenomenon is not difficult to explain.

In previous work (2008) I have identified common explanations as: "something to do with masculinity," variously defined; the psychologies of men; "social constraints on men removed," thesis; "backlash of patriarchy"; and the material gain of men. The "social constraints removed" thesis suggests that somehow it is inevitable and natural that all men will become brutish during wars or in weak or collapsed states. The "backlash of patriarchy" particularly refers to new forms of violence which are perpetrated against women at the ends of wars, particularly where women have had to take up previously male roles during wartime.

The use of the term masculinity is rather more complex and is used to mean different things to different people. It can refer to behavior and practice, ideology, ideal types, and sometimes, but not always, all of these together. There is a significant literature on the concept written largely by sociologists studying men in peacetime, and not specifically focusing on violence. Some writers argue that men's behavior changes over time, and in particular that there is a shift in what society expects of them (what it is to be a man) in the build up to and during wars. The new expectations are said to include certain types of behavior which are violent, particularly against women. I have referred to this view as the "masculinity in the ascendancy" thesis. Others also point out that men act out frustration through violence against women (on both sides) during and after wars and tend to refer to this as "masculinity in crisis," because men are seen to be unable to fulfill their masculinities (such as in protecting children, homeland, providing a living, etc.). These conceptual frameworks are often vague and imprecise yet are also often taken as self-evidently true.

The primary problem with these approaches is that "masculinity" is used inconsistently (sometimes by the same authors) and they tend to ignore research in "non-war" settings, especially from psychology. Also the types of violence under scrutiny here are not committed by all men, even when by all of those who are instructed to do so within a military hierarchy. Furthermore very little empirical research is undertaken with men themselves. No one disagrees that specific masculinities, however defined, are created and maintained through social relations. What is rarely acknowledged, however, is that one very important site for the reproduction of social relations is the family, where of course women in many societies have very strong influence (an important exception being Pearce [2006]).

Heightened violence among young men after wars is now also often seen as a key security and development problem for many post-war states, and their international supporters. Post-war violence is overwhelmingly inflicted by young, poor men against each other, and to a lesser extent against women (World Health Organization 2002, 10). They often do not have much stake in the post-war economy or society, and often suffer from many health impacts of war. What they do have is their sense of masculinity tied to that of being a fighter, and the physical and other forms of power that this can give them. Some interesting observations follow from accounts and analyses of this phenomenon (see El Bushra and Sahl 2005 for further analysis):

1. Such young men, usually have access to guns, and are a potential threat to all civilians, but they are often of most threat to each other. They usually constitute the group that suffers most violence and death both during and after wars.
2. "Young" in some international contexts can mean up to thirty-five years old so it is a confusing category, but it is also commonly assumed that a history of high levels of child soldiers during the war is likely to intensify this phenomenon.
3. Sometimes this violence is manifested through gang activity, and is analyzed alongside studies of gangs, rather than compared with other post-war studies.

## WOMEN AS PERPETRATORS OF VIOLENCE

While it is clear that women never commit anything like the amount of violence that men commit—in any social setting—that is not to say that we should not pay attention to it when it does occur. Women's roles in group violence are often hidden, or even denied, and their victim identities eclipse their agency. During wars, especially where there is no "front line," women's agency still tends to be highlighted by most observers as being exclusively peaceful and anti-violence, although there is a considerable critical feminist literature which shows how this tendency is sometimes misleading.

On the ground women normally play a wide range of roles in conflict (as they do at other times), including that of combatants and gang members, but also as supporters and influencers of men committing violent acts. Such realities present difficulties for some audiences who struggle to recognize women's agency as anything but working for peace, and all their other actions as somehow being determined and controlled by men.[2]

Women have been prosecuted for genocide in Rwanda; are celebrated as heroes for their violent acts in nationalist movements; and seen as martyrs in various Islamic-based groups and movements. In all these different roles, the image of a woman as mother is often used with powerful effect on both sides of antagonistic groups, whereas the women of "the other" are sometimes portrayed as being less than human, sexually promiscuous, untrustworthy, and such. The important volume of Jacobs et al. (2000) gives clear examples of women as protagonists in violent contexts, but also attempts some theorizing about how they engage in this as women. On a rather more subtle note, as mentioned above, if we accept that masculinities shape the way in which men commit violence, then we surely have to consider the roles that women play in shaping them.

## GENDERED IMPACTS OF GROUP VIOLENCE: WOMEN

During and after wars men often commit increasing violence against many women, sometimes in new forms—as soldiers, policemen, peacekeepers, and also partners. Data is once again highly problematic. First we have the definitional problem of "casualties" mentioned above, and this becomes even more muddled and potentially unreliable when we discuss its gendered impacts. There has also been a realignment of the identity of war casualties as being predominantly civilian since the end of the Cold War, so that women and children have come to be seen as the major casualties in war, whereas once they were much less so (Giles and Hyndman 2004b, 3–5). Typical of these is Cockburn (2001, 21), who cites the oft-quoted figure that 90 percent of the casualties of today's wars are civilians. This shift in perception is problematic for a number of reasons. First it has sometimes led to the elision that women are victimized by war to a greater extent than men, because the majority of civilians are women, and when their numbers are added to those of children (as they often are) they often do make up the majority—although the chapter on Sri Lanka in this volume illustrates that between 2000–2008 the deaths were overwhelmingly combatants on both sides, but that in 2009 this overwhelmingly consisted of civilians. This complicated picture is probably more the norm these days although it is rarely reported in this nuanced way, let alone analyzed.

Nonetheless, some analysts have undertaken careful statistical analysis of gender differentials (Stewart et al. 2001, 93; Beaumont 2006), and the calculations of Plümper and Neumayer, 2006 show that more women than men die, or suffer serious disease, as a result of war when a broader interpretation of "war-related deaths" is deployed (Plümper and Neumayer 2006, 3), even if there are more male "battle deaths." On balance then, the extent of women's war-related mortality remains controversial (Pankhurst 2008).

Not surprisingly, more detailed data on the gender balance of survivors and heads of household for instance, are also very difficult to obtain and are often contested, although in this case it is less controversial to assert that there tend to be more women than men who survive major conflicts. Moreover, the plight of women during war, particularly the scale of their sexual violation, has attracted international attention, and is often used to characterize the barbarism of mankind or brutality of particular "enemy" groups of men.

A post-war backlash against women is so common as to be seen now as almost normal (Pankhurst 2008). It often includes some or all of the following elements: sexual and domestic violence does not stop (and often in-creases); new forms of violence against women (e.g., from soldiers, police, peacekeepers, youth partners); an anti-women discourse (with or without the state involvement); measures to restrict women's lives (particularly in the public sphere) legally and socially; calls to "return," or "restore" to a differ-ent gender order (sometimes one which is imagined/invented), especially around motherhood; identification of women's agency as "Western" phe-nomena.

There is however, significant variation in the intensity and duration of a backlash, and sometimes it does not feature strongly in the discourses of commentators. It is rarely anticipated in policy or political terms, even though there has been a significant literature about this for over a decade. There are several notable points about the way in which it is discussed:

1. To my knowledge no meta-analysis has been undertaken to explore possible correlations between the nature of the backlash and, for ex-ample: pre-existing levels of violence against women; pre-existing socioeconomic and political indicators for women *vis á vis* men; the extent of change in women's socioeconomic-political status during war *vis á vis* men.

2. This lack of analysis does not prevent many observers, and partici-pants, making claims as to the causes.

3. Many of the causes are seen as including those thought to cause sexual and other violence against women during war, even where these tend to be assertions, rather than the outcome of testimonies, or other em-pirical research.

4. Scanty data on domestic violence against women after wars suggests that it is not unusual for this to increase to levels not only higher than prior to, but also during, wars. Explanations for this tend to be specu-lative rather than being based on empirical research.

5. Speculative claims are often made regarding the rates of violence, and particular "victim rates," or "casualty rates," for women which are misleading. Confusion about the data is sometimes to do with defini-tions (casualty may or may not indicate death); conflation between categories of women and children; and conflation of the category "ci-vilian" with "women." Such confusion sometimes continues for analy-ses of the post-war period, even where it is acknowledged that women usually outnumber men at this moment.

## GENDERED IMPACTS OF GROUP VIOLENCE: MEN

It is indeed the case that more men than women die directly from violence across the world in general, as well as directly from war (Pearce 2006; WHO 2002) and none of those authors who cite the 90 percent civilian deaths figure, or who highlight the burdens of women, actually refute this directly, although there is certainly ambiguity in some accounts. In other forms of violence exerted by groups, such as gang violence, it is not contested that men constitute the majority of victims, whether they are active in other groups or not.

Men also experience sexual violence during wars (usually committed by other men), but as they are thought to constitute far smaller numbers, there is very little analysis of the victim-survivor impact (and certainly not of the perpetrators).

Some feminist writers are beginning to argue that the ways in which men are encouraged, rewarded, or coerced, to behave in certain ways (as "masculine") also constitutes a kind of victimization. Where this is most obvious is where men openly challenge these norms, such as by refusing to engage in violence against women during wars, and those who actively work for peace and human rights issues, including the reduction of gender inequality.

## CONCLUSION

This is a quote from a piece I wrote eight years ago and sadly is still true:

> The persistent reluctance of many analysts and advisers to take on board lessons about gender analysis and its incorporation into policy processes in the post-war setting needs to be recorded, and further effort is needed to overcome this thoughtless, or deliberate, resistance. This can itself be seen as part of the backlash against women, helping to allow, if not facilitate, the playing out of intense gender politics in households, communities and the wider world. Feminist histories of conflicts, and feminist studies of development, provide a rich store of relevant experiences, both positive and negative. These have been collated and analyzed for several years and comprise a significant literature; but they are still not taken sufficiently seriously by many of the key international actors in the context of post-war activity. (Pankhurst, 2008, 26)

But perhaps we can now be more optimistic that we are closer to finding a synthetic approach to understanding violence amongst academics! We are nonetheless a long way from this enlightenment feeding into policy. As regards the particular violence I have highlighted here, there is still a great deal of what I call "making it up," where writers without having undertaken reading of scholarly works, let alone having developed expertise in this area, not only publish their views based on little more than personal judgment but also advise policymakers from this point of view.

There is a debate to be had about the extent to which we can say that a) intensely unequal gender relations actually cause wars and b) specific types of masculinities are themselves therefore behind the conditions that lead to mass violence, but even adding a "gender lens" to existing analyses of group and individual violence adds a further layer of understanding. Perhaps the more we bring together different perspectives to consider the causes and consequences of group violence, the closer we will get to being able to see ways in which we can break what seems otherwise to be the inevitability of war and post-war violence.

## NOTES

1. I use this term to reflect a) the fact that I am not just talking of people who die and b) the political position taken by many in this category that they prefer to be referred to as survivors rather than victims.

2. Of course women do also exert influence to limit the extent and type of violence committed by men, and often display extreme bravery in doing so, but as this receives more attention I do not explore this further here.

## REFERENCES

Beaumont, Peter. 2006. "Hidden victims of a Brutal Conflict: Iraq's Women," *The Guardian*, 8 October 2006.

Cockburn, Cynthia. 2001. "The Gendered Dynamics of Armed Conflict and Political Violence." In *Victims, Perpetrators Or Actors? Gender, Armed Conflict and Political Violence*, edited by C. Moser and F. C. Clark, 13–29. London: Zed Books.

El-Bushra, Judy and Ibrahim MG Sahl. 2005. *Cycles of Violence: Gender Relations and Armed Conflict*. Nairobi, Kenya: Acord.

Galtung, Johan P. 1969. "Violence, Peace and Peace Research," *Journal of Peace Research* 6: 167–91.

Davies, Gavyn. 2006. "How many Have Died in Iraq?" *The Guardian*, 19 October 2006.

Giles, Wenona, and Jennifer Hyndman. 2004. "Introduction: Gender and Conflict in a Global Context." In *Sites of Violence. Gender and Conflict Zones*, edited by Wenona Giles and Jennifer Hyndman, 3–23. London: University of California Press.

Jacobs, Susie, Ruth Jacobson, and Jennifer Marchbank. 2000. *States of Conflict: Gender, Violence and Resistance*. New York: St. Martin's Press.

Pankhurst, Donna (editor). 2008. *Gendered Peace. Women's Struggles for Post-War Justice and Reconciliation*. New York and London: Routledge.

Pierce, Penny. 2006. "The Role of Women in the Military." In *Military Life. The Psychology of Serving in Peace and Combat: Military Culture Vol. 4*, edited by Thomas Britt, Carl Andrew Castro and Amy Adler, 97–118. Westport, CT: Praeger Security International.

Plümper, Thomas, and Eric Neumayer. 2006. "The Unequal Burden of War: The Effect of Armed Conflict on the Gender Gap in Life Expectancy." *International Organization* 60: 723–54.

Stewart, F., C.Huang, and M.Wang. 2001. "Internal Wars: An Overview of the Economic and Social Consequences." In *War and Underdevelopment*, edited by Frances Stewart and Valpy Fitzgerald, 67–103. London and Oxford: Oxford University Press.

World Health Organization. 2002. World Report on Violence and Health. Geneva, Switzerland: World Health Organization.

*Chapter Thirteen*

# Communities

*Examining Psychological, Sociological, and Cultural Consequences after Mass Violence Tragedies*

Pekka Räsänen, Atte Oksanen, and James Hawdon

Acts of group-targeted violence such as rampage shootings are distressing and extreme tragedies. Over the past decades, several attacks of rampage violence have occurred in the United States, Europe, Asia, South America, and Australia. The scripts of these acts are well known: someone who has been considered harmless enters a public institution, a school, a workplace, or a shopping mall, and kills several innocent people. Typically, the perpetrators of these acts commit suicide or are shot by rescuing police officers (e.g., Newman et al. 2004).

Rampage violence differs from other types of lethal violence. The perpetrators are rarely considered dangerous criminals before their deeds, and perhaps most importantly, they do not fear dying themselves. This is exceptional since the vast majority of people committing homicides do not wish to die as a result of their assaults. Based on American numbers, nearly 40 percent of mass shooters commit suicide and an additional 10 percent by intentional provocation or threatening of the police (Kelly 2010). While approximately one half of mass shooters whose victims are mostly strangers commit suicide, just 4 percent of all American murderers commit suicide (Lankford 2013, 2). In addition, what is noteworthy is that most prefer to perform their attacks on "public stages before an audience" (Newman et al. 2004, 330). Many of the rampage killers have also wanted to add extra shock to their actions by disseminating media packages consisting of videos, pictures, and even straightforward manifestos through the Internet or other mediums. These facts make acts of group-targeted rampage violence something that is practically impossible to understand.

School shootings can be considered particularly tragic acts. Not only are the victims children or youngsters, but the offenders are often children or youngsters themselves. Many of the offenders are also fellow members of the school class and junior citizens of the nearby neighborhood community. In this way, mass violence brings with it several implications that connect to group processes. These processes take place within families, within peer groups, within neighborhoods, and at broader levels of social life. School-shooting massacres shock the whole nation and often lead to breaking news on a global level (e.g., Hawdon et al. 2012a; Muschert and Carr 2006; Oksanen et al. 2010). Despite this, however, we can argue that local communities particularly suffer from this form of violence.

This chapter examines the consequences of group-targeted rampage violence at a community level. In previous literature, scholars have referred to the term "community" in many different ways. For some, community is just an analytical category, which can be used for conceptualization. For others, however, it is an empirical entity that can be detected on the basis of its physical space and social structure. We understand communities as empirical phenomena that typically (but not necessarily) have a distinct geographic location and physical infrastructure. We also understand communities as consisting of human members, who are at least partly interdependent and who form social networks with each other. We also acknowledge that many communities have a symbolic dimension, which enables people to give emotional attributes to physical locations and people around those locations. Therefore, our use of the term is in line with sociological conceptualization of communities and space (see, e.g., Campbell 2000; Giddens 1991; Hawdon and Ryan 2012).

In this chapter, we first identify the key psychological, sociological, and cultural consequences that group-targeted rampage violence likely generates in communities. We then examine the impact of two Finnish school shootings. On November 7, 2007, an eighteen-year-old student killed eight students, staff, and faculty in Finland's Jokela High School. Nine months later, on September 23, 2008, a twenty-two-year-old student entered Seinäjoki University of Applied Sciences in Kauhajoki and committed Finland's deadliest school shooting in history, killing eight and injuring eleven others. Our primary focus is on small communities, but we aim to also consider larger communities. In addition to traditional social communities, we also discuss briefly the implications for Internet online communities. We build our insights on empirical results from the project *Everyday Life and Insecurity: Social Relations after Jokela and Kauhajoki School Shootings.*[1]

## IMPACTS OF GROUP TARGETED VIOLENCE

We begin our investigation by asking how communities are affected by group-targeted rampage violence. As we know, there are different kinds of consequences and they occur at the different levels of community members' lives. For instance, there can be changes in people's psychological mood, mental well-being, and their attitudes. On the other hand, behavior of community members may be affected in many ways, changing how daily routines are performed in the community. In addition to these consequences, there can also be long-term effects in the sense of cultural and moral standards. For example, certain values agreed on by a majority of the community members may change for long periods. Even the social status and the reputation of a community can be completely altered after an incident of mass violence.

We also need to acknowledge that the type of community plays an important role in determining the consequences of group-targeted rampage violence. Small communities are likely to be more vulnerable to these disasters than are larger ones. A community that is tight-knit and highly solidified is often more shaken by acts of mass violence than are communities with weaker social bonds. Physical proximity of the victims and shooters can be another influential factor, as can many other social and demographic characteristics. We may also consider Internet communities as specific communities that provide a strong source of social identification for many people even though they do not exist outside virtual space. We will return to questions regarding size and type of communities later in this chapter. In the meanwhile (as well as for the sake of simplicity), however, we distinguish three analytical levels according to which we will examine the community-level impacts of group-targeted rampage violence: psychological, sociological, and cultural consequences. Figure 13.1 summarizes the basic attributes that are used to distinguish the three levels. We begin our framing with psychological consequences.

### Psychological Consequences

First, it is well established that mass violence often has powerful psychological effects on individuals. These effects reach beyond those individuals who were injured or who experienced direct exposure to violence. In general, nearly all who witness tragic incidents, either directly or indirectly, become more fearful and worried about their safety. They also tend to be more likely than others are to experience mental distress. All of these effects have implications not only for those individuals who experience them, but also for social life in local communities.

In the aftermath of rampage violence, feelings of personal security often decline and many surviving people are traumatized. Posttraumatic stress dis-

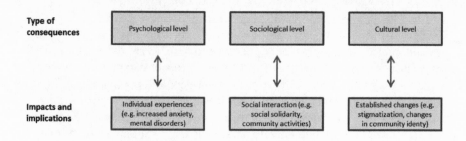

**Figure 13.1. Levels of Analysis for Community Consequences of Group Targeted Violence.**

order (PTSD) symptoms have been reported to increase dramatically. Systematic studies have been conducted to follow students and staff at the schools and universities that experienced shooting rampages (e.g., Brener et al. 2002; Hughes et al. 2011; Haravuori et al. 2011). After the Virginia Tech shootings in 2007, for example, a survey of nearly five thousand Virginia Tech students was fielded to assess the extent to which students suffered PTSD symptoms. The results indicated that over 15 percent of respondents experienced PTSD symptomology soon after the shootings (Hughes et al. 2011). Highly similar findings have been reported from other locations. After the Jokela shootings, which took place soon after Virginia Tech, PSTD symptoms were experienced by approximately 19 percent of those students who participated in the study (Suomalainen ym. 2011). In most similar studies, the effects of the mass violence are related to respondents' age, gender, and other demographic background.

Some researchers have relied on other types of measures when studying psychological impacts of mass tragedies. Sleeping disorders, increased anxiety and feelings of fear and insecurity have been reported after school shootings (e.g., Newman et al. 2004; Haravuori ym. 2011). Similarly, exposure to crimes that attack the collective can increase fear of other types of crimes (Hawdon and Ryan 2009). This indicates that those affected by mass violence are more likely than others to associate their experiences with other crimes. It has been argued that crime can fracture a community's social network, lead residents to withdraw from civic life, and eventually foster an environment that promotes more crime (e.g., Gray et al. 2011; Jackson and Gray 2010).

What is noteworthy is that since the tragedies frequently take place at schools, non-attendance at classes is likely to increase. This is well documented in a comprehensive study conducted after the Columbine school massacre (Brener et al. 2002). The traumatized students are afraid to return to classrooms and schoolyards where the tragedies occurred. In this way, psychological effects are related to other types of problems such as decreasing learning and lower grades among traumatized students.

## Sociological Consequences

In addition to negative psychological outcomes and even psychiatric symptoms, school shootings affect people's daily activities and the ways they relate to their surrounding neighborhood. We consider these effects as sociological consequences. Social solidarity, social capital, social cohesion, social networks, social norms, and trust have been used to capture the essential features of social life. Literature suggests that after major tragedies, individuals' associations with their community can change dramatically. Research on social solidarity is most systematic in this respect. Several studies indicate that social solidarity increases after tragic incidents such as natural disasters, terrorist attacks, or other mass tragedies (e.g., Collins 2004; Hawdon and Ryan 2012; Smelser 2004; Turkel 2002). Yet, how and why does this happen?

Scholars generally agree that mass violence increases solidarity because acts performed by grieving community members are intensely symbolic and focus participants' attention on the damage the violence had on the community. Since such tragedies disturb collective feelings, the community produces a collective response. This original idea stressing the strength of the community and its resiliency dates to Durkheim's seminal writings (1893/1964). According to him, the collective response to crime and related tragedies is due to the collective nature of the sentiments crime offends. As a result, a unique "public temper" emerges, which becomes visible as people seek to come together to talk to each other about the acts (Durkheim 1893/1964, 102). From this perspective, social solidarity is similar to collective efficacy, in which neighborhood members mutually participate and come to each other's aid. It is thus something that is considered as everybody's concern without being anyone's in particular.

It is often assumed that social solidarity benefits survivors of a grieving community. Indeed, solidarity can be an important source of trust, engagement, support, and well-being in normal times; however, it probably plays a more important role in promoting well-being after mass tragedies (e.g., Collins 2004; Hawdon and Ryan 2012). This is because embeddedness in strong social networks tends to develop attachment with others that, in turn, contributes to well-being. After experiencing stressful events, solid networks and relations based on trust can decrease feelings of insecurity and even the likelihood of occurrence of PTSD and other psychological symptoms (e.g., Galea et al. 2002; Hawdon et al. 2012b). Therefore, as a collective feeling of community attachment, solidarity can counteract the harmful effects of stressors by providing emotional resources and encouraging effective coping strategies for individuals.

In empirical studies, social solidarity is frequently understood as a sense of community and engagement in local activities. For this purpose, standardized instruments measuring collectivity and social interaction patterns have been used in survey-based studies. Questions on whether the respondents are proud to be a member of their community, trust their neighbors, and if people collaborate to get things done for their community are held as reliable measures of solidarity. These types of items reflect a sense of belonging to a local community and a healthy sense of attachment to that community (e.g., Bachrach and Zautra 1985; Hawdon et al. 2012b). While social solidarity is often assessed using subjective ratings, the levels of solidarity associates well with related behavioural measures. In a longitudinal study collected before and after the 2007 shootings at Virginia Tech (Hawdon and Ryan 2011), it was found that involvement in parochial-sphere activities of the local community generated and sustained social solidarity. The parochial sphere consists of local stores, schools, and clubs. This is why involvement in such general relations often correlates strongly with a high level of solidarity (Hawdon and Ryan 2011).

Psychological and sociological effects can be immediately experienced after group-targeted rampage violence. However, longer-term consequences may also result from such tragedies. For example, a feeling of collective guilt may arise among the survivors or a taboo against the discussion of the event can become a silent norm. Tragic events can even lead to a cultural shift in the community's traditions and the community members' identity.

## Cultural Consequences

It is well established that mass violence can have enduring consequences. In this respect, we can talk about cultural traumas. According to Erikson (1976, 154), collective trauma "does not have the quality of suddenness normally associated with trauma," but instead it is a slow process. If only a few individuals in the community experience a tragedy, the rest of the community is able to support the victims. In the case where the entire community is struck by a tragedy, the community can no longer offer support, and the trauma becomes collective (Erikson 1976).

A common interpretation is that communities can experience a cultural trauma when its members are subjected to a horrible tragedy, which leaves an inevitable mark on their memory and fundamentally changes the way they think about identity (Alexander 2004). A cultural trauma is thus considered as something that relates to the shared consciousness or social memory of a traumatized social group. While some theorists see cultural trauma merely as a conceptual metaphor (e.g., Kansteiner 2004; Sztompka 2000), the concept is useful when trying to interpret how complex and long-lasting traumatic experiences can be for small groups of residents and even larger communities. It is possible that a trauma, stored in collective memory, becomes a cultural heritage that is passed from one generation to another. Long-lasting traumas have been widely discussed in connection to colonization and slavery (e.g., Eyerman 2004; Ross 2009), but also in connection to tragic events such as wars, natural disasters, or terrorist attacks (e.g., Alexander 2004; Smelser 2004).

Different issues regarding tragedies can initiate trauma processes even years after the events by bringing back negative feelings such as shame, disgust, or guilt (Smelser 2004). From this perspective, cultural trauma processes have also been referenced when analysing communities that have experienced school shooting tragedies (e.g., Nurmi et al. 2012; Larkin 2009). Cultural trauma is a useful framework if it can offer plausible interpretations about what has happened and how community life changed after the tragedy.

Next, we examine how two Finnish communities experienced the psychological, sociological and cultural consequences of school shootings.

## EXAMINING THE CONSEQUENCES OF FINNISH SCHOOL SHOOTING TRAGEDIES

Our project investigated community responses to the shootings with repeated survey data and interviews. The data were collected over a period of two years, from 2008 to 2010. Comparability was the main criterion in the collection of the survey data. The themes covered in the data dealt with social relations in the local communities, descriptions of the local communities, residents' personal experiences of the school shootings, and the consequences of the shootings for community life. The questionnaires included items meauring psychological well-being, community participation, social solidarity, and beliefs as to whether or not the tragedies could have been prevented. Interview data were collected to allow us to further understand how Jokela and Kauhajoki residents experienced the shootings.

We fielded the first mail survey in Jokela between May 15 and June 15, 2009, approximately six months after the school shooting. The sampling frame for the Finish survey was seven hundred Jokela residents between the ages of eighteen and seventy-four selected from the Population Register Database. The second wave of Jokela data using the same procedures as the first wave were collected eighteen months after the shooting in May and June 2009. The minimum response rates of the Jokela surveys were 47 and 40 percent, respectively. Kauhajoki data were collected using identical techniques for seven hundred randomly selected respondents living in the Kauhajoki area. The first wave of data were collected in March–April 2009 and the second in March–April 2010, approximately six months and eighteen months after the tragedy. The minimum response rates were similar to those in Jokela at 46 and 48 percent, respectively.

To supplement the survey data, we also conducted three types of interviews. The first type of interview was with individuals who participated in crisis work or aftercare after the incidents. Six interviewees were from Jokela and five were from Kauhajoki. These interviews were conducted in January–March 2009 in Jokela and in September–November 2009 in Kauhajoki. The second type of interview involved residents of Jokela and Kauhajoki. A total of forty-three people participated in the interviews, twenty-one in Jokela and twenty-two in Kauhajoki respectively. In addition, a third type of interview was with the parents of the Jokela shooter. His parents were interviewed twice, in January 2010 and in June 2011. The interview themes for the shooter's partners were basically the same as in the other interviews with residents.

With these data, we are able to offer a relatively well-documented interpretation of how the local communities experienced the mass shootings. Responses were examined from an *ex post facto* perspective because we did not have any data prior to the shootings. We summarize our main finding using the three level approach introduced in the previous section (see figure 13.1). We start from our research findings regarding psychological impacts and then move to sociological findings. Finally, we make interpretations about the cultural consequences of the shootings. Our results suggest that the impact of mass tragedies varies by community characteristics. We will return to this question at a more general level in the following section of this chapter.

## Psychological Consequences of Jokela and Kauhajoki Shootings

A number of studies investigated the psychological effects of the Jokela and Kauhajoki shootings. The most important contributions focused on trust in institutions being able to prevent future school shootings, personal anxiety, depressive mood, and fear of crime.

Oksanen et al. (2010) examined the residents' reactions to school shootings. In general, the study asked what implications the shooting incidents may have for Finland as a Nordic welfare society. It is important to know people who were near the tragedy, but perhaps not personally involved, reacted to the shootings. Since Jokela and Kauhajoki are relatively small communities, it was assumed that many of the inhabitants knew at least one of the victims, the perpetrator, or at least their family members. The main findings show that as many as one-third (34 percent) of the respondents in Jokela said they knew someone who died in the shootings. In contrast, less than one-fifth (18 percent) of Kauhajoki respondents knew someone who died in the tragedy. Forty-four percent of the Jokela respondents believed that the incident could have been prevented. In Kauhajoki the proportion was smaller, with 41 percent of respondents believing this. Thus, the results suggest that the majority of local residents do not believe that the school shootings could have been prevented. In other words, respondents generally did not trust that the system could prevent future school shootings. This widespread lack of trust contradicts many of the basic beliefs regarding the general trust Finns have toward the insitutions of the Nordic welfare state.

Psychological effects of the shootings were examined from a more traditional framework in Oksanen et al. (in press). Acknowledging preceding research showing that PTSD, depression, and anxiety frequently emerge after mass violence, the study focused on how social support and solidarity provide protection from the harmful effects of school shooting experiences. In both Jokela and Kauhajoki, approximately 16 percent of the respondents reported depressive mood. Social support was associated with psychological well-being after the tragedies. In addition, the finding further demonstrates that social support has a function even after traumatic and rare life events. The results also underline the meaning of belonging to one's community, which proved to be a resource of well-being. Those respondents who had a strong sense of community reported less symptoms of depression.

Fear of crime is also an important psychological consequence that can increase in the aftermath of mass violence tragedies. Dramatic incidents may particularly afflict vulnerable groups such as people suffering from depression or having experienced severe personal losses. Vuori et al. (2013) examined levels of fear about the recurrence of school shootings among adults in Jokela and Kauhajoki. The results were in line with prior studies indicating that women, particularly aged eighteen to thirty-four, expressed greater concerns about the recurrence of mass violence at schools. At the same time, however, younger men were the least worried respondents about the recurrence of such incidents. Moreover, respondents at the lowest quartile of income were more concerned about crime than the financially better off respondents. Thus, fear of collective-targeted crime is grounded in the everyday lives of local residents. The Finnish school shootings, which were followed by numerous threats of similar assaults, resulted in vicarious effects, which made risk more concrete for certain social groups.

## Sociological Consequences of Jokela and Kauhajoki Shootings

A body of sociological research shows that social solidarity aids the afflicted community's residents' recovery process after mass tragedies (e.g., Collins 2004; Galea et al. 2002; Hawdon and Ryan 2011). Simultaneously, however, we also need to recognize that solidarity can have a "dark side" (Hawdon, Oksanen, Räsänen, and Ryan 2012). There can be several negative consequences of social solidarity such as the exclusion of outsiders, excessive claims on group members, and restrictions on individual freedoms. In this way, the social control created by heightened solidarity that leads to beneficial outcomes for some can have the opposite effect for others.

Nurmi et al. (2012) analyzed how negative aspects of social solidarity evolved in Jokela after the tragedy. This study explored the kinds of behavioral expectations towards grieving that emerged as the community tried to recover from the disaster. The data consisted of a mail survey of local adult residents and interview data from six professionals who were working in Jokela during the crisis. The survey data suggest that Jokela was a community in which residents liked to live; however, resident cooperation and participation in community activities were not common. The interviewed professionals also said that certain aspects of solidarity, such as collective guilt and stigmatization, were clearly present when the collective identity was being revised. In particular, the town's youth formed tight networks that excluded others, including their own parents. Therefore, the results indicate that increased solidarity also has restrictive effects on individuals. An additional study (Nurmi 2012), which was based on local residents' interviews from both Jokela and Kauhajoki, came to a similar conclusion.

One important dimension of school shootings deals with speculation about the causes behind the tragedies. Many researchers studying mass killings adopt a psychological approach and analyze the perpetrators hoping to decipher their motives. Others take a security and policing studies approach and attempt to understand how our security systems were avoided and how they can be improved to prevent future acts of mass violence. Lindström et al. (2010) brought these kinds of approaches to a sociological level of analysis by examining residents' perceptions of the shootings' causes. The analysis was based on comparable survey data from both communities. Respondents were asked to rank potential causes that entered Finnish public discourses. The respondents rated items such as the increase in the use of the Internet, deterioration of traditional community, and cuts in health care services as the primary causes for the shootings. The overall results, however, suggested that the shootings were understood as an "international" phenomenon, rather than a "national" one.

## Cultural Consequences of Jokela and Kauhajoki Shootings

It is evident that certain impacts of school shootings are long-term. For example, people all over the world still associate the word "Columbine" with a high school shooting that took place in 1999, and there is little that can be done to change that. In fact, typing Columbine into any Internet search engine offers you hundreds of web pages devoted to the massacre. It has been even argued that after the shootings, Columbine became a "keyword" for a complex set of youth troubles in public discourses (Muschert 2007, 365). While it is perhaps too early to understand what long-term cultural consequences the Jokela and Kauhajoki shootings will have, some of our findings are worth considering from such a cultural perspective.

In a study by Nurmi et al. (2012), Jokela residents worry about the stigmatization of the community. According to the results, a clear labelling phenomenon was also witnessed in everyday language as the word Jokela became a synonym for school shootings. People in Jokela felt that whenever outsiders heard their town's name, they immediately thought of the shootings. Jokela was thus associated with a negative phenomenon, which has damaged the community's image. At the time of the interviews, there was talk in the village about the decline in property prices and the difficulty of selling houses in the area. The fear of social stigmatization led some inhabitants to feel that it was easier to hide their residential identity when they were outside their community. One revealing anecdote regarding this was that some of the Jokela residents said they were ashamed to tell outsiders that they live in Jokela when buying tickets for the commuter train; as such, these residents would purchase tickets for the next closest stop.

The Jokela and Kauhajoki tragedies may also have an effect on dimensions of culture at a national level. Finland and other Nordic countries are associated with a high-quality education system, equality between sexes, low rates of poverty, and small income disparities. Although Finland is generally considered a secure, peaceful, and attractive country in which to live, the two school shootings might have affected the country's public image (Räsänen et al. 2012). The incident created a wave of threat messages in educational establishments all over Finland. In 2012, more than fifty such threats were reported to the Finnish police (Savolainen 2013). Therefore, it is possible that the incidents have added not only to the potential distress and feeling of insecurity of many residents, but also changed their local and national identities.

## Differences in Consequences among Community Types

Examining group-targeted violence, and school shootings in particular, as violence occurring in communities, we may assume that the consequences vary considerably by community characteristics. Statistics show that many of these incidents happened unexpectedly in small communities. In the United States, for example, as many as 60 percent of all school shootings between 1974–2002 occurred in rural areas (Newman et al. 2004, 232–34). Because rural and suburban areas are considered peaceful and safe compared to big cities, the collapse of this sense of security following school shootings make them extremely shocking for local residents.

The comparison of the consequences between Jokela and Kauhajoki shows that the communities responded differently to the shootings. Of course, both communities were severely traumatized as the shootings disrupted the routine of everyday life, and most community members defined the event as affecting the entire collective. Despite this, however, the Jokela tragedy will always remain Finland's first large-scale shooting. Compared to Kauhajoki, it will probably be remembered as a "unique" or an "isolated" tragedy.

Second, in Kauhajoki, a significant number of community members considered the incident as not affecting Kauhajoki, per se. Instead, they saw it as affecting the direct victims and not the local community. This contrasts significantly with the understanding of the event in Jokela. This difference is because, unlike in Jokela, the shooter and most victims were not defined as community members; rather, they were defined as outsiders who came to Kauhajoki simply to continue their education (e.g., Lindström et al. 2010; Oksanen et al. 2010). We believe this difference is the key reason why the group effects that emerged were of a different nature in Kauhajoki compared to Jokela.

Third, one of the most significant differences between the communities deals with young people's behavior. In Jokela, youth formed tight networks with each other and expressed grief together. In Kauhajoki, on the other hand, many residents felt they were excluded if they showed too much grief. Several respondents indicated that they felt those who were openly displaying grief were being too dramatic (Nurmi 2012). Some residents even believed that "public" grieving prolonged the tragedy instead of helping recover from it. In this case, the tragedy did not bind the community together; it acted as a barrier between the groups of residents.

In general, one can assume that the size of the communities as well as physical proximity between the communities has something to do with the effects of group-targeted rampage violence. Even by Finnish standards, Jokela is a small town with less than six thousand residents, and it belongs to a larger Tuusula municipality. With a population of over fourteen thousand, Kauhajoki is clearly a larger community than Jokela, both geographically and in population.

While the effects of a tragedy may vary by community size, it is important to realize the concept of community does not refer solely to physical communities. On the contrary, virtual communities create important sites of social participation, communication, and social identification, especially for young people (e.g., Lehdonvirta and Räsänen 2011; Näsi et al. 2011; Williams et al. 2006). While the terms "virtual community" and "online community" are often used loosely to refer to any interactive Web site where marketers hope to attract visitors, there are many instances where genuine group identity is formed (Lehdonvirta and Räsänen 2011). By increasing the number of social relationships and improving opportunities for communication, the participants of online communities can develop strong interpersonal ties. Emotional support, friendship, social support, and other processes that are associated with traditional offline groups are frequently observed in studies of online groups. Moreover, urbanization and the changing job market challenge the efficacy of traditional peer groups, such as neighborhood groups, work colleagues, and even families. One important difference between online and offline groups is that online groups are "communities of choice" as opposed to communities of geographically proximate.

Regarding the impacts of mass-targeted rampage violence, it is important to acknowledge that people participate in several loosely structured social groups during an average day. Many of these groups are primarily constituted through an interest in shared leisure activities and preferences. Despite this, participation in such groups can be intensive and experienced by the participating members as being extremely important. Thus, we should address the consequences that these communities may go through after tragedies. They can exist in either the physical or virtual world, or probably more frequently, in both. Such investigations are critically important areas for future researchers.

## CONCLUSION

As noted earlier, school shootings are difficult tragedies to understand. We consider them distressing because they represent extreme acts of violence and because they tend to occur in public places. In addition, unlike "normal" violence between individuals or between rival gangs, acts of group-targeted rampage violence occur unexpectedly. Consequently, public attention is often focused on the psychological characteristics of the killers instead of profiling social contexts and community characteristics that increase the likelihood of shooting rampages. Given there is still relatively little research examining how local communities experience such tragedies, what have we learned from our research on the Jokela and Kauhajoki shootings?

We argue that when examining community recovery, it is necessary to consider the consequences at different levels community. This is important since community life takes place and has significance at many different levels. Community consists of physical infrastructures and social interactions among the residents, and involves a variety of symbolic elements. Based on the published research, we suggest psychological, sociological, and cultural frames for distinguishing different types of community experiences after tragedies.

In psychological terms, both Jokela and Kauhajoki were traumatized, at least temporarily. For instance, since trust towards the prevention of school shootings was very low in both communities, the tragedies probably increased the anxiety of local residents. Although the fear of crime was generally more intense in Kauhajoki than in Jokela, the fear of crime was relatively strong in both communities after the tragedies. In addition, approximately the same proportion of the community residents showed at least mild symptoms of depression.

The most important sociological consequences of the shootings related to social solidarity. A rise in solidarity was experienced in both Jokela and Kauhajoki. The shootings were described as a shared crisis affecting the whole community, and interrupting the everyday routines of many of its inhabitants, and the functioning of several municipal institutions. However, these observations were more visible in Jokela than in Kauhajoki. In other words, the Jokela collective experienced more clearly the sense that they were the victim of a crime. The incident strengthened social solidarity inside the community and this at least temporarily strengthened the inhabitants' identification with the collective. The findings also show that although the increase in social solidarity often follows a tragedy, it does not solely result in positive outcomes for the community. Negative aspects of solidarity, such as collective guilt and stigmatization, are also present when the collective identity is being revised after a mass tragedy.

Regarding cultural consequences, the tragedies show us that school shootings can lead to cultural trauma. Perhaps most importantly, the shootings touched the roots of everyday social interaction, especially feelings of security. In addition, school shootings were seen as having social origins in contrast to accidents or natural disasters. Moreover, in Jokela, the offender was a community member, which forced the community to confront issues of collective guilt. Although the traumas were difficult for both communities, they allowed the communities to redirect the course of community life. The process will undoubtedly take several years and possibly decades, but during this process, the local communities' collective identities are likely to change.

At a societal level, the Jokela and Kauhajoki school shootings, as well as the subsequent threats of other school shootings, pose an additional problem for Finnish society. We live in a world of uncontrollable risks, and unexpected violence is an issue that might be difficult to prevent, no matter how well Finland has adapted to other social risks of the twenty-first century.

## NOTE

1. We wish to acknowledge generous research grant from Emil Aaltonen Foundation, which made our efforts possible. The project, which ran between 2009–2012, was led by Atte Oksanen and Pekka Räsänen at the University of Turku, Finland. In addition, Johanna Nurmi,

Miika Vuori, and Kauri Lindström participated in the project as researchers. The project collaborated closely with the American National Science Foundation funded projects *Campus Violence: Exploring a Community's Response to Tragedy* and the *Social Relations and Community Solidarity: An International Comparative Analysis* projects. These two projects were led by James Hawdon and John Ryan at Virginia Tech in the United States.

## REFERENCES

Alexander, J. C. 2004. "Toward a Theory of Cultural Trauma." In *Cultural Trauma and Collective Identity*, edited by Jeffrey C. Alexander, Ron Eyerman, Bernhard Giesen, Neil J. Smelser, and Piotr Sztompka, 1–30. Berkeley, Los Angeles and London: University of California Press.

Bachrach, K. M., and A. J. Zautra. 1985. "Coping with a Community Stressor: The Threat of a Hazardous Waste Facility." *Journal of Health and Social Behavior* 26: 127–41.

Brener, N. D., T. R. Simon, M. Anderson, L. C. Barrios, and M. L. Small. 2002. "Effect of the Incident at Columbine on Students' Violence- and Suicide-Related Behaviors" *American Journal of Preventive Medicine* 22: 146–50.

Campbell, C. D. 2000. "Social Structure, Space and Sentiment: Searching for Common Ground in Sociological Conceptions of Community" In *Research in Community Sociology*, edited by D. A. Chekki, 21–57. Stamford, CT: JAI Press.

Collins, R. 2004. "Rituals of Solidarity and Security in the Wake of Terrorist Attack." *Sociological Theory* 22: 53–87.

Durkheim, E. 1964. *The Division of Labor in Society*. New York: The Free Press, Originally published in French, *De la division du travail social*. (Paris: Les Presses Universitaires de France, 1893).

Erikson, K. T. 1976. *Everything in its Path: Destruction of Community in the Buffalo Creek Flood*. New York: Simon and Schuster.

Eyerman, R. 2004. "Cultural Trauma, Slavery and Formation of African American Identity," in *Cultural Trauma and Collective Identity*, edited by Jeffrey C. Alexander, Ron Eyerman, Bernhard Giesen, Neil J. Smelser, and Piotr Sztompka, 60–96. Berkeley, Los Angeles and London: University of California Press.

Galea, S., J. Ahern, H. Resnick, D. Kilpatrick, M. Bucuvalas, J. Gold, and D. Vlahov. 2002. "Psychological Sequelae of the September 11 Terrorist Attacks in New York City." *New England Journal of Medicine* 346: 982–87.

Giddens, A. 1991. *Modernity and Self-Identity. Self and Society in the Late Modern Age*. Cambridge: Polity Press.

Gray, E., J. Jackson, and S. Farrall. 2011. "Feelings and Functions in the Fear of Crime." *British Journal of Criminology* 51: 75–94.

Haravuori, H., N. Berg, O. Kiviruusu, and M. Marttunen. 2011. "Effects of Media Exposure on Adolescents Traumatized in a School Shooting." *Journal of Traumatic Stress* 24: 70–79.

Hawdon, J., A. Oksanen, and P. Räsänen. 2012a. "Media Coverage and Solidarity after Tragedies: Reporting School Shootings in Two Nations." *Comparative Sociology* 11: 845–74.

Hawdon, J., A. Oksanen, P. Räsänen, and J. Ryan. 2012. "School Shootings and Local Communities: An International Comparison between the United States and Finland." *Working Papers in Economic Sociology* (IV). Turku: Turun yliopisto.

Hawdon, J., P. Räsänen, A. Oksanen and J. Ryan. 2012. "Social Solidarity and Wellbeing after Critical Incidents: Three Cases of Mass Shootings." *Journal of Critical Incident Analysis* 3: 2–25.

Hawdon, J. and J. Ryan. 2011. "Social Relations that Generate and Sustain Solidarity After a Mass Tragedy." *Social Forces* 89: 1363–84.

———. 2009. "Social Capital, Social Control and Crime." *Crime and Delinquency* 55: 526–49.

———. 2012. "Wellbeing after the Virginia Tech Mass Murder: The Relative Effectiveness of Face-to-Face and Virtual Interactions in Providing Support for Survivors." *Traumatology* 18: 3–12.

Hughes, M. L., M. Brymer, W. T. Chiu, J. Fairbank, R. Jones, R. Pynoos, V. Rothwell, A. M. Steinberg, and R. Kessler. 2011. "Posttraumatic Stress Among Students after the Shootings at Virginia Tech." *Psychological Trauma: Theory, Research, Practice, and Policy* 3: 403–11.

Jackson, J., and E. Gray. 2010. "Functional Fear and Public Insecurities about Crime." *British Journal of Criminology* 50: 1–22.

Kansteiner, W. 2004. "Genealogy of a category mistake: a critical intellectual history of the cultural trauma metaphor." *Rethinking History: The Journal of Theory and Practice* 8: 193–221.

Kelly, R. 2010. *Active Shooter Report: Recommendations and Analysis for Risk Mitigation.* New York: New York City Police Department.

Lankford, A. 2013. "Mass Shooters in the USA, 1966–2010: Differences Between Attackers Who Live and Die." *Justice Quarterly* 30: 1–20.

Larkin, R. W. 2009. "The Columbine Legacy. Rampage Shootings as Political Acts." *American Behavioral Scientist* 52: 1309–26.

Lehdonvirta, V., and P. Räsänen. 2011. "How Do Young People Identify with Online and Offline Peer Groups? A Comparison between United Kingdom, Spain and Japan." *Journal of Youth Studies* 14: 91–108.

Lindström, K., J. Nurmi, A. Oksanen, and P. Räsänen. 2010. "Jokelan ja Kauhajoen asukkaiden arviot koulusurmien yhteiskunnallisista syistä." *Sosiologia* 47: 270–85.

Muschert, G. W. 2007. "Research in School Shootings." *Sociology Compass* 1: 60–80.

Muschert, G. W., and D. Carr. 2006. "Media Salience and Frame Changing across Events: Coverage of Nine School Shootings." *Journalism and Mass Communication Quarterly* 83: 747–66.

Näsi, M., P. Räsänen, and V. Lehdonvirta. 2011. "Identification with Online and Offline Communities: Understanding ICT Disparities in Finland." *Technology in Society* 33: 4–11.

Newman, Katherine, Roger Simpson, and William Coté. 2004. *Covering Violence: A Guide to Ethical Reporting about Victims and Trauma.* New York: Columbine University Press.

Nurmi, J. 2012. "Making Sense of School Shootings: Comparing Local Narratives of Social Solidarity and Conflict in Finland." *Traumatology* 18: 16–28.

Nurmi, J., P. Räsänen, and A. Oksanen. 2012. "The Norm of Solidarity: Experiencing Negative Aspects of Community Life after a School Shooting Tragedy." *Journal of Social Work* 12: 300–319.

Oksanen, A., P. Räsänen, and J. Hawdon. In press. *Psychological Wellbeing after School Shootings in Local Communities: Examining the Role of Social Support and Sense of Community.*

Oksanen, A., P. Räsänen, J. Nurmi, and K. Lindström. 2010. "This Can't Happen Here! Community Reactions to School Shootings in Finland." *Research on Finnish Society* 3: 19–27.

Räsänen, P., M. Näsi, and O. Sarpila. 2012. "Old and New Sources of Risk: A Study of Societal Risk Perception in Finland." *Journal of Risk Research* 15: 755–69.

Ross, R. 2009. *Dancing with a Ghost: Exploring Indian Reality.* New York: Penguin Global.

Savolainen, M. 2013. "Koulu-uhkaukset heikentävät oppilaitosten ilmapiiriä." *Haaste* 2. Accessed August 2, 2013. www.haaste.om.fi/Etusivu/Lehtiarkisto/Haasteet2013/Haaste22013/1368801768595.

Smelser, N. J. 2004. "Psychological and Cultural Trauma." In *Cultural Trauma and Collective Identity*, edited by Jeffrey C. Alexander, Ron Eyerman, Bernhard Giesen, Neil J. Smelser, and Piotr Sztompka, 31–59. Berkeley, Los Angeles, and London: University of California Press.

Suomalainen, L., H. Haravuori, N. Berg, O. Kiviruusu, and M. Marttunen. 2011. "A Controlled Follow-up Study of Adolescents Exposed to a School Shooting—Psychological Consequencess after Five Months." *European Journal of Psychiatry.* 26: 490–97.

Sztompka, P. 2000. "Cultural Trauma: The Other Face of Social Change." *European Journal of Social Theory* 3: 449–66.

Turkel, G. 2002. "Sudden Solidarity and the Rush to Normalization: Toward an Alternative Approach." *Sociological Focus* 35: 73–79.

Vuori, M., A. Oksanen, and P. Räsänen. 2013. "Local Responses to Collective and Personal Crime after School Shootings." *Crime, Law and Social Change* 59: 225–42.

Williams, D., N. Ducheneaut, L. Xiong, Y. Zhang, N. Yee, and E. Nickell. 2006. "From Tree Houses to Barracks: The Social Life of Guilds in World of Warcraft." *Games and Culture* 1: 338–61.

*IV*

# Reflections on Group Violence

*Chapter Fourteen*

# Group Violence Revisited

*Common Themes Across Types of Group Violence*

James Hawdon

The chapters in this volume address numerous types of violence. From school bullies to revolutionaries and international terrorists, these chapters tell of a variety of actors and a variety of acts. It is likely that many would argue the schoolyard bully has little in common with the international terrorist. Many may argue that the perpetrators and victims of these acts are as distinct as the acts themselves. Yet, it is possible such arguments fail "to see the forest because of the trees." I argue below a number of factors cut across these types of violence.

## VIOLENT SITUATIONS

In one sense, people are not violent, situations are. If we think about the amount of time one spends on the planet, most of that time is spent being nonviolent, even if the person is an "extremely violent person." Most theories of violence focus the characteristics of the individuals enacting violence; however, these theories fall in the category of "covering theories" and are not "causal" in nature. Indeed, theories that focus on one's psychosocial traits, status position, self-control, differential associations, or strains lack the dynamic nature that causal theories require. Contrary to Gottfredson and Hirschi's (1990) claim that self-control is the cause of all crime, it cannot be the "cause" of any crime. As the authors assert, self-control is invariant. If true, it cannot cause anything because constants cannot cause variation. Instead, theories such as self-control theory specify conditions under which crime, or violence more specifically, occurs.

While I lack the space to develop this argument here, I contest that most theories of crime and violence are, either implicitly or explicitly, rational choice theories. Few theories identify a "causal mechanism" that, when triggered, leads to violence (for similar arguments, see Wikström 2012; Black 2012). Instead, they identify characteristics of people that are likely to respond to a given situation violently—that is, rationally decide that violence is in his or her best interest in this given situation. Thus, those with low self-control act violently when presented with a situation to do so because low self-control inhibits their ability to calculate the long-term consequences of one's acts (see Gottfredson and Hirschi 1990). Similarly, associating with deviant peers does not cause crime in the same sense that adding sugar to water causes it to be sweet. Instead, those who associate with deviant peers learn that crime is acceptable or desirable; thus, when an opportunity to commit a crime presents itself, these individuals are likely to commit the crime. Of course, they are probably more likely than others are to seek such opportunities too. The point is this: we lack a good causal explanation of violence. We have, however, identified conditions that, when the cause is present, makes some more likely to act violently than others.

The chapters on the perpetrators of group violence can help identify some characteristics that are associated with group violence. I am concerned here more with the characteristics of situations than with individuals, because, in many of these cases, groups, not individuals, behave violently. It is unlikely that all the perpetrators of the Darfur genocide or the LTTE terror attacks had a particular personality trait or psychosocial characteristic or even social profile. These murders varied in personalities and social standing; some were undoubtedly poor while others were relatively wealthy; some had a broad network of friends while others were likely social outcasts. The individuals varied; however, the situations seem to have some similarities. I focus on four here: a relative lack of effective state control, the processes of group formation and boundary maintenance, the importance of social mobility, and the role of status in group violence.

## INEFFECTIVE STATE CONTROL

Although states can be efficient and effective killers, violence is extreme in the absence of a strong state (see, e.g., Cooney 1997). Hobbes (1651) was undoubtedly correct in noting that in the absence of central authority, violence pervades social life. Similarly, Weber (1922) points to the state's monopolization of violence as an effective means of restricting violence. Elias (1939) argues that the state is primarily responsible for the long-term civilizing process, and Pinker (2011) provides convincing evidence of the state's role in the decreasing rates of violence in everyday life. Several of the chapters in this volume offer additional support for this contention.

As I argue in chapter 2, vigilantism occurs when state control is absent or ineffective. It emerges when the state has failed or is perceived of as failing (Abrahams 1998; Pfeifer 2004). It is a response to the state's incapacity to police and secure citizens' rights when the system is challenged. If the groups in control find governmental efforts to confront the challenge insufficient, vigilantism is common. Of course, as Rymond-Richmond notes in chapter 4, a common explanation for genocide is that insecure states use it as a means to thwart insurgent threats. Such was the case in Darfur as the Sudanese government responded to armed threats by the Sudan Liberation Army (SLA) and Justice and Equality Movement (JEM) by mobilizing the Janjaweed militia groups against farming villages throughout Darfur. Although the genocide was ethnically based as Rymond-Richards argues, it was nevertheless a response by a weak state to a challenge to its rule. Thus, both vigilantism and genocide occur when states are ineffective at meeting challenges to their control.

Although school bullying, vigilantism, and genocide obviously differ in many ways, they are nevertheless similar in that they occur more frequently in settings with ineffective state controls. School bullying is most prevalent in schools with larger class sizes and with fewer resources (see Agnich and Miyazaki 2013). It is also more prevalent in schools that lack well-developed professional cultures among the teachers (Roland and Galloway 2004). These findings suggest that bullying occurs in schools where teachers are less able to monitor students effectively.

Thus, group violence often occurs when states are ineffective. Yet, we should recognize the curvilinear nature of this relationship. As Cooney (1997) documents, the relationship between state centralization and violence is U-shaped. Indeed, the state is by far the most effective killing machine known to humanity, as evidenced by the mass killing in Nazi Germany, Mao's China, or Stalin's Soviet Union, the Ottoman Empire's Armenian concentration camps, the killing fields of Cambodia, or the death camps of North Korea.

We also should recognize the state's indirect role in generating group violence. Even if the state's policy does not directly promote or use violence as a means of control, state policies can induce violence through oppression. Such was the case in the Sudan (see Rymond-Richmond's chapter). The chapters on the Sri Lankan civil war also document how the conflict was fueled by the Sinhala-dominated state's policies that failed to consider the needs of the Tamil minority (see chapters 5, 10, and 11). Similarly, the violence in Syria is largely a result of state oppression, and while the rebel groups share some blame, the state's response has hampered the success of nonviolent actions (see the chapter by Chang and Clott). Even in societies with relatively effective and responsive states, there are pockets of society where the state is largely absent and, when present, is often oppressive. As Kennedy notes in his chapter discussing street gangs, "it is essentially unheard of to find any meaningful density of or problem with violent street groups outside this broad context of oppression, deprivation, and schism with the rest of local society." Indeed, these are the neighborhoods in which the state has failed to address issues of poverty, where they are forced to take a combative role that emphasizes distributive or outcome justice over procedural justice, and, where, therefore, the state largely lacks legitimacy (see Hawdon 2008).

Thus, ineffective states are dangerous places. While too much state power can lead to untold acts of repression and mass violence, it would be a mistake to argue that stateless societies are less violent than stated societies. Pinker (2011) provides indisputable evidence of this, as do the recent conflicts in nations with weak and ineffective states, such as Somalia, Democratic Republic of the Congo, Central African Republic, and South Sudan. As Cooney (1997, 316) says, "High levels of violent conflict are found when state authority is weak or absent and when it is extremely strong or centralized. Between these extremes, in less centralized states, low and intermediate amounts of violence are found."

## THE DANGERS OF GROUP IDENTITY
## AND BOUNDARY MAINTENANCE

Other factors mentioned in many of the chapters are sources of group violence are the processes of group formation, definitions of group membership, and the maintenance of group boundaries. As discussed by Oksanen and Räsänen, group processes are at the core of human life, and they are at the core of group conflicts. As the primary source of our identity, the groups to which we belong significantly shape our understanding of the world and our understanding of our place in that world. As social identity theory (which several of the authors in this volume use) notes, group memberships provide a sense of self, a sense of pride, and self-esteem (Tajfel and Turner 1979). Yet, groups, by definition, create members and non-members; they create "us" and "them." This "othering" can be a dangerous phenomenon, as numerous scholars of violence have argued. Social identity plays a role in intergroup conflict because group members define themselves in contrast to other groups, and one's position within his or her group can be elevated by discriminating against outsiders. In situations where group membership is a valuable asset, the motive for "othering" increases, thereby increasing the divide between "us" and "them." This situation provides context and motive for intergroup bias, hatred, and violence. As noted by Rymond-Richmond, the "need" to distinguish "us" from "them" (that is to separate perpetrators from victims) often plays a role in genocides, such as in Rwanda, in Nazi Germany, and in Darfur.

Indeed, the construction of group identities and intense group identification are at the root of most of the violence discussed in this book. Group identity is at the heart of the analysis of the Darfur genocide. Similarly, Udalagama and de Silva argue that the root causes of the rebels' war against the Sri Lankan state are deeply rooted in the construct of ethnic identities. Hettige also argues that identity issues were root causes of the Sri Lankan civil war. Oksanen, Räsänen, and I make the argument that school shooting fans use a common language and codes to maintain their group and its solidarity. Kennedy notes the group dynamics that drive gang violence, and Juergensmeyer notes how terrorists are "soldiers in a cosmic war" defending their group against forces of "evil." According to him, even "lone wolf" terrorists such as Timothy McVeigh and Anders Breivik imagined themselves as members and defenders of some larger group. Indeed, as Matheis and his associates argue, when a-rational drives based on group identity and group loyalty supplant rational drives, group identity and loyalty often serve as epistemic justifications for violence. Whether it is in defense of their ethnic group, social class, race, religion, culture, homeland, turf, or way of life, group loyalties provide de facto justifications for engaging in violence. Gang members, school shooter fans, Syrian rebels, the LTTE, and modern terrorists are all in a "cosmic war" that pits their "good group" against those who embrace "evil."

## SLOW RATES OF SOCIAL MOBILITY AS A ROOT CAUSE OF GROUP VIOLENCE

A third common theme throughout the chapters on the causes and correlates of group violence is the prominent role of immobility (or, more accurately, slow rates of mobility; nothing social is truly immobile). As discussed in detail by Matheis and his associates, mobility is linked—and perhaps causally related—to intense group loyalties. Since restricted mobility heightens the exit costs associated with leaving one's group, it increases the importance of group membership (see Hawdon 1996; Hawdon 2005). And since restricted mobility decreases heterogeneity, reduces pluralism, heightens differences among "insiders" and "outsiders," it increases the probability of "othering" and the use of violence to control, punish, reap vengeance, or exterminate the "others."

As discussed in several chapters in this volume, group violence often erupts when social mobility is limited. Whether this is among urban gang members, refugees in IDP camps or London slums, Syrian protestors, Tamil rebels, or combatants in Darfur, when a group's access to resources and the avenues to get them are blocked, violence is a common consequence. This is of course reminiscent of Merton's (1957) strain theory. Many times, of course, frustrated dreams, hopes, goals, and aspirations lead people to strike out against those who they see as standing in their way. Indeed, when your options are limited, violence may seem like a good option. Yet, we should recognize that it is not always those whose mobility is limited that strike out in violence. At times, violence is used as a means to limit the mobility of others, especially when those others are seen as threatening the status quo that privileges one group. People do not typically give up their advantages without a fight, and sometimes that fight turns violent. Thus, instead of negotiating with the Tamils, the Sri Lankan government responded with violence. The same is true in Syria and in the War on Terror. Black (2012) is correct in noting that challenges to authority, or what he calls "underinferiority," are a major source of conflict.

Thus, slow rates of social mobility produce dangerous situations. When groups are locked into position—be it in a social system such as a stratification system or a physical location such as a neighborhood or refugee camp—group boundaries become clearer, group membership becomes more important, and the struggle for resources becomes more intense. These are dangerous conditions. These become violent when one group's existence—either literally or symbolically—becomes threatened. When life, limb, or respect is on the line, not only for you but also for your group, the battle becomes cosmic.

## THE SYMBOLIC NATURE OF VIOLENCE
## AND THE GROUP

Our violent fights become cosmic largely because they are over power. As rational choice theorists tell us, violence is rational. Several theorists have developed a far more elaborate rational choice model than presented here (see, e.g., Wikström 2012); however, the basics of that model contend that actors weigh the potential costs and rewards of their actions and select a course of action that they believe will maximize the rewards while minimizing the costs. Assuming this is the case (and there really are very few alternatives to this perspective for understanding the causal mechanisms that lead to violence), it logically follows that violence is a function of power. Power is the ability to get what one wants even against the wishes of others. There are three sources of power: force or political power, economic power, and status power (see Milner 2004). If violence is indeed the result of rational calculations, we can more accurately state that violence is the use of physical power to gain more physical power, economic power, or status power when actors calculate that engaging in such violence will result in them gaining more power than they will lose. Thus, violence is one means of pursuing power and the pursuit of power is therefore a fundamental cause of violence. Yet, violence becomes "group violence" and becomes particularly intractable when the power at stake is status power.

The insight that violence is related to the pursuit of status leads us to consider Milner's theory of status relations. According to Milner (2004, 29), "status is the accumulated approval and disapproval that people express toward an actor or object," and it "is inherently linked to the process of social construction and social meaning and evaluations." The very fact that status is socially constructed implies that groups are central to it, and, indeed, this is the case. As Milner notes, a key source of status is conformity to group norms. Simply put, group members are more likely to approve of those who abide by the group's rules than those who do not. The consequences of this aspect of status are profound: those with higher status tend to elaborate and obfuscate the norms to make it difficult for outsiders and newcomers to conform to the rules to compete for status honor. Another point of the theory is that social associations are key sources of violence (Milner 2004). Thus, if one associates with high status persons, his or her status increases; however, one's status decreases when they associate with low status persons. These two factors clearly highlight the central importance of groups in the world of status.

In addition, the third pillar of the theory of status relations holds that status is inalienable in that "it is located primarily in other people's minds" (Milner 2004, 32). It therefore cannot be appropriated or easily exchanged. The inalienability of status makes it a "very desirable resource" (Milner 2004, 32). It also makes changing the status system difficult. To do so requires changing peoples' hearts and minds, which can be extremely difficult to do for reputations are not easily altered. The difficulty of altering a status system protects the status of those on top and perpetuates the stigma of those at the bottom.

Finally, status is inexpansible. While other types of power can be expanded, status is a relative ranking and therefore cannot be expanded without devaluing that which allegedly grants status. That is, the status system cannot be expanded with producing "status inflation." As Milner (2004, 33) says:

> If a thousand Nobel prizes were awarded each year or every soldier received a Medal of Honor, the status value of these would be greatly diminished. . . . Because status is relatively inexpansible, when the status of some is increased, the status of others will eventually decrease; if someone moves up, someone will eventually have to move down.

These last two facts about status relate to group violence. Because status is such a valuable and desired commodity, it is often considered worth defending or pursuing. This is especially true when other sources of power are limited. As Milner (2004, 30) states, "when groups are excluded from economic and political power and given little respect, they may build a new identity rooted in a new status system." As argued earlier, when mobility is limited and access to power is blocked, group identity becomes increasingly important. In addition, the inexpansible nature of status makes preserving the group's integrity paramount; thus, efforts to clearly mark and protect group boundaries intensify. To fail to do so risks diluting the importance of membership; it risks status inflation. Because status is inexpansible, if others gain it, those with it lose it. Thus, those of higher status fight to maintain the status hierarchy that provides them privileges. Conversely, those without it try to alter the system by rejecting the values of the established order (Milner 2004). Because there is so much at stake, the battle for the ability to define the status hierarchy is always intense and often violent.

## TARGET SELECTION AS A GROUP PROCESS

One other point emerges from these chapters. In addition to demonstrating the group nature of violence, the chapters herein also demonstrate that the selection of a target is also a group process. I argue that many acts of violence such as bullying, online hate, and terrorism are forms of group violence, regardless if an individual or a group performs it. These violent acts are group-level phenomena on many levels, but they can be, and indeed are, often carried out by "lone wolves," individuals acting alone. While the chapters by Oksanen and Räsänen and by Juergensmeyer call this claim into question since even these "lone wolves" are typically part of a supportive network or imagine themselves as part of a larger group. Yet, even bracketing this important insight, there is another aspect of the act that is, I argue, a function of groups. Selecting the target of violence is fundamentally a social construction and therefore a group process.

The group dimension of violence is inherent in the leading theory of victimization. Routine activity theory argues that victimization occurs when a motivated offender and a suitable target converge in an environment that lacks capable guardianship (Cohen and Felson 1979). The original article defines several components of target suitability (value, visibility, accessibility and inertia, which includes the ability to defend oneself); however, of all the components of routine activity theory, "suitable targets" has received the least theoretical attention and conceptual development. Yet, flushing out the social and group aspects of target suitability clearly shows that this is typically a social, indeed a group, phenomenon.

Finkelhor and Asdigian (1996, 6) argue that personal characteristics of individuals increase their vulnerability to victimization because these characteristics "have some *congruence with the needs, motives or reactivities* of offenders." That is, offenders are drawn to certain types of victims; therefore, people possessing certain characteristics are more vulnerable. This process is what they call "target congruence." Target congruence is a function of *target vulnerability, target gratifiability,* and *target antagonism* (Finkelhor and Asdigian 1996). Target vulnerability is a function of victim characteristics that compromise his or her ability to resist or deter victimization (e.g., small size, physical weakness). Target gratifiability refers to victim characteristics that increase risk because they appeal to the wants or desires of an offender. An obvious example would be expensive goods such as diamond rings are more appealing than less expensive commodities such as costume jewelry would be. Finally, target antagonism refers to victim characteristics that arouse hatred, jealousy or destructive impulses in offenders. These characteristics can be ascribed statuses that engender bigotry or jealousy or they can be achieved status that perpetrators deem offensive or provocative.

It logically follows that targets are selected because they are "gratifiable." Yet, Augustine, Wilcox, Ousey, and Clayton (2002) note that a target's gratifiability can be either tangible or symbolic. While both tangible and symbolic rewards likely play a role in most—in not all—acts of violence, the symbolic value of targets makes most acts of violence "group violence." What makes a target symbolically gratifiable? In short, something is symbolically gratifying because it either grants the perpetrator status or lessons the status of the victim. Bullying in schools provides an excellent example of this process.

As argued by Lagerspetz and her associates (1982) over forty years ago, there are two important features of bullying that make it group violence. First, it has a distinct collective character. Second, if one is a victim, offender, or bystander depends on one's social relationships in the group. While a large body of work on identifying what sets bullying victims apart from non-victims focus on psychological characteristics such as self-esteem, self-efficacy, and self-confidence (see, e.g., Olweus 1994; Zapf and Einarsen 2011 for reviews). Others note how social networks relate to guardianship and, consistent with routine activity theory, find that children are far more likely to be victimized if alone or in small networks. For both males and females, those selected for victimization tend to be socially rejected and belong to relatively small friendship networks (e.g., Salmivalli et al. 1996; Pellegrini, Bartini, and Brooks 1999; Mouttapa et al. 2004; Kingston 2008; Huitsing and Veenstra 2012; Rivers and Noret 2010). Indeed, we know bullying is a group process whereby individuals adopt various participant roles (see Salmivalli et al. 1996; Rivers and Noret 2010) and assume specific locations within their social networks (Huitsing and Veenstra 2012). Indeed, network position even influences bystanders (Kingston 2008). Thus, even what may appear to be individualized violence is highly patterned by social groups and networks.

So, why would "fat" and "slow" or "too tall" or "too short" matter in selecting whom to bully? Marcel Danesi (1999) notes that "small cruelties" occur with high frequency and regularity in adolescent culture. He notes that these frequently are insults focused on bodies, but the phenomenon is more general. These "small cruelties" happen all the time. But why? Peguero and Kahle's analysis in this volume illustrates the process. Since status is inexpansible, those of higher status fight to maintain the status hierarchy. Hence, bullying is used to establish and protect groups. It is particularly gratifying to pick on the weak because this is the easiest way to maintain the group boundaries without risking violating some other dimension of adolescent stratification (i.e., athletic ability or intellectual ability or wealth). Thus, if I am an "elite" and I pick on a non-fat kid, I can keep you "in your place" and maintain my status position. However, if my victim is "cool" because he is a good athlete, for example, I risk alienating his associates, thereby threatening my elite position. However, since "everyone" picks on fat kids, my bullying at fat child will not only maintain the status hierarchy, it builds allies for me. Thus, "fat kids" are not only vulnerable because they may lack the physical abilities to fend off an attack, they are also gratifiable; therefore, they are frequently targeted.

Thus, Peguero and Kahle find that weight and height are related to victimization because these are indirect measures of target gratifiability. Beating up the "right" victim conveys status and makes doing so gratifying. The characteristics that define suitable targets then become essentialized, and the entire group learns who should and who should not be targeted. Therefore, these characteristics make those possessing them suitable targets not only because they make *individuals* more vulnerable, but also because the *group has defined these as* gratifiable because they establish the group's boundaries. These characteristics define "us" in opposition to "them." If we hang with "us," our status is reaffirmed; if we beat, belittle, or otherwise demean "them," our status increases because theirs decreased.

Consequently, group violence often relates to status. Since status is inherently a cultural and therefore group-defined phenomenon, all violence that is used to defend or advance one's status has a very real group dimension to it. This process is relatively easy to see in American schools because the sole power to which students have access is status. The importance of status to high school students is why they protect their groups so vehemently (Milner 2004). Yet, this process is also evident in every other form of violence discussed in this volume. The online hate group member is protecting his group's reputation (see McNamee et al. 2010; Duffy 2003), and street gangs respond violently if their gang is disrespected or "dissed." Maintaining the ethnic and cultural identity was the motive behind the state-led Arabization ideology in Sudan, and this policy reified a status system that placed Arabs above black Africans. Establishing this status system required creating social distance between the two groups, and, as Rymond-Richmond argues in her chapter, these status distinctions laid the foundation for the genocide in Darfur. Indeed, status, status seeking, and status protection are roots of violence from bullies to terrorists.

## SUMMARY AND IMPLICATIONS

The chapters in this volume discuss a wide range of phenomena; yet, if viewed collectively, they highlight several aspects that cut across types of violence. They also demonstrate similarities in the causes of violence and the selection of targets. I have identified what I believe are four fundamental root conditions of violence: ineffective states, intense group identity and loyalties, social mobility, and the pursuit and protection of status. Consequently, *slow rates of mobility* create conditions where group membership is essential to *identity*. The group's importance is elevated because, lacking access to political favor or commodities, group membership is a symbolic marker of the only power to which one has access: *status*. Group membership, then, becomes an epistemic justification for violence because the group is the source of status and therefore must be protected. This situation is exacerbated when the ultimate killing machine, *the state*, is either ineffective at managing the frustration caused by immobility or the root cause of the immobility.

I believe recognizing these factors as fundamental sources of conflict and, ultimately, violence sheds light on the relative effectiveness of attempts at conflict resolution. Assuming violence is a result of rational calculations, perpetrators of *rational violence* can be negotiated with, "bought off," or deterred. Providing alternative paths to the desired reward should tip the equation in favor of peace. That is, if we provide the desired rewards without forcing the actor to use violence, the rational actor will accept the offer since violence has high potential costs. Of course, this assumes that those offering the rewards do not attach conditions to the offer that incur such high costs so that the actors deem the costs of violence are less than costs associated with the alternative. The point is, however, that it is possible to turn a rational choice to commit violence into a rational choice to avoid it by making the desired rewards accessible to the person or group contemplating violence.

However, this is far easier to do when the reward being sought is political or economic rather than status. In other words, it is possible to make rational violence irrational when the desired rewards are tangible and expansible (or at least plentiful). If access to education is the goal, this can be made available to everyone, at least theoretically. If it is food, we can produce enough food to feed everyone and therefore get food to those seeking food. However, when status is the wanted reward, we cannot produce more of it without diluting that which exists because it is inexpansible. Often groups claim they are only seeking "respect" or "to be left alone." Peace studies scholar Johan Galtung, for example, says that when he asked leaders of the Taliban what they wanted, they simply said, "to be given respect and left alone" (Personal communication, November 2012). This seems easy enough to do until one considers what this would mean for those living in their lands. The Taliban's rigid gender hierarchy, embracing of Sharia law, dismissal of democracy, and (probably most importantly) rejection of consumer capitalism offends Western sensibilities. To tolerate their worldview and just leave them alone would elevate their status at the expense of the West. Apparently, this is asking too much.

Another example of the inexpansibility of status is the debate between religious fundamentalist and non-fundamentalists. A common plea of non-fundamentalists—even seen on bumper stickers—is that religions should co-exist. This seems reasonable enough, right? Well, it does if your status is linked to a non-fundamentalist group because, by having fundamentalists accept this solution, you win! Deuteronomy (13:1–9) tells the pious that anyone who attempts to lure you away from your religion should be killed. According to John (2 John 1:10–11), to greet those with "wrong beliefs" is to be in league with evil. Christians learn from the Epistle of Jude that those who have erroneous beliefs are ungodly, sinful, and in need of being rescued from the fire. Given these and similar pages in the bible devoted to the importance of maintaining the faith, asking a fundamentalist who devotedly believes these commands are the word of god to tolerate and coexist with those who believe differently is asking that person to forsake his or her god. This is not asking for compromise; it is demanding the person accepts a more inclusive worldview. Similarly, asking those who embrace the notion of accepting difference and tolerating diversity to concede that the fundamental-ist must be intolerant toward sinners because that is god's wish is asking them to tolerate intolerance. Yet, to tolerate the intolerance of fundamental-ists would force the tolerant to accept intolerance, which, of course, is intol-erable to them. Both cannot be right; there is no compromise possible be-cause accepting one position grants status to that worldview and reduces the status of the other. Such battles cannot be solved without someone losing status. Thus, these battles for status are symbolic battles, battles for who is right and who is wrong. These are intractable conflicts, and diplomats, nego-tiators, and peace builders would be well served recognizing this complexity.

## CONCLUSION

Arguing that the pursuit of power is a root cause of violence is nothing new. Others have also noted how seeking status and respect can lead to violence. Scholars have long identified immobility and ineffective states as sources of violence, and a vast literature demonstrates how violence relates to identity issues. These claims are not novel. What I hope this book and this chapter accomplish is to propose a relationship among these factors. Ineffective states, intense group loyalties, social mobility, and the pursuit and protection of status are possibly part of a "causal mechanism" that identifies both covering conditions (ineffective states and intense group loyalty) and triggers (the pursuit of status in a social context of slow rates of social mobility). While there are undoubtedly other factors to consider, these may be core concepts in a general theory of group violence. I have not outlined such a theory here, but I hope this stimulates further investigation into these factors as fundamental causes of violence.

## REFERENCES

Abrahams, Ray. 1998. *Vigilant Citizens: Vigilantism and the State.* Cambridge: Polity.

Agnich, Laura E., and Yasuo Miyazaki. 2013. "A Cross-National Analysis of Principals' Reports of School Violence." *International Criminal Justice Review* 23: 378–400.

Augustine, Michelle Campbell, Pamela Wilcox, Graham C. Ousey, and Richard R. Clayton. 2002. "Opportunity Theory and Adolescent School-Based Victimization." *Violence and Victims* 17: 233–53.

Black, Donald. 2012. *Moral Time.* Oxford: Oxford University Press.

Cohen, Lawrence E., and Marcus Felson. 1979. "Social Change and Crime Rate Trends: A Routine Activity Approach." *American Sociological Review* 44: 588–608.

Cooney, Mark. 1997. "From Warre to Tyranny: Lethal Conflict and the State." *American Sociological Review* 62: 316–38.

Danesi, Marcel. 1999. *Cool: The Signs and Meanings of Adolescence.* Toronto: University of Toronto Press.

Duffy, Margaret E. 2003. "Web of Hate: A Fantasy Theme Analysis of the Rhetorical Vision of Hate Groups Online." *Journal of Communication Inquiry* 27: 291–312.

Elias, Norbert. (1939) 1982. *The Civilizing Process: Power and Civility.* New York: Pantheon.

Finkelhor, David, and Nancy L. Asdigian. 1996. "Risk Factors for Youth Victimization: Beyond a Lifestyle/Routine Activities Theory Approach." *Violence and Victims* 11: 3–19.

Gottfredson, Michael, and Travis Hirschi. 1990. *A General Theory of Crime.* Stanford, CA: Stanford University Press.

Hawdon, James. 1996. "Cycles of Deviance: Structural Change, Moral Boundaries, and Drug Use, 1880–1990." *Sociological Spectrum* 16: 183–207.

———. 2005. *Drugs and Alcohol Consumption as a Function of Social Structure: A Cross-cultural Sociology.* Lewistown, NY: Mellen Press.

———. 2008. "Legitimacy, Trust, Social Capital and Policing Styles: A Theoretical Statement" *Police Quarterly* 11: 182–201.

Hobbes, Thomas. *Leviathan.* (1651) 1909. Oxford, England: Clarendon Press.

Huitsing, Gijs, and René Veenstra. 2012. "Bullying in Classrooms: Participant Roles from a Social Network Perspective." *Aggressive behavior* 38: 494–509.

Kingston, Shauna. 2008. *Bullying as a Social Process: Factors Influencing Bystander Behaviour.* Saarbrücken, Germany: Lambert Academic Publishing.

Lagerspetz, Kirsti MJ, Kaj Björkqvist, Marianne Berts, and Elisabeth King. 1982. "Group Aggression among School Children in Three Schools." *Scandinavian Journal of Psychology* 23: 45–52.

McNamee, Lacy G., Brittany L. Peterson, and Jorge Peña. 2010. "A Call to Educate, Participate, Invoke and Indict: Understanding the Communication of Online Hate Groups." *Communication Monographs* 77: 257–80.

Merton, Robert K. 1957. *Social Theory and Social Structure*. London: The Free Press of Glencoe.

Milner, Murray, Jr. 2004. *Freaks, Geeks, and Cool Kids: American Teenagers, Schools, and the Culture of Consumption*. New York: Routledge.

Mouttapa, Michele, Tom Valente, Peggy Gallaher, Louise Ann Rohrbach, and Jennifer B. Unger. 2004. "Social Network Predictors of Bullying and Victimization." *Adolescence* 39: 315–35.

Olweus, Dan. 1994. *Bullying at school*. New York: Springer US.

Pellegrini, Anthony D., Maria Bartini, and Fred Brooks. 1999. "School Bullies, Victims, and Aggressive Victims: Factors Relating to Group Affiliation and Victimization in Early Adolescence." *Journal of Educational Psychology* 91: 216.

Pfeifer, Michael. 2004. *Rough Justice: Lynching and American Society 1874–1947*. Champaign, IL: University of Illinois Press.

Pinker, Steven. 2011. *The Better Angles of our Nature: Why Violence Has Declined*. New York: Viking.

Rivers, Ian, and Nathalie Noret. 2010. "Participant Roles in Bullying Behavior and Their Association with Thoughts of Ending One's Life." *Crisis: The Journal of Crisis Intervention and Suicide Prevention* 31: 143–48.

Roland, Erling, and David Galloway. 2004. "Professional Cultures in Schools with High and Low Rates of Bullying." *School Effectiveness and School Improvement* 15: 241–60.

Salmivalli, Christina, Kirsti Lagerspetz, Kaj Björkqvist, Karin Österman, and Ari Kaukiainen. 1996. "Bullying as a Group Process: Participant Roles and Their Relations to Social Status within the Group." *Aggressive behavior* 22: 1–15.

Tajfel, H., and J. C. Turner. 1979. "An Integrative Theory of Group Conflict." In *The Social Psychology of Intergroup Relations*, edited by W. G. Austin, S. Worchel, 33–47. Monterey, CA: Brooks/Cole.

Weber, Max. (1922) 1968. *Economy and Society: Vol. 1*. New York: Bedminster.

Wikström, Per-Olof. 2012. "Does Everything Matter? Addressing the Problem of Causation and Explanation in the Study of Crime." In *When Crime Appears: The Role of Emergence* edited by Jean Marie McGloin, Christopher Sullivan, and Leslie Kennedy, 53–72. New York: Routledge.

Zapf Dieter, and Ståle Einarsen. 2003. "Individual Antecedents of Bullying: Victims and Perpetrators." In *Bullying and Emotional Abuse in the Workplace: International Perspectives in Research and Practice*, edited by Ståle Einarsen, Helge Hoel, Dieter Zapf and Cary Cooper, 165–184. London: Taylor and Francis.

*Chapter Fifteen*

# Humanistic Reflections on Understanding Group Violence

## Marc Lucht

Exegesis or interpretation would be impossible if the expressions of life were utterly alien. It would be unnecessary if there were nothing alien in them.

—Wilhelm Dilthey (1977b)

Finding oneself in a new and bewildering place can be an exhilarating as well as daunting experience. Exhilarating is the opportunity afforded to discover and explore the riches of an unfamiliar territory. Daunting, of course, are the efforts required to overcome one's ignorance of and orient oneself with respect to a vast and complicated field, as well as the real risk of going astray.

As a humanist whose academic background is in philosophy and as a newcomer to sociological investigations of issues such as group violence, the introduction to scientific approaches to illuminating the causes and implications of the phenomenon of group violence I received at the conference out of which this book emerged was both exhilarating and daunting. That experience was intensified by the awareness of the pressing importance of the work on which the contributors to this volume were reporting. It would be difficult to exaggerate the moment of the attempt to clarify the origins of bullying, gang violence, hate groups, and terrorism, or the importance of thinking through effective ways to reduce their incidence and harmful consequences.

Also contributing to the excitement of my introduction to the ways in which social scientists work to understand group violence was the repeated recognition of similarities and connections between what these scientists were saying and the ideas of many people who work in philosophy. Thus, for instance, much of the discussion at the conference centered on questions about the best way to define concepts such as "violence," or "gang," or "terrorist," or "peace," and whether generating commonly agreed upon definitions would be even possible. Professional philosophers too spend a great deal of time attempting to define what at first might appear to be quite basic or clearly understood terms.

To take another example, several participants stressed that many investigations into group violence hitherto have been plagued by unwarranted assumptions, and that much less is known about its origins and incidence than one might expect. Donna Pankhurst detailed some of the ways in which assumptions about the identities of perpetrators of violence, and in which sex and gender stereotypes inflect our conception of agency, have led to a dearth of research into the roles played by women as perpetrators of violence. In keeping with such remarks, when discussing her contribution to this volume she stated:

> Women's roles in group violence are often hidden, or even denied, and their victim identities eclipse their agency. During wars, especially where there is no "front line," women's agency still tends to be highlighted by most observers as being exclusively peaceful and anti-violence, although there is a considerable critical feminist literature which shows how this tendency is sometimes misleading.
>
> On the ground women normally play a wide range of roles in conflict (as they do at other times), including that of combatants and gang members, but also as supporters and influencers of men committing violent acts. Such realities present difficulties for some audiences who struggle to recognize women's agency as anything but working for peace, and all their other actions as somehow being determined and controlled by men.

Similarly, David Kennedy argues that failures to define the notion of "gang" adequately, to specify the relationship between violence and gangs in a noncircular way, and to isolate causal connections between gang membership and the occurrence of violence, have frustrated attempts to make meaningful progress in researching the ways in which gangs are connected with violence. This sort of recognition of the necessity to uncover and reflect repeatedly upon the cogency of the assumptions guiding one's thought is a very important part of philosophical work. And the sense I got that a great deal of very recent research into group violence indicates that much less is known about its origins than had been thought, that the world is far more complicated than for too long had been assumed, and that social scientists were arguing for the critical importance of recognizing our ignorance about some very basic questions within the field, recalled for me the venerable Socratic insight that the recognition of one's own ignorance is the beginning of wisdom, signaling one's readiness for making genuine moral and conceptual progress.

These points of reference, among others, made me hopeful that I could contribute something not entirely unhelpful or irrelevant to our discussions about group violence. In what follows I use a discussion of Wilhelm Dilthey's distinction between "explanation" and "understanding" to suggest that the prevailing commitments to the collection and analysis of quantitative data and the isolation of causal determinants of phenomena such as group violence ought to be supplemented by the project of pursuing "understanding" of the lives and cultures of perpetrators of group violence. Indeed, some researchers already are doing this, and reflection upon the nature of understanding will indicate the great salutary potential of that pursuit.

Dilthey was a philosopher who wrote in the late nineteenth to very early twentieth centuries. He played an important role in the development of the discipline of hermeneutics, made important contributions to the philosophy of history, anticipated many of the insights about language, meaning, and experience achieved by later thinkers such as Martin Heidegger, Hans-Georg Gadamer, and Ludwig Wittgenstein, and often is thought to be the foremost philosopher of "life" and of the *Geisteswissenschaften*, or human sciences.

Dilthey conceives of the scientific exploration of the physical world of nature in a very different way than the investigations of culture, history, and human psychology. In an article from 1894 entitled "Ideas Concerning a Descriptive and Analytic Psychology," he writes:

> The human studies are distinguished from the sciences of nature first of all in that the latter have for their objects facts which are presented to consciousness as from outside, as phenomena and given in isolation, while the objects of the former are given originaliter from within as real and as a living continuum [*Zusammenhang*]. As a consequence there exists a system of nature for the physical and natural sciences only thanks to inferential arguments which supplement the data of experience by means of a combination of hypotheses. In the human studies, to the contrary, the nexus of psychic life constitutes originally a primitive and fundamental datum. We explain nature, we understand psychic life. (Dilthey 1977a, 27)

Dilthey holds that the encounter with the natural world in the physical sciences is an encounter with what originally are isolated, discrete, unconnected facts or bits of data. Those facts may be related to each other through hypotheses postulating causal linkages, and it is such causal explanation that works towards providing our experience of physical nature with systematic coherence or unity. He claims that with respect to the life of consciousness, however, matters are different. The stream of conscious life is experienced or lived immediately as a "coherent whole" (Dilthey 1977a, 28), a coherence that does not need to be achieved subsequently through intellectual representation in some kind of theoretical model. Psychic connectedness is revealed not through an explanation, but it is lived, it is experienced directly. Whereas "we must impute connections and totalities to sensory stimuli," we directly

and "continually experience a sense of connectedness and totality in ourselves" (Dilthey,1977a, 28). Dilthey therefore claims:

> [p]sychic life-process is originally, and above all, from its most elementary
> forms to the highest, a unity. Psychic life does not grow together from parts; it
> is not composed of elements; it is not a composite nor is the result of the
> collaboration of sensory or affective atoms: it is originally and always a com-
> prehensive unity. Psychic functions are differentiated from it while all along
> remaining bound to their nexus. This fact, whose highest expression is the
> unity of consciousness and of the person, radically distinguishes psychic life
> from the entire corporeal world. (Dilthey 1977a, 92)

Coming to grips with such psychic holism—and with the sorts of cultural
phenomena originating in conscious life—requires a different mode of investigation from that appropriate to the physical world, and this investigation
seeks what Dilthey entitles understanding (*Verstehen*).

Instead of chaining observation statements to each other by means of
hypothesizing causal connections, and instead of explaining observations by
subsuming their descriptions under universal statements of causal law, the
sort of understanding appropriate to the human sciences involves the relating
of parts to wholes. As Rudolf Makkreel (1977) notes, Dilthey's psychological works (such as the 1894 essay quoted above), posit the "fundamental task
of description in the human studies" to lie in "articulating an indeterminate
nexus rather than in synthetically combining elements," and, in his later
works, this idea evolves into the view that "the kind of inference involved in
[humanistic] interpretation differs from that of naturalistic explanation because it is conceived in light of the reciprocal whole-to-part and part-to-
whole relations of the hermeneutic circle" (7, 15). In each case, the specification of the ways in which (hitherto indeterminate) moments of a continuum
are connected with each other and the ways in which parts relate to their
whole is the clarification of a structure of meaning. Because of this sensitivity to "the whole of psychic life," and to the even more encompassing whole
of the cultural "milieu" with which one's lived experience "stands in reciprocal interplay," Dilthey claims that humanistic understanding "opens up a
world" (Dilthey 1989, 439; 1977a, 92; 1977b, 123).

I would like to clarify this idea a bit further. As Dilthey sees it, the
meaningful wholeness of conscious experience cannot be reduced to causal
explanations. For him, as for phenomenologists and hermeneutic thinkers
after him, meaningful wholes cannot be built up out of antecedently discrete
bits of data, and thus the explanatory focus on causally relating to each other
a number of atomic facts is incapable of shedding light on a meaningful
system.[1] Meaningful wholes should be approached not through the relating
of facts through hypothetical causal connections, but hermeneutically. Meaning is achieved in part through the circular relation of parts and whole. To see

this point, one need only consider something like a sentence, or a story. In order to understand the meaning of the sentence as a whole, one must understand the meanings of each word in the sentence. At the same time, in order to understand the meaning of any individual word in a sentence, one must understand already the context in which those words occur—the sentence as a whole. Interpretation lays bare the interrelations of these parts and wholes. Similarly, in order to understand the full meaning of any individual sentence within a story, one already must know the story as a whole. In fact, it is only the sentence's place within the context of the whole story that allows it to mean what it means; there is no reason to think that, isolated from the story, the sentence will mean anything like what it did when embedded within the story-context. The better it is that one understands a story, the better one will understand the sentences composing it. At the same time, one only understands a story if one understands each of its sentences. Textual interpretation requires one to move in a sort of spiral fashion, moving from parts to whole, then whole to parts, and then back again from parts to whole, achieving deeper or richer understandings the better one recognizes the precise relation between each word or sentence and the increasingly determinate text as a whole.[2] For Dilthey, the same point holds for the narratives investing a life or a culture with meaning. As Hans-Georg Gadamer puts it, Dilthey conceived of the "historical world as a text to be deciphered" (Gadamer 1992, 240).

On Dilthey's view, there is another difference between explanation and understanding. Whereas explanation involves hypothesizing causal connections and logical reasoning, understanding is an affective as well as intellectual activity. He writes:

> The processes of the whole psyche operate together in this experience. . . . In the lived experience particular occurrence is supported by the totality of psychic life and the nexus in which it itself stands, and the whole of psychic life belongs to immediate experience. The latter already determines the nature of our understanding of ourselves and of others. We explain by purely intellectual processes, but we understand through the concurrence of all the powers of the psyche in the apprehension. In understanding we proceed from the coherent whole which is livingly given to us in order to make the particular intelligible to us. Precisely the fact that we live with the consciousness of the coherent whole, makes it possible for us to understand a particular sentence, gesture, action. All psychological thought preserves this fundamental feature, that the apprehension of the whole makes possible and determines the interpretation of particulars. (Dilthey 1977a, 55, italics deleted)

> There is something irrational in all understanding, just as life itself is irrational. It can be represented through no logically-derived formulae. (Dilthey 1977b, 137).

Any particular aspect of human consciousness is what it is because of its relation to the entire "nexus" or context of conscious experience. This means that any attempt to understand that particular aspect cannot rely on just one isolated psychological faculty or ability, but requires the "concurrence" of all of them. Understanding, in other words, is not just a rational or purely intellectual activity, but requires the involvement of the affective and imaginative dimensions of conscious life as well. To attempt to understand the richness of someone else's conscious experience requires the bringing to bear of the wholeness of one's own conscious life. To attempt to understand Prince Hamlet's motivations, for instance, it is not enough to think or calculate; one must also feel. One must enlist one's own experiences and feelings of loss, love, frustration, anger, solitude, betrayal, anxiety, duty, and uncertainty.

In this way the attempt to understand another person is in part the relating of that person's "life-context" to the entirety of one's own experience. Dilthey thinks that one must relate the other person's experience to the ultimate wholeness of one's own life. This is accomplished through a sort of "projection of oneself . . . be it into a person or a work," and the "highest form in which the totality of psychic life is effective in the understanding" is achieved through a "re-creation or re-experiencing" or "fully sympathetic reliving" of the other's life experience (Dilthey 1977b, 132–33). Dilthey thus gestures towards a sort of dialogue between the life of the investigator and the text, person, or cultural phenomenon to be understood.[3] For him, the opening up of a world that this imaginative projection makes possible is the condition for a kind of freedom. By this projection, understanding "opens up to him a broad realm of possibilities which are not available within the determination of his actual life," and "our horizons" are enlarged to

> include possibilities for human life which can be made accessible only in this way. Thus the man who is determined from within can experience many other existences in his imagination. Strange beauties of the world and regions of life which he can never attain appear before him who is limited by circumstance. . . . Man, bound and determined through the reality of life, is transposed into freedom not only through art . . . but also through the understanding of what is given in history. (Dilthey 1977b, 134–35).

Dilthey holds that understanding the life of another consciousness and the distinctive possibilities open to that consciousness is liberating, for it can disclose limitations stemming from my own circumstance as well as possible alternative ways of living. As an example, he describes the way in which the investigation of Martin Luther can enable the humanistic historian to participate in "a religious process of eruptive passion" exceeding "anything that a present-day man could possibly experience" (Dilthey 1977b, 134). Below I shall suggest that the process of sympathetically reliving the experience of another person has important methodological implications and promise for the project of coming to grips with the origins of group violence.

For Dilthey, the wholeness and significance of one's conscious life must be approached hermeneutically, that is, interpretively, as must those cultural phenomena that arise out of human consciousness and as such are meaningful. He says that just as "the system of culture . . . [arises] from the living nexus of the human soul, so [the psyche's achievements must] be understood only by reference to it" (Dilthey 1977a, 31). An "inner meaning" "comes to expression" in all cultural achievements, whether they are works of art, or laws, or religion, or family, or nation, and which then constitute a realm of significant, "objective spirit" (Dilthey 1977b, 137 and 127). If Dilthey is right about the characteristics of conscious life, there are limits to naturalistic or causally explanatory approaches, which are unsuited to the disclosure of psychological and cultural meaning. Thus he writes:

> Since the rise of the mechanistic conception of nature, literature has preserved the great feeling of life in nature, which is mysterious and inaccessible to explanation. Similarly, poetry everywhere protects the content of lived experience which cannot be conceptualized, so that what is experienced will not vanish in the analytic operations of abstract science. (Dilthey 1989, 206).

If conscious life and cultural significance indeed are irreducible to discrete bits, if understanding meaningful phenomena requires the bringing to bear not only cognitive categories but also one's affective capacities, and if the various moments of conscious experience and cultural achievements only are what and how they are because of the ways in which they are embedded within larger and never fully determinate contextual wholes, then causal and quantitative approaches to cultural phenomena such as group violence ought to be supplemented by humanistic, interpretive approaches.

I want to suggest that Dilthey's turn to dialogical hermeneutics can be of great benefit to social scientists interested in illuminating the origins and implications of group violence. As are works of literature, occurrences of group violence are cultural phenomena that are meaningful, and are meaningful in different ways to perpetrators, victims, and observers. It would be surprising indeed if the ways in which acts of group violence were meaningful to their perpetrators did not contribute to their motivations for engaging in such acts, and if perpetrators' awareness of or beliefs about the ways in which their acts will be received by their community or the larger society did not factor into their deliberations. Making sense of the consequences of group violence must include the attempt to understand the ways in which the meanings of the lives of victims and survivors, as well as the societies in which those people live, have been changed by violent events. The sense of any act of group violence is context bound, and that context itself is always modified by the various occurrences of group violence: there are part/whole relations obtaining among individual and group, group and (various small and large) societies, and each violent incident and culture. Understanding those various relations is essential for understanding the roots and import of occurrences of violence. My suggestion is that research into group violence should incorporate not just causal explanation but in addition methods appropriate to the disclosure and analysis of meaningful phenomena.

Indeed, in his contribution to this volume, Mark Juergensmeyer argues that acts of terrorism usefully can be regarded as a kind of theater, for which there are different audiences (including those meant to be terrorized as well as pools of potential recruits), a performance, a system of symbolic meanings, and reference to phenomena and aspirations of larger cultural and cosmic significance. Juergensmeyer claims that whereas political terrorism traditionally has been characterized narrowly in terms of strategic calculation, one must also understand terrorism as performance "done not to achieve a strategic goal but to make a symbolic statement. . . . Such explosive scenarios are not tactics directed toward an immediate, earthly, or strategic goal, but dramatic events intended to impress for their symbolic significance. As such, they can be analyzed as one would any other symbol, ritual, or sacred drama." Juergensmeyer notes too that the analysis of such performances must be sensitive to the larger religious and cultural contexts in which they arise, for it is their place and role within such contexts that charge them with the significance they possess. The symbolical dimension of terrorist acts, in this example, must be understood in terms of their cultural contexts, and the ways in which individuals take themselves to be oriented by and contributing to the shaping of those contexts.[4] As Juergensmeyer notes, humanistic techniques more often used to interpret religious ritual and drama should be brought to bear in the scientific investigations of terrorism.

Again and again, participants in the conference giving rise to this volume stressed the importance of talking with the perpetrators of group violence. I think that this emphasis on first hand conversation and dialogue indicates recognition of a need to better understand the lives of the perpetrators of violence. It is through conversation that a world as a system of significance is opened, that one can begin to make sense of a life, that one can disclose and orient oneself with respect to the rich experience of others. The collection of bits of quantitative data and the formulation and testing of causal hypotheses are not sufficient for this sort of understanding. As Marcus Aurelius reminds us, we should practice "really hearing what people say," and that listening will enable us to "get inside their minds" (Aurelius 2002, 81).[5] If we seek to make sense of the personal and cultural origins of group violence, the practices of dialogue and interpretation of what is said in that dialogue are essential. Dilthey reminds us of the suitability to that end of hermeneutic techniques for illuminating meaningful wholes, and of the methodological importance of sympathetically relating one's own experience to what is disclosed in the conversation.

I want to close by claiming that the humanistic project of understanding others has important and salient moral consequences. To my suggestion that scientists should attempt to understand the perpetrators of group violence, one might object that such understanding may lead to a morally perilous sympathy, postulation of false moral equivalence, or even forbearance. On this view, perpetrators of violence do not deserve the compassion that understanding may bring with it, and better would be just to fight back, to imprison or eliminate the most dangerous human threats to security and social well-being.

In his novella *Death in Venice*, Nobel Prize winning author Thomas Mann offers a clue to what may be a more appropriate measure of the moral implications of understanding. While characterizing the authorial motivations and goals of the story's main character, writer Gustav Aschenbach, the narrator states that the "weight of the words with which the writer of that work reviled the vile announced a decisive turn away from all moral skepticism, from all sympathy with the abyss, a rejection of the laxity inherent in the supposedly compassionate maxim that to understand everything is to forgive everything" (Mann 1994, 11).[6] For Aschenbach, understanding does not necessitate forgiveness. Similarly, Martha Nussbaum argues for the moral and political importance of the imaginative capacity to place oneself in someone else's shoes. She claims that:

> narrative imagination is an essential preparation for moral interaction. Habits of empathy and conjecture conduce to a certain type of citizenship and a certain form of community: one that cultivates a sympathetic responsiveness to another's needs, and understands the way circumstances shape those needs. . . . [Such sympathetic responsiveness requires too] a sense of one's own vulnerability to misfortune. To respond with compassion, I must be willing to entertain the thought that this suffering person might be me. (Nussbaum 1997, 90–91)

As does Dilthey, Nussbaum thinks that the capacity to use one's own experience to orient the understanding of the experience of others is cultivated especially by humanistic pursuits such as literature and the arts. But she does not think that such understanding ought result in an uncritical forbearance of morally troubling cultural practices. Thus whereas Nussbaum argues for the importance of "sympathetic responsiveness" to the experience and needs of others, at the same time she is troubled by the risk that an "identity-politics view" (Nussbaum 1977, 110) leads to the mere affirmation of difference just because it is difference, and by the ways in which certain approaches to teaching multiculturalism lead to a cultural relativism or moral skepticism fostering "weak-spirited citizens" who fail to respond appropriately "when they encounter evil elsewhere in the world" (Nussbaum 1977, 137). She notes that:

> When they encounter violence against women, or assaults on democracy, or discrimination against members of a religious or ethnic minority, [such people] are likely to say, 'Well, that is their culture, and who are we to speak?' In this way, Americans all too frequently lack conviction about evil elsewhere.... Students tend to think that skepticism is a way of being respectful to others. But ... to refuse all application of moral standards to a foreign person or culture is not really a way of treating that person with respect. When we refuse to make judgments that we make freely in life with our own fellow citizens, we seem to be saying that this form of life is so alien and bizarre that it cannot be expected to be measured by the same set of standards. This is another way of being patronizing. (Nussbaum 1977, 137–38).

For Mann and Nussbaum, sympathetic understanding need not lead to forgiveness or tolerance of wickedness. On the other hand, understanding another person requires one to relate that person's life to one's own affective, cognitive, and material experiences, it requires one to "project oneself" into the situation of someone who might at first appear to be quite alien. Such understanding need not result in forgiveness of the unforgiveable, but it will prompt the recognition of what we share: a common humanity.

All too often we are tempted to demonize perpetrators of great horrors, representing them as monsters or evil aliens with whom we share nothing in common. There is something comforting about such an attitude. If those who commit terrible crimes are monsters who are completely different from me, I do not need to recognize and face up to the implications of my own potential for doing terrible things. I can rest content with a sense of my own righteousness. Of course, there is a moral cost to this contentment: fastidiously ignoring my own dark side makes it less likely that I would reflect carefully about or actively strive to resist my very human—surely universally human—potential for wickedness.[7] What is more, the demonization of perpetrators of horror may serve to legitimize forms of response to or treatment of those people that might otherwise be beyond the pale, justifying the most extreme sorts of countermeasures—and thereby coarsening and degrading us as we permit ourselves to treat our fellow human beings in morally unacceptable ways. Considered pragmatically, the demonization of those with the predilection for committing great crimes may well be counterproductive, insofar is it prompts those doing the demonizing to cut themselves off from those others, establishing a cultural apartheid that can reinforce dangerous resentment and alienation. Also counterproductive is the way in which representing others as monsters or as radically other may incline us to think that their lives and motivations are completely opaque to us, in principle un-understandable; demonization thus frustrates the attempt to mitigate the likelihood of violence, because it bolsters the idea of the hopelessness of the attempt to understand the perpetrators of violence and in turn develop effective responses on the basis of that understanding. But such research is not hopeless, for the lives of those human beings responsible for even great horrors are not utterly alien. One way of overcoming the temptation to demonize others is to work towards understanding by engaging in exactly the sorts of dialogue that the conference participants were advocating.

Understanding the perpetrators of violence can help us make sense of their motivations and purposes, guiding us as we think through ways to address the sorts of concerns, beliefs, needs, values, moral commitments, affective factors, and worldviews which lead them to make the choices they make. Such understanding need not ground any kind of toleration of the intolerable. But recalling our common, shared humanity can orient us in our attempt to find better ways of responding not just effectively but also humanely to violence, without resorting to an all too comforting, simplistic, theoretically incapacitating, and morally risky demonization.

## NOTES

1. For a detailed account of Dilthey's rejection of Wilhelm Wundt's "bottom up," constructionist psychological view, a view which starts with "elementary facts that operate in isolation and [uses them as building blocks to] gradually [build] up more and more complex levels of psychological activity to account for . . . cultural life . . . ," see chapter 4 of Makkreel (1975). Quotation from Makkreel (1975), 161. More recent treatments of the incapacity of psychological and ontological atomism to account for the richness of meaningful experience may be found in Martin Heidegger's *Being and Time* and Hubert Dreyfus's *What Computers Still Can't Do*.

2. For a richer account of the process of hermeneutic interpretation, see Gadamer (1992), especially 291–307, and 324.

3. Cf. Gadamer (1992), 298–99, and 361–79.

4. David Kennedy, in his contribution to this volume, also expresses a concern with exploring such part/whole relations. He contrasts his approach with a more traditional attempt to isolate deterministic causal connections between gang membership and violence, and describes instead an "ethnography" of criminal justice agencies, communities, and individual offenders "and their interactions." He also stresses the methodological importance of "embedded partnerships" enabling sustained "exposure" to communities and conversations with individuals at multiple levels.

5. Mark Juergensmeyer (2003) expresses the same sort of commitment to opening up the minds and worlds of others through dialogue as do Aurelius and Dilthey. In the preface to his *Terror in the Mind of God,* for instance, he says, "To those activists I interviewed and who are named in the list at the end of this book, I extend my appreciation. I know that many of them, especially those who have supported acts of violence for what they regard as personal or moral reasons, will feel that I have not fully understood or sufficiently explained their views. Perhaps they are right. An effort at understanding is just that, an attempt to enter other people's worlds and recreate the moral and strategic logic of the decisions they make. The effort is always, perhaps necessarily, imperfect" (xvii, cf. 7, 10–14). For Juergensmeyer, this recreation will require sensitivity to the importance of the cultural, historical, and ideological contexts of terrorist acts.

6. It is likely that Mann here intends to offer a rejoinder to Madame de Staël's famous and often quoted line from the eighteenth book of *Corinne ou l'Italie* (1807), *"Car tout comprendre*

*rend très indulgent, et sentir profondément inspire une grande bontée"* ("To understand all makes one very tolerant, and to feel deeply inspires great kindness"). It seems that this phrase is often misquoted as "To understand is to forgive."

7. Hannah Arendt reflects upon the temptation to attribute an inhuman monstrosity to war criminals such as Adolf Eichmann, in whom there was no "diabolical or demonic profundity," in *Eichmann in Jerusalem: A Report on the Banality of Evil.* Quotation from Arendt (1994), 288.

# REFERENCES

Arendt, Hannah. 1994. *Eichmann in Jerusalem: A Report on the Banality of Evil.* New York: Penguin Books.

Aurelius, Marcus. 2002. *Meditations.* Trans. Gregory Hays. New York: The Modern Library.

Dilthey, Wilhelm. 1977a. "Ideas Concerning a Descriptive and Analytic Psychology." Translated by Richard Zaner, in *Descriptive Psychology and Historical Understanding,* 23–120. The Hague: Martinus Nijhoff.

Dilthey, Wilhelm. 1977b. "The Understanding of Other Persons and Their Expressions of Life." Translated by Kenneth Heiges, in *Descriptive Psychology and Historical Understanding,* 123–144. The Hague: Martinus Nijhoff.

———. 1989. *Introduction to the Human Sciences,* in *Wilhelm Dilthey: Selected Works,* vol. 1. Edited by Rudolf A. Makkreel, and Frithjof Rodi. Princeton: Princeton University Press.

Gadamer, Hans-Georg. 1992. *Truth and Method,* second revised edition. Translated by Joel Weinsheimer and Donald G. Marshall. New York: The Crossroad Publishing Corporation.

Juergensmeyer, Mark. 2003. *Terror in the Mind of God: The Global Rise of Religious Violence.* Berkeley and Los Angeles: University of California Press.

Makkreel, Rudolf. 1975. *Dilthey: Philosopher of the Human Studies.* Princeton: Princeton University Press.

———. 1977. Introduction to *Descriptive Psychology and Historical Understanding.* The Hague: Martinus Nijhoff.

Mann, Thomas. 1994. *Death in Venice.* Trans. Clayton Koelb. New York: W.W. Norton & Co.

Nussbaum, Martha C. 1997. *Cultivating Humanity: A Classical Defense of Reform in Liberal Education.* Cambridge: Harvard University Press.

# Index

9/11 attacks, 102, 131, 132, 134, 136, 137, 138

Atrocities Documentation Survey, 71, 78, 79

audience, 15, 26, 34, 125, 126, 132, 134, 135, 136–137, 138, 138–139, 214, 221, 256, 262

Aum Shinrikyo nerve gas attack, 131, 135

backfiring, 113, 114

Boston Gun Project, 50–52, 55

Boston Marathon bombing, 125, 126, 127

bullying, 143–145, 146–149, 149–150, 151–158, 159–162. *See also* cyberbullying

civil war, xi–xii, xiii, 21, 25, 92, 93, 95, 98, 99, 100, 101, 104–105, 110, 129, 184, 185, 186, 191–192, 243, 245

coercion, 113–115, 118

Columbine school shooting. *See* school shootings

community, xiii, 10, 11, 13, 22, 28–29, 30, 37, 41, 43, 52, 61–66, 67, 74, 87, 94, 96, 100, 102, 103, 126, 137, 144, 169, 192, 200, 202, 203, 206, 222–223, 223, 225–227, 228, 229, 230, 231, 231–63, 233–234, 261, 263

consciousness, 94, 133, 136, 226, 257–258, 259–261

context, 15, 25, 27, 29, 30, 63, 77, 91, 95, 104, 110, 117, 118, 121, 133, 161, 183, 184, 192, 207, 210, 211, 214, 215, 217, 233, 244, 245, 253, 259, 260, 261–262; cultural, 262; social, 133, 233, 253

Convention on the Prevention and Punishment of the Crime of Genocide, 73, 87–88

cosmic war, xii, 127, 128, 129–130, 245

crimes against humanity, 74

culture, 11, 15–16, 29, 32, 43, 54, 71, 73, 84, 92, 93, 136, 183, 185, 210, 231, 243, 245, 250, 257, 259, 261, 262, 264

cyberbullying, 29

Darfur, 71, 74, 74–76, 77, 78–80, 81, 82, 83, 84, 85, 87–88, 192, 242, 243, 245, 246, 251

dialogue, 95, 128, 260, 262, 265, 265n5

Dilthey, William, 255, 257–259, 260–261, 262, 263, 265n1, 265n5

displaced, 71, 74, 87, 93, 104, 185, 186

drama, 130, 131, 132, 135; dramatic, 62, 129, 130, 131, 132, 139, 262

ethnicity, xii, 15, 16, 22, 23, 75, 76, 91, 93, 95, 105, 147, 151, 154, 155, 156–158, 162, 166, 172, 174, 175, 175–176

explanation, 62, 76, 78, 121, 160, 187, 193, 211, 212–213, 216, 242, 243, 256, 257, 258–259, 261, 262

Galtung, Johan, 3–4, 91, 210, 252

Gang Reduction and Youth Development Zones, 65

Gang Resistance and Education Program (GREAT), 65

gangs, x, xi, 6–7, 9, 10, 12–15, 16, 17–18, 49–50, 51–52, 53, 54–57, 58, 59, 60, 62, 66, 187, 188, 189, 190, 191, 192, 210, 211, 214, 217, 233, 244, 245, 246, 251, 255, 256; Bloods, 54; Crips, 54; definition of, 12, 49, 63, 255, 256; La Eme, 55; Latin Kings, 55; MS-13, 55

gender, 23, 34, 99, 143, 144–146, 147–148, 150, 151–152, 152, 153–154, 156–158, 159–162, 166, 170, 172, 174, 176–177, 183, 193, 209, 210, 212, 215–216, 217, 218, 224, 252, 256

genocide, xi, 8, 71–75, 75–76, 77–78, 80, 82, 84, 87–88, 192, 215, 242, 243, 245, 251; Bosnian, 73–74, 77; Convention. *See* Convention on the Prevention and Punishment of the Crime of Genocide, definition of, 71, 72–74, 76

Genocide Convention. *See* Convention on the Prevention and Punishment of the Crime of Genocide

group formation, xiv, 23, 57, 104, 167, 242, 245

group identity, xiii, 183, 189–190, 192, 195, 233, 234, 244–245, 248, 251

group violence, definition of, x, xi, 8, 9, 10, 17–18, 58, 59, 93, 95, 111, 125, 183, 210, 241, 242, 247, 248, 250, 253, 255–256, 261

hate crimes, ix, x, xi, 9, 22

hate groups, x, xi, xii, 9, 22, 25, 25–27, 27, 29, 30, 43, 166–168, 169, 177, 178, 179, 251, 255; online, xi, 22, 27, 28, 30, 43, 166, 167, 168, 169, 178

hate speech, xii, 21–22, 26, 27, 29, 43, 132, 165–167, 168–169, 169, 170, 171, 174, 175–178

hermeneutics, 257, 261

Holocaust, 72, 75; denial, 22

homicide, 4, 8, 13, 50, 51, 53, 54, 57, 60, 61, 66, 68, 191, 221

identity, xiii, 12, 23, 43, 75, 76, 77, 93, 94, 105, 177, 185, 188, 199, 202, 204, 206, 215, 226, 230, 231, 244–245, 248, 250, 251, 253, 263. *See also* social identity theory (SIT); social identity model of deindividuation effects (SIDE)

ideology, 5, 21, 25, 32, 34, 83, 92–93, 96, 126, 128, 129, 133, 167, 204, 213, 251

immigration, 187

insecurity, xiii, 202, 203, 205, 222, 224, 225, 231

intergroup social contact, 71

International Criminal Tribunal for Rwanda, 72

Internet, 27, 27–29, 30, 32, 43, 128, 136, 165, 166, 167, 168, 169, 170, 177, 178, 221, 222, 223, 230, 231

interpretation, 177, 215, 226–227, 228, 255, 258, 259, 262, 265n2

intolerance, 22, 71, 168, 178, 204, 252

Janjaweed, 74, 75, 78, 80, 84, 85, 243

Ku Klux Klan (KKK), 22, 25–26

law, 5, 6, 12, 16, 18, 21–22, 26, 58, 64, 73, 77, 133, 178, 252, 261

law enforcement, xi, 51, 52, 53, 53–54, 55, 56, 58, 59, 60, 62, 63, 64, 65–66, 66, 67

Lemkin, Raphael, 71, 72, 73, 76

Liberation Tigers of Tamil Eelam (LTTE), xi, xiii, 91, 92–93, 94, 95, 103, 104–105, 105n4, 185, 186, 192–193, 200, 202, 203, 204, 242, 245

lifestyle exposure theory, xii

lone-wolf terrorist/terrorism, 15, 17, 28, 32, 43, 125, 125–126, 127, 138, 245, 248

loyalty shifts, 113, 114–115, 119, 121

Mann, Thomas, 263, 264, 265n6

masculinity, 213

meaning, 257, 258, 261, 262

meaningful, 139, 206, 258, 261, 261–262, 265n1

meaningful whole, 258, 262

migration, xiii, 13, 202, 205

minorities: ethnic, xi, 21, 22, 26, 55, 63, 93, 94, 103, 104–105, 117, 119, 149,

170, 185, 202, 206, 212, 243, 264; sexual, 26

mobility, 51, 183, 184, 185, 186, 187, 187–188, 190, 191, 193, 194, 195, 245, 246, 248, 251, 253. *See also* social mobility

Newtown Elementary School shooting. *See* school shootings

nonviolence, 111, 114, 117, 121–122

nonviolent movements, xii, 94, 109–111, 111–112, 112–113, 113–115, 116, 117–118, 118, 119, 120–123, 243

Nussbaum, Martha, 263–264

Oklahoma City bombing, 31, 33, 41, 125, 127, 135, 136, 137–138

online hate groups. *See* hate groups

Operation Ceasefire, 67

performance violence, 129, 130, 132–133, 138–139

police, xi, 5, 7, 11–12, 14, 17, 29, 49, 51, 53, 57, 58, 61, 63–65, 67, 68, 95, 97, 113, 114, 129, 187, 215, 216, 221, 231, 243

poverty, 5, 185, 187, 188, 231, 244

power, 4, 6, 8, 11, 12, 16, 24, 26, 57, 87, 95, 100, 111, 116, 127, 129, 131, 132–133, 138, 162, 186, 210, 214, 246–247, 247, 248, 250, 251, 253. *See also* state power

race, 72, 75, 76, 83, 91, 94, 147, 149–150, 151, 153, 154–155, 156, 162, 166, 174, 176, 245

racial epithets, 72, 75, 77–78, 78–80, 80, 81, 85, 86

rampage, 7, 9, 31, 129, 221–222, 222, 223, 223–224, 226, 232, 233

rape, 4–5, 7, 17, 60, 71, 72, 74, 75, 77, 80, 81, 84, 86, 87, 184, 191–194

rational violence, 251

refugees, xiii, 71, 78–80, 81, 84, 87, 96, 103, 109, 121, 184, 185, 185–186, 187, 188, 190, 191, 194, 205, 245–246

religion, xi, xii, 15, 22, 23, 72, 74, 91–92, 93, 127, 129, 133, 149–150, 156, 166, 184, 193, 245, 252, 261

resistance movements, 111, 112, 115, 117, 118, 122

revolutions, xi, 9, 109, 111, 121, 128, 202, 211, 241

routine activity theory, 169, 248, 249

Rwanda, genocide, 21, 72, 74, 75, 77, 191, 214, 245

school performance, 150

school shootings, x, xiii, 30–31, 32, 33, 172, 222, 224, 225, 227, 228, 229, 230, 230–231, 232, 233, 234; Columbine, 30, 32, 33, 34, 37–42, 43, 146, 224, 230–231; fans of, xi, 22, 31, 31–32, 33, 34, 35–42, 43, 245; Newtown Elementary School, 125, 127; Virginia Tech, 125, 224, 226

sexual orientation, xi, 22, 166, 172, 175, 177

sexual victimization, xi, 71, 78, 81, 86, 88

sexual violence, 54, 74, 81, 86, 87, 191, 193, 212, 217

significance, 24, 131, 132, 133, 138, 233, 261, 262. *See also* meaning

Sinhalese, 93, 94, 96, 96–97, 98, 102, 104, 105n5, 184–185, 200–201, 202, 203, 204, 205, 206

social identity model of deindividuation effects (SIDE), 30

social identity theory (SIT), 23–24, 77, 244

social mobility, xiii, 184, 187, 188, 189, 190, 194, 194–195, 201, 242, 245, 245–246, 251, 253

solidarity, xiii, 10, 18, 23, 43, 112, 116, 121, 188, 225–226, 227, 229, 229–230, 234, 245

Southern Poverty Law Center, 26, 167

state, x, xi, xii, xiii, 10, 13, 14, 15, 16, 17–18, 25, 29, 63, 73, 75, 76, 83, 92–93, 93–96, 96, 97, 100–102, 102, 103, 104–105, 109, 110, 111, 112, 113, 114, 115, 117, 118–119, 120–121, 121, 132, 185, 199–202, 202–203, 204, 205, 206, 211, 213, 216, 229, 242, 243, 243–244, 245, 250, 251, 253

state power, xiv, 12, 17, 25, 84, 93, 94, 102, 110, 113–114, 115–116, 118, 184, 202, 204, 242–243, 244 status, xiv, 4, 7, 11, 12, 14, 15, 16, 77, 133, 147, 151, 188, 216, 223, 241, 242, 246–248, 249, 250–251, 251, 251–252, 253; inexpansible, 247–248, 250, 252

status quo, 4–5, 12, 13, 113, 117, 138, 246

subculture, 30, 43

suicide, 144, 221; bombings, 91, 95, 98–100, 101, 105, 130

suitable targets, xiv, 159, 169, 191, 248, 250

symbol, 22, 43, 76, 131, 133, 139, 193

symbolic, 13, 14, 15, 32, 74, 87, 129, 131–132, 132–133, 133, 138, 222, 225, 233, 246, 249, 251, 252, 262

sympathy, 103, 263

Syrian Civil War, xii, 109–110, 111, 116–119, 119, 121–122, 243, 245, 245–246

tactical diversity, 113, 115

Tamils, xiii, 91, 92–93, 93, 94, 95–96, 96–97, 98, 99, 102, 103, 104–105, 105n5, 183, 184–185, 185–188, 188–189, 190–191, 191, 192–193, 193, 194, 200–201, 202, 204, 243, 245–246

target antagonism, 146, 249

target gratifiability, 146, 249, 250

target selection, xii, xiii, xiv, 183–184, 184, 188, 195, 248

target vulnerability, 146, 159, 249

technology, 16, 26, 28, 43, 168, 169–170

terrorism, ix, x, xi, xii, 4, 7, 8, 9, 10, 12, 15–16, 16–17, 31, 98, 109, 111, 118, 120, 121, 127, 129, 130, 131–132, 133, 134–136, 136–137, 137, 138–139, 172, 203, 225, 227, 248, 255, 262, 265n5

terrorists, 15, 15–16, 16, 22, 25, 31, 32, 43, 91, 105, 111, 120, 125, 128, 129, 130, 135, 138, 167, 212, 241, 245, 251, 256

tolerance, 63, 88, 264

torture, xi, 74, 80, 84–85, 88

urban, xi, 12, 14, 201, 233, 245

victimization, xi, xii, 17, 52, 56, 71–72, 75, 76–77, 78, 78–80, 80–81, 84, 86, 87, 88, 143, 144, 145, 146, 147–148, 148, 149–150, 151–152, 152, 153–154,

156–159, 159, 160, 161, 169–170, 190, 217, 248–249, 249

vigilantism, x, xi, 7, 8, 9, 10–12, 13, 14, 16, 16–17, 243

violence: causes, vii, x, xi, xiii, xiv, 3, 4, 6, 8, 16, 25–26, 33, 42, 71, 77, 93, 104, 110, 184, 187, 194, 209, 210, 212, 216, 230, 242, 245, 251, 253, 255; collective, x, 8, 9, 9–10, 15, 18, 77, 138, 166, 183, 199, 229, 249; definition, xi, 3, 3–4, 6, 8, 111, 121, 210, 255–256, 256; domestic, 8, 17, 53, 60, 216; and ethnicity. *See* ethnicity; and ideology; ideology; institutional, 4–5, 7, 188; interpersonal, 4–5, 60, 212; and lifestyles, 147, 158, 159, 169; mass, xi, xiii, 15, 16, 22, 31, 41, 72, 73, 74, 97, 98, 125, 127, 129, 169, 209, 218, 221–222, 223, 224, 225, 226, 228, 229, 230, 231, 233, 234, 243, 244; and physical characteristics, xii, 143, 144, 145, 146, 147, 150, 159, 250; and physical proximity, xi, xiii, 17, 23, 71–72, 77–78, 80, 82, 83, 84–85, 86, 88, 191, 223, 232; and religion, xi, xii, 15, 22, 23, 72, 74, 91–92, 93, 127, 129, 133, 149–150, 156, 166, 193, 245, 252; and social status; status; structural, xiii, 4–5, 62, 62–63, 187, 210; and women, x, 81, 86, 87, 91, 95, 99, 105n4, 167, 184, 191, 192, 193, 211, 212, 212–213, 213, 214–216, 217, 218n2, 229, 256, 264; and youth, x, xii, xiii, 7, 12, 14, 50, 65, 66, 105, 143–144, 145, 145–146, 147, 148, 151, 153–154, 154, 158, 158–159, 160, 161, 161–162, 165–166, 168, 169, 173, 175, 177, 178, 184, 187, 188, 189, 191, 199, 200, 201–202, 203, 204, 205, 206, 206–207, 207, 216, 231, 232. *See also* and poverty; rampage

Virginia Tech school shooting. *See* school shootings

war, 7, 8, 10, 18, 24, 31, 56–57, 94, 95, 100, 102, 110, 111, 183, 191–192, 209, 210, 211, 212–213, 213–214, 214, 215, 216, 217, 218, 227, 256, 266n7

weight, xii, 143, 144, 145, 146, 147–148, 150, 151, 152, 153–154, 154–161, 161,

162, 250
World Trade Center. *See* 9/11 attacks

youth. *See* violence and youth

# About the Editors

**James Hawdon** is a professor of sociology and the director of the Center for Peace Studies and Violence Prevention at Virginia Tech. Prior to arriving at Virginia Tech in 2004, he was an assistant professor of sociology and director of the Survey Research Lab at Clemson University. His research includes a ten-year, cross-site evaluation of community-based antiviolence initiatives that focused on how grassroots community efforts and public officials can co-produce public safety, reduce crime and violence, and promote well-being in economically disadvantaged neighborhoods. He has been the lead investigator on dozens of research projects and recently completed two National Science Foundation projects focused on the relationship between tragic incidents and community solidarity. He is currently involved in research focusing on online hate groups and agent based models of gun violence. He has published dozens of articles in the areas of crime, violence, policing, drug use, survey research methods, disaster research, and media studies. His book, *Drug and Alcohol Use as Functions of Social Structure*, won the Adele Mellen Prize for Contributions to Scholarship, and he recently co-edited the *Encyclopedia of Drug Policy*.

**John Ryan** is professor and chair of sociology at Virginia Tech. He came to Virginia Tech as department chair in 2001, after serving six years as chair at Clemson University. A graduate of Vanderbilt University, his research interests include the study of culture production and consumption, as well as violence and crime control within communities. Over the past fourteen years, he researched how community cultures maintain order, produce peace, and respond to crises. Specifically, he investigates the interconnections of the three realms of communal cultural life: the public, parochial, and private spheres of life. He has applied this general approach to study the control of crime, the production of public safety, and the community's response to violence, tragedy, and disasters. This body of research has influenced scholarship across a number of disciplines including cultural sociology, criminology, criminal justice, policing, media studies, critical incident analysis, disaster research, and civil engineering. This work has also bridged the "applied science" versus "pure science" divide, as his applied studies of community organizations have been recognized for their theoretic and methodological rigor.

**Marc Lucht** is a visiting assistant professor of philosophy, and education coordinator at the Center for Peace Studies and Violence Prevention, at Virginia Tech. Holding a PhD from Emory University, his scholarly work focuses on moral philosophy, phenomenology, the philosophy of peace, environmental philosophy, and the philosophy of art, and he has published and delivered numerous conference papers on thinkers such as Martin Heidegger, Immanuel Kant, George Santayana, Arthur Schopenhauer, Friedrich Nietzsche, Plato, and Leo Tolstoy. Recently he co-edited the book *Kafka's Creatures: Animals, Hybrids, and Other Fantastic Beings*, and he currently is engaged in research on connections between inter-human violence and anthropogenic violence directed towards nonhuman animals and nature. He is a member of the board of directors of the International Society for Universal Dialogue, and sits on the editorial board of the journal *Dialogue and Universalism*. His paper "Does Kant Have Anything to Teach Us about Environmental Ethics?" won the Jacobsen Research Prize.

# About the Contributors

**Jeanne Chang** is currently in her fourth year of undergraduate study in the College of Natural Resources and Environment and the College of Liberal Arts and Human Sciences at Virginia Tech. In December 2014, she will graduate with a BS in fisheries science with a marine concentration, and two minors in international studies, and humanities science and the environment. She is particularly interested in using holistic community based management approaches to fuel economic and cultural growth in developing nations to better attain food stability. Previous research projects have focused on investigating the relationship between economic development and marine fishery health statuses in North America, South America, Europe, and Africa. In fall 2014, Jeanne will pursue a marine science education at Stony Brook University. After graduation, Jeanne hopes to pursue research in marine cetaceans, but her passions remain in teaching, traveling, and outdoor recreation.

**Alec Clott** is an undergraduate senior at Virginia Tech and will complete both a BA in international studies and BS in sociology in May 2014. In international studies his concentration includes world politics and policy, and in sociology he concentrates on crime and deviance. Much of his research interests stem from both fields, specifically revolving around conflict resolution and human rights. His undergraduate honors thesis analyzes micro and macro-level problems in the prevention of human trafficking, ultimately arguing that lack of coherence between local and international efforts is a main obstacle to effective interventions. Other research projects have focused on instances of international political violence, such as analyzing various identity constructions associated with acts of genocide throughout the twentieth century. Recently, Alec has served as a standpoint editor for an upcoming textbook, *Nations and Nationalities* by Dr. Edward Weisband and Dr. Courtney Thomas, and currently serves as an undergraduate teaching assistant for the Department of Political Science at Virginia Tech.

**Premakumara De Silva** received his BA and MA in sociology from the University of Colombo and MSc and PhD in social anthropology from the University of Edinburgh, UK. He has won several prestigious international fellowships including ones from the British Academy, the American Academy of Religion and the Wenner-Gren Foundation for Anthropological Research in New York. Currently, he is the head of sociology department and the senior student counselor of University of Colombo. His research interests include political use of religion and ritual, nationalism, local democracy, youth culture, indigenous study, violence, and globalization. He is the author of "Globalization and the Transformation of Planetary Rituals in Southern Sri Lanka" (2000), "'Second Tsunami': Lost of co-existence among Tsunami Affected Communities in Southern Sri Lanka" (2009), "Discourse and Counter-discourse(s) on the New Bhikkhuni Order in Sri Lanka: An Ethnographical Inquiry" (2010). His most recent article is, "Diminishing or Survival: Case of Veddas' Culture in Sri Lanka" (2012), and he has published a number of papers in local and English languages. He is currently working on a monograph, titled *Beyond the Sacred Journey: Varieties of Pilgrimage at the Sri Pada Temple in Sri Lanka*.

**Siri Hettige** is a senior professor and holds the chair of sociology at the University of Colombo. He is also an adjunct professor at RMIT University, Australia, and an adjunct research associate at the Centre for Population and Urban Research at Monash University, Australia. He currently chairs the National Committee on Social Sciences at Sri Lanka's National Science Foundation and has numerous publications on a range of themes that include migration, youth, social policy, political economy of development, identity politics, and education. Professor Hettige has been a visiting scholar at numerous universities in countries such as the United States, United Kingdom, Finland, Switzerland, Germany, the Netherlands, Australia, and India. He has been a senior Fulbright Visiting Scholar at the University of Pennsylvania, British Academy Fellow at the University of Edinburgh, visiting fellow at the Centre for Development Research, Bonn, distinguished visiting scholar at the University of Adelaide, and senior visiting fellow at Melbourne University. He has also held the positions of dean of Faculty of Arts, head of the Department of Sociology, and director of the Social Policy Analysis and Research Centre, all at the University of Colombo. Professor Hettige earned a bachelor's degree from the University of Colombo, and he received his PhD in social anthropology in 1980 from Monash University. He has been teaching at the University of Colombo since 1986.

**Mark Juergensmeyer** is professor of sociology and global studies, affiliate professor of religious studies, and director of the Orfalea Center for Global and International Studies at the University of California, Santa Barbara. He was previously coordinator of the Religious Studies Program at the University of California, Berkeley, and dean of the School of Hawaiian, Asian, and Pacific Studies at the University of Hawaii. He is author or editor of over twenty books, including *Global Rebellion: Religious Challenges to the Secular State* and *Terror in the Mind of God: The Global Rise of Religious Violence,* which was cited by the *Los Angeles Times* and the *Washington Post* as one of the most notable books of the year. He is also editor of the *Oxford Handbook of Religion and Violence* and *The Princeton Readings in Religion and Violence.* He was president of the American Academy of Religion, and has received honorary doctorates from Lehigh University (United States) and Roskilde University (Denmark). He has been awarded the Grawemeyer Award in Religion and the Silver Medal of Spain's Queen Sofia Center for the Study of Violence.

**David Kennedy** is the director of the Center for Crime Prevention and Control at John Jay College of Criminal Justice in New York City. He directed the Boston Gun Project, whose "Operation Ceasefire" intervention was responsible for a more than 60 percent reduction in youth homicide victimization. His work has won two Ford Foundation Innovations in Government awards, two Webber Seavey Awards from the International Association of Chiefs of Police, and the Herman Goldstein International Award for Problem-Oriented Policing. He was awarded the 2011 Hatfield Scholar Award for scholarship in the public interest. He helped develop the High Point Drug Market Intervention strategy; the Justice Department's Strategic Approaches to Community Safety Initiative; the Treasury Department's Youth Crime Gun Interdiction Initiative; the Bureau of Justice Assistance's Drug Market Intervention Program; and the High Point Domestic Violence Intervention Program. He is the co-chair of the National Network for Safe Communities, an alliance of more than sixty cities and jurisdictions actively implementing the center's strategies and dedicated to reducing crime, reducing incarceration, and addressing the racial conflict associated with traditional crime policy. Professor Kennedy is the author of *Deterrence and Crime Prevention: Reconsidering the Prospect of Sanction,* co-author of *Beyond 911: A New Era for Policing,* and a wide range of articles on gang violence, drug markets, domestic violence, firearms trafficking, deterrence theory, and other public safety issues. His latest book, *Don't Shoot, One Man, a Street Fellowship, and the End of Violence in Inner-City America* was published in September 2011.

**Lindsay Kahle** is a second year PhD student in the Department of Sociology at Virginia Tech. Her two areas of specialization are women and gender studies and crime and deviance. Prior to pursuing a PhD, she obtained a bachelor's degree in psychology and a masters of arts in sociology from Indiana University of Pennsylvania. Her prior research included a master's thesis entitled *Testing the Effects of Bullying and Cyber Bullying Using the 2009 PAYS Survey,* which investigated the effects of bullying on adolescent cigarette and alcohol use. Her current research interests involve youth violence; women, gender and sexuality studies; crime and deviance; and LGBTQ identity. Her current research projects include work focuses on areas of gender, sexuality, and youth violence. She has co-authored several publications appearing in journals such as: *Violence and Victims, Journal of Criminology,* and *Gender, Place, and Culture.* She was the 2006 recipient of the Edinger Shay student leadership award, and the 2012 graduate recipient of the Indiana University of Pennsylvania women's leadership award.

**Christian Matheis** is a doctoral candidate (ABD) at Virginia Tech conducting research in ethics and political philosophy in the Alliance for Social, Political, Ethical and Cultural Thought (ASPECT). He holds a BS in psychology and an MA in applied ethics with graduate minors in ethnic studies and sociology, both from Oregon State University. Among his research interests are feminist philosophies, philosophies of race, border epistemologies, and Latin American philosophies. In his dissertation he complements traditional moral and political notions of solidarity by arguing specifically for a liberatory conception of solidarity as "relational," primarily a matter of what happens to people when they relate with one another. This, he contends, can serve as a resource for disparate, oppressed social movements who must nevertheless organize in order to effectively challenge the dominance of oppressive moral and political regimes. His broader research projects include a Dusselian critique of the hegemony endemic to contemporary whiteness studies, proposing moral criteria for evaluating the treatment of refugees who endure institutionalized petitions for asylum, and an analysis of the logical implications of Hegel's lord/bondsman dialectic showing that the hypothetical agents seek not to fulfill a desire for recognition, but instead aim at reproduction of will in the beliefs and actions of the other. Christian teaches in both the Departments of Philosophy and Political Science at Virginia Tech, as well as for the Department of Philosophy at Radford University.

**Atte Oksanen** has studied the well-being of young people in changing cultural and societal situations. His doctoral dissertation in social psychology (2006, University of Tampere, Finland) explored violent and vulnerable identities in contemporary culture. Oksanen's research interests and projects have centered on the fields of social psychology, sociology, and cultural studies. He has published in a variety of areas including youth studies, drugs and alcohol use, mass shootings, and cultural studies. Oksanen is currently an associate professor of social psychology at the University of Tampere, Finland. He recently led the Emil Aaltonen funded research project *Everyday Life and Insecurity*, together with Professor Pekka Räsänen. Currently Oksanen and Räsänen are leading a Kone Foundation Project *Hate Communities: An International Comparison*.

**Donna Pankhurst** is the associate dean for teaching and learning at the University of Bradford's School of Social and International Studies. Her central area of research interest is gender issues in conflict and post-conflict settings, which includes men's experiences, issues of masculinity, and the experiences of women. She is part of a network of scholars who are developing this area and her edited book, *Gendered Peace: Women's Struggles for Reconciliation and Justice*, is a pioneering work in the field. She is currently working on approaches to peace-building with regard to truth commissions, justice, and reconciliation and when these strategies are most appropriate to use. Her research history concentrated on fieldwork in Southern Africa, particularly Zimbabwe and Namibia, but she has also worked in Sudan and other countries in east and west Africa. She has recently concentrated on Uganda as a case study. She has worked with a number of NGOs and international organizations as advisor and consultant, and she is a founding member of the University of Bradford's Programme for a Peaceful City.

**Anthony Peguero** is an assistant professor of sociology and research affiliate of the Center for Peace Studies and Violence Prevention at Virginia Tech. His research interests include youth violence, socialization and marginalization, schools, and the adaptation of the children of immigrants. He is also a National Institute of Justice W. E. B. Du Bois Fellow and member of the Racial Democracy, Crime, and Justice Network which holds the dual goals of advancing research on the intersection of race, crime, and justice and of promoting racial democracy within the study of these issues by supporting junior scholars from underrepresented groups. He serves as a consultant on the Cartoon Network's campaign against bullying, and the editorial board for the journal of *Youth Violence and Juvenile Justice, Sociology of Race and Ethnicity, Journal of Criminal Justice*, and the Crime and Deviance Section of *Sociology Compass*. Dr. Peguero's research has been published in *Crime and Delinquency, Journal of Youth and Adolescence, Youth and Society, Sociological Spectrum, Punishment and Society, Journal of Ethnicity and Criminal Justice, Victims and Offenders*, and *Journal of Interpersonal Violence*.

**Virginia Roach** is a senior in civil and environmental engineering with a minor in twenty-first-century studies at Virginia Tech. Her research interests include sociological impacts on transportation, the impact of immobility on the likelihood towards violence, and transportation and culture. After graduation, she plans to pursue a graduate education.

**Wenona Rymond-Richmond** is an assistant professor of sociology at the University of Massachusetts-Amherst. Her research focuses on genocide, race and ethnicity, and the sociology of law, with particular expertise on the genocide in Darfur. She is the author, with John Hagan, of *Darfur and the Crime of Genocide*, which received the Albert J. Reiss, Jr. Outstanding Book Award for the Crime, Law, and Deviance Section of the ASA and the Michael J. Hindelang Outstanding Book Award for Distinguished Scholarly Publication from the American Society of Criminology. She co-authored several articles on the Darfur genocide published in the *American Sociological Review*, *Criminology*, and *American Journal of Public Health*.

**Pekka Räsänen** is a professor of economic sociology in the Department of Social Research at the University of Turku, Finland. He has studied consumer behavior, mass violence and media, and attitudes towards various welfare issues for more than ten years. Räsänen has experience in comparative research methods and in analyzing large-scale quantitative data. He has published widely in international scholarly journals. He recently completed a project analyzing the social responses to mass violence in two Finnish towns that experienced school shootings. His current research focuses on how new information technology influences modern life, including how online hate groups operate and influence youth. He has also conducted extensive research on ICT use, new media, and ageing.

**Michelle Sutherland** graduated from Virginia Tech with a degree in political science and a second major in philosophy. During her tenure at Virginia Tech, she worked in the School of Education assisting with research on the recruitment and retention of women in science, technology, engineering, and mathematics. She is currently the advertising adviser at the Educational Media Company at Virginia Tech, Inc., the parent company of the university's independent student media organizations, and occasionally does freelance writing. She recently published in *The Atlantic*.

**Tharindi Udalagama** graduated from the Department of Sociology University of Colombo in 2010 with first class honors in sociology and is currently a lecturer in sociology at the University of Colombo. She has been working with the project *Biomedical and Health Experimentation in South Asia* from

2010–2012 as a research fellow, managing the fieldwork in Sri Lanka, which included observation at case study sites, in-depth interviews with respondents, writing, and presenting from the project outcomes. Her research interests include science and technology studies, bioethics, policy studies, and suicide and self-harm in rural settings.